Of Other Thoughts: Non-Traditional Ways to the Doctorate

Of Other Thoughts: Non-Traditional Ways to the Doctorate

A Guidebook for Candidates and Supervisors

Edited by

A.-Chr. Engels-Schwarzpaul
AUT University, Auckland, Aotearoa/New Zealand

and

Michael A. Peters
University of Waikato, Hamilton, Aotearoa/New Zealand

SENSE PUBLISHERS
ROTTERDAM/BOSTON/TAIPEI

A C.I.P. record for this book is available from the Library of Congress.

ISBN: 978-94-6209-315-7 (paperback)
ISBN: 978-94-6209-316-4 (hardback)
ISBN: 978-94-6209-317-1 (e-book)

Published by: Sense Publishers,
P.O. Box 21858,
3001 AW Rotterdam,
The Netherlands
https://www.sensepublishers.com/

Printed on acid-free paper

Cover image: Ross Jenner, "Micronesian Map and New World Wall Frame", University of Auckland School of Architecture winning entry, *The Venice Prize 1991 – Forty Three Schools from round the World.*

All Rights Reserved © 2013 Sense Publishers

No part of this work may be reproduced, stored in a retrieval system, or transmitted in any form or by any means, electronic, mechanical, photocopying, microfilming, recording or otherwise, without written permission from the Publisher, with the exception of any material supplied specifically for the purpose of being entered and executed on a computer system, for exclu sive use by the purchaser of the work.

TABLE OF CONTENTS

Endorsements ix

Acknowledgements xi

1. Non-Traditional Ways to the Doctorate: Introduction 1
   A.-Chr. Engels-Schwarzpaul

Part 1: Non-Traditional Candidates

2.1. Ruku – Dive: A Physicality of Thought 17
   Moana Nepia

2.2. Western "Sentences that Push" as an Indigenous Method for Thinking 23
   Carl Mika

2.3. A "Psychedelic Method": Spatial Exposition,
   Perspectivism and Bricklaying 27
   Albert L. Refiti

2.4. Fantasy, Resistance and Passion as Important Aspects
   of the Doctoral Writing Process 35
   Lynley Tulloch

2.5. Unaware that I Was Walking Backwards 39
   Richard Heraud

2.6. Contributing to the Field of Design Research
   A Brief Personal Wrap-Up 43
   Christian Wölfel

2.7. The Trademan's Door to the Ivory Tower: Doing Research as
   Just Another Kind of Practice 47
   Katharina Bredies

2.8. Sticky Advice for Research Students 51
   Sarah McGann & Barbara Milech

3. Spaces of Other Thought: E kore e piri te uku ki te rino 53
   Shane Edwards

TABLE OF CONTENTS

4. Culture as a Place of Thought: Supervising Diverse Candidates 67
   Catherine Manathunga

5. Transfer and Translation: Negotiating Conflicting Worldviews 83
   King Tong Ho

6. The Colour of Thought: Advising Ethnic Minority
   Candidates through a Radical Ethic of Pedagogical Love 101
   Roland W. Mitchell & Kirsten T. Edwards

7. Transforming the Academic Field: Field-Reflexivity and
   Access for Non-Traditional Doctoral Candidates 115
   Susanne Maria Weber

8. Queer as a Two-Bob Watch: The Implications of Cultural
   Framing and Self-Declaration 131
   Welby Ings

9. Anxieties of Knowing: Renegade Knowledges – of Choice and Necessity 147
   Michael A. Peters

10. Emerging Knowledge, Translation of Thought 163
    A.-Chr. Engels-Schwarzpaul

Part II: Emerging Fields of Research

11. Alternative Design Doctorates as Drivers for New Forms of Research,
    Or: Knowing and Not-Knowing in Design 183
    Wolfgang Jonas, Rosan Chow & Simon Grand

12. Thought out of Bounds: Theory and Practice in Architecture Doctorates 203
    Ross Jenner

13. Thinking through Moving Image and Performance 221
    Sarah O'Brien

14. Thinking through Art, Creating through Text:
    "I Think I May Be Finding My Own Voice" 239
    Barbara Milech & Ann Schilo

15. Spaces between Indigenous and Non-Indigenous Knowledge
    Systems: Deep Listening to Research in a Creative Form 259
    Laura Brearley & Treahna Hamm

TABLE OF CONTENTS

16. "Not All Academics Can Do It": The Haunted Spaces of Post-Colonial Supervision 279
Barbara M. Grant

17. A Creative Journey: By Māori for Māori.
Interview with Robert Jahnke 297
Robert Jahnke & A.-Chr. Engels-Schwarzpaul

18. Emergent Knowledges and Non-Traditional Candidates: Conclusion 311
A.-Chr. Engels-Schwarzpaul & Michael A. Peters

Index 325

ENDORSEMENTS

This is a much-needed book, designed to drive conversations that we can no longer avoid: how to imagine new forms of research training offered to doctoral students from a variety of non-traditional backgrounds. Given the growing diversity of such students, interested in creating new knowledge at the intersection of the dominant and their own cultural and epistemic traditions, this collection of essays does not only provide rich accounts of the experiences of doctoral students but also sophisticated theoretical analyses suggesting new ways of establishing intellectual communities among supervisors and students based on the principles of openness, trust and reciprocity.

Fazal Rizvi | Professor of Education | University of Melbourne | Australia

Wonder or doubt opens up the possibility of new understanding and yet it is something that happens to us; we cannot make or force it to happen. Yet wonder is a pre-condition of research, so must we merely wait for it to present itself or can we facilitate its appearance? In this book we find accounts of situations where the habitual practices of the participants involved, "traditional" and "non-traditional", were tested and challenged. And in this I find the book's appeal: assuming wonder is promoted when we find ourselves in unfamiliar situations, then here is a valuable resource for inquiry into wonder and the conditions of its emergence.

Steven Scrivener | Professor, Graduate School | UAL: University of the Arts London, Camberwell | UK

This is an excellent book for students and supervisors navigating the often tremorous routes to a doctoral degree. For students who fear having to sacrifice their souls in order to become distinguished holders of a doctoral degree, this book can allay fears and offer new avenues for creative success.

Peter McLaren | Professor, University of California, Los Angeles | Distinguished Fellow in Critical Studies, Chapman University | USA

ACKNOWLEDGEMENTS

This book has been produced by many, of whom some were directly involved, others indirectly. Our thanks to all!

Tina: Thanks are due to AUT University's grant of a sabbatical leave, which helped substantially to progress the editing and paid for a research trip to the UK to speak with practice-led PhD supervisors about their experiences. I would like to thank the authors for their generous sharing of thought and for their occasional encouragement. They clearly invoked the feeling of a virtual community of scholars oriented by a common goal. I would like to thank Bob Jahnke (my external PhD advisor) and Michael Peters (primary PhD supervisor) for participating. To work with them on this book marked something like a belated closure on my own PhD and the beginning of a new type of collaboration. Particularly the discussions with Michael focused my thinking regarding some core issues of this book and sowed the seeds for a future project.

Michael: I would like to thank Tina for inviting me to coedit this important collection with her: it has been a pleasure to spend time with her, discussing issues and problems based on important political and epistemological exclusions of non-traditional students. It has been an opportunity to work and collaborate with Tina for the first time since she completed her PhD, and I realise in retrospect how much I benefited from that relationship.

Cover image credits: "Micronesian Map and New World Wall Frame", University of Auckland School of Architecture winning entry, *The Venice Prize 1991* – Forty Three Schools from round the World. Ross Jenner, Rewi Thompson, Chris Adams, Andrew Barry, Helen Furjan, Mary Jowett, Richard McGowan, Glen Watt, Anthony Hoete and Kerry Morrow. The installation combined timber framed according to the NZ Code of Practice and a Micronesian navigation map: one frame from and of technology, one from the flux of wind and water. The two systems and cultures slid obliquely through each other to form an intricate entanglement – something between drawing, built form and drifting cloud. Photo: Ross Jenner

A.-CHR. ENGELS-SCHWARZPAUL

1. NON-TRADITIONAL WAYS TO THE DOCTORATE

Introduction

An intellectual community able to stimulate new ideas and development is one with an appreciation for the generative potential of multiple perspectives. (Walker et al., 2008: 125)

I felt dissatisfied with the prevailing discourse of representationism, with the computational model of mind, and with the dominant epistemology. Why? I am not really sure myself. ... One reason may have been that I came from another country with a different culture and, therefore, never really belonged; in addition, I had not been educated in the standard U.S. way. It helped, I suppose, that I really came to the United States from another planet. ... I spent my early childhood with my family in a small village in the mountains where everything I had was the sky and the animals. (Francesco Varela in Gumbrecht, Maturana, & Poerksen, 2006, pp. 43–4)

The growth of PhD thesis enrolments over recent years has been astounding (see Halse & Mowbray, 2011: 516-7). It has been accompanied by an increasing number of books guiding supervisors and candidates through changing processes and environments. Most of these guides are written for, as one author terms it, *traditional candidates* ("disproportionately male, from high-status social-economic backgrounds, members of majority ethnic and/or racial groups, and without disability", Taylor & Beasley, 2005: 141). Over the last three decades, though, student populations internationally have changed significantly: new funding regimes and life styles have led to an increase of mature and part-time students; at the same time, identity politics over the last decades of the twentieth century articulated the positions of women, sexual minority researchers, and Indigenous, ethnic or diasporic communities (Hardt & Negri, 2005: 86).[1] Globally, the internationalisation and commercialisation of university education led to a marked increase of students from non-English speaking backgrounds in English language programmes.[2]

Candidates in *non-traditional disciplines* have always come from diverse backgrounds. In education and health, for instance, the "typical first class honours graduate" entering doctoral studies arguably never was the norm (Thomson & Walker, 2010a: 13). Often, these *non-traditional candidates* have research interests that do not fit easily into the traditional organisation of universities. Their concerns, or those of their supervisors, are not usually discussed at length in the doctoral guide

A.-Chr. Engels-Schwarzpaul and M. A. Peters (Eds.), Of other Thoughts: Non-Traditional Ways to the Doctorate: A Guidebook for Candidates and Supervisors, 1–14.
© *2013 Sense Publishers. All rights reserved.*

books. They have to 'translate' the available literature for their particular needs and purposes.

In postgraduate, particularly PhD supervisions, pedagogy and research intersect intensely and in highly personal ways, but non-traditional candidates' interests, circumstances and needs do not sufficiently enter into a consideration of this distinctive pedagogical configuration. If they address the supervision of non-traditional candidates at all, most PhD guidebooks summarily deal with it in one or two chapters – entitled, for instance, "Dealing with difference" (Wisker, 2005) or "Responding to diversity" (Taylor & Beasley, 2005). Managerial and pedagogic ad-hoc responses to the growing numbers of inherently diverse candidates tend to squeeze them (inadvertently or not) into an oversimplified model of homogenised difference (i.e., all that is 'Other'). Further, institutional thinking about what might be particular to their interests and needs is, too often, conceptually underpinned by a "deficit model" (Cunningham, 2011; Ryan & Zuber-Skerritt, 1999; Slee, 2010). The assumption, then, is that the same standards are valid for everyone, and that it is the students' differences (cultural or other) that cause unsatisfactory performance.

This perspective misses out on a significant and important aspect of changing student populations: as new groups of non-traditional students mature into postgraduate researchers, they enrich academic culture and research by bringing their own, distinct ways of knowing and getting-to-know into the research situation. Granted, the divergence of non-traditional candidates' epistemological perspectives and approaches to knowledge from those that prevail in most Western universities can, if they are not adequately represented in mainstream frameworks, produce "pedagogical alienation" (Aspland in Ryan & Zuber-Skerritt, 1999, 37). However, the very same conditions imply also that non-traditional candidates can contribute new knowledge and new approaches to research. They usually bring with them the "appreciation for the generative potential of multiple perspectives" that George E. Walker and his co-authors consider so crucial for an intellectual community to be "able to stimulate new ideas and development" (2008: 125).

An interest in exploring precisely such diverging epistemic potentialities is prevalent, though, in some newly emerging or recently established fields of academic engagement. Researchers in those fields want to relate theory and practice in new ways and/or undertake research collaboratively in, across and beyond disciplines where the individual, disciplinarily committed researcher is still the norm. Here, candidates from non-mainstream backgrounds can render visible new aspects of many researchers' simultaneous embeddedness in different and potentially conflicting or complimentary research networks (for instance, those of a mainstream university, those of other knowledge communities, and those within in the communities being researched). If it is considered important to monitor PhD education from outside the University (Shulman, 2010), then non-traditional candidates' involvement with communities can create a counterweight to a primarily instrumental concept of relevance. Otherwise, the orientation of professions and industries (with their particular motives, purposes and goals) could impoverish research directions and content (see Kehm, 2007). In any event, contemporary universities need to engage with these often contradictory issues and be inspired by them to initiate change.[3]

As I was editing this book, two of the doctoral candidates I have worked with over the last years submitted their creative practice-led theses and went to examination. Their successful completions not only changed their *way of being, but also mine: they are now 'doctors' and I have 'supervised to completion'. For them and for me, their success confirmed that it can be worthwhile (while risky) to deviate from safe and certain formats, methods and procedures. On the way, though, there were many anxious moments caused by concerns about the potentials and limits of disciplinary knowledge-gaps in supervision. It was these moments of intense feelings of uncertainty that ultimately led to the conception of this book.*

During a break enforced by an operation, I tried to educate myself as a PhD supervisor by reading guide books on doctoral supervision. The advice offered in several books I read barely touched on, and often completely missed, the conditions and concerns of most of the candidates I worked with. It turned out, as I was reading, that they were nearly all non-traditional *(part-time and mature candidates, of 'ethnic minorities', second-language international students and/or gay). I found this highly disconcerting, not least because I found reading guidebooks as a PhD student helpful: when I became seriously stuck (probably 2-3 times in a year), I went to the library and borrowed 'how to' books (just as I would consult car repair manuals when necessary). This pragmatic way of dealing with problems of organisation, structure or process helped me keep the panic at bay – I would also find useful tricks and tips. On another level, the reading helped me establish a distance from which I could look at my messy situation and see it in a larger context. In a peculiar way, it made me aware of the conditions of possibility for my thesis, and it helped me think through my options within a system that I could change only marginally.*

This time, on the other side of the fence as it were, the need to educate myself was initially motivated by my lack of disciplinary competence concerning the project of a candidate whose supervision I had just accepted. I had previously been somewhat sanguine about the importance of expert knowledge in supervision, since my experience with my own PhD supervisor, Michael Peters (who knew nothing about the specific aspects of my thesis), had been excellent. Nevertheless, my lack of disciplinary knowledge had already prompted me earlier to investigate various theories, for instance Jacques Rancière's account of Joseph Jacotot's strategies in The Ignorant Schoolmaster *(e.g., Engels-Schwarzpaul, 2007).[4] This time, the matter was urgent enough for me to contact Michael in the South Island, and then to fly to Christchurch to meet with him to discuss the conundrum of knowing and not-knowing as a supervisor.*

I suspect that when we look for models of supervision, we often turn to our own good and bad experiences to make sense of undecided or ambiguous situations. My doctoral supervision relationship with Michael had been as successful as that with my Masters supervisor had been disastrous. I wanted to find out how Michael had made it work:

how had he handled the ostensible problem of not-knowing in supervising my PhD research? Out of this discussion came the idea of editing a book on non-traditional PhD candidatures – a matter I wanted both to think through and learn more about, and one that seemed to be in need of addressing beyond my personal interest.

Some remarks about the book's orientation and assumptions, its terminology, some themes and its structure are in order. *Of Other Thoughts* takes its bearings from the position of non-traditional candidates like Francisco Varela, who come (literally or metaphorically) from "another country with a different culture and, therefore, [may] never really belong". Candidates who, "in addition," have not been "educated in the standard ... way", even arriving at their university "from another planet" (Varela in Gumbrecht et al., 2006, p. 43).

The book consequently opens with a series of short reflective pieces by PhD candidates: Indigenous scholars, creative practice-led researchers, educationalists, designers and an architect give insights into the challenges of their PhD journeys and write about their moments of wonder. The authors of the main chapters scrutinise and contextualise Indigenous, postcolonial, sexual and ethnic minority, international (second-language), educational and counselling, and creative practice- or design-led research PhDs – taking a stance and proposing their version of non-traditional PhD candidatures. The authors' ontological and epistemological outlook and their experiences in academic research in newly emerging disciplines inform their analysis and advice to PhD candidates and their supervisors. Between them, they cover first-nation epistemes and protocols; creative practice-led research in art, design, architecture, performance and writing; transdisciplinarity and/or collaboration in the creative field and other disciplines that continually re-invent themselves, such as education or public and cultural policies. The range of contributors is considerable, even though it could have been even more plural,[5] and the differences between their positions and perspectives are sometimes significant. What they share, however, is their viewpoint (which often translates into a distinct view of the world) from outside the mainstream and a sometimes acute sense of marginality. They also share a keen interest in ways of being, seeing, moving, reflecting, thinking and advancing that are not currently common in mainstream research. So they have in common an attentiveness to alternative ontologies and epistemologies and a commitment to different aesthetics and ethics. They are, in that sense, oriented towards a shared goal – even as they provide multiple perspectives from which to test and elaborate alternatives, and from which to "build, in place of a single argument, a structure of possibilities" (Ulmer, 1994: 94). In the juxtaposition of different conditions of possibility, they create collectively, in Hannah Arendt's words, the possibility for "worldly reality truly and reliably [to] appear" in research and scholarship by contributing to the

> ... simultaneous presence of innumerable perspectives and aspects in which the common world presents itself and for which no common measurement or denominator can ever be devised. For though the common world is the

common meeting ground of all, those who are present have different locations in it, and the location of one can no more coincide with the location of another than the location of two objects. Being seen and being heard by others derive their significance from the fact that everybody sees and hears from a different position. ... Only where things can be seen by many in a variety of aspects without changing their identity, so that those who are gathered around them know they see sameness in utter diversity, can worldly reality truly and reliably appear. (Arendt, 1958: 57)

An intellectual community then arises whose members know that a single common measurement and a single common denominator is stifling. Their diverse locations in different cultures leave them dissatisfied with prevailing discourses and dominant epistemologies, and they know that the Western world as we know it – however much it may seem to be the only one there is – is only one of many. And so, they look for different ways of knowing and getting to know, which better nurture the generative potential of multiple perspectives. It is precisely in the interface of idiosyncratic, and culture or discipline specific perspectives that creative approaches can be initiated and developed, without or with less anxiety concerning the foreign than under 'normal' academic circumstances (see Hüther, 2011: 131-2). Not only does this co-presence of approaches amplify aspects that are considered vital to science (the "systematic comparison of one knowledge with another for the sake of gaining a third", Baecker, 2012: 70). It also helps overcome the limitation of each local knowledge, namely that each "particular, historically and regionally bounded culture, ... permits certain questions and not others" (70). Perhaps one has to leave a country for some time, and become denaturalised, in order to appreciate these limitations. During the editing of this book, both Michael Peters and I returned to our native countries after extended periods overseas. We were both struck with what Michael called the "dark side" to our respective cultures: the unawareness of a gap in knowledge that was so obvious to outsiders like us. But all cultures have a blind spot: they cannot see that they do not see what they do not see (Baecker, 2012: 109). In academia, as much as outside of it, that lack of awareness is unfortunately more often than not accompanied by an epistemological certainty that verges on arrogance.

The authors in this book are strangers to each other's locations. They write from Aotearoa/New Zealand, Samoa, Australia, the USA, England, Germany and Switzerland. Their collective epistemological interests include Mātauranga Māori and Māori Curriculum Research; Policy, Cultural and Social Studies in Education; Philosophy of Education; Educational Theory Policy and Practice; Higher Education Administration and Research; Higher Education, Vocational Education and Adult Community Education; Social Sciences; Creative Writing; Visual Arts; Dance Performance and Choreography; Performance for Live and Recorded Media; Photography; Architecture; Spatial Design; Media and Graphic Design; Design Studies (*Designwissenschaft*); Management Research and Organisational Development. They identify with Māori, Samoan, Chinese, Australian, New Zealand,

Canadian, Black American, German, and Gay communities – or consider themselves as being between worlds. They are at the beginning or in the middle of their PhD candidature, or they have recently completed; they are in the middle of their first supervision, have just completed it, or have been supervising for many years.

Despite all the differences, we propose they share a connection: non-traditional candidates' approaches to the production of new knowledge have an affinity with the trajectories of many new and emerging research fields. The uncertainty they experience in the confrontation with knowledge systems that do not provide an easy fit for their research interests is matched by another: through their work, they raise questions that unsettle what has hence been taken for granted. And, whatever cannot be taken for granted any longer "can then be mistaken; and what can be mistaken can be translated into entirely different contexts through different interpretations" (Baecker, 2012: 159). In this condition of productive uncertainty, epistemological and methodological pluralism helps create an opening, or unfurl a horizon, in which different knowledges can be seen and shared. The co-presence of similar aspects in different phenomena then afford potential for new comparisons and new discussions (Siegesmund & Cahnmann-Taylor, 2008: 241).

Such discussions will reveal the instability and contested nature of much terminology. It is important, I believe, that the differences between language games (Wittgenstein) are kept visible. For example, diverging interpretations of the political situation in Aotearoa/New Zealand led authors deliberately to deploy different notations: *Aotearoa New Zealand* indicates a hope for, even if not the reality of, a united nation. Authors who perceive the presence of two separate cultures or societies within the nation state prefer the notation of *Aotearoa/New Zealand*. A related issue is the capitalisation of *Indigenous*: some authors prefer capitalisation, to give the term parity with its equivalent, *Western*. Others prefer not to capitalise it when referring to indigenous people who have a proper name by which they are known (e.g., Māori).

One of the central figures of this book also bears diverging names: some authors tend use *candidate*, others *student*, others again prefer *researcher*. The terms connote different status conditions, also in relation to the complementary figure, called the *supervisor* in Commonwealth countries, *advisor* in the USA and *Doktorvater/-mutter* in Germany. These terms, too, have different implications regarding the power relationships structuring the supervisory relationship, and some authors deploy those implications deliberately. Where an author did not take an explicit position, I have produced some consistency throughout the book and normally used *candidate*, *supervisor*, *Indigenous* and *Aotearoa/New Zealand* in the editing process.[6]

A central term, *non-traditional* arose originally from the reading of Stan Taylor and Nigel Beasley's *Handbook for supervisors* (2005). The terms *traditional* and *non-traditional* have a peculiar sound in Aotearoa/New Zealand, where a good part of the (colonial/anthropological) discourse of difference between Māori and Pākehā has always been concerned with what is traditional or not. Initially, calling Māori candidates non-traditional was a bit mischievous: it brushes against the grain of an automatic and unthinking tendency in the New Zealand public to assign the mark *tradition* to Māori. Later, I realised that the term is reasonably well established in the educational literature (e.g., Kiley & Liljegren, 1999; Martin, 2012; Petersen, 2012; E. Phillips & Pugh, 2005), but still I believe that it has not been theorised thoroughly. Perhaps the chapters in this volume can add to the conceptualisation of *non-traditional* students and projects.

In a sense, however, we have also assumed that we are part of a tradition, even though perhaps on its fringes: the tenor of the book assumes that qualitative research is well established, and that the premise that different kinds of interest in knowledge will require different research paradigms is widely shared today. I have therefore encouraged authors to devote their time and words to the discussion of specific aspects of their research and supervision engagements – rather than to long and general justifications of, for example, creative practice-led research *vis à vis* rationalist and/or positivist research paradigms.

In any event, even though non-traditional candidates and emerging research fields are often defined in opposition to mainstream populations, standard methods, and academic conventions, not all authors in this book define themselves and their research engagements in a similarly oppositional manner. Many seem to share awareness that "a way of seeing is also a way of not seeing" (Burke, 1984: 49) and that "every insight contains its own special kind of blindness" (41). Eliot Eisner believes that multiple perspectives are generally needed in educational research since "[e]ach template or lens one engages to see can make vivid what other lenses obscure" (2008: 22). Even if culture is, indeed, bias (Douglas), the chapters of this book promote, taken together, a cultural and thereby epistemological and methodological pluralism.

The book falls into two parts. Chapters in the first part adopt the viewpoint of non-traditional PhD candidates in exploring the specific frictions and openings they may encounter in mainstream academic life. Connecting the first and second part, two chapters outline relevant theoretical, practical and personal aspects impacting on supervision relationships and processes in non-traditional constellations. Chapters in the second part focus on questions about standards, values, methods, procedures and access that trouble and energise new and emerging research fields. An overview of these contributions is provided in chapter 10. The final chapter attempts a critique of institutional knowledge from within the institution, examining notions of the literature and scholarship; practice and research; thesis requirements and potentials for change. Contributors to the first part of the book not only provide accounts of experiences but offer alternative ways to conceptualise and theorise the PhD journey. While they cannot provide recipes, they offer choices: their reflections and provocations attend to the many insecurities prevailing in new and emerging fields of knowledge that trouble candidates' progress at times. They investigate philosophical concepts germane to their field of engagement, attempt a critical review of the extant literature, and (sometimes) offer 'how to'-tips and hints.

Chapter 2 consists of observations by eight doctoral candidates whose experiences relate to Aotearoa/New Zealand, Samoa, Germany and Australia. Moana Nepia, a dancer/choreographer/visual artist, describes how he overcame anxieties caused by the perception of his candidature as 'other' by adopting a creative way of writing. In "Ruku – dive: A physicality of thought" he explains how the clear positioning of his thesis as an exploration of a Māori concept through creative practice allowed him to develop focus and cohesion. Carl Mika, similarly, maintained a creative encounter of disparate elements. In his piece, "Western 'sentences that push' as an Indigenous method for thinking", he gives an account of his PhD engagement (across German Studies, Māori Studies and Philosophy) with Friedrich von Hardenberg (Novalis)'s concept of *Stoßsätze* (sentences that push), through which he developed a creative method of thinking about Māori ontology that retained the latter's integrity. In "A 'Psychedelic Method': Spatial exposition, perspectivism and bricklaying", Albert Refiti describes his theoretical and methodological dilemmas in trying to give an exposition of Samoan concepts of space. He found that, to account for their complexity, he had to take an approach that allowed the stitching-together of heterogeneous materials. Lynley Tulloch narrates her experience of *the scream* (Holloway) of emotional opposition and resistance when facing the dilemma of diverging perspectives between her and her supervisors. She reflects on deeply emotional aspects of academic research and how her *scream* has shaped the relationship with her supervisors and the direction of her research. In his PhD in education, Richard Heraud wants to investigate the problem of how creative thinking implicates individuals in the political process of their own formation (Negri, 1989). In "Unaware that I was walking backwards" he reflects on the first part of his candidature as an "older student", and how previous encounters with academic role models impacted his research interests. More pragmatic in orientation, Christian Wölfel sketches the story of his candidature, as the second PhD enrolment in his department of Industrial Design in a German university. His "personal report" lucidly relates the PhD journey to networks of relations between academic institution, mentors and peers, work relationships, friends and family. Katharina Bredies is another very early PhD candidate in design in Germany, in her case for a practice-led PhD. In "The tradesman's door to the ivory tower", she looks back on what she now considers a highly unusual trajectory, which renders an informative picture of early German practice-led research in the academy. Lastly, in "Sticky advice for research students" Sarah McGann and Barbara Milech reflect on key lessons learned over the course of a candidature. Sarah compiled the notes on graduation (after talking with Barbara); Barbara wrote the preface (after talking with Sarah). This piece reflects, they think, the kind of collaboration supervision at its best can be.

In chapter 3, Shane Edwards scrutinises the environment into which many Indigenous students and faculty enter. He finds that the University, its habitudes and agents continue to be ignorant of or even to resist Indigenous ways of knowing and being. Through personal narrative and an eclectic account of the emergence and development of Māori scholarship in Aotearoa/New Zealand, Edwards animates various positions and experiences of Māori doctoral learners and their connections with mainstream and Indigenous knowledge and research.

Similarly, Catherine Manathunga observes that Western/Northern academic paradigms and practices rarely consider the interests of culturally diverse international and domestic PhD candidates who make the West/North the site from which to conduct research. Manathunga explores in chapter 4 how culture can become a place of thought from which these candidates build unique contributions to new knowledge by delving into their own stores of cultural knowledge. Supervisors, then, become learners who engage with their own ignorance *as* supervisors. Despite many unhomely (Bhabha) moments of ambiguity, tension and uncertainty, this rich, creative place for new thought may open the academy up to Eastern/Southern theory. She sketches possible avenues for this journey.

In chapter 5, King Tong Ho addresses the difficulties and opportunities of a Chinese academic in a Western university, both as a PhD candidate and supervisor, in the context of art & design practice-led research. As part of a minority, in terms of research context *and* cultural identity, Ho offers his views on resolving the paradoxes surrounding marginal researcher identities and research approaches. His aim is to contribute to a more balanced stance between marginal positions and dominant Western frameworks and to the development of confluent new knowledge.

Roland Mitchell and Kirsten Edwards discuss in chapter 6 aspects of supervising/advising candidates of colour. Mitchell is a black American supervisor in a majority white higher education context in the US (where student populations are increasingly diverse, while the professoriate remains remarkably homogeneous). Students from historically disenfranchised populations are initiated into knowledge communities that devalue minority communities' ways of being and knowing. Edwards (at the time of writing a black woman advanced doctoral candidate under Mitchell's supervision) recently completed her PhD. The chapter explores epistemologies that challenge majority culture and support black graduate advisors' practice drawing on Freirian scholarship. It challenges supervisors to explore their im- or explicit epistemologies, and candidates to start the same while being socialised as the next generation of supervisors for increasingly diverse student populations.

In chapter 7, Susanne Maria Weber addresses the doctorate as an institutionalised and cultural configuration. From a Bourdieuian sociological perspective on social and cultural inequalities, the hidden agendas and rules of the game in the University and higher education are crucial. The doctorate comes into view as a process of institutional socialisation: "becoming an academic" unfolds between *habitus* and *field*, in which it is critical to acquire a *sense for the game*. The chapter suggests transformational strategies, methods and designs for epistemological interventions, the "conversion of thought" and a "revolution of the gaze" of doctoral candidates, supervisors – and academic institutions generally.

Welby Ings offers in chapter 8 a narrative critique of queer candidates and their supervisors' positions by highlighting often overlooked issues. For instance, researchers who self-declare as queer run the risk that their research is automatically considered Queer research, and there is an assumption that Queer research is aligned with tenets of Queer theory (which has a parallel in the stereotyping of Māori researchers who declare themselves as Indigenous). The often involuntary position on the fringes of academic research frequently leads queer PhD candidates to customise personalised research methodologies, which establish the 'self' as a singularity and thereby avoid generalising. Simultaneously, though, queer researchers need to consider questions of community and frequently find themselves with one foot outside the academic environment.

Creativity, like research, has a lot to do with changing the rules of the game. A creative work (written, designed, made, performed), for instance, will exceed the already known criteria and rules. It cannot be "wholly described in terms of its audience or context, because this would imply that we knew beforehand what kinds of social relation it would invoke or entail, and to what intellectual purposes it might be put" (Howard, 2007). Nevertheless, the engagement in creative research does require an outward-looking disposition, beyond the experiments of the project itself, to develop an "explicit interpretative-contextual (relational) understanding" (Franz in Durling & Friedman, 2000: 66). Since one's own empirical ability to encounter multiple points of view is limited, part of the material from which to build such understanding will be derived from reading, observing, listening, and from a "process of imaginatively thinking from standpoints not one's own; thus forming what Kant called an 'enlarged mentality'" (*eine erweiterte Denkungsart*) whose "condition of possibility is not the faculty of understanding, but imagination" (Zerilli, 2005: 161, 175). This thinking is based on what Hannah Arendt thought of (in *Lectures on Kant's Political Philosophy*) as an imagination trained to go visiting and thinking critically "from the standpoint of others" by bringing them to presence (1992: 42-43). The space of the visiting imagination is "open to all sides" (43), allowing different particular conditions to stand next to each other, never becoming the same.

Our imagined readers are doctoral candidates and their supervisors. We want the book to serve as a resource for their collaborations, a "thing in common" (Rancière, 1991: 13) to refer to individually and together. Shared reading and discussion of a relevant chapter might stimulate, we hope, not only the research process but also reflection and adjustments to the supervisory relationship (a "learning alliance", as Halse and Bansel term it, 2012: 378). The discussion of third-party advice about specific aspects of supervision relationship or process is likely to open up a shared space, in which both parties can consider how best to address needs, respond to interests, assuage anxieties. When I was a student, I thought at times that books written for supervisors were much more informative regarding the institutional aspects of supervision, while guide books for doctoral candidates helped me in other ways.

We decided to call this book a guide book, rather than a handbook, not only because of its small size (compared to the volume of most handbooks). More importantly, the term *guide book* triggers different connotations. Interestingly, several contributors (when – hopefully gently – pressed by me to extend their 'useful advice' section)

NON-TRADITIONAL WAYS TO THE DOCTORATE

insisted that theirs was not a general case, and that there was little useful advice they could give that would be generally valid: "there are more ways than one". Many shared, clearly, a reluctance to proffer PhD recipes. In any event, the diversity of our imagined readers certainly means that, whatever useful thoughts, facts or tips they find, they will probably need to translate them into their own context. This is not a bad thing since translations compel engagement and critical enquiry that simple reading often fails to elicit. The differences between even the US, UK and European systems are significant, despite periodic attempts to achieve some degree of co-ordination. While this book provides specific questions and insights related to projects in Aotearoa/New Zealand, Australia, UK, Germany and the USA, it will (as open to translation) be of more general interest, given the internationalisation of education world-wide.

A guide is, to start with, good at watching and observing (*witan*: to watch, observe) and thereby comes to know (Skeat, 1883: 247). In Old English, "*wīsian*, to render knowledgeable or shrewd, hence to guide or advise" is intimately related to *wise*. In Frankish, *witan* is more immediately related to *guide*: it means "to show the direction to" (Partridge, 2006: 3693). In Aotearoa/New Zealand, we have the tradition of Māori guides who conveyed to nineteenth century European explorers knowledge of their country, drew maps for them and often fed and carried or canoed them.[2] Early tourism relied heavily on Māori guides like Sophia Hinerangi and Kate Middlemass (and later Mākereti Papakura and Rangitīaria Dennan) – all of whom have become objects of the popular imagination (Diamond). Māori guides were hosts who imparted knowledge and understanding to their visitors, they were cross-cultural and (at least) bi-lingual mediators who knew how to deal with diversity. Good guides will only tell you about the ways they know. And while all roads may lead to Rome, we also know that each is different. That, it seems to us, is a good place from which to set out to find alternative ways to the doctorate.

NOTES

[1] Between 1998 and 2006 in Aotearoa/New Zealand, for instance, the number of Māori doctoral enrolments grew by 79%, and that of Pacific doctoral enrolments by 187% (Çinlar & Dowse, 2008: 68). Knight commented already in 1999 that the student body in Australian universities had grown much more diverse in terms of ethnicity and native language (1999: 93), and this will have continued from undergraduate to doctoral studies.

[2] For figures of PhD enrolment in non-English speaking countries, see Halse & Mowbray (2011: 516).

[3] See, for instance, Denicolo and Pope (1999 69ff). Already, an increasing diversity amongst student populations and research interests, along with a heightening sense of the implications of globalisation and neo-colonial influences on local communities or multitudes, has directly or indirectly led to changing research paradigms and epistemologies (see Halse & Mowbray, 2011: 516-7). They have initiated new fields of scholarly engagement: women's studies and postcolonial studies are two early examples, Indigenous research paradigms and gay and lesbian approaches more recent. These changes finds expression, for instance, in the inclusion of two chapters on kaupapa Māori methodologies by Linda Tuhiwai Smith and Russell Bishop in *The Sage handbook of qualitative research* edited by Norman Denzin and Yvonna Lincoln (2005: 85-138). It is staggering that the epistemological

or methodological innovations non-traditional candidates bring to academic research are seldom acknowledged.
4 The engagement with the requirements of this particular supervisory relationships later gave rise to a joint publication with the candidate, Azadeh Emadi (Engels-Schwarzpaul & Emadi, 2011).
5 Chapters on off-campus and part-time candidatures, interactivity design and on collaboration in new media productions, for instance, were planned, but the authors were unable to fit them into their lives and schedules. These configurations are addressed at various levels of details in Thomson & Walker (2010b).
6 That process was different in different cases. While some authors submitted nearly print-ready drafts, in which case my editing amounted to not much more than copy editing, it was more like a collaborative process in some others. Typically, and not surprisingly, chapters from authors who write from outside the Anglo-Saxon language and educational research sphere involved more clarification and translation. Translation, actually, is also a major theme of the subject matter of this book. I will return to this aspect in chapter 10.
7 The explorers, in turn, then defined new routes, mapped the territory differently and named the landscape in their image. Often unfaithful to their hosts' intentions, "[t]hey helped bring 'Māori land' … increasingly under European authority" (J. Phillips).

REFERENCES

Arendt, H. (1958). *The human condition.* Chicago, IL: The University of Chicago Press. (1958)
Arendt, H. (1992). *Lectures on Kant's political philosophy. Edited and with an interpretive essay by Ronald Beiner.* Chicago, IL: The University of Chicago Press.
Baecker, D. (2012). *Wozu Kultur?* Berlin, Germany: Kadmos.
Burke, K. (1984). *Permanence and change: An anatomy of purpose.* Berkeley, CA: University of California Press.
Çinlar, N., & Dowse, J., &. (2008). *Human resource trends in the tertiary academic workforce.* Wellington, New Zealand: Tertiary Education Commission, Te Amorangi Mātauranga Matua.
Cunningham, C. (2011). Chapter 11: Adolescent development for Māori. In *Improving the transition. Reducing social and psychological morbidity during adolescence. A report from the Prime Minister's Chief Science Advisor* (pp. 145–152). Auckland, New Zealand: Office of the Prime Minister's Science Advisory Committee.
Denicolo, P., & Pope, M. (1999). Supervision and the overseas student. In Y. Ryan & O. Zuber-Skerritt (Eds.), *Supervising postgraduates from non-English speaking backgrounds* (pp. 63–74). Maidenhead, England: Open University Press.
Denzin, N. K., & Lincoln, Y. S. (2005). Epilogue: The eighth and ninth moments: Qualitative research in/and the fractured future. In N. K. Denzin & Y. S. Lincoln (Eds.), *The Sage handbook of qualitative research* (pp. 1115–1127). London, England: Sage Publications, Inc.
Diamond, P. (22 September 2012). *Te tāpoi Māori - Māori tourism. 20th-century Māori tourism.* Retrieved from http://www.TeAra.govt.nz/en/te-tapoi-maori-maori-tourism/page-2
Durling, D., & Friedman, K., &. (2000). *Doctoral education in design: Foundations for the future.* Stoke on Trent, England: Staffordshire University Press.
Eisner, E. (2008). Persistent tensions in arts-based research. In M. Cahnmann-Taylor & R. Siegesmund (Eds.), *Arts-based research in education: Foundations for practice* (pp. 16–27). New York, NY: Routledge.
Engels-Schwarzpaul, A.-Chr. (2007, 6 - 9 December). Traversing the distance between the known and unknown: Fastening one's seatbelt in postgraduate creative-practice research supervision. *PESA - Philosophy of Education Society of Australiasia* symposium *Creativity Enterprise and Policy - New Directions in Education,* Wellington. Retrieved from http://www.academia.edu/attachments/31270726/download_file
Engels-Schwarzpaul, A.-Chr., & Emadi, A. (2011). Thresholds as spaces of potentiality: Non-traditional PhD candidatures in art and design. *ACCESS Critical Perspectives on Communication, Cultural and Policy Studies, 30*(2), 1–14.

Gumbrecht, H. U., Maturana, H. R., & Poerksen, B. (2006). Humberto R. Maturana and Francisco J. Varela on science and the humanities: The Poerksen interviews. *Journal of Aesthetic Education, 40*(1), 22–53.

Halse, C., & Bansel, P. (2012). The learning alliance: Ethics in doctoral supervision. *Oxford Review of Education, 38*(4), 377–392.

Halse, C., & Mowbray, S. (2011). The impact of the doctorate. *Studies in Higher Education, 36*(5), 513–525.

Hardt, M., & Negri, A. (2005). *Multitude: War and democracy in the age of empire*. New York, NY: Penguin Group USA.

Howard, P. (2007). Creative writing and Schiller's aesthetic education. *The Journal of Aesthetic Education, 41*(3), 41–58.

Hüther, G. (2011). Was wir sind und was wir sein könnten. Ein neurobiologischer Mutmacher. Frankfurt a.M., Germany: S. Fischer.

Kehm, B. M. (2007). The changing role of graduate and doctoral education as a challenge to the academic profession: Europe and North America compared. *Key Challenges to the Academic Profession*, 111–124.

Kiley, M., & Liljegren, D. (1999). Discipline-related models for a structured program at the commencement of a PhD. *Teaching in Higher Education, 4*(1), 61–75.

Knight, N. (1999). Responsibilities and limits in the supervision of NESB research students in social sciences and humanities. In Y. Ryan & O. Zuber-Skerritt (Eds.), *Supervising postgraduates from non-English speaking backgrounds* (pp. 93–100). Maidenhead, England: Open University Press.

Martin, A. (2012). Supervising doctorates at a distance: Three trans-Tasman stories. *Quality Assurance in Education, 20*(1), 42–53.

Partridge, E. (2006). *Origins. A short etymological dictionary of modern English*. London, England: Routledge.

Petersen, E. B. (2012). Re-signifying subjectivity? A narrative exploration of 'non-traditional' doctoral students' lived experience of subject formation through two Australian cases. *Studies in Higher Education*, 1–12.

Phillips, E., & Pugh, D. S. (2005). *How to get a PhD: A handbook for students and their supervisors*. Maidenhead, England: Open University Press.

Phillips, J. (13 July 2012). *European exploration. Discovery and exploration*. Retrieved from http://www.teara.govt.nz/en/european-exploration/page-1

Rancière, J. (1991). *The ignorant schoolmaster: Five lessons in intellectual emancipation* (K. Ross, Trans.). Stanford, CA: Stanford University Press.

Ryan, Y., & Zuber-Skerritt, O. (1999). *Supervising postgraduates from non-English speaking backgrounds*. Maidenhead, England: Open University Press.

Shulman, L. S. (2010). Doctoral education shouldn't be a marathon. *Chronicle of Higher Education, 56*(30), B9–B12.

Siegesmund, R., & Cahnmann-Taylor, M. (2008). The tensions of arts-based research reconsidered: The promise for practice. In M. Cahnmann-Taylor & R. Siegesmund (Eds.), *Arts-based research in education: Foundations for practice* (pp. 231–246). New York, NY: Routledge.

Skeat, W. W. (1883). *An etymological dictionary of the English language*. Oxford, England: Clarendon Press.

Slee, J. (2010). A systemic approach to culturally responsive assessment practices and evaluation. *Higher Education Quarterly, 64*(3), 246–260.

Taylor, S., & Beasley, N. (2005). *A handbook for doctoral supervisors*. Milton Park, UK: Routledge.

Thomson, P., & Walker, M. (2010a). Doctoral education in context: The changing nature of the doctorate and doctoral students. In P. Thomson & M. Walker (Eds.), *The Routledge doctoral student's companion: Getting to grips with research in education and the social sciences* (pp. 9–26). Milton Park, England: Routledge.

Thomson, P., & Walker, M. (Eds.). (2010b). *The Routledge doctoral student's companion: Getting to grips with research in education and the social sciences*. Milton Park, England: Routledge.

Ulmer, G. L. (1994). *Heuretics: The logic of invention*. Baltimore, MD: The John Hopkins University Press.

Walker, G. E., Golde, C. M., Jones, L., Bueschel, A. C., Hutchings, P., & Shulman, L. S. (2008). *The formation of scholars. Rethinking doctoral education for the twenty-first century*. Standford, CA: Jossey-Bass.

Wisker, G. (2005). *The good supervisor*. Basingstoke, England: Palgrave MacMillan.

Zerilli, L. M. G. (2005). "We feel our freedom": Imagination and judgment in the thought of Hannah Arendt. *Political Theory, 33*(2), 158–188.

AFFILIATION

A.-Chr. Engels-Schwarzpaul
School of Art and Design
AUT University, Auckland

PART 1

NON-TRADITIONAL CANDIDATES

MOANA NEPIA

2(1). RUKU – DIVE

A Physicality of Thought

Take one deep, final breath.
Flip over and duck under the surface.
Dive quickly towards the bottom,
blow out.

Feel mask press in on face.
Turn to look up.
Watch bubbles rise.
Listen.
All seems quiet.

Let air from lungs,
and listen again.
What sound is this?

Stay still.
Let more air from lungs.
Sink further.
Drop legs,
but stay floating,
deeper.

Let knotted kelp unfurl slowly across your body.

Rest.
exhale further.
Empty.
Still.

Turn from the warmth of the sun.

Lift up,
and lower
to shadows' silent dance ...
four armed
slink-ripples
across rocky floor.

A.-Chr. Engels-Schwarzpaul and M. A. Peters (Eds.), Of other Thoughts: Non-Traditional Ways to the Doctorate: A Guidebook for Candidates and Supervisors, 17–22.
© *2013 Sense Publishers. All rights reserved.*

Turn to follow a silvery flash.
Clutch kelp, and kick.
Watch boggle eyed shrimps hovering casually past.
Other feelers retreat into darkened crevice.

Seaweed curtain washes silence back over.
Relax and stay calm.
Running out of breath?
Stretch legs,
and kick off with arms stretched for surface.

Unexpected surge from above pushes down,
flips over rock, and down once again.

Disorienting white noise,
heart thuds loud,
lungs about to burst,
in side searing pain.

Will to relax
and will to make air.
Feel rock with feet,
and kick off again.

Rise, blow, gasp and spit.
A salty taste, in afternoon sun.

Gather breath.
Relax.

Empty shell wind pours from ears,
to sea-breathing clouds,
unstoppable force.

Lay back in waves,
soften, light,
joints up and over
through head into spine,
femur, knees,
shins, ankles, feet.

Breakers recede in level response,
to cool heeled pleasures ...
recover and stand.

Tai...hoa.

(Nepia in Blank, 2012).

Ruku likens the emotional, physical and sensory experience of my doctoral journey to diving. At times, this felt like running out of breath while being tossed out of control or held underwater by a churning wave. At other times, the ebbs and flows of mood or creative energies, the experiences of exploration, discovery and revelation were much calmer. Adopting a creative approach to writing as part of my practice-led investigation proved beneficial in several ways:

- it brought the action of writing closer to the creative investigation I was pursuing in the project as a whole;
- it provided me with a way to articulate, reflect upon and share insights with others, including my supervisors;
- it deepened my level of engagement with the main kaupapa, or subject, of my investigation and key source material – poetic texts and art works that I referred to;
- it drew upon kinaesthetic, choreographic and sensory ways of knowing through the body I was familiar with as a performer and choreographer;
- it followed cultural precedents of synthesising and positioning knowledge in relation to the environment;

This approach also helped me overcome anxieties that my candidature might be perceived as 'other' or 'non-traditional'. I did not want to feel distanced or 'other' in relation to my subject, the project or its methods, but normal and connected to it. To reach this state was not easy.

Midway through my doctoral journey, I received a warning from one of my supervisors that my project seemed to be "drifting" or "floating". My combined use of dance, creative writing, performance, video and installation was identified as a potential weakness unless I could "consolidate" my thinking, develop a stronger theoretical "framework" for what I was attempting to do, and "ground" the investigation in relation to existing approaches and bodies of knowledge that "others" could recognise, I had a serious problem. If I could not make enough sense to my supervisors, how could I expect other "others", including potential examiners, to comprehend what I was doing?

I accepted the criticism but struggled with some of the terms used to convey this message. "Framing" and "consolidating" seemed counter-intuitive to my choreographic and kinaesthetic senses and desire to centralise the body. "Floating" and "drifting," on the other hand, seemed potentially useful terms to describe phases within a creative process – moments of heightened sensory perception. I needed to reconcile potentially divergent interpretations of terms I was using and radically reassess my use of language in order to be understood. Eventually, terms I found problematic, such as "frameworks", "methodology" and "epistemology", were either rejected or temporarily put to one side while I searched for others that were more aligned with the cultural context in which the thesis was positioned. In this process, writing became less of an emotional struggle.

An interpretation of *thesis* as a *positioning* of knowledge is aligned with the Māori concept of *whakapapa*, a genealogical paradigm in which people and ideas are positioned through relationships. As a concept, whakapapa was also used to determine cultural relevance, validity and appropriateness of methods and sources. The methodology was titled *Aratika* to indicate an appropriate (tika) pathway or methodological approach (ara), exploring metaphors related to *takutai moana* (foreshore). In this geographical, historical and theoretical realm, drifting, floating, advancing and receding, building up and washing away could be understood as actions familiar to the choreographer, dancer and swimmer.

The term *kaupapa* was adopted to describe the subject matter of my investigation because of its alternative interpretations as platform, plan or schedule, as well as its associations with movement and grounding: *kau* translates as both ancestor or swim, and *papa*, an abbreviation of Papatūānuku (Earth Mother), also translates as grounding or layering. Swimming, floating and drifting could be thought together with grounding, layering and consolidation.[1] The investigation proceeded as a cumulative process of layering based on knowing one-self and what has gone before. From an ancestral and bodily grounding, it then moves to explore 'other' horizons.

Poetic texts and *whakapapa* from nineteenth century Ngatī Porou[2] *tohunga* (scholar), Mohi Ruatapu were identified as key source material for my thesis, which investigated *Te Kore* – the Māori concept of *void*, *absence* and *nothingness*, also understood as *potentiality*. His *kōrero* (narratives) informed my understanding of the main *kaupapa* and the development of *Aratika*, but this process was not entirely straight forward because I am not a native Māori speaker. I had to refer to expert translations of terms offered by others, consult with native speakers, and compare Ruatapu's interpretations of *Te Kore* with those from other contexts, including *maramataka* (Māori lunar calendars), personal and *whānau* (family) narratives, and artwork by Māori artists. Some of Ruatapu's propositions about *Te Kore* differ from those offered by other tribal accounts, and coming to terms with this layer of difference or *otherness* was complicated by my lack of fluency in the Māori language. My two main supervisors were not fluent in Māori either, and neither of them were dance or performance specialists.

At times, my grappling with specific cultural content was at odds with their concerns to focus on structure, frameworks and consolidation. A specialist Māori supervisor may have helped me much earlier to consider Ruatapu's kōrero as a source of precedents for articulating my methodology from a basis in *mātauranga Māori* (Māori knowledge), but this was not an option at the School of Art and Design at AUT. Instead, I sought advice from various *whānau* (relatives), who were also repositories of tribal knowledge – a process I continued after a third Māori supervisor, Wiremu Kaa,[3] was eventually appointed. They helped me to consolidate my understanding of key concepts and texts, and reassured me that I needn't feel *at odds*, *other* or insecure about what I was attempting to do. The approach I was developing made sense to them as part of a continuum – my creative proposals and approach could be perceived in relation to inherited traditions of creative practice and thought.

The *gap* in my knowledge about Te Kore, and the lack of suitable inter-disciplinary creative practice-led models based on mātauranga Māori (Māori knowledge), eventually presented themselves as *creative opportunities* – realms of *potentiality*, rather than as sources of anxiety, *emptiness, lack* or *void*. Through perceiving my own predicament in terms of Te Kore, I found ways to align and differentiate my project as Māori (normal), not *other*. This practical application of knowledge could not have been achieved or demonstrated without having first found a deeper level of connection and understanding with my subject matter. *Aratika*, as a methodology, also remained open, so that others adopting this approach could develop their own creative proposals and interpretations of Te Kore.

Although I felt encouragement and support from my supervisors to pursue this pathway, at times I also felt very much alone within what Carola Conle might describe as a personal *quest* to understand origins. This quest was not an entirely introspective process but an artistic and intellectual journey that included "explorations of contexts and social interactions" (2000, pp.191-193). Fortunately, my supervisors were sufficiently conversant with the broader political and cultural issues contextualising my project to recognise that it could not succeed without additional specialist guidance and support within the areas of performance and mātauranga Māori. They agreed to steer me through the relevant academic processes on this basis, offering extensive critique of both written and practical work. As designers, they also encouraged and assisted me to make core themes of my thesis explicit in the design and layout of the exegesis. This was eventually presented as three inter-related volumes. Volume one, a compilation of video imagery and creative texts including *Ruku*, offered a sensory introduction to the thesis. Other more 'traditional' sections, including a review of knowledge and methodology chapter, were included in the other two volumes, together with a DVD of video and performance work.

The reconciliation of inter-disciplinary, emotional, physical and intellectual issues in this project was partly an issue of design: reconciling otherness with self through poetic approaches to writing, choreography and performance. Adequate provision of support, from outside as well as within the University, eventually helped me to overcome personal and institutional limitations, including the risk that my project may have been perceived as *other*. The quest to overcome the distance and separation of not knowing was eventually achieved through recognising that creative thought entangles emotions with physical and sensory experiences. As "essential elements of human intelligence," emotions are, as Martha Nussbaum suggests, "not just the fuel that powers the psychological mechanism of a reasoning creature" but "highly complex and messy parts of this creature's reasoning itself" (Nussbaum, 2001, 3).

NOTES

[1] Vapi Kupenga, a Māori broadcaster and repository of tribal knowledge to whom I am also related, sheds further light on this possibility via reference to the Ngāti Porou saying *Ko koe te papa o āhau mahi*. Elaborating on a literal translation, *you are the foundation (*or *ground) for your own work*, she suggests more poetic interpretations – you must be grounded first in order to move or, alternatively, once the groundwork is established, the kau (ancestor) swims, comes into view, or goes on from there (Nepia, 2012, p115).

[2] Ngāti Porou is one of the iwi (tribes) I belong to.
[3] Wiremu Kaa is a retired Māori educationalist, Ngāti Porou tribal elder and repository of tribal knowledge to whom I am related.

REFERENCES

Blank, A. (2012). *Ora Nui. 2012. Māori Literary Journal.* Auckland, Aotearoa/New Zealand: Anton Blank Ltd.
Conle, C. (2000). Thesis as Narrative or "What Is the Inquiry in Narrative Inquiry?" *Curriculum Inquiry, 3*(2), 189–214.
Nepia, P.M. (2013). *Te Kore – Exploring the Māori concept of void.* [Unpublished PhD thesis]. Auckland, Aotearoa/New Zealand: AUT University.
Nussbaum, M.C. (2008). *Upheavals of thought. The intelligence of emotions* (8th ed.). Cambridge, England: Cambridge University Press.

AFFILIATIONS

Moana Nepia
Te Whānau ā Te Aotawarirangi, Te Whānau ā Ruataupare, Te Whānau a Hinerupe,
Te Aitanga ā Hauiti, Ngāti Porou, Rongowhakaata, Ruawaipu.
AUT University, Auckland

CARL MIKA

2(2). WESTERN "SENTENCES THAT PUSH" AS AN INDIGENOUS METHOD FOR THINKING

Indigenous doctoral students in the humanities are often faced with the gruelling task of representing the worldview/s of their people as sympathetically and correctly as possible. This holds true both for students who are undertaking qualitative research to address a particular problem, as well as for those who wish to engage in an entirely philosophical or theoretical inquiry. In the case of the former, a challenge lies in presenting interviewees' voices in ways that closely correspond with what the interviewees intend their responses to mean; in the latter, the literature of the key philosopher must be put forward accurately, but the Indigenous writer must be capable of melding the philosophy with his or her own, possibly very different voice.

My own method of inquiry fell into that latter category, with my thesis seeking to explore the reclamation of mystery through Novalis' notion of Being.[1] Novalis (the pen name of Friedrich von Hardenberg) was an eighteenth century, Early Romantic German poet and philosopher, and it quickly became apparent to me that, although I was referring to a philosopher at a distant remove from my own culture, I was nevertheless engaging with notions of ontology that deserved respect. Not only did Novalis make assertions about Being, he also encouraged the reader to critique an excessive focus on certainty. For that reason, I felt compelled to follow suit and mimic his style of critique in a Māori context. I had to find a method that would allow me to somehow retain the uniqueness of my own position, and the Indigenous culture that situates it, whilst immediately engaging with a Western philosopher.

I had always planned to refer to Novalis as an impetus, and had figured from quite early on that this approach would retain the integrity of a Māori worldview. As luck would have it, Novalis himself proposed this same method quite explicitly, by stating that any of his fragments should act as "sentences that push", or *Stoßsätze* (1960b, p. 374), but that they should not step forward as constraining thought in advance of the writer. The aim, for him, was to get the writer to think "in the wake of" his sentences, and to transform banal perceptions of things in the world within the social and philosophical horizon of the writer (which may be different to that of Novalis). He called this active method *poeticisation*, where the world could be 'romanticised'. As a Māori writer, my method turned entirely on intellectually and emotionally responding to his sentences, to discuss the colonisation of Māori philosophy and metaphysics, and also to romanticise scientised Māori terms.

A.-Chr. Engels-Schwarzpaul and M. A. Peters (Eds.), Of other Thoughts: Non-Traditional Ways to the Doctorate: A Guidebook for Candidates and Supervisors, 23–26.
© 2013 Sense Publishers. All rights reserved.

Thus the challenge for me was twofold. First, I had to interpret Novalis' sentences in the wider context of what he calls "the Absolute" (cf. Wood, 2007, p. 195) or "Seyn" (Being) (1960a, p. 266). This is not widely carried out in Romantic scholarship. Novalis' fragments are known to be at times contradictory, but this is meant to reflect the paradoxical nature of that overarching phenomenon of Being. Then, I had to explore current Māori scholarship in light of those fragments – and this exploration had to be as relevant for a Māori audience as possible. One particularly poignant example was my interpretation of a Māori notion of Being itself, brought about by a conversation between Novalis' assertion that "*Absolute absolute* or *absolute*² is the highest and the ultimate" (cf. Wood, 2007, p. 195), Heidegger's maxim that "das Nichts nichtet" (1998, p. 39) ("the nothing noths"; Inman, 1999, p. 274), and the Māori phenomenon of *korekore* ("thorough negativity"/ Being; Marsden, 2003, p. 20). If Novalis had provided a system of thought that prescribed my approach to Being then I might have 'applied' his system to a Māori assertion of Being. Instead, his idea served as an impetus, illuminating for me what the active nature of Being was for Māori but not prescribing my description of it within the limits of his own philosophies. In that example, Novalis brought to my attention the possibility of a type of chaos within Being: it is so negative that it evidences positive attributes. Heidegger deepened my exploration (and extended Novalis' assertion) by speculating that even what is considered to be 'nothing' has a negative action. On the push of those sentences, I could consider *korekore* within the possible realms of negative and continuous action. The jolt that Heidegger and Novalis provided for my thinking took place in an analysis of the term *korekore* through Māori scholarship.

In the sentence that pushes, the Māori concern, spurred on by the Western philosopher, has alighted on the Western fragment and carried it onward to an apparent conclusion. The outcome is manifestly Māori in flavour, as it retains to it some very vibrant Māori metaphysical aspects – but what has happened to the initial sentence that liberated the Māori writer and, in a sense, allowed the Māori writer to take flight to begin with? In essence, this sentence endures, but in a hidden way. That first principles, such as provocative sentences, persist, is an element of both Novalis' and Māori metaphysics. Māori notions of *wana* (awe), for instance, allow for the thrill of an object to shine through, despite its concealment. It is perhaps even its hiddenness that revitalises thinking; the term *whakaaro*, which refers to an active "becoming of thought" as much as to "think" in a cognitive sense, also implores the thinker to cast their concern towards what cannot be discerned, because one is constantly becoming (*whaka*), concerned about (*aro*) something, with the implication that this process is one always in the making. Thus to overlook the continued presence of Novalis' work, simply because I describe a Māori phenomenon, would deny the reality of that becoming. And it would rely precisely on a way of thinking that Novalis recoiled from – the final, systematic and overly cognitive approach to a thing that provides an outcome for my consumption. Novalis' fragments flourish underneath, and indeed within, the Māori product.

In that light, then, a sustained reference to a Western philosopher in my doctoral studies – particularly to glean some ontological orientation on existence – carries with it both promise and concern. The method holds promise because it can bring to our Indigenous attention matters of colonisation and enable us to propose theories that confront it from an Indigenous perspective. Perhaps disquieting for some Indigenous writers, however, is that such a reference yields a surface of writing with some undeniably 'Other' undercurrents. Yet, arguably, kaupapa Māori research methods – which are regularly invoked in masters and doctoral studies – are no different, because they are still sustained by, and infused with, some highly discernible Western philosophical discourses and frames of thought, despite their obviously Māori visage and the fact that the responsible philosophers aren't mentioned. The continuing presence of colonisation that Indigenous peoples are met with pervades even everyday life, from everyday general discussions to writing a thesis.

FREE THINKING IN THE SUPERVISION PROCESS

Everyday general discussions and writing a thesis are two apparently unrelated activities. In part, I chose them as contrasting examples of the extent to which Indigenous peoples, generally speaking, must participate in a reality that is never entirely divorced from Western metaphysics. They appear to lie far enough from each other on a spectrum for me to be able to insert another activity somewhere in between them: doctoral supervision. Doctoral supervision, from my perspective as a Māori student, brings together the voices of text, self, other, and ancestor, into one space. Again, as with writing, casting one's awareness towards a focused dialogue illuminates what is not immediately apparent, but is nonetheless extant: the essence of what one has been reading; the current concern that either plagues or pleases the self; the *whakapapa* (inheritance) that has gone before and the events associated with that; and the presence of the supervisor (and indeed their own concerns and inheritances). Novalis, along with the other Early German Romantics, emphasised that one should be aware of expressive mystery, and supervision certainly competes with any other activity for its orientation towards the hidden.

My supervision experience leads me to emphasise that the Māori student shouldn't be afraid of supervisors from other cultures, just as they shouldn't disdain philosophies from without. The student and supervisor who create an open space for thinking are immediately involved in compelling sentences, regardless of the political views or cultural knowledge they bring with them. For Māori, supervision should therefore be treated with some respect, although obviously the experience should not be a dourly humourless one. Indeed, a doleful approach to supervision would not be a respectful one. At times when even the bleakest features of colonisation would confront me, when I was contemplating its darkest ontological depths, there was room for laughter at some frequently vague absurdity. Sentences that push in supervision – where supervisor and student creatively bounce ideas off each other – have the capacity, for Māori students, to highlight the poetic nature of the world alongside its highly constrained opposite, and to that extent give rise to a certain dark irony. I imagine that Novalis, being a Romantic, would have been sympathetic to that outcome. Moreover, his text was at the centre of supervision meetings; he may have been amused himself that he was being referred to *so* centrally in a Māori doctorate.

NOTE

[1] I started my thesis in 2007, enrolled in German Studies, University of Waikato. The thesis was examined in 2012.

REFERENCES

Heidegger, M. (1998). *Was ist Metaphysik?* Frankfurt am Main, Deutschland: Vittorio Klostermann GmbH.
Inwood, M. (1999). Does the nothing noth? In A. O'Hear (Ed.), *German philosophy since Kant* (pp. 271–290). Cambridge, UK: Cambridge University Press.
Marsden, M. (2003). *The woven universe: Selected writings of Rev. Māori Marsden*. Otaki, Aotearoa/New Zealand: Estate of Rev. Māori Marsden.
Novalis. (1960a). Philosophische Studien der Jahre 1795/96: Fichte-Studien. In P. Kluckhohn & R. Samuel (Eds.), *Schriften: Das philosophische Werk I* (Vol. 2, pp. 29–296). Stuttgart, Deutschland: W. Kohlhammer.
Novalis. (1960b). Philosophische Studien des Jahres 1797: Hemsterhuis und Kant-Studien. In P. Kluckhohn & R. Samuel (Eds.), *Schriften: Das philosophische Werk I* (Vol. 2, pp. 299–395). Stuttgart, Deutschland: W. Kohlhammer.
Wood, D. (Ed.). (2007). *Novalis: Notes for a romantic encyclopaedia*. Albany, NY: State University of New York Press.

AFFILIATION

Carl Mika
Tūhourangi, Ngāti Whanaunga
Faculty of Education, University of Waikato

ALBERT L. REFITI

2(3). A "PSYCHEDELIC METHOD"

Spatial Exposition, Perspectivism and Bricklaying

To undertake research on customary Samoan knowledge of space and architecture from the perspective of a Samoan architect or spatial designer requires a rethinking of methodology. As I am about to draw together my research to write up my PhD, I put together the materials and sources on Samoan culture that I have revisited and reviewed to generate an alternative narrative of Samoan notions of space and the architecture of the traditional *faletele* (meeting house). I found that, to account for the complexity of Samoan concepts of space, I had to take an approach that enabled the stitching-together of heterogeneous materials from many archives: theology, cosmology, anthropology, sociology, archaeology, cultural studies, philosophy and architecture. In my attempt to stitch together the many pieces, seams were left exposed, in places even untrimmed. The result so far is 'patchy', having a 'psychedelic effect' that is not altogether unexpected. The patchiness reveals a PhD project still in process, but it would not be surprising if (some of) this mottled effect were retained in the final thesis submission, for its potential to produce daring concepts.

My thesis, *Spatial Exposition of Samoan Architecture*, evolves from a consideration of the role that space has played recently in the quest to construct a Samoan identity in the New Zealand, Australian and the US diasporas.[1] This quest is motivated by the desire to create alternative spaces of relations, which maintain customary Pacific heritage in the diaspora and can serve as a platform from which to assert Pacific values and heritage in a new home.[2] This positive ideological project mines traditional Pacific ideas, forms and concepts – to transform them into symbols of identity that have already become characteristic markers and icons of the *Pasifika* community in New Zealand.[3] In relation to this project, my PhD attempts to provide a contextual history of the way in which a particular type of space, now used in this search for identity, came about in Samoa. This attempt required, first of all, an understanding of the genesis of the concept of space in Samoan thought, and then of the way in which Samoan identity became bonded to it. Only with that understanding would I be able to probe the question of whether architectural form emerged in Samoa from the desire to bond space to identity or whether it is a consequence of something else.

A.-Chr. Engels-Schwarzpaul and M. A. Peters (Eds.), *Of other Thoughts: Non-Traditional Ways to the Doctorate: A Guidebook for Candidates and Supervisors*, 27–33.
© 2013 Sense Publishers. All rights reserved.

Cosmological perspectivism

A. L. REFITI

At the heart of my project is a particular *perspectivism*, a Samoan perspective in my research question that situates the work firmly within Samoan thought. With this perspectivism, an account of the concept of space, a *spatial exposition*, from within this tradition becomes possible. In it, I seek to *exhibit*[4] the contents of the concept of space, rather than provide a definition of space. The exposition is an engagement with social space and lived situations, in which concepts, identities and polities are continually produced and consumed from within Samoan culture and society, in what Brazilian anthropologist Eduardo Vivieros de Castro termed "cosmological perspectivism".[5] Cosmological perspectivism opens and orients the researcher to many possible worlds in which beings (animals/humans/environment) and objects circulate. It encompasses a *cosmocentric* perspective that supposes "a spiritual unity and a corporeal diversity [where] culture or the subject would be the form of the universal, whilst nature or the object would be the form of the particular" (Vivieros de Castro, 1998: 470).[6]

Samoan cosmogony was, therefore, one place in which to start locating a cosmocentric view of the world, as well an understanding of the birth of space in Samoan thought.[7] Accordingly, I carried out an exposition of the *Solo o le vā*, a chant and narrative account of the birth of the world.[8] The text provides a perspective on how the world was born and became differentiated into many parts, constituting the firmament, the environment, and humans – each part arising from a bifurcation of Papa, the original matter. In this cosmogony, each being can trace its lineage to the original being, and all human beings have a genealogy connecting directly to the ancestor gods.

There are two aspects of space I was interested in. First, the spatial relations bonding the Samoan social sphere, or *vā*,[9] and, second, the shape, form and material realities of such a bonding. Exposition is a method of 'exhibiting', in the sense of 'something opening up' (or, to expose or exposit), as in the Samoan notion of *teu* (to reveal and embellish, to ornament and adorn in a public manner). What *teu*, as exposition, highlights is the crucial link with 'publicness'. This publicness prevails in the form of an openness, everywhere in a traditional Samoan settlement,[10] which is most effectively felt at the centre of a *faletele*, where an invisible force always seems to inhabit the centre that never escapes our gaze.[11]

Thus, in my form of spatial exposition, a territory is a meshwork (Ingold) that takes place within social organisations, in every culture, according to and within its own particular perspectivism.[12] The meshwork interprets the operations of a particular spatial language and its coding of the comings and goings of different forms of cultural milieu. This interpretation, too, becomes an exposition, as a methodological task that unfolds an understanding of Samoa spatial concepts. And this, in turn, will show how Samoans make and think about their architecture.

What characterises the origin and shaping of the Samoan world is a predisposition for things to unfold (*māvae*) into rampant diversity; periods of such growth are followed by periods of extreme order (*tōfiga*), during which responsibility is brought to bear on every element that was created: the task to organise, to group and to

A "PSYCHEDELIC METHOD"

facilitate relations. *Vā*, the Samoan concept of space,[13] is an image of this 'toing and froing' from divergence/divarication to the orderly/unitary, from the smooth to the striated, from lines of flight to knots and entanglement. These movements facilitate the coming into being of *tagata* (humans), who are agents of both growth and inertia.

This pulsating image of confinement and release is like the rolling motion of the ocean, which gathers and pushes up a stair-casing energy of water into a bulging restrained force that, once released, causes an almighty clamour. It shapes the concepts ordering the Samoan world, which is made up of the following: *noa*: free and unrestrained, often characterising things and people outside the known polities; *mana*: divine qualities enabling people and things to be close to the ancestor gods; *tapu*: ensnaring and capturing *mana*, holding it in place so that we can access its potency. *Noa* is the impulse to untangle the constraints of *tapu* and thereby to discharge lines of flight in all directions, creating and inventing new genealogies.[14] *Tapu* establishes 'circles of control' (*fono a matai*),[15] pulling people and resources into foci regulating and distributing roles (*nofoāga*)[16] and functions (*tautua*).[17] *Mana* is the elevated and invisible seat of power and prestige emanating from the ancestor gods, which both *noa* and *tapu* aspire to.[18] *Noa* looks for *mana* in the unstructured free-space of the extended periphery beyond the social circle. *Tapu* tries to capture and control *mana* within the centre of its socialising operations. The spatial exposition at the centre of my thesis takes account of these Samoan notions of the world, which enable Samoans to talk about 'being in the world'; sustain their existence in the space given to Samoan thought by its traditions and limits; and open up *and* constrain one's ability to engage with one's tasks. At the heart of Samoan thought is a notion of space that is a 'problematic', a question of identity of how one can relate to the divine.

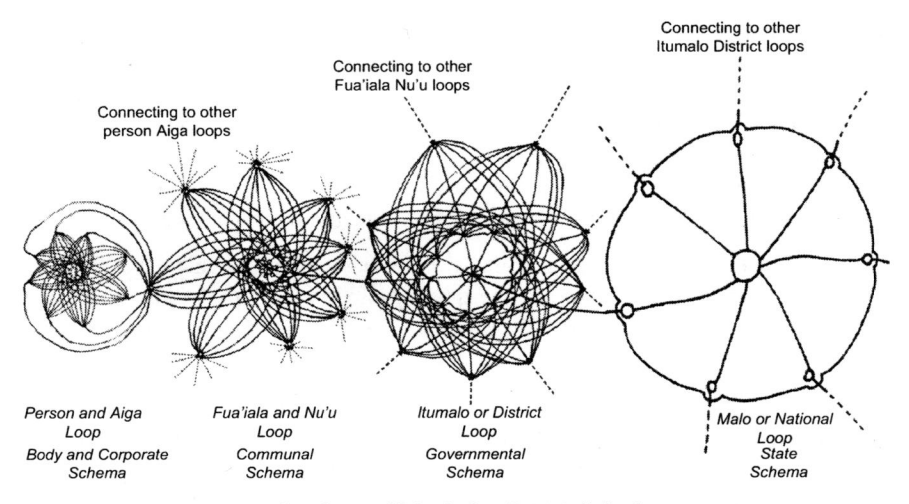

Person and Aiga Loop
Body and Corporate Schema

Fua'iala and Nu'u Loop
Communal Schema

Itumalo or District Loop
Governmental Schema

Malo or National Loop
State Schema

Connecting to other person Aiga loops
Connecting to other Fua'iala Nu'u loops
Connecting to other Itumalo District loops

Alaga System of Belonging from Person to National

Today, I can more confidently talk about my concepts in terms of the swelling and ebbing of confinement and release, as in the rolling motion of the ocean. When I started my PhD in 2009, though, I had no clearly defined methods that were suitable for my approach,[19] except for a wonderful notion by the poststructuralist philosopher Gilles Deleuze and the psychoanalyst Felix Guattari, who had twisted Claude Levi-Strauss' concept of *bricolage,* or bricklaying, into a 'smooth' desiring-machine (Deleuze & Guattari, 1983: 7; Levi-Strauss 1966: 17). One of my supervisors termed this a "psychedelic method", intimating that it must include the idealistic abandonment of a 'straight method' for madness, as when one is on a hallucinatory trip. The most renowned exponents of the psychedelic method have to be Deleuze and Guattari. Over the course of my research, they have become silent authors in the writing of a thesis on Samoan concepts of space and architecture. Deleuze and Guattari rejected the notion of a history that orders and subsumes events underneath its project. They truly believed that history should be a machine that works for the events that are usually subsumed underneath history.

Deleuze and Guattari termed this re-engineering of history *nomadology* (1988a: 23). History operates as a State-like apparatus (associated with striated or gridded space) that orders events (already existing in many pieces) into discrete components and insists on a particular order. Nomadology, on the other hand, is immersed in the changing state of things in such a way that the whole of history can be present. It works by avoiding sedentary perspectives of history by operating a strategy of interrupting the past (ordering the present) and instead activating 'the past *in* the present', picking up the pieces irrespective of the 'right' order. This strategy requires stitching many parts together, while each part retains its own consistency, its own voice. The "psychedelic method" is my attempt at 'activating the past in the present'. Deleuze and Guattari strove for an art of inventing and creating new concepts. Rather than bringing things together under an existing concept, they were interested in relating variables according to new concepts to create productive connections (1995: 5). This approach allows our view of things to "move beyond experience so as to be able to think anew, rather than 'standing apart' from experience, ... concepts *must* be creative or active rather than merely representative, descriptive or simplifying" (Stagoll, 2005: 51). One strategy Deleuze suggested as a way of rehabilitating the history of philosophy, and thereby creating new concepts in the process, was a form of 'buggery' or 'immaculate conception'.

> I saw myself as taking an author from behind and giving him a child that would be his own offspring, yet monstrous. It was really important for it to be his own child, because the author had to actually say all I had him saying. But the child was bound to be monstrous too, because it resulted from all sorts of shifting, slipping, dislocations, and hidden emissions that I really enjoyed (Deleuze, 1995: 6).

This practice of buggery distinguishes Deleuze from the operation of deconstruction. Rather than approaching texts with suspicions, Deleuze advised his students to "trust the author you are studying. Proceed by feeling your way. You must silence the voices of objection within you. You must let him speak for himself, analyze the frequency of his words, the style of his own obsessions" (Colombat, 1999: 204). The philosopher Slavoj Žižek contrasted the different approaches of deconstruction and Deleuze's nomadology by suggesting that Derrida's deconstruction proceeds in the mode of critically undermining the interpreted text or author, while Deleuze's buggery "imputes to the interpreted philosopher his own innermost position and endeavors to extract it from him" (Žižek, 2004: 47). Derrida engages in a "hermeneutics of suspicion" while Deleuze practices an excessive benevolence toward the text or author. This benevolence, Žižek intimates, is much more violent and subversive than the Derridean reading, because "his buggery produces true monsters" (47).

The reason for my adoption of a Deleuzian methodology is not to give birth to a 'bastard child', but to unfold an approach that is akin to a 'sympathetic reading', an approach concerned with the 'sensible'. I want to develop a *feeling for and towards the text*,[20] rather than a critical reading that becomes obsessed with limits, so typical of the intrusive and clinical workings of deconstruction:

> A text is merely a small cog in an extra-textual practice. It is not the question of commenting on the text by a method of deconstruction, or by a method of textual practice, or by other methods; it is a question of seeing what *use* it has in the *extra-textual practice that prolongs the text* (my emphasis) (Deleuze, 1998b: xvi).

This bricolage approach has enabled me to account for the many forked and varied pathways originating in the diverse texts from several disciplines that have something to say or ask of my topic. It also allowed me to 'pry' into them (as in: breaking an entry) and then to attempt to make these texts productive in narrating a new story. I found that you have to have sympathy with and for the materials you look at. You therefore have to 'feel the text', to read along and with the grain of its texture. From it *alight* images that will enable you to *align* images (next-to or over-laid) with other, possibly connective images. The construction of a perspectival position has not yet been helpful or easy for the writing process, though: there were and are so many conflicting situations that can easily pull one from one side to another. There is also my personal desire to account for: the ambition to take a Samoan position that is sensitive to the past but also relevant for the future. The difficulty has been, perhaps above all, a felt obligation to account for most, if not all aspects of Samoan thought. This was an error, I now believe, beginning to realise that a single work couldn't possibly account for a vast historical phenomenon.

NOTES

I want to acknowledge my supervisors Dr Tina Engels-Schwarzpaul and Dr Ross Jenner for their constructive comments on early drafts of this paper, and also my colleague Andrew Douglas who first alerted me to the idea that one has *to feel for and towards the text*.

[1] See Karlo Mila-Schaaf (2010), Melani Anae (2007) Sailiemanu Lilomaiava-Doktor (2009), Tevita Ka'ili (2008), I'uogafa Tuagalu (2008).

[2] Traditional island polities and village spaces function differently in these new settings.

Cosmological perspectivism

A. L. REFITI

3. The traditional Samoan *fale*, an architectural type predating European contact has been recruited, for instance, as the iconic representation of Samoan identity (see Engels-Schwarzpaul & Wikitera, 2009), by the Samoan government in the 1980's design of the Maota Samoa banquet room in Auckland (see Gatley, 2008), and for a Pan-Pacific meeting place at the Fale Pasifika at the University of Auckland (see Refiti 2011).
4. Exposition comes from the Latin *ponere*, originally to put aside, to put or place or set. Conjoined with the prefix 'ex' yields the Latin *exponere*: to put out, to interpret or explain. This then becomes exponent or 'to exposit'; exposition is therefore to exhibit, to publicly display (Partridge, 1966: 2509).
5. "Cosmological perspectivism" treats the world as being inhabited by different sorts of subjects or persons, human and non-human, which apprehend reality from distinct points of view, often at right angles or "perpendicular" to the opposition between relativism and universalism view of the world, which seeks to resolve partial and multiple views into a stable picture (De Castro, 2012: 45).
6. A cosmocentric perspective differs from an egocentric, sociocentric and anthrocentric perspective because it accounts for many possible ways, scales and dimensions of world that Indigenous peoples have invented.
7. There are a number of extant versions recorded by the missionaries, see Turner (1884); I have relied on a particular tradition from in Manu'a, commonly understood to be the oldest in Samoa.
8. Powell and Fraser published the interpretation of the chant first (Powell & Fraser 1892), and the chant itself five years later (Powell & Fraser 1897).
9. There are two types of *vā*: *feiloa'i* (everyday social relations) and *tapua'i* (consecrated).
10. Bradd Shore used the 'structural' image of concentric circles that converges to a centre to describe a Samoan settlement; a *malae* meeting place is located here surrounded by the *faletele* meeting house (Shore 1996: 271).
11. See Refiti (2009) for a detailed explanation of this.
12. *Meshwork* is a concept generated by Tim Ingold, who suggested that "[o]rganisms and persons ... are not so much nodes in a network as knots in a tissue of knots, whose constituent strands, as they become tied up with other strands, in other knots, comprise the meshwork" (2011: 70).
13. For the Pacific diaspora, *vā* has become an important concept by which to describe the many relationships that Pacific people have to 'navigate' and 'negotiate' in order to create (albeit temporarily) a unified Pacific identity outside of the island nations themselves (Wendt 1996, Anae 2005).
14. Bradd Shore characterised *noa* as "free", "nothing or "unmarked" to describe action that is unguided and without purpose or destination (Shore 1988: 150), while *tapu* is engaged with fa'alavelave, which is "'to tangle' or 'to make complicated'" (151).
15. Samoan villages contain a number of meeting places or *malae* lorded over by circles of *matai* or leaders made up of *ali'i* (chiefs) and *tulafale* (orators).
16. *Nofoāga* is the land on which the *matai* resides with his extended family.
17. *Tautua* pertains to services every member of a family pays to the *matai* and the village.
18. *Mana* is commonly referred to as *sā* or the sacred, which takes the form and image of a circle when applied to a family or clan.
19. I had completed a Bachelor of Architecture with Honours in 1990, which had taught me hardly more about methodologies than to be suspicious of them.
20. *Feeling* relates to Deleuze's notion of 'affect', which I interpret as reading along – rather than against – the grain of the text.

REFERENCES

Anae, M. (2007). Teu le va: Research that could make a difference to Pacific schooling in New Zealand. Paper commissioned by Ministry of Education for *Is your research making a difference to Pasifika education? Symposium*. November 2007, Wellington, Aotearoa/New Zealand.

Colombat, A. (1999). Three powers of literature and philosophy. In Ian Buchanan (Ed.), *A Deleuzian century?* (pp. 199–218). Durham, N.C.: Duke University Press.

Deleuze, G. & Guattari, F. (1983). *The anti-Oedipus: Capitalism and schizophrenia*. (Robert Hurley, Mark Seem & Helen R. Lane, Trans.). Minneapolis, MN: University of Minnesota Press.

Deleuze, G. & Guattari, F. (1988a). *A thousand plateaus: Capitalism and schizophrenia*. (Brian Massumi, Trans.). Minneapolis, MN: University of Minnesota Press.
Deleuze, G. (1995). *Negotiations 1972–1990*. (Martin Joughin, Trans.). New York, NY: Columbia University Press.
Deleuze, G. (1998b). *Essays critical and clinical* (Daniel W. Smith & Michael A. Greco, Trans.). London, England: Verso.
Engels-Schwarzpaul, A.-Chr. & Wikitera, K. (2009). Take me away … In search of original dwelling. *Interstices: A Journal of Architecture and Related Arts, 10*, 42–54.
Gatley, J. (2008). *Long live the Modern: New Zealand's new architecture, 1904–1984*. Auckland, Aotearoa/New Zealand: Auckland University Press.
Ingold, T. (2011). *Being Alive: Essays on movement, knowledge and description*. London, England: Routledge.
Ka'ili, T. (2008). Tauhi Vā: Creating beauty through the art of sociospatial relations (Unpublished PhD Thesis in Anthropology). University of Washington, Seattle, USA.
Lilomaiava-Doktor, S. (2009). Beyond "migration": Samoan population movement (malaga) and the geography of social space (vā). *The Contemporary Pacific, 21*(1), 1–32.
Mila-Schaaf, K. (2009). Pacific health research guidelines: The cartography of an ethical relationship. *International Social Science Journal, 60*(195), 135–143.
Lévi-Strauss, C. (1966). *The savage mind*. Chicago, IL: University of Chicago Press.
Partridge, E. (1966). *Origins: A small etymological dictionary of modern English*. London, England: Routledge.
Fraser, J. & Powell, T. (1892). Folk-songs and myths from Samoa. *Journal of the Polynesian Society, 6*(1), 19–36.
Fraser, J. & Powell, T. (1897). The Samoan story of creation. *Journal of the Polynesian Society, 1*(3), 164–189.
Refiti, A. (2009). Whiteness, smoothing and the origin of Samoan architecture. *Interstices: A Journal of Architecture and Related Arts, 10*, 9–19.
Refiti, A. (2011). Other Places / Other Spaces: Space and Samoan identity. Paper presented at *Tracing Footprints of Tomorrow: past lessons, present stories, future lives - Samoa Conference II*, July 4–8, 2011. National University of Samoa, Apia.
Stagoll, C. (2005). Concepts. In A. Parr (Ed.), *The Deleuze dictionary* (pp. 50–52). Edinburg, Scotland: Edinburg University Press.
Shore, B. (1989). Mana and Tapu. In A. Howard & R. Borofsky (Eds.), *Developments in Polynesian ethnology* (pp.137–175). Honolulu, HI: University of Hawaii Press.
Shore, B. (1996). *Culture in Mind: Cognition, culture, and the problem of meaning*. New York, NY: Oxford University Press.
Tuagalu, I. (2008). The heuristics of the vā. *Alternative: An International Journal of Indigenous Peoples, 4*(1), 107–126.
Turner, G. (1884). *Samoa a hundred years ago: Notes on the cults and customs of twenty-three other islands in the Pacific*. London, England: Macmillan & Co.
Vivieros de Castro, E. (1998). Cosmological deixis and Amerindian perspectivism. *The Journal of the Royal Anthropological Institute*, Vol. 4, No. 3, 469–488.
Vivieros de Castro, E. (2012). *Cosmological perspectivism in Amazonia and elsewhere*.
Viveiros de Castro, E. (2012). Cosmological perspectivism in Amazonia and elsewhere. *HAU: Masterclass Series, 1*, 45–168.
Wendt, A. (1996). Tatauing the post-colonial body. *Span, 42–43* (April–October), 15–29.
Žižek, S. (2004). *Organs without bodies: Deleuze and consequences*. New York, NY: Routledge.

AFFILIATION

Albert L. Refiti
AUT University, Auckland

LYNLEY TULLOCH

2(4). FANTASY, RESISTANCE AND PASSION AS IMPORTANT ASPECTS OF THE DOCTORAL WRITING PROCESS

MY EXPERIENCE OF RESISTANCE

The role of fantasy is central to a candidate's investment and attachment to the doctorate (Johnson, Lee & Green 2000). My particular fantasy of the academic that I aspired to be when I initially enrolled in my doctorate is associated with my background in critical social theory. My fantasies are also based on my deep respect and admiration for the radical critical scholars who taught me at both undergraduate and post-graduate level. But the fantasy of a radical scholar on which I based my dreams was challenged in the very earliest days of my doctorate. Through this challenge, I have come to realise that identity work, resistance and passion are central to the commitment of a PhD candidate when carrying out this extensive body of research. For me, this went further than an interest (strong or otherwise) in the research problem. Embodied passion and rage bring my fingers to the key board, but paradoxically can also freeze them.

So what exactly am I raging against? Through my academic work in social and political educational studies, I have identified with those who critique the devastating features of the current advanced capitalist social order. This includes the human and environmental carnage of capitalism and its justification through an instrumental rationality (see Giroux 2001). In addition, critiques concerning the 'truth claims' of science are central to the critical project. I have engaged in these theoretical debates over the years of my undergraduate and post-graduate studies and developed an academic positioning that relies heavily on Marxian critical theory. I have taken an interest in eco-socialism and, drawing inspiration from the Frankfurt school of critical theory, I have also become committed to the struggle for subversive social change. This raises questions that are not normally asked in the natural sciences (or in some areas of the social sciences and humanities), questions concerning the relationships between "knowledge, power, ideology, class, and economics" (Giroux 2001:170). A central point of resistance for me is that environmental sustainability research is currently predominantly located in the positivist science paradigm, with all its associated assumptions and truth claims. This is paradoxical, as sustainability is an overtly value-laden and political enterprise, whereas environmental science lays claim to neutrality and objectivity. Ontologically, the physical sciences generally hold a technical view of the environment and eschew the broader political context as subjective. These very

A.-Chr. Engels-Schwarzpaul and M. A. Peters (Eds.), *Of other Thoughts: Non-Traditional Ways to the Doctorate: A Guidebook for Candidates and Supervisors*, 35–38.
© 2013 Sense Publishers. All rights reserved.

inconsistencies became my research problematic. I base my doctorate on the Frankfurt school of critical theory, according to which what counts as knowledge is inherently political as it represents certain interests, and 'truth claims' are problematic.

Further, while I was interested in teasing out the links between ideologies of the environment, neo-liberal economics, and domination and power in the educational arena, I was also fostering a deeper objection. The oppression of humans through capitalist processes is linked to the oppression of non-human nature. The two are intricately connected, and science is staking its claim in what may well be the last vestige of human resistance: "the invention and reinvention of nature [is] perhaps the most central arena of hope, oppression and contestation for the inhabitants of planet earth in our times", according to Donna Haraway (1991: 1). The notion that non-human nature is on one level an invention, or a social construct, need not be antithetical to an exploration of non-human nature through the natural sciences. Nevertheless, the truth claims of natural science have effectively established a physical 'natural reality', which has a powerful grip on the minds and hearts of those in the West. Henri Giroux (2001) proposes that science as a form of rationality is integral to Enlightenment thought, and he takes this idea further to link the knowledge it produces with broader hegemonic power relations. This extends also to research in the social sciences, prompting feminists to call the imposition of quantitative research methods from the natural sciences onto the social sciences *malestream* research. Ann Oakley argues for the social and historical appreciation of divergent ways of knowing and the necessity of embracing them in emancipatory social science research (Oakley 1998: 707). Thus, the tension and pressure, felt by women researchers and others involved in the critical and emancipatory field of social inquiry, can lead to feelings of alienation. Struggling to swim upstream for legitimacy, against the current of mainstream/*malestream* research paradigms, is both a strengthening and a lonely experience. My resistance to Enlightenment ideology (with its hallmarks of objectivity and instrumental reason) is based on its critique as a master narrative generating assumptions that have destructive consequences for both humanity and non-human nature (Giroux 2005; Haraway 1991). This resistance is central to my passion for my research. It is a position and a way of being that almost seems independent of my conscious thought. It is as one: an emotional, ethical, academic, physical and spiritual drive.

THE CANDIDATE-SUPERVISOR RELATIONSHIP

My initial doctoral panel included three supervisors (one in the biological sciences and two in the social sciences and humanities). One of the potential advantages of the diversity of my supervisors' orientations might have been an enlarged dialogue across research paradigms, perhaps even a crossing of academic boundaries resulting in new and rich insights. However, this process is complicated and can be difficult to negotiate for supervisors and candidates alike. One of its potential dangers is the exacerbation of power disparities between candidate and supervisor, especially if their adopted research paradigms, methodologies and knowledge claims diverge. It can also have recognisable advantages: one of the most powerful is the strengthening of the candidate's voice through the successful challenge of normative research paradigms. My experience of writing a doctorate has involved the making and remaking of myself as an 'eco-socialist-feminist' human being (Haraway 1991). This identity work inevitably led to academic *and* emotional challenges. Having supervisors from different research paradigms meant that we had some stimulating discussions about our different approaches. However, this was a double-edged crossing of swords. Many academically stimulating team meetings with my supervisors left me struggling to reconfigure and reposition the direction of my PhD and battling with a sense of disjuncture. In those discussions, my focus on broader political relations was questioned, for example. I knew I had to find a way to allow my voice to surface, but I felt intimidated by the more sophisticated and coherent positions held by my supervisors. I also had to resist adopting their voices to replace my own.

I experienced this disjuncture as a silent, but familiar *scream* of resistance (Holloway 2002). Initially, my response was to freeze academically as I dealt with the emotions and passions that had been roused. At the root of my discomfiture was a sense that I had to justify my doctorate as a political project (as well as an educational one) whereas, for me, its political nature was the whole point. The fact that I felt unable to explain and justify this on my own terms left me floundering. Images of the traditional doctoral candidate flitted through my consciousness. That fantastical, elusive and increasingly autonomous scholar ("normatively masculine elite") haunted me (Johnson, Lee, & Green 2000: 137). My academic (and hence personal) self-image took a dive. If one of the key goals of the doctorate is the "production of the autonomous scholar self" (143), then I was falling well short at this stage. But then, one supervisor's encouragement to pursue the overtly political focus of my work gave me the much needed encouragement that my PhD research could be a valid expression of academic resistance against the oppressive features of the current global social order.

CANDIDATE IDENTITY WORK

The normative ideals of traditional research enterprise (independence, rationality, and originality) become particularly problematic when the doctoral candidate locates him- or herself outside this dominant mode of inquiry (Johnson, Lee, & Green 2000). Anna Yeatman (1995) refers to the importance of imagined possibilities for doctoral candidates, on the one hand, and the exclusionary features of the normative ideals of academic research culture, on the other. According to Yeatman, the increasing number and diversity of doctoral candidates, due to the rapid development of mass higher education, means that the traditional elitist notion and apprenticeship model of doctoral study is no longer viable. She writes, "[i]t is especially inadequate to the needs of many new PhD aspirants who, by historical cultural positioning, have not been invited to imagine themselves as subjects of *genius"* (Yeatman 1995: 9). And she adds that the "new PhD aspirants" include women and all those others who are excluded and marginalised, for example due to their class or ethnicity.

It is clear from the above that the intricate identity work of the doctoral candidate involves diverse aspects, such as forms of rationality and gender (Johnson, Lee, & Green 2000). To allow for a truly open process, the supervisor-candidate relationship needs to move beyond the traditional apprenticeship model of master and student and make space for a genuine consideration of the student voice – and, if necessary, the student's scream.

A WAY FORWARD

Through the process of exploring literature concerning my problems with doctoral relationships and processes, I have been increasingly drawn to feminist scholarship, and in particular eco-feminism. One supervisor in particular encouraged me to pursue this approach and it has proved to allow me to express my voice, and my scream. As Lesley Johnson, Alison Lee and Bill Green argue, feminism can contribute to a new PhD pedagogy that resists the old dualisms of "rationality and irrationality subject and object, autonomy and dependence" (2000: 140). I can imagine myself in this space. I can identify with feminist struggles against male dominance in narratives about non-human nature and female experience. I can write again as my fingers fly of their own accord – sometimes gently, sometimes furiously, sometimes thoughtfully and painfully – but always reflecting my own voice and recording my scream of resistance. I am whole again.

REFERENCES

Arnold, J. (2005). The PhD in writing accompanied by an exegesis. *Journal of University Teaching and Learning Practice, 2*(1), 34–50.
Cherryholmes, C. (1980, September). Social knowledge and citizenship education: Two views of truth and criticism. *Curriculum Inquiry*, 115–141.
Giroux, H. (2001). *Theory and resistance in education.* Westport, CT: Bergin and Garvey.
Haraway, D. (1991). *Simians, cyborgs and women. The reinvention of nature.* New York, NY: Routledge.
Holloway, J. (2002). *Change the world without taking power. The meaning of revolution.* London, England: Pluto Press.
Johnson, L., Lee, L., & Green, B. (2000). The PhD and the autonomous self: Gender, rationality and postgraduate pedagogy. *Studies in Higher Education, 25*(2), 135–147.
Oakley, A. (1998). Gender, methodology and people's ways of knowing: Some problems with feminism and the paradigm debate. *Sociology, 32*(4), 707–731.
Yeatman, A. (1995). Making supervision relationships accountable: Graduate student logs. *The Australian Universities' Review, 38*(2), 9–12.

AFFILIATION

Lynley Tulloch
Faculty of Education, University of Waikato

RICHARD HERAUD

2(5). UNAWARE THAT I WAS WALKING BACKWARDS[1]

INTERROGATING MY HISTORY AS IF IT WERE A PRESENT
(AN INTRODUCTION)

Returning to university as an older student is a paradoxical experience: my 23 years out of university presumed knowledge of experience, and yet it was this very knowledge that initially inhibited my theorising anew the experience that produced this knowledge. Such a paradox cannot be played out in private; every lecture, every tutorial, every conversation presents itself as an opportunity to test the relevance of such knowledge, an experience that not only led to a consciousness of my theoretical limits but also made me aware of how an older student's experience can set him apart in the company of a younger cohort. The paradox is not merely internal; it is a public and potentially hostile situation. Younger students understand the purpose of being at university according to how society has prepared them, and also how the University has been designed to meet their ends. From this perspective, an older student's participation can appear irrational and illogical.

I wouldn't have returned to university if I could have just as well learnt the same thing in the work environment. My motivation for returning was not about changing my professional status but was driven by a personal necessity to learn to think under different conditions. My consciousness of this necessity helped me to begin to think about what I had brought with me to university as a problem of thought. In order to identify this problem in greater detail, I turned away from the majority of my cohort and, instead, situated my enquiry within the interactions with my tutors and lecturers.

Albert Camus, in *The Myth of Sisyphus* (2000: 15), makes a simple but seismic claim that "[w]e get into the habit of living before acquiring the habit of thinking". The problem with a habit of living is that it relies on implicit assumptions, which are rarely scrutinised unless one's behaviour is brought into question. This inattentiveness that precedes thought leads to the commitment of errors and the formation of problems of interpretation. When I returned to university, I saw that I was unable to implicate myself intellectually in my own formation – in the way that I had come to constitute myself – and that I needed to assume responsibility for this history of my thought; this insight was no doubt influenced by my reading of Michel Foucault.[2]

A.-Chr. Engels-Schwarzpaul and M. A. Peters (Eds.), Of other Thoughts: Non-Traditional Ways to the Doctorate: A Guidebook for Candidates and Supervisors, 39–42.
© *2013 Sense Publishers. All rights reserved.*

R. HERAUD

ONTOLOGICAL FACETS OF POSSIBLE LEARNING: I DON'T SAY THAT I HAVE

Three lecturers influenced my formation as an undergraduate and, ultimately, my formation as a postgraduate: Professor Pita Sharples,[3] Professor Linda Smith and Professor James Marshall.

The first thing that struck me about Pita Sharples was that he spoke to us rather than lectured; he spoke as if our presence made us an essential party to his exposition. The lecture was about the disproportionate number of Māori in New Zealand's jails and the fact that we students were implicated in the reproduction of this reality. Pita Sharples described this situation as being symptomatic of education's creation of an inequality in society and that we, as the privileged ones, had a responsibility to address the manner in which we participate in the politics that governed this situation. While I may not agree with his analysis,[4] this does not detract from the significance of the challenge he extended. Today, while less theoretically naïve than then, I would say that it was not about the need to orient our studies explicitly towards solving this problem. Rather, it was a reminder that we continue to play a role in the reproduction of this situation, whatever our area of study, and that this situation says something about our vision for Māori.[5] For me, Pita Sharples' lecture highlighted the dysfunctional relationship that education and society shared. This reality was not unfamiliar to me; my earliest education had begun in such a socio-cultural paradox! My first experience of education was at a country school, where eighty per cent of the students were Māori.

Professor Linda Tuhiwai Smith was another significant lecturer during my undergraduate years. A superb orator, she lectured barefoot. This was an image that encompassed the relationship of feeling and thought. For myself as an older student, who had neither the tools to effectively interpret how my absence from academia had conditioned my thinking, nor the means to recognise where my future interests should lie, this experience was strangely vital. The aesthetic experience that conditioned her discourse seemed to facilitate my recognition of my theoretical interests. This fact became much clearer to me later on, when I read the biographies of Michel Foucault. At this point, I understood that my task was not to connect theory to practice, but to situate life within a practice of theory!

During the ten years prior to returning to university, painting had been what I would call my reason for being. My approach to this work comprised both an experience of *search* and *adventure*, attitudes that I always sought to maintain in relation to one another, with the intention that each should mutually condition the value of the other. These orientations functioned as *ad hoc* "truth procedures" (Badiou, 2005: xxxi); the search and the adventure being capable of their own particular truths. When painting, this approach encouraged me to seek an equivalent and yet intellectual (as against purely aesthetic) orientation to my studies. The task I had created for myself on my return to university, if formulated as a question, would be: how could I continue to be creative in my thinking, when the tasks posed by my studies required a rational description of the relation between the known and the unknown?

Furthermore, how could this relationship continue to be held in suspension? It is in this respect that Linda Smith has been a significant influence on my intellectual development. Reading her texts and attending her lectures affected an invitation to take the role of my feelings in this intellectual work as seriously as I had taken the role of my feelings in my painting. You might ask where I saw this invitation. Her lectures spoke of the relationship between the formal and the informal in a manner that seemed to be achieved through the role given to her imagination. Linda Smith taught me to trust my imagination in my intellectual work.

What drew my attention to Professor James (Jim) Marshall's was his anger, the cause of which I could not understand in the beginning. My best guess was that it related to the complex role of philosophy in education. Jim's lectures seemed to involve him playing the catalyst for a catharsis that might or might not have been consciously experienced by the student cohort. The emotions involved alluded to positivist developments that frustrated the role of philosophy in education. That said, Jim was not calling us to action or to take up his problem. He was calling us to think, that is, to consider not only the role of academic work in our formation as intellectuals, but also that this process presumed the formation of political actors. Jim's anger during his lectures, and later in his office, transmitted the notion that my studies implied the need to act; that thinking was a problem of action. To me, this was of fundamental importance; something that led me to want to study as a postgraduate.

For an older student, the choice to research a particular question is far from arbitrary. A question of a theoretical nature is very likely to have significant genealogical content. Research therefore becomes a means of re-working, within an academic framework, one's understanding of a problem that has been historically formed.

THE INTERACTION OF SUBJECT AND SUBJECT

My research problem of the present (my doctoral thesis) occupies me with theorizing the formation of political subjectivities; something I am intent on doing from the subject's perspective. While a genealogical explanation of this problem will inevitably take me beyond the scope of both subjects (the individual and the problem), a few things could be said. The thresholds in one's intellectual development do not necessarily follow an academic logic. I began by recognising the need to see the place of creativity in my studies – in the hope that it would stretch to an engagement with a social problem (the contestation of the political narrative that governs my learning), and that this would be done with a determination to grapple with the question of what it might mean to think independently. In my academic work, creativity came to suggest the need for political subjectivity; and that my internal preoccupation with questions about how we constitute ourselves should become an "operant of the outside" (Deleuze, 1999) and, as such, my problem when I taught. Taking this problem to the theory and philosophy of education, I have realised that creativity in academia means nothing if it does not lead to a political subjectivity, where our expression of how we are implicated in social problems should be made to be a problem for politics. In academia, we toy with self-deception, unaware that we are constantly moving away from the relationship between truth and subject, and therefore away from an understanding of how the individual is constituted as a political subject. Returning to university has taught me to fear the possibility that I am merely participant in my own formation; that I am constituted as an object of politics!

NOTES

[1] This text is dedicated to Rod Hamel and Merryn Greenwood who, without realizing it, made it possible for me to understand the manner in which friendship facilitates the development of philosophical thought. Significant others who have accompanied me in this nexus include Andrew Gibbons, Xavi Laudo, Yanina Welp, Kirsten Lock, Marek Tesar and Carl Mika.
[2] See, in particular, Foucault (1997).It was in one of those moments in which I felt cut off from what I had created in life that I decided to return to university, believing that I needed to learn to think again.
[3] Now the Hon. Dr. Pita Sharples, Minister of Maori Affairs, Associate Minister of Corrections, Associate Minister of Education. Iwi affiliations: Ngāti Kahungunu, Ngai Te Kikiri o te Rangi, Ngāti Pahauwera. The course was 'Schooling, Education and Society', the same course that both Linda Smith and James Marshall taught.Professor Linda Smith is now at the University of Waikato. Iwi affiliations: Ngāti Awa, Ngāti Porou. James Marshall is Emeritus Professor at The University of Auckland and Research Professor at The University of North Carolina at Chapel Hill.
[4] I now think of the relationship between equality and inequality as being much more paradoxical; see, for instance, Jacques Rancière's (1999) theorizing of equality and inequality, Biesta & Bingham (2010), or Simon & Masschelein (2011).
[5] While the numbers of Māori in New Zealand prisons significantly exceeds their part in the national population, the number of Māori in the lecture theatre that day most likely fell significantly short of their demographic share.

REFERENCES

Badiou, A. (2005). *Metapolitics*. (Jason Baker, Trans.) London: Verso.
Biesta, G., & Bingham, C. (2010). *Jacques Rancière: Education, truth, emancipation*. New York, NY: Continuum.
Camus, A. (2000). *The Myth of Sisyphus*. (Justin O'Brien, Trans.). Auckland, Aotearoa/New Zealand: Penguin Books (NZ) Ltd.
Deleuze, J. (1999). Foucault. (Sean Hand, Trans.). London: Continuum.
Foucault, M. (1997).Polemics, politics, and problematizations. (Lydia Davis, Trans.). In P. Rabinow (Eds.) *Ethics* (pp. 111–120). London: Penguin Books. Rabinow, P. (Eds.) (1997). *Ethics: subjectivity and truth. Essential works of Foucault, 1954–1984, Vol. I.* Auckland, Aotearoa/New Zealand: Penguin Books (NZ) Ltd.
Rancière, J. (1999). *The ignorant schoolmaster: Five lessons in intellectual emancipation*. (Kristin Ross, Trans.). Stanford, CA: Stanford University press.
Simons, M. & Masschelein, J. (Eds.) (2011). *Rancière, Public education and the taming of democracy*. London, England: Wiley-Blackwell.

AFFILIATION

Richard Heraud, University of Waikato

CHRISTIAN WÖLFEL

2(6). CONTRIBUTING TO THE FIELD OF DESIGN RESEARCH

A Brief Personal Wrap-Up

This is a personal report on the thesis or dissertation project of a trained designer at a university in Germany (where a PhD thesis is called a dissertation). Germany is known for its long tradition in design, and design research has a long tradition there as well, one prominent example being the work of Horst Rittel, who was also a teacher at the HfG Ulm. (e. g. Rittel 1972, see Rith & Dubberly 2007). However, design research developed rather loosely connected to traditional sciences in Germany. One reason for this is that design education used to take place at *Fachhochschulen* (roughly equivalent to polytechnics) and Universities of Art and Design, neither of which were given research missions or the right to grant doctorates. For various reasons – including EU-wide harmonisation ("Bologna process") and international trends in design (research) – this has started to change in recent years. Accordingly, more and more designers enrol in newly established (partly practice-based) PhD programmes, e. g., at the Bauhaus-Universität Weimar and other art schools. Before these distinctive opportunities were created, though, designers always had the chance to submit a dissertation/thesis at traditional universities – according to *their* rules. And some did.

My personal story lies somewhere in-between: I was trained in industrial design at an engineering faculty within a traditional university (very roughly equivalent to the Industrial Design Engineering programme at TU Delft or Product Design Engineering at Swinburne University). On the one hand, the programme was rather practice-focused. On the other, I graduated as a *Diplom-Ingenieur* (equivalent to a M.Sc.) instead of *Diplom-Designer*, which was still the standard at art schools at that time. This gave me the opportunity to start a doctorate without problems: I easily met the faculty's requirements. But how could I know I was able to write a PhD thesis? My Diploma (Masters) thesis had been a small test of my interest and skills in scientific (empirical) research. However, my decision to start a PhD was also encouraged by my personal background: my older sister, as well as some good friends (also trained in a rather practice-based field), had finished their PhDs a few years earlier, and my (back then, soon-to-be) wife had started her own research career at the philosophical faculty. Last, but not least, the position of a research associate was advertised at the industrial design department, which included the expectation of "interest in design PhD research". At universities, research associates are usually employed to conduct

A.-Chr. Engels-Schwarzpaul and M. A. Peters (Eds.), Of other Thoughts: Non-Traditional Ways to the Doctorate: A Guidebook for Candidates and Supervisors, 43–46.
© *2013 Sense Publishers. All rights reserved.*

specific research and/or teaching. In this case, the position included supervising students' design projects, teaching fundamentals of design, as well as conducting practice-based design research in interdisciplinary projects. However, there always is a formal (and mostly real) request for undertaking and completing a PhD thesis while being a research associate – in this case, the requirement was explicitly written into the job advertisement by the head of department. I applied for it.

In contrast to the structured PhD programmes now established at some universities, my own doctorate was somewhat of a private project – as it is for most PhD students in traditional academic disciplines in Germany. According to the rules, a PhD thesis had to provide "proof of scientific competence beyond masters level and exceptional qualification for independent scientific work" that should "promote the particular scientific field, its theories and methods". There are no further explicit rules on what and how one must proceed in doctoral studies. There is no curriculum, no training in scientific work – just the general requirement of submitting a written thesis to the faculty. Anything more specific must be learned from the literature, particularly other theses. Most importantly, all specifics must be discussed and arranged with the 'doctoral parents' (this term goes back to the title *Doktorvater*, for the – traditionally usually male – supervisor, doctor father).

In accordance with my position at the interface of theory and practice, as well as design and engineering, my doctoral supervisors were a designer from my engineering faculty and an art school design researcher whose formal training had been in engineering. Both assessed my thesis after my faculty's doctorate committee accepted the submission of my thesis draft. I eventually defended my research and successfully completed the oral *rigorosum* exam. Although I could have done so, I was not required to give evidence of publications in my name.

When I started my doctoral research, I was given descriptions of research problems from which I could select my topic. I then had to develop my body of literature, research methods and hypotheses work from scratch. Since there were no role models for such dissertations, I had to find my own way or adapt other existing ones. My personal starting point for getting into the international design research community was the Design Research Society conference in Lisbon (Friedman et al. 2006), followed by a number of international conferences in the following years. Presenting the state of my work, as well as meeting interested and interesting people, helped me a lot. One important advice to PhD students is: talk about your dissertation project. Do it at conferences, do it with friends and family. Even if a conference submission is not accepted, the reviewers' feedback can be valuable. And explaining the project to non-experts helps clarifying and simplifying the shape of the research, identifying gaps or just realising the amount of work already done. Although I conducted my PhD research part-time, in parallel to my work as lecturer and researcher in (other) funded research projects at my university, I always stayed connected to my project. Thus, I hardly became aware of my own progress, made step by small step. Opportunities of presenting my research, formally or informally, always made me realise how far I had moved forward, compared with the starting point. This has always been a good source of motivation.

Midway through my doctoral research, there was already a growing number of designers enrolled in doctoral studies in Germany. At my industrial design department, there had been a long period after the early 1990s' transformation of the East German academic system, during which doctoral research had ceased. In the wake of this period, I was the second candidate to enrol after the first had started just six months earlier in 2006. Thus, there were no role models to follow. But soon we discovered that there were almost ten designers spread across the faculties among the 2,900 doctoral students of our university. We started regular evening meetings for the exchange of experiences, where the fellow sufferers could provide help and motivation to each other.

In contrast to the multitude of international conferences, there were no national networks of (junior) design researchers in Germany. Within the recently established German Association of Design Theory and Research, and together with Katharina Bredies (from Universität der Künste Berlin (UdK), see chapter 2(7) in this book) I established the *Design promoviert* forum in 2008. Since then, we have organised regular biannual colloquia for doctoral design students that were held at various universities in Germany and Switzerland. In the last five years, approximately one hundred PhD candidates, most of them beginners, presented at the colloquia (cf. Bredies & Wölfel, forthcoming). We observed that most of PhD students expect to develop extensive theories or to produce fundamental, ground-breaking findings. However, my experience was that I eventually realised how many people had already devoted themselves to similar research problems – if one does not address the questions and interests of other members of the research community, one is not likely to make a significant contribution.

The impact of persona and narrative scenario methods on product character descriptions acquired from individual knowledge of the designers. The font size represents the quantity of the words' naming in the control group (left) and test group (right).

The larger part of my thesis comprises a theoretical chapter, where I discuss and develop a model of individual design knowledge that is applied by industrial designers in the early design stages. The slightly smaller part of the thesis consists of the application of the developed model to four smaller empirical studies (Wölfel, 2012). The findings of the empirical studies were neither overwhelmingly surprising, nor ground-breaking: in one study, for example, I assessed the impact of personal narrative scenario methods in industrial design processes. Meanwhile, these methods have become state of the art in many design studios – there is no need to convince anyone of their value. However, I was able to prove empirically the impact of the methods, even on a statistical basis. According to my literature review, this had not been done before. Accordingly, this is one of the small contributions I made to the field of design (research).

Finally, it must be said that many of the challenges, motivations and experiences of designers enrolled in PhD programmes are not that different to those of doctoral students in other disciplines (cf. Wölfel & Melles 2011, Melles & Wölfel 2014). Many, for instance, undertake their doctoral research in the 'rush-hour of life'. My dissertation was one project amongst several, not only in the work-related context of my life: especially if children can be counted as projects. To most PhD students, not only to those researching in the area of design, the dissertation project is a *wicked problem* (Rittel 1972) – just as any other design project. In the beginning, they don't know their way, and they don't know the result. How could they? Research is almost always a process of learning. Anyway, for trained designers – even if they are not trained or experienced in scientific research – it should not be too hard to cope with the uncertainty and surprises on the way through the doctoral research candidature.

REFERENCES

Bredies, K., & Wölfel, C. (forthcoming) Long live the late bloomers: Current state of design PhD in Germany. *Design Issues*.

Friedman, K., Love, T. & Côrte-Real, E (Eds.): *WonderGround. Design Research Society International Conference 2006*. Lisbon, Portugal: IADE 2006.

Rith, C. & Dubberly, H. (2007). Why Horst W. J. Rittel Matters. *Design Issues, 23*(1), 72–74.

Rittel, H. W. J. (1972). On the Planning Crisis: Systems Analysis of the 'First and Second Generations'. *Bedriftsøkonomen*, 390–396.

Melles, G. & Wölfel, C. (2014). Postgraduate Design Education in Germany: motivations, understandings and experiences of graduates and enrolled students in Master's and Doctoral Programs. *Design Journal, 17*(1).

Wölfel, C. (2012*). Designwissen: Spezifik und Unterstützung der Akquise durch reflexive und narrative Methoden*. Technisches Design, 7. Dresden, Germany: TUDpress Verlag der Wissenschaften.

Wölfel, C., & Melles, G. (2011). Investigating motivations and experiences of design doctoral students: Research design and results from a study in Germany. In N. Roozenburg, L.-L. Chen & P. J. Stappers (Eds.), *IASDR2011: Diversity and unity. 4th World Conference on Design Research*. Delft, Netherlands: TU Delft.

AFFILIATION

Christian Wölfel
Center for Industrial Design,
Technische Universität Dresden, Germany

KATHARINA BREDIES

2(7). THE TRADEMAN'S DOOR TO THE IVORY TOWER

Doing Research as Just Another Kind of Practice

The circumstances of my PhD thesis in Design are a bit extraordinary in several ways: they were exceptionally good concerning practicalities, even though they were somewhat political concerning the disciplinary establishment of design as research practice. As a result, I might have had more freedom to experiment, but I also had a constant feeling of risk and uncertainty due to the lack of role models. Although this last point applies to some extend to all original research, it is amplified by the still emerging status of design research.

As for financial and moral support, I was well equipped. When I started my PhD in 2007, I was employed by a newly founded research institute in Berlin, surrounded mainly by engineers and computer scientists, with my supervising 'Postdoc' being the first and only design researcher in the team at that time. Over the years, more design PhD students joined, who were all able to define their own research topic. We could also apply for internal funding from our employer for our design projects and received support to do empirical studies, such as access to databases to recruit test subjects for interviews. Our engineer colleagues had to face much more exact and exacting expectations regarding the outcome of their work. By comparison, the 'exotic' nature of design research gave us ample room for experiment. A design research group such as ours, endowed with sufficient funding and the freedom to develop their own topics, was quite rare in Germany at the time.

However, over the past years, German design research at PhD level has gained momentum. My official supervisors had still obtained their doctoral degrees in domains other than design: one as an engineer, the other – a professional designer – in rhetoric; one out of interest, the other (not only, but also) out of necessity. Now they were actively promoting the possibility of genuine design doctorates, which include design practice as an integral part of the research process. I was literally surrounded by well-organised proponents, both theoretically and institutionally, of design research. At the same time, more and more German universities offered designers the opportunity to enrol in doctoral degrees (other than classical PhDs) or in structured PhD programmes. It seemed that, finally, designers interested in research were joining forces and had reached sufficient critical mass to push the institutions for the doctoral degrees in their discipline.

Although I also witnessed the need for constant justification for practicing designers, as well as researchers from more established disciplines, design research felt like a matter of fact in the environment created by my fellow PhD students and advisors, a normal thing to do rather than an exotic venture. I witnessed the political reservations my supervisors faced while trying to introduce the right to grant PhD degrees, but I was not affected. The first year, I was still very busy writing an exposé for my PhD project. When I was finally ready to enrol, my main supervisor had joined the university in Braunschweig, one of the first universities in Germany to offer a PhD to designers. My enrolment there went smoothly. I learned about definitions of design as a disciplinary field already established by others, and benefitted from their thoughts regarding the difference between research in design and that in other disciplines. Consequently, doing project-based research made perfect sense to me, right from e beginning. Also, I was lucky enough to have the resources to do so.

My main problem was how to do it, exactly. While one might expect problems with poor funding, or institutional or personal conflicts in a weakly established academic field, my most serious concern was the lack of role models and exemplary research processes. Theoretical justifications for Research Through-Design (RTD) were available and convincing, but only in very few cases had the idea been implemented and exemplified in PhD theses. Therefore, I was aware of the potentially exemplary status of my project and the critical examination it might have to bear up to. I felt obliged to comply with existing standards of academic research and deliver high quality design at the same time. There was a realistic possibility that design practitioners would not appreciate the theoretical considerations behind the design, and that theorists would consider the theoretical discussion to be shallow.

Methodological struggles and uncertainties are probably common during a PhD thesis, even in well-established academic fields. Without the support of well-established methodological handrails, however, the uncertainty increases significantly. Like for many designers, my studies focused on methods for idea generation, not for observation and (text) interpretation. I had to make myself familiar with theories and methodological premises while I was in the middle of my design project. It felt like chopping my way through the undergrowth, occasionally bumping into discourses in human-computer interaction and sociology of technology without proper knowledge of their history; on the way discovering things like epistemology and ontology while trying to develop an appropriate research process for my questions; and constantly translating the findings from other disciplines back into a design perspective. My PhD thesis was the first research project I have ever engaged with, and I had to pick up the necessary tools as I was moving along. Without the close supervision I had, the situation would have been an even bigger mess.

My aim was to set up and follow a research process in which analysis of the existing was tightly coupled with projection, and theoretical concepts with designing. Design actions should be an interpretation of, and be implied by, a particular theoretical perspective and allow a revision or reflection of those theories in turn. My sense of RTD as a concrete practice remained blurry until the end, until my thesis project was almost finished. It was telling that one of my supervisors, who had accompanied my project for several years, told me after he had read the introductory chapter of my thesis that he finally understood what I was trying to do. I found the verbal articulation of my experiences difficult, not only because I had not practiced it before, but also because part of my thinking was non-verbal. It took several iterations of sketching, prototyping and trying different design processes to work out my theoretical concepts. It was a painful process without the guarantee of a happy ending.

Having experienced the same troubles, my supervisors were well aware of the difficulties and limits in expressing experiential knowledge verbally. They took care that I had plenty of opportunities to practise my scientific writing: I was always involved in other research projects at the institute, about which I could then publish or present at conferences. I was also advised to deliver intermediary written reports on my thesis project roughly every six months, sticking to a basic project structure of problem definition, methodology, empirical study, analysis and conclusion. My supervisors considered this structure a common denominator in scholarly research in general, and a benchmark for rigor in design research in particular.

The peculiar thing about this structure is that it appears to be static and inappropriate for practice-based research. At the beginning of a project, it forces designers into the libraries, not into the workshops, where they feel at home. It therefore represents the academic ivory tower perspective that designers often consider irrelevant for their practical work (and for a reason). But once I understood theories and concepts to be just another material for designing, I appreciated the scaffolding that the structure provided to organise my thoughts. It served as a link and a translation tool between design practice and research practice.

This is why I am rather optimistic about adopting and appropriating established academic rules to new areas of research. Sure, writing research papers was awful at first, but at the same time, my intermediary thesis reports resembled the project reports and documentations I had done for all my design projects. Research was just another craft to be learned and practiced, and in this aspect, it was suddenly very similar to designing.

Some prior education in scholarly routines of information handling, however, would have saved me a lot of time. When I started out as the first and only design PhD student at the institute, I spent hours over boring and irrelevant literature before I knew how to identify the relevant authors in a field and become familiar with a particular disciplinary discourse. Developing critical reading skills only became much faster and easier when more PhD students joined and we started to have weekly colloquiums to discuss relevant literature in the group. Now, after about five years of work, I am close to handing in my thesis. Looking at my extremely comfortable situation during my PhD, I wonder whether it was the luxury of not being rushed, doubted, or put in a narrow frame of expectations that made an experimental thesis possible. Not having to worry about practicalities left far more time and energy to worry about the actual content. My supervisors trusted and supported me, despite the fact that they had to work hard to understand my intermediary work reports. I think these conditions were exceptional and extremely fortunate, and I am not sure if my thesis would have possible in a more established academic setting.

However, my impression is that the acceptance of design research has significantly increased since I started my PhD. Future design researcher will probably not need to rely on so much luck to undertake a successful practice-led PhD thesis in design. They will get research training during their undergraduate studies, have scholarships to apply for, role models to follow, and peers to complain to, just like any other discipline.

AFFILIATION

Katharina Bredies
Universität der Künste Berlin, Design Research Lab

SARAH MCGANN & BARBARA MILECH

2(8). STICKY ADVICE FOR RESEARCH STUDENTS

The sticky advice for doctoral students reproduced on the following page represents our sense of the collaboration between doctoral student and supervisor when all goes well. For Sarah, it represents her sense that the doctoral student moves from a position of learning to teaching – the sticky notes come from a presentation she gave to current doctoral students in her department shortly after graduation. For Barbara it represents her sense that the supervisor moves from a position of teaching to learning, with the supervisor's last best job being to be the best editor possible. This particular supervision was carried out across disciplines – Sarah's field is architecture, Barbara's cultural studies. Their interdisciplinary collaboration reinforced their separate convictions that a thesis comprised of an exegesis and a production (novel, building, paintings, etc.) should be a whole – that the two parts of such a thesis are connected through a response in each component to the same significant research question.

Even more, their collaboration reinforced their separate experiences of similarities in the processes of creating both components of a creative-production thesis – production and exegesis. Neither process is linear; both depend on a sense of structure. That is, both start from a core intuition/idea/answer-to-a-research-question that develops, after studio/library work (via sketches, concept maps, and the like) into related frameworks for both production and exegesis (1:500 site map in architectural terms, a provisional chapter plan in exegetical terms). Those related plans are then tested and revised, again and again, through working between the framework/s and the details of production (the 1:50 plan) and research (more reading/viewing/talking). In both instances – in work related to the production *and* the exegesis – the process is circular/reciprocal/creative, a process in which framework/s are (continually) refined, and details (continually) find a cogent place in work and text. The special challenge and excitement for creative-production research students is that they work in this (essential) way, not only within one genre (production or text), nor only in two genres (production and text), but crucially between two genres (production and text). The result – in our experience – is a rich reciprocity that makes creative-production degrees, at their best, potent contributions to the disciplines from which they arise.

A.-Chr. Engels-Schwarzpaul and M. A. Peters (Eds.), *Of other Thoughts: Non-Traditional Ways to the Doctorate: A Guidebook for Candidates and Supervisors*, 51–52.
© 2013 Sense Publishers. All rights reserved.

10 things I learnt doing a PhD.

a PhD is....[1]
A test. It is not a book.
2 supers + 2 examines + MAYBE other students read it.
A book comes later.

On Rigour....[2]
Photocopy, Post-it + keyword everything. File in topic folders — breath depth + date. Start formatted Refs.

On Doing...[3]
A phd is like designing a building.
You Diagram, sketch, Design, Design Dev Detail + Document.

On writing...[4]
Writing is like drawing.
Do rough outlines/sketch Design as you draw / think as you write Render / fill in detail

On mapping...[5]
The table of contents is like a road map. It starts with all the details + end up as a series of essay titles.

On reading...[6]
Take your reader on a journey.
Tell them where you're going, why you're going, now we're getting there + who we'll meet

On structure...[7]
A PhD: has Intro/body/conc
A chapter: Intro: body: conc
A section: Intro: body: conc
A para: topic sentence: body: wrap sentence

On time...[8]
A Phd shouldn't take 4ever. Don't hold back or wait. Write as you read read as you write. [Longer time: Longer Lit]

On Editing...[9]
or The pleasure of Polishing!

On Enjoyment...[10]
A Phd is an indulgent luxury.
You grow, learn, teach and actually get Paid to do so.

SHANE EDWARDS

3. SPACES OF OTHER THOUGHT

E kore e piri te uku ki te rino[1]

INTRODUCTION

For an Indigenous person, the doctoral experience brings contrasting knowledge systems into relationship. Indigenous people involved in doctoral study will begin a deep relationship with the Academy. The Academy is not neutral; it has a history, a character, an identity. This identity is formed in the image of Europe and is Eurocentric in character and design. The Academy's traditional values are different from the values and traditions relating to Indigenous peoples' knowledge and knowledge systems. The Academy conveys an image of neutrality – but when Indigenous people participate and engage in it, ideological differences become apparent. Ideas of intention, purpose, collectivity, validity, authority and power are brought into focus.

As Indigenous people, we recognise that when we enter into doctoral study we bring our relations with us. We bring our status as tāngata whenua, first peoples; our history of a long association with people and place; a history of colonisation and displacement, of ruptured and fractured knowledge systems; but also a desire to serve our people and a belief in our own humanity and place, our(many)selves, our study, our passions, our dreams and our work efforts in the context of contemporary academic systems. The experiences of many Māori doctoral students show that the modern University, its habitudes and agents, maintains and advances an epistemic ignorance of Indigenous worldviews, combined with a resistance to acknowledging their valid place in institutions of knowledge building and sharing. This is the space many of us confront from the moment we enter into it, but which reveals its character and nature more fully as we engage in the doctoral journey. The structures of the Academy, which infer a regime of truth, powerfulness, and masterfulness, present an(other) complex nature and set of realities to Indigenous intellectuals within the Academy.

This chapter calls on 'testimony' (Smith, 1999), relaying lived personal realities. Testimony is an important element of truth telling, it is a knowing often also called, amongst other things, talking story, narrative, re-membering lived and personal experience. Experience recursively reinforces constructions of reality, as part of centrifugal thought and practice. Jody Byrd explains this approach well in the context of reading: "Such a reading practice understands indigeneity as radical alterity and

A.-Chr. Engels-Schwarzpaul and M. A. Peters (Eds.), Of other Thoughts: Non-Traditional Ways to the Doctorate: A Guidebook for Candidates and Supervisors, 53–66.
© 2013 Sense Publishers. All rights reserved.

uses remembrance as a means through which to read counter to the stories empire tells itself." (2011: xii-xiii).

My own experiences, as both a doctoral candidate and doctoral supervisor, are called on as part of this eclectic dialogue. As an urban-born Māori who has experienced educational success in academic spaces, and who just over a decade ago returned to live permanently in his ancestral homelands, I am able to speak from at least two divergent worlds. Experiences of working with and supporting Māori students in educational contexts have certainly helped me formalise insights into the tensions many Māori experience in their studies, particularly at the higher end of formal education and scholarship. My own experiences have included attempts to help non-Māori, who grappled with their assessments and judgments of our work, to understand our worldviews by showing that our ways of knowing and being are rigorous, even when they differ from Eurocentric norms. These attempts were about opening up spaces for the recognition of the validity of Māori ways of building, transmitting and sharing knowledge. The constant efforts to include, meet and balance the demands of the Academy and te ao Māori (the Māori world), both for myself and the students I have been engaged with, remain a dilemma that frustrates me like many other Māori. It makes me feel that there are clear limits to the inclusion of Māori worldviews in New Zealand society.

The chapter begins by detailing a history of Māori participation in Academia in Aotearoa/New Zealand, before exploring the University system's epistemic racism and the resulting challenges and opportunities for Māori scholars/students/practitioners whilst suggesting approaches and possible solutions for dealing with these realities.[2]

MĀORI PARTICIPATION IN THE ACADEMY: A BRIEF SYNOPSIS

The history of Māori scholarship in the Western Academy[3] is recent, less than one hundred years. I would argue that the work and focus of the first generation of prominent Māori academic scholars (including Peter Buck, Apirana Ngata, Maggie Papakura and Maui Pōmare) mirrored that of their contemporary non-Māori colleagues in the same field elsewhere in the world. As anthropologists, they centred their attention on recording accurate accounts of the culture and practices of our people, as well as on correcting the work of early European writers such as Elsdon Best, Percy Smith and John White, all early Eurocentric amateur ethnographers and anthropologists.

Ngata and Pōmare, academics and politicians of note in the 1900's, lived dichotomous existences. They were well educated in European style schooling and attended University, but they were also intimately raised and steeped within Māori worldviews. Subsequently, they attempted to reconcile the jagged edges of their dichotomous lives and times, as they sought to ameliorate the lot of their people, who suffered from the ravages of colonial order. A combination of government policies and the Second World War (1939-1945) delayed further Māori penetration into the

Academy, until Maharaia Winiata was appointed a tutor in Māori adult education at Auckland University in 1949. His appointment inaugurated what might be called the first generation of Māori academics, who were primarily concerned with the *survival* of Māori as a people and a culture. Winiata was followed by Bruce Biggs as lecturer in Māori language in 1951, Matiu Te Hau in 1952 and later arrivals, many of whom are still living today but have reached advanced stages of life and "active duty" (Deloria, 2004: 16) in institutions.

The second generation of Māori scholars were/are concerned with creating space for Māori students in the University, and advocating for inclusion of things Māori in mainstream society, as part of the Māori *revival* movement. Many of the second-generation academics are now also retired. However, they participate in furthering Māori causes as advisors, distinguished fellows, and in other leadership roles. Today's Māori academic intellectuals are the third and fourth generation who participate in an increasing force to push forward the acceptance of Māori ways of viewing and interacting with the world as valid practices. Across many disciplinary fields, one now finds a large number of Māori transforming the world – each from their specific strategic points and positions. They infiltrate the Academy and create spaces for others, which provide the freedom to explore and create change for Māori well-being.

They are only the latest group who have created spaces for us to dream of other ways of being and knowing. This is part of an unwritten agenda of Māori scholarship, which is committed to transforming Eurocentric philosophy, theory and practice (Battiste, 2000), whilst at the same time advancing Māori worldviews and life ways. This does not mean, though, that there is 'one way' and that we, as Māori, are all agreed on how and where the challenges should be made. The spaces from which people contribute to the cause are now far more dispersed than they have ever been. This reflects both our diverse colonial realities and the diversity of our resistance strategies and efforts. The legacy of those who came before us is the inheritance of privileges we enjoy; likewise, those of us in privileged positions now (largely) recognise our obligations – to those who created space for us and to those coming now and in the future. To succeed, we need to be clear and coherent about the system we operate, how it came to be this way, how we can change this constellation, and how we can use it to support our agendas.

UNMASKING AND DE-ROBING THE ACADEMY: AN INDIGENOUS PERSPECTIVE

A critical examination of the Academy or the University – that place where doctoral studies occur – is the prerequisite of any discussion of Indigenous and Māori relationships with doctoral study programmes. This critical examination challenges the status quo by questioning whether the Academy serves Indigenous interests or perpetuates domination and control: it initiates an inquiry into academic decolonisation, or what I have termed academic exorcisms. The scrutiny of some ideologies and contestations that pervade this environment is likely to make visible the realities Indigenous doctoral candidates face. It will also help (re-)locate and affirm Indigenous knowledge in the Academy, as part of the general push for affirmation of Māori epistemologies and life-ways, and advance the development of ideas such as tradition, orality, ancestors, time, space, non-universality and authenticity.

The task of critiquing and challenging *dominant orthodoxies* (Findlay, 2000) from a peripheral and marginalised position always carries risks, as it places the historically dominant under threat and challenges some people's positions in the structure. Bringing Indigenous worldviews, ideas and discourses into academic life can critically interrupt normality and encourage questioning introspection and reflective examination of established worldviews and understandings (Brown & Strega, 2005).

Arguably, academic normality is characterised by the prevalence of a particular kind of epistemic ignorance (Kuokkanen, 2007; Denzin, Lincoln and Smith, 2008), an ignorance that constructs "cognitive prisons" (Battiste, 2000: xvii). Marie Battiste's term refers to the continued operation of practices and discourses in Eurocentric thought that exclude minority groups and, in particular, Indigenous epistemic and intellectual traditions (Smith, 1999: 65). At its core, Eurocentrism is racist in its emphasis on real or imaginary differences and its assignment of differential values to the racists' advantage, using *European* as the standard measure. Eurocentric thinking has a tradition of making its values absolute, general and final – often to justify privilege and/or the use of aggression, at the victims' expense.[4] Canadian scholars Marie Battiste, Lynne Bell, Isobel Findlay, Len Findlay and James (Sákéj) Henderson illuminate this idea:

> If one thinks of "thinking place" as a place *for* thinking, the history of "the" university can and should be read as a history of promoting orthodoxies and punishing heresies, a pattern that continued long after the institution diluted or revoked its allegiance to specifically theological notions of right and wrong thinking. (2005:10)

This view of an epistemically ignorant and Eurocentric Academy becomes clearer when we unpack its origins and history – which have informed its character and identity. The Academy has its origins in the Mediterranean and features in both Greek and Roman accounts. The *Akademia* was sited at Akademeia, a grove of sacred olive trees outside the walls of ancient Athens. On the Roman invasion, c.86BC, the grove of olive trees was axed down to build siege engines. Around 410AD, the Academy was re-founded but closed again in 529AD. Raphael's Renaissance interpretation of the Academy in his fresco for the Vatican, *The School of Athens* (ca. 1510),[5] shows people who will seem familiar to us (though uncomfortably for some), such is our inherited intimacy with this educational tradition. The prevalence in this painting of white, well-off men provides a powerful picture of the ideology in which the modern Academy has its foundations. Significantly, Plato, founder of the Athenian Academy, proposed an individual epistemic agency that was instrumental in the construction of Euro-Western paradigms of knowledge.[6]

SPACES OF OTHER THOUGHT

Understanding this history helps us realise its contemporary manifestations in the New Zealand Academy, which is still dominated by the views of rich, white, Christian males. It is the continuation of a tradition (although proponents may argue it is neutral) which continues to be considered by many as the major institution of valid knowledge. By default, it is an extension of Empire, operating as the Governor of knowledge and of the institutions charged with creating it. By default, it enforces and validates some groups' orthodox knowledge and doctrines and, at the same time, relegates and subjugates other knowledges (Foucault, 1972; Goldberg, 1993; Smith 1998; Denzin, Lincoln and Smith, 2008). Knowledge and power are inextricably connected, and the Academy and universities continue to buttress knowledge as a discourse of power.

> Each society has its régime of truth, its 'general politics' of truth; that is, the types of discourse which it accepts and makes function as true; the mechanisms and instances which enable one to distinguish true and false statements, the means by which each is sanctioned; the techniques and procedures accorded value in the acquisition of truth; the status of those who are charged with saying what counts as true. (Foucault, 1972: 131)

For Māori participating in the Academy as part of their doctoral experience this is important to understand, as it helps us to know what we might expect to have to contend with and to prepare for the dominant habitats, culture and identity. It aids Indigenous candidates/scholar practitioners in thinking about how best we might prepare for the challenges of the doctoral journey and, importantly, it asks personal questions about our purposes and intentions regarding our occupation and participation in this area.

OUR OCCUPATION IN EMPIRE

Māori students/scholar/practitioners' reasons for engaging in doctoral study, with all its inherent challenges and opportunities, are never universal. A very common thread, though, is the aspiration to improve the lot of others, to achieve a freedom from the levels of dis-comfort and dis-ease commonly experienced by Indigenous peoples.

Within Māori epistemology, ideas of wisdom, knowledge, power and identity contribute to a discourse and agenda of radical freedom in contemporary contexts (Delanty & O'Mahoney, 2002: 6). The notion of radical freedom requires many of us in the context of academic study to re-think how we know the world as Māori, and why our ways of knowing are powerful catalysts for healthy and satisfying living and existence. Our occupation is most commonly first and foremost to better serve our people. The doctoral journey, and the spaces and places within which it is contained, become potential sites of struggle, but also of liberation. This is not easy work, as it asks us literally to dismantle, or at least renovate, the Masters' house with a combination of his own and our tools.

S. EDWARDS

The Academy at its best offers some possibilities for Indigenous peoples, for instance: a space shaped by Māori worldviews, interfacing with historically Eurocentric spaces; recognition of, and focus on, kaupapa Māori and mātauranga Māori; conceptualisation of modes of accountability in Aotearoa/New Zealand society; the nurturing and widening of Māori and non-Māori minds through co-location and co-operation; and participation in the wealth of resources that academic sites offer. The Academy can be helpful by offering a place of intellectual engagement for solution finding, for the advancement of cultural recovery and reclamation (Takino, 1998: 288), and for positive development and sustainability. In this regard, an adaptation of the four recommendations provided by Cherokee writer Daniel Justice can be useful for Indigenous scholars.

– This is Indigenous country – we are not invaders, this land is our inheritance and we belong to it. We have a right and a place in meaning making.
– We must not forget to be humble, respectful and dedicated to the pursuit of truth and its connection and effectiveness to people in marginalised positions.
– It is important to be generous of spirit in peace, as well as in war – do not act with raw prejudice but be generous, even if it is to enter into an unavoidable battle with the goal of healing at its end, rather than destruction.
– The world hasn't always been what it is, and it will be something very different in the future; look backward and forward as you go – ensure our work honours our ancestors and ask yourself whether it will it help or hinder those who follow.
(adapted from Justice, 2004: 102-103)

Through our occupancy, our intellectual journeys act as catalysts for the reshaping of what counts as knowledge, what knowledge counts, who counts, and who says so. Occupancy of the Academy by Indigenous people through doctoral study allows for a critical review and remaking of the Academy by rendering visible and engaging our distinctly Māori forms of knowledge, methodologies, and intellectual capital.

As a doctoral student and supervisor, I have found the most powerful and inspirational research to be that which invites te ao Māori into the work. Māori supervisors and students who support this idea, and purposefully seek to engage in the utilisation of Māori worldviews, create frameworks that incorporate Māori methodologies, Māori ethics, Māori references. Thus, they address the needs and aspirations of te ao Māori in highly impactful and satisfying ways.

WHO'S AT THIS PARTY?
THE BIO-POLITICS OF BEING MĀORI IN THE ACADEMY

The most obvious figures on the doctoral journey are the Indigenous doctoral candidate, the supervisor, other Indigenous faculty and other non-Indigenous faculty.

Indigenous doctoral students will be asked a number of fundamental questions by and of us, their contemporaries, family and communities. A key one is about their reasons for being a doctoral candidate, their, purpose, motivation and intentions. Candidates' responses to the probing questions vary, from serving our people, to completing our educational journey and gaining status for personal and/or collective gain. It's from understanding a candidate's sense of purpose that family and community, so critical to our success and often our motivation for our doctoral journey, are able to discern and shape our progress. Knowing that we have the backing of *our people* is critical: they give rigour to our work, as they act as arbitrators of our motivations; clarify whose interests we want to serve; and assess the utility of our work for the needs of our marginalised peoples. They thus help us (the group members with privileged access) disrupt and change the status quo, with its uneven levels of wellbeing and the disadvantages experienced by many Māori people. Their questions not only get to the heart of a candidate's motivations for this expedition, but they also help us recognise potential challenges and risks. One such challenge is an over-exposure to Western ideals and ideologies, which can occur to the detriment of Māori candidates' identities if they are not fully secure. During the course of the thesis research, our own people, inside and outside Academia, will question our motivation, our purpose and our intent. On completion, we will be judged by our people according to how well we have used the benefits of our privilege in nurturing our own communities. We must be clear from the outset about our intent and purpose and ascertain that it is tika – good and right.

The relationship with the other central figure(s), the supervisor(s), will determine to a large extent how a candidate's journey will unfold. Almost inevitably, most supervision relationships are characterised by a power differential between supervisor (expert) and supervised (candidate), which challenges both parties. Many candidates will complain about such things as the direction in which their work is being taken by the supervisor; that their supervisors' own work is being promoted or further researched for them by the candidates; or that candidates must do what their supervisors say or risk failure. When candidates and supervisors are aligned and dare to challenge the systems and structures that maintain academic traditions and privileges, they may face backlash from others. Colleagues may feel threatened by emerging doctoral scholars and often react with direct or indirect ethno- or bio-politics. In many cases, these colleagues are our own Indigenous people. I have seen and heard Māori academics describing the work of our people as "non-academic", as "low order academic thought", or simply "not academic enough". In many cases, the people making these judgments want to ensure that others conform to their particular, subjective views of academic activity. The standards against which these kinds of value judgments are made, though, have often been set by non-Indigenous academics; they may be the norm in the institution they are employed by; or they happen to be their personal convictions, out of which they judge Indigenous ways of knowing. In my experience, such standards are most commonly non-Indigenous constructs and used predominantly to perpetuate the power differential between supervisor and candidate, master and apprentice, or the powerful and the powerless (Denzin, Lincoln and Smith, 2008).

Such actions attempt to colonise our own people, just as their agents claim to have been colonised. Rather effectively, some of the benefits of the dominant society are given to "Indigenous elites" in Academia, in return for their contributions to pacifying Indigenous dissenters (Friesen & Friesen, 2002: 23). We must be aware that those in similar positions within the Academy are most likely to hire, honour and appoint to positions of power Indigenous scholars whose work is unthreatening to them (Mihesuah & Wilson, 2004: 32). As a result of this insidious practice, the transformative potentials of Indigenous scholarship have been defused by the advancement of those seen as non-threatening. Our goals of transforming the Academy, its covert and overt operational conventions and the conventions of academic training, occur within the wider paradigm of challenging those in dominant positions who have spent large parts of their lives benefiting from and actively constructing these conventions (Gone, 2004: 125). It is not uncommon, in my experience, to hear about academics, who protect their preferred interests for personal benefit, partially by denouncing as inferior, non-academic or not robust such practices and knowledges that do not conform to the standards that underpin their power. When they supervise doctoral candidates, they are likely to attempt to shape the candidates in their own image, or to use PhD research to further their own. These acts of defining what counts as knowledge and who is entitled to say so are attempts to maintain control and dominance.

Whatever the politics, there are many different motivations which take on different characteristics. Many candidates become involved in the doctoral journey to engage with and subvert the very systems set up to frame it. Some do so to attempt to enlarge space for Indigenous thoughts and knowledges that are respected by and useful to Indigenous communities. Some do so for power and privilege. In relation to privilege in and via the Academy, Linda Smith of Ngāti Awa states that the "insulation of disciplines, the culture of the institution which supports disciplines and the systems of management and governance all work in ways which protect the privileges already in place" (1999:133). Supervisors, Māori and non-Māori, who recognise this will respond in different ways. They are likely to presume that it is worthwhile to indigenise the Academy, because something productive will result (Cordova, 1997; Mihesuah & Wilson, 2004: 5). When we, Māori and non-Māori, attempt to do so, we strive to contribute to liberatory education that informs Indigenous peoples and educates non-Indigenous people, so that both oppressed and oppressors are liberated by our inquiries. Our goal is that higher learning institutions, the bastions of the Academy, might be turned from centres of colonialism to centres of decolonisation.

But perhaps it is necessary first to discuss the question of contemporary Māori identity – or, rather, identities – since there are frequent debates about who is Māori, who is not, who is authentic, who is not, and who says so. In Aotearoa, ethnic identity is officially established by self-declaration, rather than measured by Government-defined blood quanta as in other countries. For Māori, identity is almost entirely based on ancestry and orientation. Debate continues about the relationship between individual identity and the level or degree of connection to a distinctly Māori identity – even about what that identity does and does not signify.

Ashis Nandy (1983) touches on an aspect of cosmopolitanism to this question when she writes about intellectuals abroad who live outside traditional contexts. They will have different degrees of meaningful contact to the spaces, places and people of the ancestral domain. Some will have acquired an academic education, occupy positions in mainstream academic institutions, or work as 'servants' of the government. When these intellectuals attempt to work with our Indigenous communities, identity frequently becomes an issue since degrees of belonging can be central to acceptance. The proposition I present here in brief, which crucially belongs to current debates (Durie, 2003; Borell, 2005), is that 'Māori unity' is a colonial phenomenon, in many regards and on many levels. I argue that diversity is an organic feature of Indigenous experience.

What is of some concern to many, though, is the large number of third and fourth generation urban Māori academics (who were largely raised in metropolitan contexts and formed by the corresponding experiences and ideas) compared with the relatively small number of those who occupy positions of knowing and relating to urban/metropolitan *and* rural/hapu environments. This situation causes a dilemma, namely that more and more thinking and debates in neo-colonial/Eurocentric environments are informed by one-dimensional experiences. This is likely to limit the breadth of thinking and action that would be possible if wider perspectives were available, which could be made available by those connected very firmly to the knowledge found in the ancestral domain. The dilemma becomes even more complex, though, when the thought and protocols of urban environments take root in places belonging to the Māori ancestral domain, to the point that these environments become largely unrecognisable. They then look, sound, smell, taste and feel like their urban creators, reflecting their lived realities and environs. As a result, only remnants and small traces of Māori society and identity remain visible. These markers, the elements of ancestral Māori identity (land, language, story, peoples and places) that contain the breadth of our knowledge, these legacies for succeeding generations, become located at the margins of the cities and towns and are constantly under threat of land development, for instance, for purchase and use by the sprawling urban domain. Those of our people who occupy such places struggle to remain Māori in environments that seek to displace them, to move them to areas of employment that alter our physical, psychological, spiritual and cultural states, often to our detriment.

My aim here is not to promote an 'authentic' identity of ancestrally connected Māori, who occupy what I call "home spaces" (Edwards, 2009: 78), over and above that of Māori leading largely urban lives, who may in many regards be less connected to ancestral environments and ways of knowing. People who are located away from ancestral domains make hugely valuable contributions. However, I acknowledge that many of our people occupying the home spaces would not want colonial oppression to be replaced by oppression from our own, by a pastoral welfare-ism of sorts, that

Deloria V. (2004) Marginal and submarginal, in DA. Mihesuah and CA. Wilson [Eds]. Indigenizing the Academy.

is, by those of us who may tend to write for, speak for and appear for those of our people who occupy these older spaces of our distinctive identities.

Vine Deloria (2004: 17) refers to some of his own people who occupy the urban/metropolitan spaces as 'new Indians.' This term, I believe, detracts from the valid contributions of a large sector of people, but I nevertheless agree that it would be difficult for my urban relations to access in depth some parts of the rich repository of Māori knowledge. There are distinct differences between Indigenous ways of knowing, which are influenced by the ancestral domain, and ways of knowing that are strongly influenced by metropolitan epistemologies. This creates great challenges and tensions for those who live outside their ancestral location, particularly for those studying at doctoral level, when they return home and attempt to share their research or participate in community projects. The challenges from their rural relations concerning their rights and their identity can make returning home and being actively involved an un-enjoyable experience for Māori PhD candidates. The potential of 'applying' the wrong kind of knowledge is a real one, though, and we, as Māori, need to be ever mindful that the dominance of Western or urban epistemologies can be debilitating and oppressive.

Despite the great variance of opinions regarding these issues, I am continually reminded of an African saying that helps ground those of us on doctoral journeys:

Ubuntu – I am because we are. (Ladson-Billings & Donnor, 2005)

Pragmatically speaking, the very real possibility of seeing te ao Māori through the values and ends of an incompatible knowledge system requires Māori doctoral students to be strategic in their selection of supervisors. It is my experience that institutions will often assign a supervisor who happens to be available from within the institution, often because of fiscal reasons. I recommend students identify what their specific needs are, be that writing style or content/subject matter, and then select the most appropriate person to supervise. In my own doctoral project, I was not in desperate need for content knowledge, for I had my elder participants for that. What I needed was help with writing and composition (removing duplication, condensing into one sentence what I had originally written in three, and the development of clarity in my language use). For me, this meant using a European supervisor as my primary supervisor, primarily to help develop my English language writing skills. The choice of writing in English for Indigenous doctoral students is often a double edged sword. Most commonly, we will write in English to reach a wider audience, to speak with our own who are still recovering from language loss, or because we ourselves are more proficient in the language of our colonisers. This challenge is amplified when we attempt to write from cultural spaces and express Indigenous ideas in English – a language that 'thinks' the world from a different space and place than we as Māori do. It is a very big achievement to think Māori and write English and still produce high quality work that is honourable.

Of equal importance for me was that I already knew my supervisor to a degree. It is important to know the person with whom one is going to spend the next several years together in an intimate relationship – at least to some extent. For me, there needs to be a match of values, the potential for friendship and a common inclination – otherwise the journey will be un-enjoyable.

HABITUDES: MASKING THE ACADEMY, A NON- INDIGENOUS ELEMENT

A unique experience awaits the Indigenous intellectual who enters the Academy and embarks on his or her own doctoral journey or supports that of others. This experience is often tension filled and strained by many unmarked contradictions. Some of our colleagues in the Academy will perceive of us as 'having been saved' or 'having seen the light'. We spend large amounts of time in our marginalised and peripheral spaces within universities, the bastions of the Western Academy, but also in wānanga and polytechnics in Aotearoa/New Zealand. Wānanga, as essentially Indigenous tribal institutions, are an example of spaces that offer 'other' views and approaches to being. A feature of wānanga is that they render and create knowledge and shape thought by utilising the inherent value of mātauranga Māori, Māori knowledge and worldview. In these spaces, there is no need to argue aggressively for the right, firstly, to be Maori and, secondly, to utilise Māori thought, practices and approaches to knowledge. This is helpful for those Indigenous students who want to immerse themselves in Indigenous philosophy, theory and practice, or even want to create it! This radical freedom is balanced by the rigour of Māori worldviews that guide us in our work and ensure its appropriateness and utility. Here, we attempt to speak about positive difference and tolerance, about Māori history and worldview, to those who may not fully know in order to make change for our people. Elsewhere, a common Māori strategy is to become so diplomatic and cautious that parts of the story are compromised and sanitised. Because we are in the minority, and because we are aware that our actions for change come under scrutiny from a majority, we often begin to feel under threat. For many, it then becomes a political strategy to support the status quo, rather than to resist and fight it (Mihesuah & Wilson, 2004: 12).

There is risk in succumbing to this type of pressure because we cannot be the doctor if we are the disease; we cannot advance our Indigenous causes while we uncritically serve the Master. However, we can become the vaccine (Battiste, 2000); we can act as agents of change and challenge unequal power relations by creatively making transparent many of our dis-eases to promote change and positive transformation, so that equity and social justice amongst and by us support our own agency. The supervisor and other faculty who mediate and support Indigenous doctoral students will find this journey challenging, and we will all encounter rough seas like those highlighted above. Despite these challenges, though, many continue to develop powerful initiatives to counter perilous experiences of Māori in the Academy, building Indigenous worlds and cadres of new Indigenous scholars. For those of us who wish to remain in the Academy and who consider ourselves academics, the goal is aptly articulated by Mihesuah & Wilson:

handwritten note: DA Mihesuah & CA Wilson (2004) Indigenizing the Academy.

> As academics committed to our nations, we must resist institutional co-optation and continue to challenge the dominant conventions of our disciplines, and at the same time we must use whatever authority, benefits, and power that derive from our positions to further promote the causes of our people. Our research skills, methodological training, and access to audience and resources can become instruments of power for our nations, if we choose to wield them in that way. However, we must simultaneously work to ensure that we don't in the process become colonizing agents for colonizing institutions. (2004:14)

Many Māori students have bemoaned the 'game playing' they had to endure to 'pass' and 'get' a doctorate. They often followed the requirements of the Academy and those of their supervisors in a complicit fashion – to the point that many felt they were simply doing whatever is needed to 'get through'. At the end, they felt hollow and retained a sense of having been conditioned, rather than freed, by the doctoral experience. There is a warning here for supervisors who may feel the need to shape students, even to the point that a student becomes a 'creation in their own image'. This practice is detrimental to the self-esteem of any doctoral student.

In a conversation, leading Māori Academic, Ranginui Walker reminded me of our greater purpose in doctoral study:

> You take me, I never did a classic anthropological study of going, say, to a place like Tikopia and writing about the Tikopians. I just went out to Otara and wrote about the Māoris in Otara. What's wrong with that? Nice easy suburb, manageable size. ... it's what you do afterwards that matters. ... The doctorate is just your union ticket to work at the University, that's all a doctorate is. It's your credential that qualifies you to work at the University. And it's the work you do afterwards that matters.

CONCLUDING DISCUSSION

Indigenising the Academy is a dynamic course of action. It is social, but more importantly it is political. It is concerned with imagining a location from which we can combat the powerful forces of colonialism. This can be done most successfully, I would argue, if Indigenous and non-Indigenous scholars alike reconfigure the colonial structures and frames of mind that pervade our thoughts and actions, and which ensure that we conform as the "Master's tools" (Lorde, 1981). If we can successfully rupture and subvert the Academy in thought and action, we may see a wealth of applicable resources and practices that can return health and wellbeing to Māori communities and individuals (Clark, 2004). In some cases, we may need to consider using the Masters' tools to actually destroy, or at least critique and destabilise, the foundations of the Master's house (Kuokkanen, 2007: 8).

There is a growing need for Indigenous scholars and intellectuals to actively engage in this agenda. The Indigenous intelligentsia, for its part, needs to be grounded in tikanga and ahuatanga Māori, Māori custom and tradition. We must beware of the pervading force of Western ideologies if we want to alleviate the burden of our people and present them in ways that preserve and enhance their mana, their power and integrity. The keys for this are located within our own episteme, our ancestral ways of knowing and their meaningful engagement and application in contemporary contexts.

NOTES

This chapter is partially based on my 2009 PhD thesis, *Titiro whakamuri kia marama ai te wao nei: Whakapapa epistemologies and Maniapoto Māori cultural identities*.

[1] This whakatauki (proverbial saying) comes from the Taranaki region of New Zealand and literally means, "clay will not stick to iron". Its fuller interpretation means that clay will not stick to metal as it begins to dry. It refers to an idea in which Māori cultural inheritance is the iron that must be preserved to maintain Māori integrity, whereas Western culture (the clay) fails to provide full support.

[2] Māori is the name for the collective Indigenous people of Aotearoa/New Zealand.

[3] I wish to acknowledge at this point that this statement refers to scholarship in the Western Academy. Scholarship has always existed in Māori society, and today in parallel to Māori academic scholarship.

[4] I am indebted to and grateful for the discussions I had, in September 2012, with Sákéj Henderson from the Faculty of Law at the University of Saskatchewan in Canada, when I was a visiting scholar there. These discussions informed the ideas of Eurocentrism and the links to racism presented here and were part of a wider discussion relating to ideas of Western Humanities and Indigenous Humanities.

[5] Available at http://en.wikipedia.org/wiki/File:Sanzio_01.jpg

[6] Plato (427-347BC) is recognised as the first systematic Euro-Western philosopher and the first person to establish a university in the Euro-Western world (Thayer-Bacon, pp. 34).

REFERENCES

Battiste, M., Bell, L., Findlay, I., Findlay, L., & Henderson, J. (2005). Thinking place: Animating the Indigenous humanities in education. *The Australian Journal of Indigenous Education, 34*, 7–19.

Battiste, M. (2000). Introduction. In M. Battiste (Ed.), *Reclaiming Indigenous voice and vision* (pp. xvi-xxx). Vancouver, Canada: UBC Press.

Borell, B. (2005). *Living in the city ain't so bad: Cultural diversity of South Auckland rangatahi* (Master's Thesis). The University of Auckland, Auckland, New Zealand.

Brown, L. & Strega, S. (Eds.). (2005). *Research as resistance: Critical, Indigenous and anti-oppressive approaches.* Toronto, Canada: Canadian Scholars' Press.

Byrd, J. A. (2011). *The transit of empire: Indigenous critiques of colonialism.* Minneapolis, MN: University of Minnesota Press.

Clark, D. A. T. (2004). Not the end of the stories, not the end of the songs: Visualizing, signifying, counter-colonizing. In D. A. Mihesuah & A. C. Wilson (Eds.), *Indigenizing the academy: Transforming scholarship and empowering communities* (pp. 218–232). Lincoln, NE: University of Nebraska Press.

Cordova, T. (1997). Power and knowledge: Colonialism in the academy. *Taboo: The Journal of Culture and Education, 2*(Fall), 209–233.

Delanty, G. & O'Mahoney, P. (2002). *Nationalism and social theory.* London, UK: Sage Publications.

Deloria, V. (2004). Marginal and submarginal. In D. A. Mihesuah & A. C. Wilson (Eds.), *Indigenizing the academy: Transforming scholarship and empowering communities* (pp. 16–30). Lincoln, NE: University of Nebraska Press.

Deloria, V. & Wildcat, D. R. (2001). *Power and place: Indian education in America.* Golden, CO: American Indian Graduate Centre.

Denzin, N. K., Lincoln, Y. S., and Smith, L. T. (2008). *Handbook of critical and indigenous methodologies.* Los Angeles, CA: Sage.

Durie, M. H. (2003). *Nga kahui pou: Launching Māori futures.* Wellington, Aotearoa/New Zealand: Huia.

Edwards, S. (2009). *Titiro whakamuri kia marama ai te wao nei: Whakapapa epistemologies and Maniapoto Māori cultural identities* (PhD thesis). Massey University, Massey (Aotearoa/New Zealand). Available at http://mro.massey.ac.nz/bitstream/handle/10179/1252/02whole.pdf?sequence=1

Findlay, L. M. (2000). *Foreword.* In M. Battiste (Ed.), *Reclaiming Indigenous voice and vision* (pp. ix–xiii). Vancouver, Canada: UBC Press.

Foucault, M. (1972). *Power/Knowledge: Selected interviews and other writings.* New York, NY: Pantheon Books.

Friesen, J. W. & Friesen, V. L. (2002). *Aboriginal education in Canada: A plea for integration.* Calgary, Canada: Detselig Enterprises Ltd.

Goldberg, D. T. (1993). *Racist culture: Philosophy and the politics of meaning.* Oxford, UK: Blackwell Press.

Gone, J. P. (2004). Keeping culture in mind: Transforming academic training in professional psychology for Indian country. In D. A. Mihesuah & A. C. Wilson (Eds.), *Indigenizing the academy: Transforming scholarship and empowering communities* (pp. 124–142). Lincoln, NE: University of Nebraska Press.

Justice, D. H. (2004). Seeing (and reading) red. In D. A. Mihesuah & A. C. Wilson (Eds.), *Indigenizing the academy: Transforming scholarship and empowering communities* (pp. 100–123). Lincoln, NE: University of Nebraska Press.

Kuokkanen, R. (2007). *Reshaping the university: Responsibility, Indigenous epistemes, and the logic of the gift.* Vancouver, Canada: UBC Press.

Ladson-Billings, G. & Donnor, J. (2005). The moral activist role of critical race theory scholarship. In N. Denzin & Y. Lincoln (Eds.). *Handbook of qualitative research* (pp. 279–302). Thousand Oaks, CA: Sage.

Lorde, A. (1981). The master's tools will never dismantle the master's house. In C. Moraga & G. Anzaldua. (Eds.). *This bridge called my back: Writings by radical women of color* (pp. 98–101). Watertown, MA: Persephone Press.

Mihesuah, D. A., & Wilson A. C. (2004). Introduction. In D. A. Mihesuah & A. C. Wilson (Eds.), *Indigenizing the academy: Transforming scholarship and empowering communities* (pp. 1–15). Lincoln, NE: University of Nebraska Press.

Nandy, A. (1983). *The intimate enemy: Loss and recovery of self under colonialism.* New Delhi, India: Oxford University Press.

Smith, L.T. (1999). *Decolonizing methodologies: Research and Indigenous peoples.* London, UK: Zed Books.

Smith, T. (1998, 7–9 July). Doing research from home: Tangata whenua issues and Māori research. Proceedings of *Te oru rangahau: Māori research and development conference.* Te Putahi-a-Toi: School of Māori Studies, Massey University, Palmerston North, Aotearoa/New Zealand.

Takino, N. (1998, 7–9 July). *Academics and the politics of reclamation.* Proceedings of *Te oru rangahau: Māori research and development conference*, Te Putahi-a-Toi: School of Māori Studies, Massey University, Palmerston North, Aotearoa/New Zealand.

Thayer-Bacon, B. J. (2000). *Transforming critical thinking: Thinking constructively.* New York, NY: Teachers College Press.

AFFILIATION

Shane Edwards
Te Wananga o Aotearoa

CATHERINE MANATHUNGA

4. CULTURE AS A PLACE OF THOUGHT

Supervising Diverse Candidates

HOW CAN CULTURE BECOME A PLACE OF THOUGHT IN SUPERVISION?

My Position

Many of the candidates I have worked with as a supervisor in the area of educational research, and many of those who participated in my research on intercultural supervision, are non-traditional insofar as they come from Eastern and Southern cultures and countries. In most cases, these international or domestic, culturally and linguistically diverse research candidates have deliberately sought out a Western doctoral qualification from an Australian or Aotearoa New Zealand university. They often arrive in these Western, 'settler' postcolonial sites believing that the answers to the research questions troubling their higher education systems lie in the West, and most seek to contribute to a body of knowledge and theory that is essentially Western or, as Raewyn Connell (2007) suggests, Northern. They usually work with white Australian, Western or, in the Aotearoa New Zealand context, Pākehā supervisors. Further, to gain their credentials, as researchers, they usually have to satisfy the standards and norms of several Western examiners, either through written, or written and oral examination. Very often, they can draw only on little local, culturally relevant research written in English, although, especially in the case of many Asian countries like China, Japan and Vietnam, there may be vast literatures in languages other than English (Singh, 2009).

Before we delve further into how these points of divergence from the university mainstream shape my candidates' and research participants' positions, I think it will be helpful to clarify, theoretically and practically, the broad key terms I am going to use in this chapter and to highlight some of the slippages and difficulties in finding a comfortable language that adequately captures difference. I would also like to clarify from where the background data come that I will draw upon in this chapter.

First, I am referring to both international candidates and domestic candidates from cultural and linguistic minorities when I speak about intercultural supervision here. My research and supervision has not included Indigenous candidates, although I have drawn extensively on postcolonial theory, and there are some parallels between the intercultural experiences of Indigenous and culturally and linguistically diverse candidates.

A.-Chr. Engels-Schwarzpaul and M. A. Peters (Eds.), Of other Thoughts: Non-Traditional Ways to the Doctorate: A Guidebook for Candidates and Supervisors, 67–82.
© *2013 Sense Publishers. All rights reserved.*

Second, I have chosen to use the broad and troublesome categories of Western and Eastern, Northern and Southern, and sometimes Asian and African. This decision is nourished by Connell's ideas in her book, *Southern Theory* (2007), and by Michael Singh's in his body of work on Western Anglophone supervisors working with Chinese doctoral candidates (e.g., 2009; 2012a&b). Although impossibly general to adequately capture the massive variations they include, these categories can be useful shorthand through which to begin exploring the complexities of intercultural supervision. They also allow us to investigate the peculiar positioning of 'settler' postcolonial societies, such as Australia and Aotearoa New Zealand, as traditionally Western but located in the South. As Connell (2007) and Linda Tuhiwai Smith (1999) point out, Southern knowledges, theories and experiences are generally ignored by the Northern academy, where the real Theory is made. The South is a giant research lab, where data are gathered and Theory is tested and applied (Smith 1999).

Then there is the vexed issue of what to call the non-Indigenous Australians and Aotearoa New Zealanders. While the Māori term Pākehā and the Samoan term Palagi are used extensively in Aotearoa New Zealand to talk about those who are not indigenous to Aotearoa New Zealand, there are no such equivalents for non-Indigenous Australians. Instead, I have used the term settler/invader scholar (Manathunga, 2011a) because the term 'settlement' can never capture the realities of colonial invasion and expansion in Australia. I will use the terms Pākehā and settler/invader scholars here to talk about white Western, non-Indigenous supervisors such as myself (Irish-Australian), who work with culturally and linguistically diverse domestic and international candidates.

I will draw upon my reflections as a supervisor of several international doctoral candidates from different Asian and African countries. These supervisions took place, or are taking place, in Australia and, since May 2011, in Aotearoa New Zealand. The reflections are based both on my outsider observations and on discussions with my doctoral candidates over the years. It is important to remember here, again, that such reflections and discussions cannot ever step outside of the complex and unpredictable power dynamics that circulate in any form of supervision (Grant, 2003) – and these dynamics are likely to be further complicated by the intercultural nature of our interactions. In particular, I will probably only ever understand and be aware of a fraction of the experiences of my non-traditional candidates, given the slippages of language and different cultural norms of politeness and communication with someone in a teacherly or supervisory position of authority (Manathunga, 2011a).

I will also delve periodically into the data I collected during several studies of culturally and linguistically diverse (and mostly international) candidates and their supervisors at an Australian university. These studies involved a total of 25 candidates and 22 supervisors from the broad fields of Education, Languages and Cultural Studies, Psychology, Engineering, Biomedical and Physical Sciences and Agriculture. Candidates from many countries in Asia, Africa, South America and the Middle East, and supervisors from varied cultural backgrounds, participated in the

CULTURE AS A PLACE OF THOUGHT

study. The latter, though, were in their vast majority from Western cultures, and all of them were supervising in Australia. The study involved separate interviews, with matched pairs or trios of supervisors and their candidates, which were analysed using a postcolonial theoretical frame, which I will outline shortly (Manathunga, 2011c). Only a small selection of particularly relevant quotes will be included in this chapter, but more details of the findings from these studies are available (Manathunga, 2007; 2011a &b; 2012).

The Candidates and Participants' Positions

All of the factors mentioned in the first paragraph shape, in different and challenging ways, the ontological and epistemological commitments and interests that culturally and linguistically diverse doctoral candidates bring to their doctoral studies and to supervision. Most of my international research candidates are academics in their home countries. They are often encouraged by their home universities, as part of a research and knowledge capacity building strategy, to embark on Western doctoral studies. Some candidates have institutional leadership responsibilities for academic development, across the university or within their faculties. Their interests, requirements, family, community and organisational obligations and engagements may thus go beyond what many universities expect of their doctoral candidates.

The participants in my studies cover a wide spectrum of disciplinary areas, career stages and interests. For some PhD candidates, an overseas doctoral candidature is part of their continuing journey into adulthood and career preparation. For other candidates, overseas studies require significant financial and personal sacrifices, such as leaving partners and children at home. Others still had to resettle their partners and children in Australia or Aotearoa New Zealand during their studies. Some could tap into ready-made networks of people from their home countries, others found few people from their regions.

Disciplines accommodate the cultural knowledge candidates bring from their (Eastern and Southern) home countries and cultures to different degrees, if they are not simply impervious to them. Interestingly, though, some differences do not fall along expected disciplinary lines: doctoral candidates in Science and Engineering disciplines, for example, do not always experience a pressure to assimilate to dominant Western knowledge paradigms. Thus, one of my studies included an interdisciplinary research centre combining various scientific and engineering disciplines, where a great deal of emphasis was placed on recruiting culturally and linguistically diverse domestic and international candidates, precisely because of the diversity of knowledges and approaches they bring:

> I think what enriches the culture is just a lot of different groups, a lot of different people from around the world ... It's not just a technical thing; it's everything you know ... [We] ...have people here from different cultures. I'm sure all the candidates think that. It's just there, it's implicit in everything they do, you

69

know, they just meet and interact and talk. That's really valuable (English male supervisor, unpublished interview transcript, intercultural supervision project, 2010: 9).

Conversely, it is not necessarily the case that candidates in some of the Social Studies disciplines are encouraged to draw upon their stores of cultural knowledge. For example, one supervisor from a Social Science discipline exhibited a highly assimilationist point of view when discussing her supervision of an Asian male student:

So, like the example this morning ... I was ... trying to get him to understand that one way to do [this] was to give me an overview of the whole theoretical area. And I was saying to him "you can't do that" and he said that is the one I want to use. I am going "NO, what you've got to do is you have to", and he begin to understand why he needed to do that (Australian female supervisor, unpublished interview transcript, intercultural supervision project, Australia, 2010: 4-5).

This supervisor had difficulty imagining what she might learn from her students and relied on a strident discourse about English language issues and standards to describe her interactions with international candidates (Manathunga, 2007, p. 107). The Penguin Dictionary of Sociology's definition of assimilation describes the principles underlying such relationships well: assimilation is "a unidimensional, one-way process by which outsiders relinquished their own culture in favour of that of the dominant society" (1984: 18). I have found postcolonial notions of assimilation or universalism (Ashcroft, Griffiths & Tiffin, 2000) helpful in understanding the experiences of some of the culturally and linguistically diverse participants in my research.

Working Together

I worry that my own culturally and linguistically diverse candidates, too, may feel under pressure to assimilate to Western research discourses and practices – after all, there are research processes in Western universities that seem to make assimilation mandatory. For example, one of my African candidates explained how the request to sign ethical consent forms arouses mistrust and suspicion in her culture, but these forms are an integral and mandatory part of the standard ethical procedures used in Western universities. By the same token, I worry about the consequences of encouraging my candidates to challenge Western thought, without adequate protection and the authority that comes with credentials and experience in research.

Some of my own culturally and linguistically diverse candidates commenced their higher education studies fully convinced of the veracity of Western knowledge and theory and its applicability to their own university contexts. As a postcolonial researcher, I have wondered how to read this strong belief in the inherent usefulness of Western knowledge and theory. Is it an instance of postcolonial self-doubt in the face of the overwhelming dominance of Western ways of knowing and thinking in many disciplines? Is it because the English language dominates the production and dissemination of knowledge in numerous fields? Is it the internalisation of colonial discourses about the so-called superiority of Western knowledge? And how am I, as an Irish-Australian supervisor now working in Wellington, Aotearoa New Zealand, to respond to this? I have argued before that my participation in a Southern postcolonial society gives me an opportunity, even an obligation, to actively facilitate the challenging of Western dominant ontological and epistemological discourses (Manathunga, 2011a). Is this possible as a settler/invader scholar and supervisor?

I have sometimes used quite a lot of persuasion, deployed guided reading and suggested revisions to a research design to make space for my doctoral candidates' Eastern or Southern ways of knowing and thinking. I think some of my candidates have greeted these efforts with relief and pleasure, while others may have been perplexed or even suspicious. I have also encouraged my candidates to create additional opportunities to gather data about the cultural, social, political and economic contexts within which their universities operate. However, enquiring too extensively into some political contexts can sometimes hurt sensitivities, even create dangers. It can be difficult for supervisors to find out about these issues, but I have gradually become aware of the need for caution in some of my candidates' cultural contexts.

Regarding theory, I have encouraged my doctoral candidates to explore the postcolonial concept of *transculturation* (Pratt, 2008) or the creative blending of Western, Eastern or Southern knowledges to create a "third space" (Bhabha, 1990) of understanding. Not surprisingly, perhaps, there were instances of transculturation in my interview data. For example, one Asian supervisor described her own difficulties as a Ph.D. student in reconciling her values about collectivity, reciprocity and holistic connections between her mind, body and spirit with Western individualistic and rational approaches to research. It was only when she came across poststructuralist theories about identity and subjectivity and blended them with her values that she felt able to produce her own culturally inflected contribution to knowledge (Manathunga, 2007: 103). Some of my culturally and linguistically diverse doctoral candidates have found transculturation a productive metaphor, in some cases even generative enough to frame their postcolonial studies, to turn their experiences and research tensions into a rich space of scholarly inquiry.

When the theoretical tools provided by postcolonial theory can be used to enable and value my candidates' diverse, tacit knowledge, they also tend to support facilitative supervision. I try to create space with my candidates and co-supervisors to interrogate our Western disciplinary norms, practices and discourses in the field of Education. I also try to be open about my desire to create space for candidates to explore their own cultural norms and discourses about Education. Nevertheless, I think there is much that remains mutually unknown between me and my candidates, and I am wary about my Western need to KNOW. As Alison Jones reminds us, as settler/invader supervisors we need "to embrace positively a 'politics of disappointment' that includes a productive acceptance of the ignorance of the other" and a "gracious acceptance of not having to know the other" (1999: 315-6).

My culturally and linguistically diverse doctoral candidates, and those who participated in my intercultural research, are simultaneously located in the research networks of mainstream universities and their own different knowledge communities of origin, which they often also research. This creates 'unhomely' tensions and challenges as well as the exciting transcultural possibilities I wrote about above. To understand what it might feel like to research across and between the Western academy and their cultural knowledge communities, I have found Homi Bhabha's (2004) concepts of *unhomeliness* and *liminality* (or between-ness) useful. Bhabha defines unhomeliness as that "estranging sense of the relocation of home and the world ... that is the condition of extra-territorial and cross-cultural initiations" (13). Liminality is the correlate of a contested and unstable, in-between space, where identities can be interrogated and engaged with and where cultural change may take place. In it, the "colonised subject ... [is located] between colonial discourse and new non-colonial identities"; as a result, liminality is a "constant process of engagement, contestation and appropriation" (130).

My research candidates' negotiations across and between the Western academy and their own communities must be exhausting and deeply troubling at times, particularly as the communities whose interest the research is designed to serve continue to grapple, in different ways, with colonial pasts and presents. As researchers, the candidates circulate across and between spaces where knowledge may be owned collectively or individually; where it may be regarded as context-specific, and only accessible to particular people or groups, or universal and for all to engage in. There are times when Western and Eastern or Southern knowledge paradigms are irreconcilable – how can these challenges and tensions be navigated, and what can productively be created from them? Sometimes, the only thing I can do as an outsider is to share readings and suggest postcolonial theoretical tools and ideas, like unhomeliness, to help candidates process and come to their own terms with these experiences. For some of my candidates these resources have created resonances and reassurances. As bell hooks reminds us, "theory is a location for healing" (1994: 59).

From the perspective of an Irish-Australian settler/invader supervisor, I have also found the notion of unhomeliness useful in thinking about my lack of knowledge, understanding and experience of my candidates' diverse communities and ways of knowing and being. I find the unsettling of my authority as a supervisor (the one who knows) productive, but also sometimes uncomfortable and challenging. Constantly, I am asking for more insights into my candidates' knowledge communities and how higher education plays out in their countries and cultures. I am deeply aware of my own ignorance and need to learn. This is where Singh's (2009) work on the generative pedagogies of ignorance in supervision becomes inspiring. Drawing on Rancière's concept of 'ignorant schoolmasters', Singh argues that "the conscientious

> Philosophy – "love of wisdom" In a broad sense, philosophy is an activity people undertake when they seek to understand fundamental truths about themselves, the world in which they live, and the relationship to it.

CULTURE AS A PLACE OF THOUGHT

but ignorant" supervisor can acknowledge their student's "co-presence" and intellectual equality, create space for "intellectual reciprocity" and assist the student to build new connections between their own cultural knowledge and that offered by Western theory (194-198). So I am relying on my candidates to advise me about how we might vary the scope and methodology of their research, to match as closely as possible the requirements of their communities and the contours of their cultural knowledge. In these ways, I seek to acknowledge and value my culturally and linguistically diverse candidates' ways of knowing and enable their agency. It is my hope that, in so doing, my candidates and I might work collaboratively to reshape Western epistemologies, methodologies, forms of collaboration and the conduct of ethical and sensitive research. Drawing on postcolonial theories and these kinds of educational philosophies, I seek to make culture a place of thought for my culturally and linguistically diverse candidates.

> Florida State University

DRAWING ON OTHER SOURCES

In addition to the texts discussed already, there are a number of recent articles and books that provide thought-provoking and productive ways to think about the experiences of non-traditional doctoral candidates and suggest respectful approaches to supervising them. In this section, I will highlight some of the most useful, recent texts and explain why my candidates and I have found them helpful. I will not critique some of the older texts that were written from a deficit discourse and some of the mainstream literature on intercultural communication. It is by now well established that, while some of the texts on intercultural communication can be helpful, their use is limited if they remain largely silent on issues of power, history and place in supervision. This silence can sometimes even make supervisors and candidates feel inadequate, as they grapple with specific tensions and challenges that are not addressed in the generic recipes for effective intercultural communication.

Singh and some of his candidates have continued his generative investigation into productive pedagogies of ignorance and published really practical and powerful examples of the possibilities of transculturation. In a recent book chapter, Singh and Chen (2012a) outline how some Chinese candidates have challenged current Western knowledge. In drawing upon their Chinese intellectual heritage, their multilingual abilities and their transnational digital communities, Singh's candidates seek to connect intellectual developments concerning school pedagogy in China and Australia. This involves a four-step process of conceptualising by taking a literal translation of a Chinese character (*kunji*), contextualising the historical and contemporary use of this character, using this Chinese character to challenge Western knowledge, and finally making transnational intellectual connections that demonstrate how Chinese concepts can provide new understandings of pedagogy. For example, Xiafang Chen (one of Singh's candidates who co-wrote a part of the book chapter with him) developed a new reading of leadership from Chinese character *li ti*[1] to capture more accurately the multidimensional nature of school leadership, where different school, regional and system-based partners operate across and between these levels, in unevenly distributed ways. Chen thus extended the Western concept of tri-level leadership, which failed to adequately capture the complexity of these partnerships.

So too, a recent article by Singh and Xiaowen Huang (2012b) demonstrates how non-Western candidates can activate their bi- or multilingual capabilities and use non-Western theoretical tools to analyse research evidence critically, to reshape Western Anglophone education. As an example, Singh and Huang explore how Bourdieu's concept of *habitus*, which he developed during an ethnographic study of the Algerian Kabyle people, emerged out of an inability to acknowledge the Kabyle people's ability to engage in critical analysis. Instead, Bourdieu argued that the Kabyle needed French critical theory to become aware of their own experience of domination. Singh and Huang also explore the slippages in language and interpretation that occur when French and Algerian ideas are consumed in Anglophone countries. They use this exploration to "interrupt Euro-American theoretical dependency by engaging in a multiplicity of critical theoretical resources" and to challenge studies, including postcolonial ones that "do not move beyond Western theories despite interested commitment in non-Western languages and cultures" (8). Singh and Huang argue convincingly that Western Anglophone educators can activate non-Western candidates' linguistic knowledge and theoretical resources – in this case, Mandarin and Chinese critical thinking, or *yin cai shi jiao*: "teachers should conduct their teaching in accordance with each individual student's characteristics and capabilities" (11).

Some recent special issues, specifically on supervision and culture (Grant & Manathunga, 2011) and doctoral education (Devos & Manathunga, 2012), provide useful reflections on supervising non-traditional doctoral candidates. I will particularly focus on an article by Barbara Grant and Elizabeth McKinley in *Innovations in Education & Teaching International* (the whole special issue provides insightful work and is worth consulting in detail) and those by Anita Devos and Margaret Somerville, Janette Ryan, and Rui Yang in *Australian Universities Review*.

Although the experiences, requirements, interests, obligations and engagements of Indigenous candidates and their supervisors differ in important ways from those of other culturally and linguistically diverse research candidates, there are some parallel lessons that candidates and supervisors can learn from the inspiring work about Indigenous supervision. In particular, the work of Barbara Grant, Liz McKinley, Sue Middleton, Kathie Irwin and Les Tumoana Williams about Māori supervision provides many valuable insights. I will focus only on three of their articles here. Grant and McKinley (2011: 377) demonstrate how history and locality in Aotearoa New Zealand "colour" supervision pedagogies differently. Their research demonstrates the diversity among Māori candidates across a range of engagements, either within Western academic research, while acknowledging their ancestral lineages, or deeply embedded in Māoritanga (Māori culture, practice and beliefs).[2] Pākehā supervisors are sometimes concerned about their lack of knowledge of mātauranga Māori

(Māori education, knowledge and wisdom), which creates similar situations to those described by Singh, above, regarding pedagogies of ignorance. Grant and McKinley also discuss the "settler grief and guilt" that supervisors may experience as they engage with Aotearoa New Zealand history, recognise how they are "part of the problem" and become conscious of their own biases and assumptions (383 & 380).

Importantly, Grant and McKinley outline the significant roles played by supervisors external to the university. These include the candidates' kaumātua (male or female elders) who may take on a grandparent-type relationship with candidates. This is the primary pedagogical relationship in Māori culture, while the candidates' tūpuna (female or male ancestor) provide spiritual guidance for the project. The authors describe how some Pākehā supervisors try to use Māori imagery with their candidates, and how candidates and supervisors trade metaphors in a mutual exchange. They also show how candidates and supervisors struggle to work through tensions resulting from clashes between Māori and Western academic knowledge. All of this "colours and thereby enriches" supervision, holding open the possibility of transformation for both candidates and supervisors (although some of these transformations may be painful (379). As I will describe below, there are some important parallels, especially in regard to the role of beliefs about spiritual guidance and ancestor involvement, with the experiences of culturally and linguistically diverse candidates. Further, as Said's (1978) work on orientalism and Elizabeth Bullen and Jane Kenway's (2003) research demonstrate, Europeans' stereotypes and misunderstandings of non-European ways of knowing and being may continue to surface, even unconsciously, in intercultural supervision.

In an article written by the whole research team (McKinley, Grant, Middleton, Irwin & Williams, 2011), Māori ways of knowing are explored – particularly Māori candidates' experiences of "working with(in) different knowledges, working with research advisors and researching as Māori with Māori" (116). The authors provide details on the guidance some candidates receive from their tūpuna (ancestors) and relate how one student sought to "give status to her grandmother's teaching" through her doctoral thesis (121). They also highlight the ways in which some Western academic practices may be contrary to Māori ways of knowing: they recount, for example, how a student was told to "unpack the stories" (121), which, however, would have been a violation of tikanga (Māori cultural protocols). The article concludes with a summary of recommendations for Pākehā supervisors, which are particularly helpful and explicate the need for Pākehā supervisors to be:

– aware of the multiple agendas some Māori candidates bring to their academic work,
– prepared for unpredictable consequences of their involvement,
– understand that some Māori candidates may be using their doctoral study to strengthen their Māori identity,
– open to the influence of community-based mentors,
– open to unfamiliar ways of knowing and thinking (127).

Expanding Pedagogical Boundaries

C. MANATHUNGA

Each of these recommendations also has ramifications for supervising culturally and linguistically diverse candidates.

In a 2012 book chapter, McKinley and Grant describe the Māori concept of *ako* (pedagogy), which is the "unified cooperation of the learner and the teacher in a single enterprise" (207). There are three traditional forms of *ako* that could be adapted to Māori doctoral supervision: formal learning, everyday exposure and apprenticeship. Each of these approaches has its 'proper setting' (in other words, place is really important), in which the learner listens, looks and imitates the teacher and which may involve a series of tests to check the learner's desire to learn. McKinley and Grant demonstrate how these pedagogies require time, care, Māori cultural knowledge and language development and recovery. They call on institutions to make space in their research higher degree programmes to facilitate these slower and deeper doctoral pedagogies. The chapter provides an important example of transculturation, which is also helpful for supervisors of candidates from culturally and linguistically diverse backgrounds and for the candidates themselves.

There are some important parallels between these explorations of Māori supervision and the supervision and examination experiences of a Cambodian doctoral student, Piphal, and her Australian supervisors. Devos and Somerville outline the latter, in which the clash of Western and Cambodian knowledge production processes and subjectivities came to a head when the student received two different examination results. Piphal's thesis in the field of Education was a memoir of Piphal's grandmother, a member of the Cambodian Royal Family, who had been exiled during the Pol Pot regime. Piphal, who had lost everything during this period of terror, including her two children, had written her grandmother's memoir in Cambodian language before she fled Cambodia for Australia. Her research was "a highly emotionally charged commitment to intergenerational and transcontinental identity work" (Devos & Somerville, 2012: 48). Piphal's supervisor writes about part of the supervisory process, which involved dressing Piphal correctly in Cambodian Royal dress and photographing her – a process the supervisor found "uncomfortable" but helpful to understand "much more of Piphal's subjectivity" (50). Just as the Māori candidates above described the spiritual guidance provided by their ancestors, Piphal, according to her supervisor, "believes that the writing ... is directed by the hands of the ancestors" (50).

While one examiner regarded Piphal's thesis as "a remarkable work of personal and academic scholarship", the other examiner recommended that substantial work needed to be done to "develop the historical and political contexts of the narrative" (51). An adjudicator, given the challenging task of making a ruling that took into account both examiners' reports, argued that, while "both examiners were competent and fair from the perspectives of the disciplinary and research spaces in which they were each located", this thesis could not be examined "in the usual ways" because "the work stands alone, in its own genre" as a work of "difference and innovation" (52 & 53). Devos and Somerville conclude that we must create space in the Academy for "non-traditional forms of inquiry and representation" (53), especially for the risky work of culturally and linguistically diverse candidates.

In a similarly vein, Ryan (2012: 55) argues for the "need for genuine intercultural dialogue" in higher education, particularly between scholars of Western and Confucian heritages. In interviews conducted in Australia, the UK, China and Hong Kong, Ryan explores the differences and similarities between Western and Chinese perspectives on 'good' scholarship and 'effective' learning and suggests that there is a great deal of "potential for mutual learning when assumptions are critically examined and the possibilities for reciprocal learning are identified" (61). Like Singh's work, her article problematizes stereotypes of Confucian-heritage education systems and encourages Western supervisors to think about how they might learn from their Chinese candidates. Yang's (2012) exploration of doctoral education in China is particularly vital, given the general lack of current English-language literature on the topic. He emphasises particularly how doctoral supervision in China is "highly debated especially over such issues as the most important qualities for good supervision and whether or not there is a Chinese way to supervise" (68). This kind of work is important for Western supervisors who work with Chinese candidates and have to consider the differences between their supervisory style and that which Chinese candidates may have experienced during earlier studies in their home country.

WORKING THROUGH SOME ISSUES

Effective intercultural supervision requires high levels of trust between candidates and supervisors. It also requires a great deal of belief in the candidates' ability and cultural knowledge, particularly, as Singh (2009) points out, when supervisors attempt to facilitate their candidates' critical and highly innovative explorations of their own cultural knowledge, without having that knowledge themselves. It takes great courage for candidates and supervisors to venture into the unknown realm of transcultural thought and ideas. For supervisors, this can create intense feelings of unhomeliness and a fear that their candidates may take the wrong direction in their research or expose themselves to examiners and other academic gatekeepers' censure – and this is not an irrational fear, as Devos and Somerville's (2012) article shows. Sometimes, the boundaries between amazing creativity and potential dead ends seem very blurry. Grant discusses these difficulties of "going into another world", when Māori "knowledge spaces could be disorientating and uncomfortable, fraught with anxiety about how to conduct themselves" for Pākehā supervisors (2010: 122).

This can also be the case in the supervision of other culturally and linguistically diverse candidates, especially when the work takes place across and between different languages and mutual comprehension and critical understanding is difficult. Some concepts and knowledges are difficult to translate fully into English, and there are times when supervisors and candidates who lack a shared first language find it hard adequately to convey unique cultural knowledge or highly innovative transcultural ideas. As Singh's research (2009; 2012a&b) has demonstrated, there are many exciting possibilities associated with harnessing candidates' linguistic knowledge to challenge Western thought, even though this work is inherently difficult and unhomely for both parties.

Then, there can be situations in which cultural knowledge is sacred or tapu, or only available to certain authorised people or groups, which might mean that supervisors are not permitted to look at raw data. This issue can especially occur in the supervision of Indigenous candidates, but could potentially impact upon the supervision of culturally and linguistically diverse candidates as well. Several Indigenous supervisors have discussed with me the difficulties they experienced with their Western co-supervisors' concerns that they were not allowed to 'see' these data. Here, Jones' (1999) reminder that we cannot always fully KNOW the Other becomes important. Again, though, this situation poses a risk to the acceptance of the candidate's research – both in the Western academy and sometimes within Indigenous communities, as well.

Sometimes, feelings of guilt and remorse on the part of Western settler/invader supervisors may get in the way of effective supervision. As Grant argues, Māori candidates may "consciously or unconsciously use the power imbalance to maintain a kind of moral authority over their supervisors" (2010: 121) to vindicate a lack of progress or to defend particular approaches they cannot really justify. A Māori academic mentioned in an interview the occasional need to "rescue non-Māori supervisors and candidates from this dynamic" (121).

There are situations when these disagreements can be difficult to resolve in a productive way. Apart from involving supervisors who share the cultural and linguistic background of the student, and may therefore be able to 'read' more effectively what is actually happening, there are no definite or watertight strategies. Instead, a complex and respectful negotiation needs to occur, in which supervisors work hard to understand the cultural and linguistic knowledge the candidate shares with them and then seek to work out collaboratively how this knowledge may be made recognisable in the Western academy. When this is not possible or appropriate, supervisors and candidates need to consider the odds and determine whether they can convincingly challenge or push the boundaries of what has come to count as knowledge, evidence, and research. Devos and Somerville's work (2012) highlights the risks, but also the possibilities, of taking this approach.

HELPING CULTURE TO BECOME A PLACE OF THOUGHT IN SUPERVISION

I have found in my own supervisory practice, as well as in my research on intercultural supervision, that postcolonial theory can provide particularly rich resources to help realise culture as a place of thought in supervision – for culturally and linguistically diverse doctoral candidates and for their supervisors. The postcolonial tropes of *assimilation, unhomeliness* and *transculturation* are especially helpful for all parties to understand and grapple with their experiences in intercultural supervision and to seek ways to reshape Western epistemologies, methodologies, and forms of collaboration. I will use these concepts to organise my thoughts about possible strategies, tactics and techniques for effective supervision of non-traditional candidates, which arise out of this chapter.

The pressure towards *assimilation* to Western research norms and ways of knowing remains very strong in Western universities. Indeed, as a settler/invader supervisor, I realise how my own biases and assumptions may surface, unwittingly, in intercultural supervision. This point was also raised in Grant and McKinley's (2011) and Bullen and Kenway's (2003) research, and it means that we must constantly and reflexively review our ways of thinking, talking and working with culturally and linguistically diverse candidates. It also means, at times, that we must seek to process our settler/invader guilt and remorse (Grant & McKinley, 2011), which may not only impact upon our work with Indigenous candidates but may also influence our supervision of other culturally and linguistically diverse candidates, with whose histories we are less directly entangled.

However, there may also be occasions when our candidates will have to adopt Western research practice standards, despite their lack of translatability across cultures. Earlier, I mentioned the requirement to follow standard ethical clearance practices in the conduct of research. These processes of informed consent and voluntary participation are very important in the appropriate and sensitive conduct of research, especially with non-dominant groups. However, as I described earlier, the ways of securing this kind of consent are often different across cultures. In some African countries, relationship building rather than the signing of consent forms is a more appropriate way of securing voluntary participation.

A far more challenging issue regarding assimilation is the strong belief of some culturally and linguistically diverse candidates that Western knowledge is more effective than their own cultures' ways of knowing; a kind of 'West is best' approach. It is hard to know whether this kind of belief is an instance of self-doubt resulting from the dominance of Western knowledge and the English language in many disciplines. As outlined above, the strategies I use to encourage candidates to think differently include guided reading (especially postcolonial work); discussion of their own cultural context, and how this shapes the issues they are studying; and suggestions that they include exploratory techniques in their research design. I have found that these tactics work to varying extents, depending on the values held by the candidates and sometimes on their disciplinary background (e.g., whether they come from an educational psychology background, with a commitment to individual, cognitive understandings of learning, or an educational sociology one, with a commitment to the group and contextual understandings of learning). Most important in dealing with possible assimilation to Western knowledge, though, is the engagement in constant and respectful discussion and negotiation.

Unhomeliness is a significant part of any intercultural supervision experience, I have found, for culturally and linguistically diverse candidates as well as their supervisors. This has been confirmed in Singh's (e.g., 2009) and Grant and McKinley's (e.g., 2011) research. The first strategy I use in grappling with these feelings of uncertainty and ambivalence is to acknowledge their existence; these disconcerting feelings of being in a strange liminal, in-between place, where home and the world are sometimes thrown upside down, are part and parcel of intercultural research and interaction. I try to talk with my culturally and linguistically diverse candidates about these experiences and encourage them to share some of their moments of unhomeliness – although I realise that there will be issues and challenges that they choose not to share with me. Instead, they may want to discuss them with their fellow candidates, and I try to provide them with opportunities to do so by including them in thesis cluster meetings that I co-facilitate with one of my colleagues, who also supervises culturally and linguistically diverse candidates. We try to retain a sense of humour about these issues (I use self-deprecating humour to tell stories of my intercultural gaffs and misunderstandings), although there are also times when tears are not very far away for either of us.

Again, I encourage my candidates to read postcolonial theory to deepen their understanding, not only of the difficult consequences of uncertainty and unhomeliness and the tensions and pain that these may bring, but also of the exciting possibilities of thinking at the limit of current knowledge. I find it useful to brainstorm with them what these possibilities might include, and what they might mean for our [inter]disciplines. It's an edgy and risky space, but that is exactly also what also makes it fun and engaging. As a supervisor, I learn to be comfortable with uncertainty and with being the one who doesn't always know – the ignorant one. With my candidates, I return again and again to hooks' (1994) powerful mantra "theory is a location for healing" (59).

Finally, I have developed a number of strategies for trying to facilitate *transculturation*. Transculturation involves moments of creativity in supervision when "culturally diverse students may carefully select those parts of Western knowledge that they find useful and seek to blend them with their own knowledge and ways of thinking" (Manathunga, 2007: 97-98). This concept draws on the work of Mary Louise Pratt (1992: 6) who argued that transculturation is when "subordinated or marginal groups select and invent from materials transmitted to them by a dominant ... culture" (Pratt, 1992: 6). I try to make space for my culturally and linguistically diverse candidates' ways of knowing, thinking and being, so that they might challenge the dominance of Western knowledge. Others have written about this (e.g., Singh, 2009; Grant & McKinley, 2011; Devos & Somerville, 2012), but these issues have also emerged from my studies of colleagues' supervisory practices (Manathunga, 2007; 2011a &b). In particular, I have found McKinley and others' (2011) recommendations for Pākehā supervisors useful in working with culturally and linguistically diverse candidates. The beginning of this process is always to try and learn, as much as I can, about the history and circumstances of my candidates' countries and cultures. As a researcher of intercultural supervision pedagogy, I have read recent work on Chinese ways of knowing and supervising (e.g., Ryan, 2012; Yang, 2012) and conducted research on supervision at a Japanese university with a Japanese colleague, Yoshiko Saitoh (Manathunga, 2012). I also constantly seek to ask my candidates about the conditions of higher education in their countries and the social, political and historical contexts within which they are situated. I provide guided reading activities on intercultural supervision and postcolonial theory and ask my candidates to write about their reactions and about possible resonances with their own experiences or research topics. As indicated above, all of these explorations then become an important part of the candidates' research design and data analysis.

All this requires an epistemological position that is open to and curious about different ways of knowing and thinking (McKinley et al., 2011). I am particularly keen to push the boundaries of my own thought and understanding and hope that my candidates similarly enjoy extending their thinking repertoires. Although this sometimes means that we journey together down dark, dead-end alleyways, it often means we can find powerful avenues for *transculturation*. Finally, I also try to find out about and respect the multiple agendas that my culturally and linguistically diverse candidates have for conducting their research (McKinley et al., 2011). Very often, these may involve many responsibilities and obligations to their own communities, themselves and their families, which go well beyond the commitments of Western candidates. The extent or meaning of some of these I may never fully know. Postcolonial theory can help supervisors to ensure that culture can become a rich, productive and exciting place of thought in supervision. By helping our students understand how assimilation continues to operate in dominant Western forms of knowledge construction, we can assist them to resist such pressures and open spaces for the recognition of other ways of knowing and being. By discussing the unhomeliness that is often part of intercultural knowledge journeys and supervision interactions, we can acknowledge our moments of mutual discomfort and explore the ways in which this can also create exciting deconstructive possibilities for innovative thought. Finally, by offering strategies for transculturation, we can make spaces for unique blendings of different ways of knowing that allow students to create genuinely original, culturally-inflected new knowledge.

NOTES

[1] Literally, upright body with length, width and thickness – three dimensional.
[2] Elsewhere, Grant (2010) describes how some Māori candidates use their research projects to reconnect with their Māori heritage and become Māori.

REFERENCES

Abercrombie, N.; Hill, S. & Turner, B. (1984). *The Penguin dictionary of sociology*. London, England: Penguin Books.
Ashcroft, B.; Griffiths, G. & Tiffin, H. (2000). *Postcolonial studies: the key concepts*. New York, NY: Routledge.
Bhabha, H. (1990). The third space: interview with Homi Bhabha. In Rutherford, J. (Ed.) *Identity: community, culture, difference* (pp. 207–221). London, England: Lawrence & Wishart.
Bhabha, H. (2004). *The location of culture*. New edition. London, England: Routledge.
Bullen, E. & Kenway, J. (2003). Real or imagined women? Staff representations of international women postgraduate candidates. *Discourse: studies in the cultural politics of education*, 24(1), 35–50.
Connell, R. (2007). *Southern theory*. Crows Nest, NSW: Allen & Unwin.

Devos, A. & Manathunga, C. (2012). Letter from the editors. *Australian Universities Review, 54*(1), 2–4.

Devos, A. & Somerville, M. (2012). What constitutes doctoral knowledge? *Australian Universities Review, 54*(1), 47–54.

Grant, B. (2003). Mapping the pleasures and risks of supervision. *Discourse: studies in the cultural politics of education, 24*(2), 175–190.

Grant, B. (2010). Challenging issues: doctoral supervision in postcolonial sites. *Acta Academica Supplementum*, 1, 103–129

Grant, B. & McKinley, E. (2011). Colouring the pedagogy of doctoral supervision: Considering supervisor, student and knowledge through the lens of indigeneity. *Innovations in Education & Teaching International, 48*(4), 377–386.

Grant, B. & Manathunga, C. (2011). Supervision and cultural difference: Rethinking institutional pedagogies. *Innovations in Education & Teaching International, 48*(4), 351–354.

hooks, b. (1994). *Teaching to transgress*. New York, NY: Routledge.

Jones, A. (1999). The limits of cross-cultural dialogue: pedagogy, desire and absolution in the classroom. *Educational Theory, 49*(3), 299–316.

McKinley, E. & Grant, B. (2012). Expanding pedagogical boundaries: Indigenous candidates undertaking doctoral education. In Lee, A. & Danby, S. (Eds.), *Reshaping Doctoral Education: Changing programs and pedagogies* (pp. 204–217). London, England: Routledge.

McKinley, E.; Grant, B.; Middleton, S.; Irwin, K. & Williams, L. (2011). Working at the interface: indigenous candidates' experience of undertaking doctoral studies in Aotearoa New Zealand. *Equity & Excellence in Education, 44*(1), 115–132.

Manathunga, C. (2007). Intercultural postgraduate supervision: ethnographic journeys of identity and power. In Palfreyman, D. & McBride, D. (Eds.), *Learning and teaching across cultures in higher education* (pp. 93–113). New York, NY: Palgrave Macmillan.

Manathunga, C. (2011a). Intercultural postgraduate supervision: postcolonial explorations and reflections on Southern positioning. *NZ Annual Review of Education*, 20, 5–23.

Manathunga, C. (2011b). Moments of transculturation and assimilation: Post-colonial explorations of supervision and culture. *Innovations in Education & Teaching International, 48*(4), 367–376.

Manathunga, C. (2011c). Postcolonial theory: enriching and unsettling doctoral education. In Mallan, V. & Lee, A. (Eds.) *Doctoral education: papers at the IDERN Research Meeting, Malaysia, 2011*, Serdang: Penerbit Universiti Purtra Malaysia, 84–99.

Manathunga, C. (2012). Supervision and culture: postcolonial explorations. *Nagoya Journal of Higher Education*, 12, 175–190.

Pratt, M. (2008). *Imperial eyes: travel writing and transculturation*. London, England: Routledge.

Ryan, J. (2012). Internationalisation of doctoral education. *Australian Universities Review, 54*(1), 55–63.

Singh, M. (2009). Using Chinese knowledge in internationalising research education: Jacques Rancière, an ignorant supervisor and doctoral candidates from *China. Globalisation, Societies and Education, 7*(2), 185–201.

Singh, M. & Chen, X. (2012a). Generative ignorance, non-Western knowledge and the reshaping of doctoral education: Arguing over internationalising Western-centred programs and pedagogies. In Lee, A. & Danby, S. (Eds.), *Reshaping Doctoral Education: Changing programs and pedagogies* (pp. 187–203). London, England: Routledge.

Singh, M. & Huang, X. (2012b). Bourdieu's lessons for internationalising Anglophone education: de-classifying Sino-Anglo divisions over critical theorising. *Compare: a journal of comparative and international education*.

Smith, L. T. (1999). *Decolonising methodologies: research and Indigenous peoples*. London, England: Zed Books Ltd.

Yang, R. (2012). Up and coming? Doctoral education in China. *Australian Universities Review, 54*(1), 64–71.

AFFILIATION

Catherine Manathunga
Victoria University of Wellington

KING TONG HO

5. TRANSFER AND TRANSLATION

Negotiating Conflicting Worldviews

INTRODUCTION

This chapter makes key references to my PhD study and my postgraduate supervision experiences in art and design, particularly of creative practice-led research projects. While I teach and research in a Western context today, I am yet influenced by how I was brought up, in a British-colonised Chinese community in Hong Kong; by how I became acculturated to the Western-dominated, multicultural society in Aotearoa/New Zealand; and by the thinking of Chinese or Asian postgraduate thesis candidates. Over time, I have adopted a fusion of these cultural views. What I would ask the readers here, irrespective of their cultural background, is to suspend their own worldviews temporarily, to enter into those of others.

In my own field of art and design, a candidate's cultural origin affects the research outcomes, since the latter usually hinge on creative resolutions that result from the researchers' artistic pursuits – and these are, in turn, influenced by their creative research processes and philosophical orientation (Tanaka, 2009).[1] In another discipline, Barbara Grant pays attention to the ethnic identities of supervisors and candidates, and the complex postcolonial politics of domination and displacement, in her exploration of Māori research, doctoral supervisions, and the differences between Western and Indigenous knowledge (2010: 506). Grant is concerned about the political imbalance in an academic community where "non-Western worldviews get little recognition". She suggests that this is particularly the case in doctoral education – "a site where dialogue is always already compromised by institutionalised power differences" (512).

Chinese and Asian candidates[2] often face a principal challenge brought about by their displacement from the research and knowledge contexts in their countries of origin – that is, by the shift from their own context to one with minority status in the West. The concomitant difficulties are aggravated by the fact that supervisors in many contemporary Western research supervision environments tend to expect controlled research outcomes and restrict the candidates' freedom of choices (Grant, 2010: 509; see also McCallin & Nayar, 2012; Wisker, Robinson, Trafford, Warnes & Creighton, 2003). This restriction may then intensify the potential for conflict between supervisors' Western views and those of non-Western candidates. For the latter, the supervisors' cultural identity is often another ambivalent and unsettling

A.-Chr. Engels-Schwarzpaul and M. A. Peters (Eds.), Of other Thoughts: Non-Traditional Ways to the Doctorate: A Guidebook for Candidates and Supervisors, 83–99.
© *2013 Sense Publishers. All rights reserved.*

aspect. It is common that aspiring researchers want to make their knowledge known and recognised in Western contexts; therefore, when choosing supervisors, they often consider supervisors' Western identities more important than their area of expertise. On the other hand, supervisors' cultural indifference may also concern them. Thus, to maintain a promising supervision relationship, it is vital for supervisors and candidates to understand the differences arising from their respective diverse cultural backgrounds.

Gina Wisker, Gillian Robinson, Vernon Trafford, Mark Warnes and Emma Creighton argue that supervision is a form of teaching, and doctoral research a form of learning; research is also a dialogue amongst experts (2003: 385). They emphasise the importance of collaboration and interaction between supervisors and candidates as collegial equals (387) in a dynamic and long-term supervisory relationship between researchers, supervisors and a body of work (396). However, if supervisors are unfamiliar with the cultural aspects of their candidates' research contexts, they may be unable to engage in a dialogue about the research project. To an extent, this will hinder interaction and collaboration between supervisors and researchers. There is sometimes a danger that a supervisor dominates the intellectual direction of the project – not so much of the candidate's creative research and its resolution, but of the contextualisation of the practice and its scholarly development. Supervisors may induce candidates to abandon their own worldviews and adapt a dominant framework, and there is a danger that the candidates' research either ends up diverted away from the original research question or context, or the creative research and its contextualisation are mismatched, which prevents the work from achieving coherence and relevance.

This chapter suggests some possible solutions to minimise conflicts arising from the differences in worldview between candidates and supervisors in a cross-cultural supervision relationship. While these solutions may be interpreted differently from different cultural perspectives, I hope that they are nevertheless transferable.

FROM "CRITICAL GAZE" TO "CRITICAL APPRECIATION": TRANSCULTURALISM AND INTERCULTURALISM

Roberto Salvadori defines transculturalism as the successful interchange of knowledge – it goes beyond interculturalism insofar as a common culture is created in the exchange, which is "different from the original cultures of both teachers [supervisors] and pupils [candidates]", "[s]omething changes in the culture of both" (1997: 188-187; see also p. 70, above). By contrast, Scherto Gill promotes intercultural adaptation, in which outsiders (candidates) learn to meet the expectations of insiders (supervisors) and, through a growing familiarity with Western systems and frameworks, develop intercultural competence and reconstruct their identity (2007: 171). Gill's views largely represent those predominant in Western academic institutions. However, while the development of intercultural competence is an indispensable survival skill for candidates, it does not necessarily advance the interchange of knowledge, nor does it reshape the knowledge of the candidates' original cultures.

To facilitate transcultural exchange and reshaping of knowledge, supervisors and candidates need to develop a new "critical appreciation of the value of critical thinking"[3] about the diversity of knowledge (Cadman, 2000: 481, 488). Yet, merely to embrace the politics of difference (477) is inadequate if the supervisory relationship does not move into a space that lies beyond the Western-centric model of the acceptance of Others. The Chinese advocacy of approaching differences with *harmony but no assimilation* (和而不同) (Fang, 2003: 1-2) suggests a reciprocal approach to creating transcultural spaces:[4] knowledge is exchanged and shared, and both sides shift their positions in the process.

The creation of a shared basis of values and understandings (Cadman, 2000: 488) ultimately requires the collaborative effort of supervisors *and* candidates. Thus, the candidate's final research will become accessible (or survives) in a form that does not compromise the position he or she would have established in negotiations with the supervisor, namely to develop confluent knowledge in a transcultural context. Respecting candidates as experienced scholars within their own cultural context is a first step to turn the (Western) "critical gaze" (Cadman, 2000: 487) into "critical appreciation" (481). However, there is little in the extant literatures that would help supervisors and candidates to progress towards more satisfying and reciprocal relationships – most texts are weighted towards the intercultural adaptation of the candidates to a Western educational system. Only rarely is the predicament of the supervisors explored, and the challenges they face as they co-construct a transcultural environment with their candidates.

As a Chinese designer and academic working in a Western university, focusing primarily on research and supervision in art and design contexts, I am interested, on the one hand, in analysing and resolving the conundrums associated with supervisory relationships between members of dominant and minority groups. On the other hand, I believe it is important to see these relationships in the global context of a shift from Western dominance to a more balanced transcultural state. While my views do not necessarily represent those of other minority Others, I hope they are useful to and adaptable by other minority researchers and their supervisors working in a Western academic context. My PhD study *The Poetics of Making* (2007) represents a sustained and in-depth study of contemporary contexts of digital art, digital technology, digital printmaking and East-West cross-cultural studies. The research sought to integrate traditional materials, aesthetics and philosophical ideas with contemporary technologies in digital art and design practice. The thesis explored connections between Eastern and Western cultural theories, philosophy, art and design practice methods, and aesthetics. My supervisors Colin Gibbs and Elizabeth Grierson are both practicing artists and educators.[5]

The trajectory of my research journey underwent constant negotiation. Initially, it was a negotiation with 'myself' (my self as existing in internal and external conceptual spaces; see Tuan (2007) about 'The Triune Roots of Identity', p. 90 below) to decide on the context of my research: was it to be my professional expertise in photography and digital technology, which I was familiar with, or was it to be Chinese art, aesthetics and philosophy, which were new to me but seemed important. It took me many months to overcome my anxieties about including the latter areas. Later, I found that I enjoyed the research, as I became more familiar with Chinese art, aesthetics and philosophy. This growing familiarity empowered me to establish my roots, and thereby my cultural identity, in New Zealand. The on-going negotiation with my supervisors concerning research contexts and different worldviews bearing on my research clarified how I saw my research (internal world) and how my supervisors perceived it (external world). Between us, we attempted to attain a basis of shared values and understandings of the research contexts and processes. These processes were challenging but inspiring, time consuming but worthwhile. In my experience, to bring about a productive tutorial session, the candidate has to take the initiative and responsibility for articulating with precision what is likely to be unfamiliar to the supervisors – be that research contexts, worldviews, or methodological issues. And the supervisors must attend with patience and refrain from premature disapproval of the candidate's propositions.

To support the shift from an unequal power balance in the West's favour to more reciprocal research relationships, I believe it is further useful to explore some philosophical differences between the systems, but also Chinese concepts of relationality (reflection and observation, interiority and exteriority) and their relationships with knowledge production. Different disciplines value different types of knowledge: anthropologist Jacques Maquet posits that sociologists are not inclined towards acknowledging the inner processes of humans, nor to trust the introspection of self. Different contexts of study, he argues, should develop their own strategies to achieve critical understanding (1986: 25-6). But even within the same contexts, a variety of approaches may be useful at different stages of the research process. In the perception of art and design, for instance, experience is a primary factor, while comparative reflection and analytical observation are integral parts of the processes towards intellectual understanding (29). I would add that aesthetic experience also involves negotiation between interiority and exteriority, both for individuals and for the relationship between internal and external worlds.

Here, art historian Hung Wu's metaphor of the *Double Screen* (1996) and his review of the function of screens in classical Chinese painting are relevant.[6] The contemporary painter Lei Xu[7] (徐累) (2011), when asked during an interview to appraise his own painting, refers to the classical painting, *Playing Chess by the Double Screen* (Figure 1) (重屏會棋圖) by Wen-ju Zhou (周文矩) (~950 AD). Xu says: "Similar to Zhou's painting, the scenes in my own paintings evolve from the people and the screens, which reflect each and everyone, real or virtual, and repetitively involute; they also reflect on the past through the present, and the reverse" (2011: 185). Xu's idea corresponds to Wu's *Double Screen*. Here, individual internal and external space, as well as the relationship between interiority (the internal world) and exteriority (the external world), are constantly negotiated. The spaces that are

TRANSFER AND TRANSLATION

created by the screens reflect the physicality and internal world of selves in relation to the external world. Here, negotiation is a strategy of embracing the other's views to attain an agreed solution, thereby achieving harmony with others. Similarly, I would argue, a balanced embracing of each other's ideas between members of minority and dominant cultures can be both a strategy and a process in supervisory relationships, for which the philosophical worldview of achieving harmony provides conceptual support (see note 4).

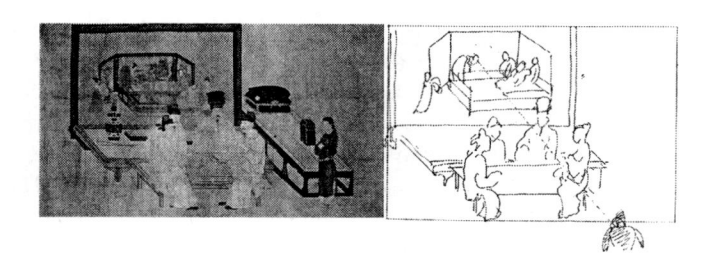

Figure 1. Left: attributed to Wenju Zhou, Double Screen, Ming copy of a tenth century work, short handscroll, ink and colour on silk. Palace Museum Beijing; right: drawing by Hung Wu showing the composition of the painting.

Embracing the other's view also underpins and sustains the Chinese traditional concept of "always adapting to change for long-lasting survival" (變則通, 通則久).[8] When Chinese candidates return home from Western countries, they are usually able to incorporate the other's (mostly Western) views to reshape the knowledge of their own culture in order to excel, irrespective of their performance in a Western environment. Having embraced the others' views, to enrich their own cultural origins they reach for a connecting worldview of achieving harmony. Japanese graphic designer Ikko Tanaka's global vision of non-territoriality in technology, culture, art, and so on (1992) further endorses a universal embracement of others.[9] However, Tanaka also points out that the pace towards the disappearance of territories is much slower in culture, art and design. In other words, the process of cross-over embracement is in progress, but the goal of fusion with harmony is yet to be accomplished.

The official primary role of China's art and design education is currently to inculcate moral principles, presumably those that have been endorsed by the Chinese Communist Party (Fielding & Chung, 1998: 316). However, in practice, teachers give preference to the development of art and design knowledge and practical skills over inculcating Party-endorsed moral and spiritual values (320) and lessons are often subject-led and outcome-oriented (318).

> A high priority is placed on training and technique, as compared with the openness and creativity valued in the West, with the result that Chinese children often achieve a much higher level of technical competence at a much younger

87

age in music and art, for example, than their Western counterparts. Perhaps this stems partly from the use of an ideographic language, which requires the rote learning of thousands of characters, and the ability to reproduce those characters with technical perfection. (Jacques, 2009: 199)

Martin Jacques concurs with American educationalist Howard Gardner and draws attention to his advocating of respect for the "fundamental difference" between Chinese and Western systems and the systems' "deep historical and cultural roots" (Gardner in Jacques, 1989: 501). Jacques agrees also that it is disastrous to inject Western "notions of education, progress, technology into alien cultural contexts" when it is far more appropriate and timely "to understand these alternative conceptions on their own terms, to learn from them if possible, and for the most part to respect (rather than to tamper with) their assumptions and their procedures" (501). In the context of design education in China, given its short history, it is pivotal for students to prove that they can master new technological skills. The fact that this proof is considered evidence of one's academic achievement is likely to induce Chinese PhD candidates to further pursue skills-led research. They will often aim for practical outcomes (subject-led and product-oriented) rather than explore uncertain potentials and possibilities.

For Asian candidates in a Western system, guidance from their supervisors that exposes them to approaches focusing on creative potential is therefore paramount. However, the greatest challenge for supervisors is not about changing their candidates' mind-set: the greatest challenge may well be their own dislocation into research contexts with which they are unfamiliar, but towards which their candidates may lean in a desire to explore the potentials of their cultural origins. When supervisors in this situation try to redirect a candidate's project into a context within their comfort zone, they may trigger a crisis: while it seems legitimate for supervisors to envision the potential of a research context through the matrix of their own expertise, redirecting their candidates into that same matrix may jeopardise the development of new and different knowledge. To tolerate a dislocation from their own research contexts, and even to thrive on the change, supervisors need to make the transition to a transcultural space. For this, an understanding of difference and duality as not necessarily opposed and mutually exclusive is essential. It helps develop a negative capability, as John Keats called it. This capability concerns not only tolerance but positive expectation towards uncertainty (see Engels-Schwarzpaul & Emadi, 2011: 10).

BEING IN-BETWEEN LANGUAGES – INTERPRETING SILENCE

The ability of both supervisors and candidates to tolerate uncertainty and to remain curious under ambiguous circumstances is also very useful when dealing with cultural and philosophical differences in communication. Examining variances between Chinese and Western philosophical views on languages, Yanfang Tang expatiates on 'metaphorical silence', as a Chinese tactic for manoeuvring a language that stresses semantics, rather than syntax. Silence renders gaps and holes in the text, which provoke the readers' imagination and encourage them to search for hidden meanings; physical marks are transformed into artistic symbols. Through silence, new horizons arise in the form of suggestion, evocation, 'quiet observation', and 'direct experience', providing Chinese philosophers and poets with a most effective means for obtaining truth or literary understanding (1999: 20).

On the other hand, Diana Bridge describes how Japanese people maintain silence as a way of disagreeing, in contrast to the use of silence in the West as a form of agreement (2008: 19-23). She also notes the significance of silence in creating distance in Chinese classical poems. Bridge further discusses her difficulty, as a poet from a Western culture, to bridge cultural gaps and to interact with people belonging to other cultures (19). Her description exemplifies complications in communication that can also arise between Western supervisors and Chinese, or more generally Asian, candidates in a Western context.[10]

One practical way of resolving the challenge of communications in a PhD supervision situation is to establish a glossary with a collection of key terms.[11] In creative practice-led PhD projects, candidates commonly struggle, in writing the exegesis, to decide between the relative importance of accessibility for the readers of their text (most of whom will belong to a culture other than their own) and that of preserving the originality of their thoughts, in their own cultural context. In my experience, both as a PhD candidate and as a supervisor of postgraduate theses, a glossary with a collection of key terms, outlining important cultural and philosophical meanings, can efficiently facilitate communication in the supervision process. As working documents, these glossaries are most effective if they clearly explain a candidate's understanding of specific terms and lay out in detail his or her justifications and critiques regarding the resolution of differences. They can become a repository of core concepts that reveal the researcher's philosophical vision and situate the research in a specific context. When integrated into an exegesis or a publication, these glossary terms can help reduce the gap between text and reader and facilitate the readers' imagination in trying to render implicit meanings (see Tang, above). In the context of examinations, glossary terms may ease, or even avoid, unnecessary debates about the critical framework of the research. Such debates are often influenced significantly by unacknowledged assumptions about what it means to do art and design research – unacknowledged, because they are so 'normal' for a dominant culture that they become invisible to its members. To most of those who do not belong to the dominant culture, though, it is quite clear how philosophical position, research ethics, critical framework, methodology, and other fundamental aspects of a PhD thesis always derive from specific cultural, disciplinary and academic contexts.

Already in the 1980s, Clifford Geertz acknowledged the shortcomings of Western semiotic theories and approaches concerning art (and design), and I believe that his observations are transferrable to design. A more adequate semiotics of art and design not only requires the engagement in "a kind of natural history of signs and symbols, an ethnography of the vehicles of meaning" (1983: 118-9). It also demands of semiotic theory's analytic powers (be that Peirce's, Saussure's, Levi-Strauss's, or Goodman's) to turn away from an abstract investigation of signs toward an investigation of signs "in their natural habitat – the common world in which men look, name, listen, and make" (119).

> A theory of art is thus at the same time a theory of culture, not an autonomous enterprise. And if it is a semiotic theory of art it must trace the life of signs in society, not in an invented world of dualities, transformations, parallels, and equivalences (109).

In Geertz' view, Western scholars commonly fail to investigate the cultural origin of signs from other cultures. This goes along with a duality, frequently observable in art and design research, whereby the world is seen in terms of the 'Western self and the others'. For me, the cultural origin of signs is the root of one's identity. Retired Chinese geography scholar Yi Fu Tuan's perspective on 'The Triune Roots of Identity' in the context of history, geography and language (2007: 158-171) is my rationale for clinging to my own cultural domain; indeed, it revives my ambition to imprint Chinese cultural marks onto the Western domain that I inhabit now. I am a New Zealand Chinese, simply because I think in my Chinese language; have no sense of rootedness in New Zealand history; and am thronged with geographical belongings to the past. However, I struggle to accept my inability to adapt to another cultural milieu and this struggle constitutes an undertow sustaining my identity. I feel imbued with the mission to ensure my Chinese identity in a Western domain, and to establish a Chinese cultural profile in my academic profession (Ho, 2007: 332).

From the Chinese perspective, space is constantly in transformation. Many Chinese PhD candidates have followed their ambition to relocate from a familiar space (China) to an unfamiliar space (in the West). Always, problems arise – if not simply from a lack of familiarity with new spaces (interior/exterior, insider/outsider spaces), then from a state of being in-between. My experience suggests that a documentation of the research processes can give evidence and provide justifications for the findings of potential knowledge of the research when the knowledge system related to a transcultural space has not yet been fully developed. In time, the accumulated documentations of individual projects will sediment to form a collective archive of discourse, which transforms the unfamiliar knowledge of this transcultural space into familiar territory, thereby making it accessible to members of other cultures. However, my view is that the archive is only an empty inactive container of documentations.[12] Only when it is accessed by other researchers and a discourse is initiated, does it become active and enables the documented contents of the archive to constantly mutate and transform in its representations and meanings.

The issues associated with cultural differences that are likely to surface in Asian PhD candidates' projects can be explicated in reference to a different philosophical stance taken in Chinese and Western art and design. For instance, some Western scholars in semiotics define the relationship between the artwork (image) and its concept (the idea that underpins the artwork), as one between two separate elements: the *signifier* (physicality or form of the artwork/image) and the *signified* (concept, intention, etc.). However, such distinctions are not integral to Chinese art practice. Chinese audiences make reference to the creative concepts or ideas [意] of others (creator or author and other existing opinions) to review the artwork (image) [象], and to integrate their experiences and opinions, in order to interpret and develop their own ideas about the artwork. While the audience and the creator might have distinct positions regarding the concept behind the artwork, their interpretations are open-ended and transformative. This can be explained by the historical developments of the pictographic system of the Chinese language, which has undergone generations of transformation. Simply put, text is image-based for the Chinese. Each Chinese character is composed of at least one pictograph. Chinese readers are able to construct their interpretation by reviewing the pictographic form(s) of the character. To become proficient, Chinese learners have to undergo a rote learning procedure of the basic meanings of the pictographic system.[13] While both Western and Chinese approaches regarding concept and image aspire to the intellectual engagement of the participants, their different philosophical stance often leads Western supervisors (and examiners) to misread Chinese candidates' resolutions of a creative work. What can further worsen the situation is an often deliberate cloaking of an originally Chinese intention in challenging the intellectual response of the audience. In an art and design thesis, this incongruence between Western and Chinese frameworks of interpretation could effectively be addressed and alleviated through mind-mapping, structural diagrams and maps.[14] The resultant processes and discussions are likely to enable candidates to sustain their philosophical approaches, while making them accessible to a broader audience.

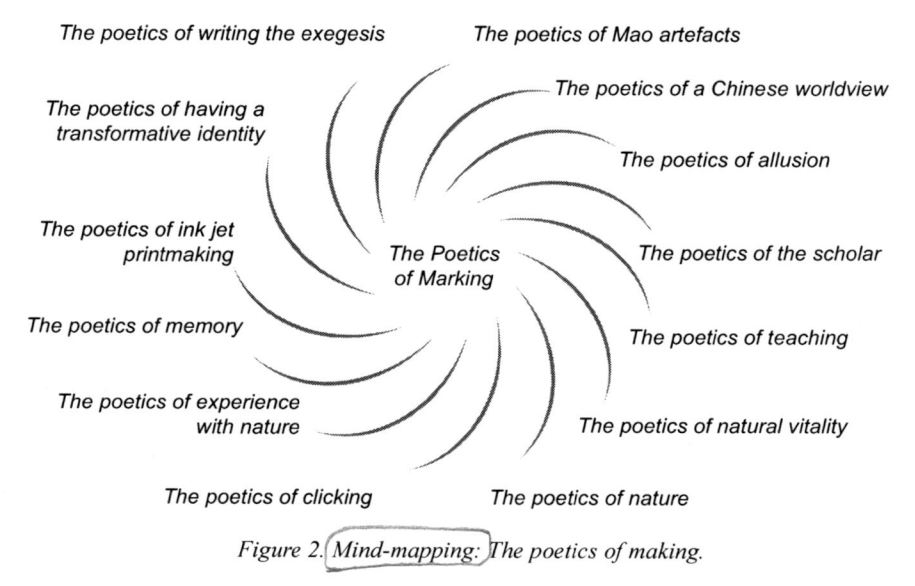

The poetics of writing the exegesis

The poetics of Mao artefacts

The poetics of a Chinese worldview

The poetics of having a transformative identity

The poetics of allusion

The poetics of ink jet printmaking

The Poetics of Marking

The poetics of the scholar

The poetics of memory

The poetics of teaching

The poetics of experience with nature

The poetics of natural vitality

The poetics of clicking

The poetics of nature

Figure 2. *Mind-mapping: The poetics of making.*

In my own PhD thesis, I devised a particular structure to anchor a transformative identity and to substantiate Chinese poetics as the centre of a space of negotiation concerning a Chinese philosophical worldview and Western technology. In the constellation of collateral concerns, activities and practices converging in a central space of negotiation, each practice deals with a specific context or content to reflect a "single, empirically determined unity of state of mind, situation, and moment" (Owen, 1992: 452) and engenders an affluent and unparalleled consideration of the cultural or philosophical significance of the Chinese worldview of poetics. Their unity not only constitutes a crossover of aesthetic perspectives, of congruent profusion, to the self (myself) (Ho, 2007: 95) but forms a system of logical structure with a Chinese spirit – Western physicality with a Chinese interiority. Collectively, these practices give rise to a place for self-enlightenment – for the my-self and others – and form a collateral wholeness within which to explore the concept of poetics of making (Ho, 2007: 21; see Figures 2 & 3). As mutative and transformative representations, these practices are intended to trigger a poetic externalisation of the self (119-120), unveiling potential knowledge through their physicality, and stimulating enlightenment through their interiority. For Westerners, this is about unveiling and enlightening; for the Chinese, it is to unveil *through* enlightening.

Culture & ideology:	The poetics of Mao artefacts
	The poetics of a Chinese worldview
Philosophy:	The poetics of allusion
	The poetics of the scholar
	The poetics of teaching
Self beliefs:	The poetics of natural vitality
	The poetics of nature
	The poetics of clicking
	The poetics of experience with nature
Emotional experiences:	The poetics of memory
	The poetics of ink jet printmaking
Identity:	The poetics of having a transformative identity
	The poetics of writing the exegesis

Figure 3. Mind-mapping: The Poetics of Making.

While philosophical worldviews may not be debatable, knowledge is (Zhuangzi, 300 B.C./1985: 216-7) and this debate may require supervisors to relocate themselves to a space-in-between cultures. Here, Western dichotomised duality poses a challenge to supervisors, for there are no absolute 'selves' or 'others' in Chinese culture, only constantly shifting identities of self and other. Jacques (2009) argues in a similar vein that the present and the past are not discrete. Current East Asian forms of modernity are layered with past and future, and in China the very old coexists with the very new (109; see also p. 93, below).[15]

But what counts as new in the context of art and design practice? Since an original and significant contribution to knowledge is a core requirement that every PhD thesis must meet, candidates are often questioned about the new contribution their project makes. 'New' is relative to 'old', or 'constant' [古], and may aim to revitalise the existing. In a transcultural space or context, the relocation of an existing concept into another context often gives rise to something new (concepts, methods, processes, etc.). In art and design, this metaphorical aspect of a relocation of cultural context creates "bridges between artists [and designers] and cultural legacies in order to secure their own paths" (Gao, 2002: 47). This new is a 'constantly new constant' in a new context (Ho, 2007: 74) that, most importantly, is engaged in a cross-cultural dialogue that interrogates existing knowledge.

The relocation requires that the candidate-researcher takes a clear position. A research statement, instead of a question, could in the early stages of the research achieve a more effective communication between candidate and supervisor. When talking through a research statement (instead of a question) with the supervisor, the candidate-researcher will have to review and defend the existing (old or constant) knowledge in a relocated context (instead of its own context). Similarly, the supervisor will be made aware of the shift in cultural space (and context). It is likely that tutorial discussions of an initial statement will give rise to research questions that are situated in a transcultural context. Ultimately, 'relocating as new' corresponds with the relocation of both candidate and supervisor as they begin to work in a transcultural space.

THE ECONOMICAL RISE OF MINORITY COUNTRIES

The economic rise of former minority countries,[16] led by China in the past decade, brings forward a global consideration of political and cultural shifts. So far, limited perspectives predominate in Western discourse, which discount the histories and cultures of countries with contrasting civilizational inheritances (Jacques, 2009: 11). They lead to a tendency to measure the unfamiliar in terms of the familiar (100), subsequently neglect others' worldviews, and will likely produce careless assumptions that China will become Western (13). While China (and other minority countries) did change its value systems rapidly to accommodate a highly developed pragmatism and flexibility (107),[17] Jacques argues that Anthony Giddens' view of Western modernity[18] does not apply to East Asian modernity where "the present and the past are not 'discrete'". Asian modernity is distinct from Western modernity in that "the present is layered with *both* the past and the future" (109). East Asian modernity is "a unique combination, in terms of social and economic realities, attitudes and consciousness, of the present, the past and the future" (110). The differences in cultural outlook instigate tensions between China (and other minority countries) and the still dominant West in the process of reshaping the global political structure. Jacques also argues that the feeling of superiority, so firmly embedded in the Western psyche and historically supported by "powerful economic, political, ideological, cultural and ethnic currents", is in crisis (144). In future, Westerners will be required to think of themselves "in relative rather than absolute terms, obliged to learn about, and to learn from, the rest of the world without the presumption of underlying superiority, the belief that ultimately it knows best and is the fount of civilizational wisdom" (145). Discourse generated by transcultural academic research will help ease these tensions. In recent years, the percentage of academic research taken up by Chinese students (and those from other minority countries) in higher education has rapidly increased.[19] In a supervision relationship with a Chinese (and Asian) candidate, it is therefore indispensable that Western supervisors expeditiously migrate to a transcultural context.

Today, China actively influences the world and the Chinese language is becoming more familiar and accessible to the West. A system of Chinese-ordered English (COE), which uses English words to represent Chinese phrases and retains the syntax of the original Chinese text, is indicative of a merging, or at least drawing nearer, of two distinct cultural spheres. COE was invented by the Confucius Institute at Michigan State University to help English speakers to learn Mandarin Chinese – possibly in recognition of the necessity of relocation into a transcultural space of supervision, which candidates and supervisors of mixed teams have to perform if they are native speakers of English and Mandarin respectively. Already in 2009, Chinese came first on the list of the top twenty languages (Jacques, 2009: 115). Yet, when promulgating the language, Chinese academics accommodate Western learners by offering them transitional strategies as they enter an unknown environment. This also aspires to developing a learning system that is sustainable in a global context.

In the long history of Chinese civilisation, collective belief is deeply rooted in Confucius' legacy, with its "emphasis on moral virtue, on the supreme importance of government in human affairs, and on the overriding priority of stability and unity" (198). It is not likely that China aspires to develop a Chinese-centric view to influence the world, but it will strive for a balance with Western-centric systems — a transcultural balance between Western ego-centric and Chinese (and Asian) collective thinking. Strategically, academic discourse is one of the spaces that are appropriate to develop this transcultural view.

CONCLUSION

When reviewing a practice-led art and design thesis that belongs to a culture unfamiliar to them, few supervisors and examiners are able to reposition themselves and enter the worldview underpinning the research context. If they cannot shift their position sufficiently, there is a danger that they may not be able to fully appraise the potential of the research. When judgement – for instance of structure, depth, or process – is partially based on the supervisor or examiner's tacit knowledge (as it frequently is in the assessment of creative practice-led research), or when scattered memories are drawn on to reach a logical inference, the supervisor's advice or the examiner's assessment could put the candidate's research at risk. This is often exacerbated in the examination process, when examiners have to assess an exhibition (as an important component of a creative practice-led thesis) within a tight timeframe.

Candidates and supervisors working together on a cross-cultural research project should acknowledge this condition early on and situate the research in a transcultural instead of an intercultural space (see Salvadori, p. 84, above). Insofar as a practice-led research project is a transformative showing in the here and now, it can provide an intellectual locale for communication and interrogation to develop new knowledge. The reflective experience of the (researcher-candidate's) self and the actualisation of the practice should be documented and discussed in ways that support transculturation (see Manathunga, p. 70, above). In this sense, the practice generates creative resolutions that stimulate visual discourse and the exegesis presents the philosophical and/or conceptual implications of the research, as well as the rationale of research processes and outcomes. New knowledge is developed through acknowledging differences between cultures. However, accepting and embracing differences is not enough. What is needed to achieve confluent new knowledge is not only a tolerance of the cultural counterpart's vision, but the cherishing of its potential to reshape existing knowledge. Relocation, in its literal and philosophical senses, is a key aspect in cross-cultural research projects: re-location of the cultural field in which both candidates and supervisors work, and re-location of the discourse of existing (constant) knowledge into a transcultural space.

On the way to a greater balance between the currently dominant Western worldview and other possibilities, Li's idea of *sedimentation of life experience* (2005: 159) through artistic practice offers the potential that, in time, the knots will untie themselves in their own way, helped by self-enlightenment. Whether this kind of knowing, which usually lacks immediacy in its effect, will supplement the Western logical stance in critical thinking is unclear. In any event, its introduction requires a process of systematic justification and documentation which, in time, becomes part of the collective archive of discourse, which will gradually transform the unfamiliar knowledge to become familiar. For instance, the strategy of my PhD thesis, which negotiates and substantiates a central idea through the constellation of collateral concerns, reflects the ambition to expand both Chinese and Western methods and to enhance critical thinking: investigating a concept within a range of different contexts, I deployed different approaches not only to achieve different aesthetics, but also to initiate different discourses. Aspects of content, and the discourses they initiated together, form an archive engaging individual selves in an intellectual dialogue, with the potential to stimulate self-enlightenment to obtain new knowledge.

Often, candidates require support from their supervisors to cope with the University's expectations, not only regarding the execution of their research but also the presentation of their ideas, without compromising the potential of the work. Joanne McClure has shown that students found adjustment to the new academic/cultural environment most difficult during the first six to twelve months. She suggests that this is due largely "to the influence of previous educational and cultural experiences" (2008: 216). Given that the Western University's expectations differ from those at Chinese and other Asian universities, it is imperative that candidates are supported early on in changing their mind-set from expecting to achieve practical outcomes to exploring potentials and possibilities. The greatest promise of cross-cultural research projects involving Asian PhD candidates and Western supervisors, though, lies in the potential of transculturation – the creative blending of different knowledges to generate a new space for knowledge. Towards this goal, it is probably necessary that researcher-candidates become more explicit about their practice, and that a wide-spread cliché, namely that art and design practice does not necessarily function to represent concepts is re-examined.

In building a transcultural space, the Chinese concepts of openness and transformative quality in art practice are valuable. In practical terms, precisely defined glossaries of research terms, critical frameworks and maps, as well as a full and reflective documentation of the experimental practice can function well as core components of the exegesis. Often, embarking upon a research statement instead of a research question at the initial stage will progress the research more effectively. What is most helpful for the transfer and translation of potentially conflicting worldviews, though, is the acknowledgement that new knowledge (not only, but particularly in a transcultural space) is relative, rather than absolute: relative to the present with its elements of past and future; relative to historical and cultural differences; and relative to a global political balance.

NOTES

1. Ikko Tanaka (Zhu, 2009: 181), who is considered the pioneer of Japanese graphic design, held the view that the cultural origins of a country are creative sources in design. He also emphasised the relationship between daily life and design.
2. Throughout this chapter, the terms "researcher" and "candidate" represent Chinese and Asian researchers and candidates, unless otherwise stated.
3. In an evaluation of the International Bridging Programme (IBP) at the University of Adelaide, data collected by Cadman (2000) from students and staff acknowledged that critical thinking is one of the key aspects that international students are concerned with and value. For example, "[u]nlike in [my country], how you think is more important than what you know" (481); "[l]earning how to criticize is very interesting for me ... Having the ability to give argument about something is considered as a way of showing our existence" (481). Cadman notes, that while "the move from 'reproductive' to 'critical' thinking is a crucial one for international students (Ballard, 1987; ... Ballard & Clanchy, 1991; Ballard, 1995), it has elsewhere been suggested that to assume a deficit because of a non-critical tradition in CHC cultures is inappropriate (Kember & Gow, 1991; Biggs, 1997; Chalmers & Volet, 1997)". Further, "to use a remediation model for addressing so-called 'problems' is a form of cultural imperialism (Birch, 1990; Benesch, 1993)" (479).
4. Fang Keli (2003) proposes the classical idea of 'harmony but no assimilation' [和而不同], which emphasises the co-existence of different cultures. "The scholars from various countries agreed that human civilization in the twenty-first century will confront many important problems, its prospect will not be the 'conflict of civilization' and the disaster caused by such conflict as some Western scholars have predicted, but rather a co-existence of various civilizations which is claimed by Chinese Philosophy as 'harmony but no assimilation' and will accord to the aspiration of the peoples from all over the world." (1-2).
5. Initially, I began my project with a different primary supervisor, but our supervisory relationship ended when the collaboration did not prove to be productive and the research could not move forward.
6. Wu (1996) analyses Wenju Zhou's painting *Double Screen*: "It is possible that this theme [of a poem by Juyi Bo] inspired the painter [Zhou] of the *Double Screen*, who literally depicts the domestic scene

TRANSFER AND TRANSLATION

described in Bo's poem on a screen. But when the poetic expression is translated into a visual illusion, its meaning, entirely changes. It is no longer a literary *simile* ('… *like* a scene on a screen'), but has become a visual *metaphor* ('… a scene on *a screen*'). This internal screen, though a flat pictorial image, entices the viewer to take it as reality" (81). The artist "has separated these two scenes with a solid screen frame, which reminds the viewer that the domestic scene within the frame is no more than a picture. When the viewer has overcome his initial confusion and declares – *yes! The scene on the screen is indeed an illusion!* – he has forgotten that it is merely an illusion within a larger illusion, which is the whole painting." (83-4).

7   I translated Xu's idea from the Chinese article. In the original: 繪畫中也一樣,像五代周文矩的'重屏會棋圖',現場的人和屏風裏的景象互為印証,虛與實不斷回旋,看到過去反照現在,或者是看到現在反照過去,這種方法不是簡單的時空觀,而是觀看心理學的挑戰,特別有現代的思辨意識 …"（ 生命雜誌, 第69期, 185頁, 2011年8月）

8   The idea of 變則通, 通則久 originates from a Chinese classical document 《系辭下》. Weng [王吉勝] (2009) exemplifies the idea in Chinese that it is the constantly changing that will last forever. The following is the excerpt from his Chinese article: "易, 窮則變, 變則通, 通則久。" "窮" 指事物發展到極端。事物發展到極端而滯礙不通, 就會發生變革, 使事物獲得新的發展余地。《系辭上》又: "一闔一辟謂之變, 往來不窮謂之通。" 所謂 "變則通" 並不是一次性的, 而是要 "往來不窮" 地變。世界由此才可以恒久"

9   "[I]n the 21st century, I foresee a fusion of the non-mainstream cultures led by West Asian, Eastern Europe and Africa. The time of East looking towards the West will end … and territories between technology, culture, art and etc., will not exist" (Tanaka, 1992, in E Zhu [朱鍔]).

10 The challenge of cross-cultural research lies not only in the appropriateness of translation at a philosophical level but, more importantly, the accessibility of cultural difference in thinking (Ho, 2007: 18). When translating Wang Fu-chih's (Wang Fu-zhi's) *Interpretations of Poetry (Shi Yi)* [詩譯] *and Discussions to While Away the Days at Evening Hall* (Yi Tang Yong Ri Xu Lun) [夕堂永日緒論], Owen (1992) says: "Much of Wang Fu-chih's sharpest critical and theoretical writing is to be found in his Broad Commentary on the Book of Songs [詩經] … There are, unfortunately, serious difficulties in presenting these works to the English reader. The Shih kuang-chuan (Shi Guang Zhuan) [詩廣傳] has deep roots in the long and complex tradition of scholarship on the Book of Song, and the issues it addresses are often comprehensible only within that tradition" (451-452). Ames (2003), when translating *Daojejing* [道德經], also acknowledged the challenge of trying to interpret Chinese philosophy: "Chinese philosophy has been made familiar to Western readers by first 'Christianizing' it, and then more recently by locating it within a poetic-mystical-occult worldview. To the extent that Chinese philosophy has become the subject of Western philosophical interest at all, it has usually been analysed within the framework of categories and philosophical problems not its own … it has presented us with the challenge of trying, with imagination, to take these texts on their own terms by locating and interpreting them within their own worldview" (Preface and Acknowledgments, p. xi).

11 Renowned sinologist and scholar Stephen Owens always includes a section of glossary terms in his translation and writing on classical Chinese literature. His glossary terms are paradigmatic in their accessibility to Western readers while preserving the 'Chineseness' of both the language system and cultural thinking of the original literature.

12 This idea is expanded from my view on photographic archive that "… photographs contained in a photographic archive are fragments of ideas and memories. It is not so much a system or record of historical evidence, but an empty container. It is the collision of these fragments of ideas and memories when placed in the public domain that has the potential to fold a discourse … Together they (photographs and discourse generated) become an active archive. It is this potential for discourse that enables the context of the archive to constantly mutate and transform in its representations and meanings." (2011: 10)

13 This unique characteristic of open-ended and transformative in meaning is primary to the survival of the ancient Chinese language. This correlates with the earlier discussion that "embracing the other's view has sustained the Chinese traditional thought of 'always adapting to change for long lasting survival" [變則通, 通則久].

14 Gray & Malins (2004) have fully utilised structural diagrams and maps in suggesting design strategies of practice-led research.

[15] In fashion design, the *qipao* [旗袍], a contemporary one-piece Chinese dress for women, is a paradigmatic example. The traditional *qipao* had a loose and wide cutting, to hide the wearer's body, and it gained its contemporary, tight fitting form in Shanghai in around 1920s, under a Western aesthetic influence for accentuating women's figures. Since then, the tight fitting *qipao* has become a global representation of traditional Chinese women's dresses. Today, the design of the *qipao* retains many Chinese traditional features and continues to evolve. The Chinese take a Western aesthetic worldview in fashion to display the Chinese tradition. Yet, for the Westerner with a worldview of dichotomised duality of self and others, the *qipao* is always a Chinese traditional dress.

[16] Minority countries refer to those countries in Africa, Asia and Latin America that are considered by the West as underdeveloped; these countries are collectively named 'the Third World'.

[17] Jacques interviewed Hung in March 1999: "As Hung Tze Jan, a successful writer who has since become one of Taiwan's leading cyber entrepreneurs, philosophically remarked: 'We have had to change our value system so many times in such a short space of time.' The result, not surprisingly, is a highly developed pragmatism and flexibility; otherwise it would be quite impossible to cope with such rapid change" (2009: 107).

[18] "In his book *The Consequences of Modernity*, Giddens seeks to draw a distinction between the characteristics of modernity and premodernity" (Jacques, 2009: 109).

[19] As an example, Li Xiaokun of China Daily reported in 2008 that Chinese mainland students have been the second largest source of foreign students at Harvard University for the past seven years; and the number has increased 81.8 % in the past 16 years. The majority of these students take postgraduate courses and focus on research work. Asian countries make up three of the five top foreign sources of students at Harvard, with South Korea and India ranking third and fourth respectively.

REFERENCES

Ames, R. & Hall, D. (2003). *A philosophical translation: Dao De Jing "making this life significant"*. New York, NY: The Ballantine Publishing Group.

McCallin, A. & Nayar, S. (2012): Postgraduate research supervision: A critical review of current practice. *Teaching in Higher Education, 17*(1), 63–74.

Bridge, D. (2008). O to be a dragon. *New Zealand Journal of Asian studies 10*(1), 8–27.

Cadman, K. (2000): 'Voices in the air': Evaluations of the learning experiences of international postgraduates and their supervisors. *Teaching in Higher Education, 5*(4), 475–491.

Engels-Schwarzpaul, A.-Chr. & Emadi, A. (2011). Thresholds as spaces of potentiality: Negotiating the supervision relationship in a non-traditional Art and Design PhD candidature. *ACCESS, 30*(2), 1–14.

Fang, K. (Ed.). (2003). *Chinese philosophy and the trends of the 21st century civilization*, vol. 4. Beijing, China: Commercial Press Ltd.

Fielding, R. & Chung, S.K. (1998). The paradox of aims in Chinese Art and Design education: Speculation on co-operation in Hong Kong, Post 1997. *Journal of Art and Design Language, 17*(3), 315–22.

Gao, X. (2002). *Return to painting* (N. Benabid, Trans.). New York, NY: Perennial.

Geertz, C. (1983). *Local knowledge: Further essays in interpretive anthropology*. USA: Basic Books Inc.

Gill, S. (2007): Overseas students' intercultural adaptation as intercultural learning: A transformative framework. *Compare: A Journal of Comparative and International Education, 37*(2), 167–183.

Gray, C. & Malins, J. (2004).*Visualizing research: A guide to the research process in art and design*. Hants, England: Ashgate Publishing Limited.

Grant, B. M. (2010): The limits of 'teaching and learning': Indigenous students and doctorate supervision. *Teaching in Higher Education, 15*(5), 505–517.

Ho, K. T. (2011). *Expanding from Dominion Road: Documentary through discourse as an active archive*. Auckland: AUT University

Ho, K. T (2007). *The poetics of making. A new cross-cultural aesthetics of art making in digital art through the creative integration of Western digital ink jet printmaking technology with Chinese traditional art substrates*. PhD thesis. Auckland, New Zealand: AUT University.

Jacques, M. (2009). *When China rules the world: The rise of the Middle Kingdom and the end of the Western world*. London, England: Allen Lane.

Kim, K. H. (2005). Learning from each other: Creativity in East Asian and American education. *Creativity Research Journal, 17*(4), 337–347.

Li, X. (2008, January 4). Chinese students flock to Harvard. *China Daily.* Retrieved February 10, 2013 from http://www.chinadaily.com.cn/china/2008-01/04/content_6369844.htm

Li, Z. & Cauvel, J. (2005). *Four essays on aesthetics: Towards a global view.* Lanham, MD: Lexington Books.

Maquet, J. (1986). *The aesthetic experience: An anthropologist looks at the visual arts.* New Haven, CT: Yale University Press.

McClure, J. W. (2007). International graduates' cross-cultural adjustment: Experiences, coping strategies, and suggested programmatic responses. *Teaching in Higher Education, 12*(2), 199–217.

Neumann, R. 2005. Doctoral differences: Professional doctorates and PhDs compared. *Journal of Higher Education Policy and Management, 27*(2), 173–88.

Owen, S. (1992). *Readings in Chinese literary thought.* Cambridge, MA: Harvard University Press.

Pye, L. W.(1992). *The spirit of Chinese politics.* Cambridge, MA: Harvard University Press.

Salvadori, R. G. (1997). The difficulties of interculturalism. *European Journal of Intercultural Studies, 8*(2), 185–191.

Tanaka, I. (1992/2009). *Awakening of design* (E. Zhu, Trans.). Guangxi, China: Normal University Press. 田中一光 (2009) 朱鍔譯《設計的覺醒》。中國：廣西師範大學出版社.

Tang, Y. (1999). Language, truth, and literary interpretation: A cross-cultural examination. *Journal of the History of Ideas, 60*(1), pp. 1–20.

Tuan, Y. F. (2007). *Coming home to China.* USA: University of Minnesota Press

Wang, J. S. (2009). 窮則變，變則通，通則久. Retrieved from http://www.zhexue.com.cn/html/ proposition/eastp/bianzhenglun/changbianguan/2009/0209/339.html
王吉勝(2009).《窮則變，變則通，通則久》檢索於2012年12月10日自　http://html/proposition/　eastp/bianzhenglun/changbianguan/2009/0209/339.html

Wisker, G., Robinson, G., Trafford, V., Warnes, M., & Creighton, E. (2003). From supervisory dialogues to successful PhDs: Strategies supporting and enabling the learning conversations of staff and students at postgraduate level. *Teaching in Higher Education, 8*(3), 383–397.

Wu, H. (1996). *The double screen: Medium and representation in Chinese painting.* Chicago, IL: The University of Chicago Press.

Xu, L. (2011). Liu, J. J. (Interviewed). *Lifemagazine, 69,* 183–5.
徐累 (2011).劉晶晶採訪.刊於《生命雜誌》. 第69期183至185頁

Zhuangzi. (1985). The sorting which evens things out (A. G. Graham, Trans.). In S. Bush & H. Shih, (Eds.), *Early Chinese texts on painting.* Cambridge, MA: Harvard University Press. (Original work published ca. 300 B.C.)

AFFILIATION

King Tong Ho
School of Art and Design
AUT University, Auckland

ROLAND W. MITCHELL & KIRSTEN T. EDWARDS

6. THE COLOUR OF THOUGHT

Advising Ethnic Minority Candidates through a Radical Ethic of Pedagogical Love

There are countless illustrations that attest to the level of rigour associated with perusing postgraduate study – some empirical (Abedi & Benkin, 1987; Bowen, & Rudenstine, 1992; Goldie, 1998, 2005; Fischer, & Zigmond, 1998), others anecdotal (Mitchell & Rosiek, 2005; Smallwood, 2004), and still others somewhere in-between (Baird, 1990; Edwards, 2010; Turner, Miller, & Mitchell-Kernan, 2002). For students of colour, the additional complication of systemic racism within institutions of higher learning only compounds their struggle towards the Ph.D. As the overall arc of the present text suggests, individuals from historically marginalised communities experience unique challenges associated with existing on the margins of formal intellectual traditions (Dancy & Brown 2011; Mitchell & Edwards, 2010; Barker, 2007), which extend beyond scholarly acumen and perseverance. This chapter conducts an inquiry into ways in which to resist the systemic oppression that influences the practice of advisors working with doctoral candidates from traditionally marginalised communities.[1]

We will situate our discussion within our own experiences as academics, educators and graduate students of colour in a predominantly white U.S. context. Mitchell is a black American tenured associate professor, seven years removed from being a doctoral candidate. Edwards is a newly minted black American scholar, weeks removed from her dissertation defence, who has recently accepted a tenure track assistant professorship. This diversity, we hope, will provide readers with a rich vantage to consider our combined, nearly two decades of experiences of being black educators studying/teaching/working in white spaces. Five years of collaboration in an advisor (Mitchell)/candidate (Edwards) relationship afford a continuum of experiences, as well as key stopping points along the way. By co-authoring the chapter in this manner, we seek to open up our candidate/advisor relationship to make visible the often messy work of building support for students of colour.

We believe that the primary way to establish meaningful candidate/advisor relationships is through community. Referencing well-documented appeals of community-building among marginalised populations (Chang, 2001; Delpit & Dowdy 2002; Gregory, 2000; Wane, Shahjahan, & Wagner, 2004), we will conceptualise a particular relational ontology that not only provides shelter, but transforms patriarchal white supremacist spaces. For us, given the institutionalised and intersecting nature

A.-Chr. Engels-Schwarzpaul and M. A. Peters (Eds.), Of other Thoughts: Non-Traditional Ways to the Doctorate: A Guidebook for Candidates and Supervisors, 101–114.
© *2013 Sense Publishers. All rights reserved.*

of oppression within U.S. higher education (Hill-Collins, 1986; Vaught, Castagno, 2008), community membership entails establishing a dialogical relationship between candidates, advisors, and the higher education context.

This relationship counters a reactionary binary, organised and structured by oppression (whether we resist or act in a complicit manner). Central is an acceptance of the strengths and limitations inherent in relationships to infinitely powerful yet amazingly frail, absolutely perfect yet perfectly flawed beings. As a result, our emphasis shifts away from preparing educators simply to react to oppression. It is our aim, instead, to build community around a critical sensibility that doggedly appeals to what we will refer to as a "Radical Ethic of Pedagogical Love"; notwithstanding the strife that arises from being socialised in a state of perpetual prejudice.

To move from reactionary relationships to proactive community membership, we will consider the work of scholars who speak directly to the issue of developing communities that resist binary and reactionary thinking. Next, we will consider what community looks like for scholars and doctoral candidates from traditionally marginalised populations, who operate under the interlocking oppressions of racism and sexism. The chapter concludes by turning from a descriptive mode to a more recommendatory one, exploring moments in our own experience when our attempts at modelling the type of community membership we are advocating (a radical ethic of pedagogical love in advising doctoral candidates) were sometimes successful, sometimes thwarted, and most commonly something in between.

SETTING THE TONE: THE IMPORTANCE OF KNOWING THE LIMITS OF OUR OWN KNOWLEDGE

The legacy of institutionalised educational apartheid curtails the ability of U.S. higher education to incorporate the diversity of the nation at large (Anderson, 1988; Smith, Altbach, & Lomotey, 2002; Watkins, 2001; Wright, 1988). This disparity is even more apparent in the strikingly homogeneous makeup of the participants in doctoral level education (Anderson et. al., 2002; Lynn & Parker, 2006). In Mitchell's case, this meant that he, like most doctoral candidates in the U.S., was advised by a white American male scholar. Edwards, on the other hand, was a rare exception in being advised by a black American male scholar. However, even in this rare exception, the interlocking discourses of systemic racism and patriarchy created a distinct set of experiences – one of the vastly different ways in which black men and women doctoral candidates experience education. The complexities associated with Mitchell and Edwards' supervisions (a black man advised by a white male advisor and a black woman advised by a black male advisor) occurred in a space rife with centuries of educational disenfranchisement. The cumulative effects of these complexities set the stage for developing a frame of reference that is vitally important for advising doctoral candidates studying in diverse settings.

We do not suggest that sharing racial or gender identity inherently promotes the development of meaningful relationships between advisors and candidates (Mitchell

& Rosiek, 2005). However, the demographically identifiable vestiges of separation and inequality, consequences of a whole history of U.S. educational policy, have significantly impacted our experiences in epistemic and material ways – across now three generations of academics. One of the most profound reflections during Mitchell's candidature was his white American advisor's profession, "I can teach you how to be an academic, but I cannot teach you how to be a black academic in a white university". Mitchell's advisor was intent on establishing a relationship with a black American faculty member, who eventually joined Mitchell's dissertation committee. Such a clear demarcation concerning the limits of one's knowledge, and the explicit acknowledgement of the value of traditionally marginalised epistemologies for survival in majority contexts, is not only rare – it is also indispensable for advisor/candidate cross-cultural relationships (Blackmore, 2010; Kirk-Kuwaye, & Libarios, 2003; Harding, 2008). Advisors' appreciation of the need to be able to vacillate between being the teacher of a specific subject-matter, and being a student of their candidates' home communities' knowledges, is vital.

It has been said that such actions indicate that the primary advisor palmed off the arduous task of working across the tumultuous lines of racial and cultural difference on a faculty member of colour. We vehemently disagree: the work of building cross-racial relationships is an on-going endeavour (Barker, 2007; Castillo & Kalionzes, 2008) and thus, even seven years removed from candidacy, the relationship between Mitchell and his advisor is an on-going project based on mutual respect and affection. The point here is that the socialisation afforded to scholars can lead to a myopic type of arrogance, which can cause one to overestimate one's own level of understanding. Even in cases where a lack of knowledge is recognised, such knowledge can be misjudged as insignificant if it is located outside the bounds of formal academic inquiry. Mitchell's advisor, we suggest, insightfully knew enough to know what he did not know enough about, and in response reached out to a community of scholars to help address this void.

This choice, to reach out to scholars of colour for assistance, sets the tone for our thinking. Mitchell's advisor's actions partially helped us recognise the importance of community. Mitchell also recognised the power of a diverse and collaborative community of scholars when he began serving as an advisor. Like his advisor before, Mitchell provided a service to a candidate (Edwards) who would be facing the brunt of educational hegemony in ways that he had not personally experienced. While Mitchell, as a man of colour, understood how institutionalised white supremacy impacts the lives of black students in general, he was unclear about specifics that relate to women doctoral students of colour. Therefore, like his advisor, he connected Edwards with a community of black women scholars. Maturation, and the understandings that arise from personal experiences associated with white supremacy, moved Mitchell beyond his advisor's initial critical recognition ("I need the support of scholars of colour"), to start the work of an in-group member of these critical communities. And Edwards, armed with, shall we say, two academic generations of critical recognition of the importance of community, and the actual wisdom that comes from being a member of a community, is in a position to push the idea forward.

The remainder of this chapter considers the culmination of *pushing forward* our combined thinking, to open up these advisory relationships, and ultimately the communities that we consider to be essential for their success, as a means to further productive questions. Our push forward is to enter relationships with candidates from traditionally marginalised communities through a practice that is directly informed by a radical ethic of pedagogical love. This approach calls for individuals to be in relation in ways that not only inoculate or resist oppression, but actually challenges advisors and candidates (regardless of their race, ethnicity, or other identity markers) to do the work of building inclusive communities. In the following section, we will situate this radical ethic of pedagogical love within the existing literature, to provide a definition first and then to highlight its potential for impacting pedagogical relationships.

CONCEPTUAL FRAMEWORK

There are several methods, ideas, and 'best practices' in the arena of, broadly defined, education for social justice. Many of these methods incorporate "exposure" to, or understanding of, the specific and problematic experiences of people of colour in the academy as a white supremacist culture (Blackmore, 2010; Cochran-Smith, Albert, Dimattia, Freedman, Jackson, Mooney, et al., 1999; Goodman, 2001; Scheurich, 2002). Conventional models of socially just pedagogy often imply that scholars and activists of colour must appeal to the humanity of their white counterparts to do the work of social justice (in other words, convince white folks that recognising the struggles of people of colour, and being compassionate towards those struggles, would be a more humane ideal and will in turn prove beneficial, see Freire, 1970). In these models, the experiences of scholars of colour become vehicles for white student learning. Two realities, we believe, are not addressed: first, humane responses are extended towards those viewed as equally human – a classification people of colour are not always afforded (Fanon, 2008; Freire, 1970; Memmi, 1965). Second, to make these models work, people of colour and white people are required to assume different roles: vehicles for learning and willing passengers on the road to becoming a more just human being.

We constantly find ourselves struggling together to consider more fruitful efforts towards the work of social justice in the classroom. Regarding our advisor-candidate relationship, we ask, "How can Mitchell best prepare Edwards not only to survive the post-secondary classroom as student and teacher, but also to transform a toxic space?" We often share our individual experiences and note how we think about the advising we individually received, and the knowledges and wisdoms offered to us as pedagogues. We discuss the multiple limitations of conventional critical pedagogy, and how those ideals have influenced our training as pedagogues. Early in these discussions, we began to question the basic premise of humanity and wondered if, instead of making general appeals to humanity, we need to begin highlighting the ways our (white and colour) humanities are *dependent* on each other (Wang, 2010). What if we all truly saw ourselves in relation, as an interdependent community? Now, the white student or colleague no longer practices social justice as a compassionate ideal for the benefit of the person of colour, she sees it as a *fundamental* and *necessary* condition of her own humanity. The person of colour is no longer a vehicle for socially just practices (another dehumanising subject-position), but a whole human being and an agent in the process towards continued betterment and wholeness. How would this interrelated sense of self/ves among academic participants influence pedagogical engagement, and particularly the training of doctoral candidates?

In all this, we have to take seriously the systemic factors that maintain white supremacy, and subsequently impede the basic premise of our model: one being the implicit belief that people of colour are sub-human.² We therefore explored theories that addressed in significant ways the assumption of sub-humanity, so essential to the continuation of systemic white supremacy. We considered the work of four scholars in detail to frame our "radical ethic of pedagogical love". They are Paulo Freire, D. Jean Clandinin, M. Shaun Murphy, and Theresa F. Latini. We begin with Freire (1970), because his work provides the most straight-forward response to mutual, interdependent humanity. In his ground-breaking book, *Pedagogy of the Oppressed*, Freire (1970) argues that the very act of hate and oppression dehumanises the oppressor. The oppressed, because of their more human, yet historically dehumanised position, have a responsibility to bring humanity back to both themselves and their oppressors. He writes,

> Concern for humanization leads at once to the recognition of dehumanization, not only as an ontological possibility but as an historical reality. And as an individual perceives the extent of dehumanization, he or she may ask if humanization is a viable possibility. Within history ... both humanization and dehumanization are possibilities for a person as an uncompleted being conscious of their incompletion ... [However humanization] is thwarted by injustice, exploitation, oppression, and the violence of the oppressors ... which marks not only those whose humanity has been stolen, but also (though in a different way) those who have stolen it, it is a *distortion* of the vocation of becoming more fully human ... This struggle is possible only because dehumanization, although a concrete historical fact, is not a given destiny but the result of an unjust order that engenders violence in the oppressors, which in turn dehumanizes the oppressed ... [I]n seeking to regain their humanity [the oppressed cannot] become in turn oppressors of the oppressors, but rather restorers of the humanity of both. This then, is the great humanistic and historical task of the oppressed: to liberate themselves and their oppressors as well. (pp. 43-44, emphasis in original)

We posit that a Freirian approach to socially just pedagogical engagement, and the first prong of a radical ethic of pedagogical love, does not appeal to the already existing humanity of white participants in the academy. Instead, it questions white humanity that does not recognise the humanity of people of colour. Further, it does not exempt people of colour from responsibility and self-reflexivity, but requires that they take their role seriously and guard the project of humanisation from continued acts of violence and oppression. As Freire states, "[Oppressed people's] ideal is to be men; but for them, to be men is to be oppressors. This is their model of humanity." (p. 45) Therefore, the task of humanisation becomes to envision a reality apart from what is known, modelled, and experienced.

Theorising a humanity beyond one's reality may seem like an impossibility. However, Freire offers a solution to the conundrum: love. He writes,

> They will not gain this liberation by chance but through the praxis of their quest for it, through their recognition of the necessity to fight for it. And this fight, because of the purpose given it by the oppressed, will actually constitute an act of love opposing the lovelessness which lies at the heart of the oppressors' violence (p. 45).

Love becomes the barrier that inoculates the oppressed from inhabiting the position of the oppressor. This is not a passive, docile, silent love, it is a love that fights – what we, the authors, would call a radical love. A radical ethic of pedagogical love involves neither eros nor romantic love, but asks for an unconditional, self-sacrificing, active, and volitional love. It is passionate about humanisation for all involved, because it recognises that liberation is not possible apart from humanisation. It is not love by "chance"; it has a "quest", a pursuit and a "purpose".

Freire highlights the importance of radical sensibilities in the effort to move beyond oppression:

> Radicalization, nourished by a critical spirit, is always creative. Sectarianism mythicizes and thereby alienates; radicalization criticizes and thereby liberates. Radicalization involves increased commitment to the position one has chosen, and thus ever greater engagement in the effort to transform concrete, objective reality (Freire, 1970 p. 37).

Our desire is not only to articulate a radical ethic of pedagogical love, but also to commit ourselves to its enactment. We believe that our efforts to implement this disposition, in and beyond our advisor-candidate relationship, as a model for other, similar relationships, will "transform [the] concrete, objective reality" of white supremacy in academe. In this, we recognise, like Freire, that a transformation is impossible without radical sensibilities and love.

However, Freire's work is limited by a dependency on people of colour as responsible for white development, which potentially disrupts mutuality. We agree with curriculum theorist Hong Yu Wang's (2010) emerging ideas concerning epistemological violence and "nonviolent pedagogy". She suggests that "understandings in working through loss have transformed [our] thinking as [we] attempt to work with students [and colleagues] to get unstuck and move forward in an endless process of subjective and intersubjective formation and re-formation" (para. 5). A commitment to pedagogical formation through intersubjective or interdependent mutuality with our students and colleagues becomes the lynchpin to the development of a radical ethic of pedagogical love.

Our search for authors who emphasise interdependence led us to the work of Jean Clandinin and Shaun Murphy (2009) and their idea of a "relational ontological commitment". Even though Clandinin and Murphy position their concept within the field of research methodology, we believe their basic principles and assumptions will aid us in theorising a radical ethic of pedagogical love, modelled in the advisor-candidate relationship and ultimately enacted in the classroom. They posit that (narrative) research should be grounded

> in a thorough understanding of ontological and epistemological commitments. These commitments are situated in the relationships generated between narrative researchers and their participants ... it is the experience of the participants with the researchers that remains the primary concern. Narrative research is relational research (2009, p. 599).

Clandinin and Murphy see narrative inquiry "as the study of people in relation who are studying the experiences of people in relation" (p. 600). Similarly, we would maintain that a radical ethic of pedagogical love is the pedagogy of "people in relation", teaching and learning with "people in relation". We also consider as primary the relationship between advisor and candidate and recognise that everything else hinges on a commitment to the existence of these relationships. Like Clandinin and Murphy, we are most concerned with how individuals "co-construct" their experiences in relation to one another.

> [An] [o]ntological commitment to the relational locates ethical relationships at the heart of narrative inquiry. The ethical stance of narrative inquirers is best characterized by a relational ethics. To consider representations primarily in a literary mode displaces the centrality of the relational ethics of research relationships. (Clandinin & Murphy, 2009 p. 600)

Clandinin and Murphy, speaking specifically about research methodology, consider a primary emphasis on representations "in a literary mode" a fallacy. We recognise a similar fallacy in scholarship associated with enactment of socially-just practice, namely, a primary emphasis on the acquisition, acceptance, and articulation of specific knowledges considered appropriate for socially-just discourse. Instead, we argue, the primary focus should be on the development of relational commitments or interrelated humanities. Only then can a radical ethic of pedagogical love mature that will transform and displace the current white supremacist paradigm. This ontological commitment is dependent on the reality of our relationships' being; meaning, we must engage each other with the understanding that we are already in relationship, and that our humanities are already dependent on each other.

Clandinin and Murphy's dispositional approach is immensely fruitful for theorising deeper levels of commitment among participants in the academy. Nevertheless, we contend that another factor is crucial – love as a response to violence. Not only is love essential in the creation of socially just pedagogical associations based on relationship, mutuality, interdependence, and ultimately community; we also insist that it must be a radical love, facing the intersecting and all-consuming nature of injustice and oppression as part of white supremacy. Therefore, we looked for examples of what a radical ethic of pedagogical love might look like in light of epistemic violence. What is the antithesis to violence, rather than a response or reaction to it? And how would it operate in pedagogical contexts?

We hope the work of Theresa Latini (2009) addressing nonviolent communication will give legs and arms to our understanding of a radical ethic of pedagogical love in practice. Latini's work is particularly fruitful because she not only theorises responses to violence. She also describes supporting communicative practices and the need to "communicate in ways that uphold the humanity of others" (p. 19). Nonviolent communication tends to "reconcile rather than alienate those of differing perspectives and beliefs", to "foster peace and respect in a diverse and complex world", so that people "stay connected to others and themselves in the midst of disagreement and dissension" (p. 19).

For us, Latini describes a method that allows individuals to "stay connected" or participate in a mutually interrelated humanity in the face of white supremacy. She posits that, in hearing non-violently, we let our presuppositions be dismantled and our suspicions suspended. There is a mutual invitation to help each other understand the other (p. 23). Then,

> [i]nstead of labeling others with disdain [or in need of fixing], we can … state what we do not appreciate about another's behavior … identify and express the feelings we experience in response to that behavior … connect with the basic need that is not being met for us. At the same time, we can empathize with the other person's feelings and needs. In this way, we enter into a dialogue marked by mutual seeing, speaking, and hearing. (p. 24)

Latini's goal of "mutual seeing, speaking, and hearing" is of particular import for our project: instead of "self-sufficiency", which "denies our basic humanity" (p. 24), we must foster spaces of relation (or, for this project, advisor/candidate relationships set in pedagogical spaces), knowing that the work cannot be done independently: we recognise our need for the Other.

A nonviolent method of communication modelling a radical ethic of pedagogical love asks the person of colour to search out loving ways to engage the injustice implicitly enacted by white academic participants. It also requires that white participants lovingly respond to the wrath held by people of colour, which develops as a result of the continued pain caused by white supremacy. This level of engagement can seem like an impossible task. However Latini (2009) offers a simple yet powerful solution, the notion of nonviolent requests that are not demands.

[T]he other person can say "no" without retribution ... they are stated in positive language; they avoid asking someone to refrain from a particular activity ... They are specific enough to be doable ... Requests are gifts ... nothing brings us greater joy in life than helping other people meet their needs while simultaneously allowing them to help meet ours. When we fail to make requests of others, we lose an opportunity not only for our own needs to be met but also for their needs to be met ... we lose an opportunity to live in mutual assistance and thus in true encounter (p. 25).

Through requests and notions of mutuality, nonviolent communication invites advisors and candidates interested in developing a radical ethic of pedagogical love to engage in practices with loving intentions, which have the potential to transform academic spaces plagued by the violence of white supremacy and injustice into spaces of love, mutual respect and interdependence, and productive learning and knowing.

A RADICAL ETHIC OF PEDAGOGICAL LOVE IN PRACTICE

We have experienced numerous instances of complications associated with attempting to be in relation and build community with candidates of colour in an environment that lacks a sense of mutuality. Constricting humanity is an inherent part of white supremacy (Hurtado, Milem, Clayton-Pederson & Allen, 1998; Yosso, 2005). The unfortunate result is a high demand by black candidates for individualised and personal attention from black advisors (Gallien & Peterson, 2004; Gilbert, 2003; Mitchell & Rosiek, 2006; Mitchell, Wood & Witherspoon, 2010). On the one hand, this demand is a predictable outcome of the scarcity of scholars of colour on campus. Candidates of colour are constantly impacted by epistemic and ontological barriers to educational success and subsequently seek out individuals whom they expect to be supportive (Gallien, & Peterson, 2004; Heisserer, & Parette, 2002).[3] On the other hand, regarding black advisors more like caregivers than scholars is problematic in a system that is notorious for valuing the detached and aloof scholar. For better or worse, the 'holistic caregiver' cliché implies that advisors of colour possess lower levels of professional and intellectual capital.

The result of establishing community in these racist educational contexts sometimes causes advisors of colour to be leery about working with candidates of colour – there is always additional pressure associated with the increased emotional investment, as well as an increased professional work load associated with righting a century-long institutional dereliction of duty. In practice, a racially imposed familiarity (which we personally experienced as breeding contempt) is expressed in comments by black candidates like, "I didn't know you were smart"; their reluctance to oblige basic doctoral candidature responsibilities when requested by advisors of colour; a sense that tokenism is the reason that an advisor of colour has achieved their place in the academy; and an overall lack of deference of advisors of colour compared to that of white scholars by candidates of colour.

Thus, when Mitchell started his first professorship, a senior colleague of colour pulled him aside and showed him a stack of twenty or thirty dissertations he had chaired. He commented that several of them were incomplete and continued, "when I was a novice professor I was willing to work with any student". However, as a result of the institution's century-old white supremacist admission practices, even after formalised segregation, the equally important work of developing infrastructure to meet the needs of this historically disenfranchised population had not even begun. Consequently, many hard-working and dedicated faculty of colour attempted (in primarily unofficial and unrewarded ways) to right a mountain of wrongs, which they had not perpetrated and by which they were even in many cases personally victimised when they were doctoral candidates. The lasting impact of nearly twenty years of navigating this system led this senior scholar of colour to comment to Mitchell,

> As a young and seemingly dynamic new black professor, black students will flock to you. Your classes will be full and numerous doctoral students will want to work with you. However, despite your willingness to want to help, be a responsible community member, or just be a nice guy, I strongly warn you, do not work with poorly prepared black students. They will sap you of vital energy and it is thankless work.

We see here how white supremacy, the dehumanisation of people of colour, and systemic injustice converge to effectually block the enactment of a radical ethic of pedagogical love in the relationships between people of colour. This senior scholar's advice to Mitchell, while pragmatic and in some regards necessary in its context, remains a reaction to racism and its constant violence in the lives of people of colour. The senior scholar's goal was to see Mitchell navigate successfully, but that navigation required a disengagement from black students that were perceived as ill-prepared. Success for a black male scholar in a white supremacist context translates into a humanity without relation.

Similarly, these same barriers to mutual humanity manifest in heterogeneous racial engagements. When Edwards co-taught a course on race and gender in education with Mitchell, she met with a difficult challenge in Addy, a Christian, white woman from the U.S. South with very conservative sensibilities. As much of Edwards' work addresses the role of a religio-spiritual epistemology in theorising, she believed the woman's enrolment would enrich the learning experience and further the conversation. One day after class, Addy asked to speak with Edwards and shared her distress about some provocative articles and discussions. She felt attacked and silenced. Edwards tried to be as gentle with her as she knew how, and expressed to her that every students' voice is valuable and necessary to the development of the class. Although the conversation ended amicably, the rest of the semester did not go as smoothly. Addy became more and more resigned and obviously angry in class. No matter how much research Edwards shared with her, Addy remained intent on convincing Edwards that her racist and overall unjust beliefs were acceptable. However, Addy responded to Mitchell differently. She was more reserved, less accusatory and less prone to vehemently stating her opinion. Mitchell encouraged Edwards not to take Addy's deference to him personally, and that Edwards' pedagogical responses were appropriate and effective. But Addy made it clear that it *was* personal. For Edwards, professional rules did not work as racism, sexism, and issues with academic authority merged on the stage of white supremacy in ways that vastly complicated Mitchell's advice.[4]

After her experience with Addy, Edwards accepted that she would not have the same experiences with students as Mitchell. She realised she had two options. One was to adapt her advisor's advice in a way that would hopefully aide her in her personal role as teacher. Yet, by doing this, she would essentially react to white supremacy by adjusting pedagogical tools to respond to the violence against her as a Black woman. Alternatively, she could attempt to engage in pedagogical methods that would rise above white supremacy and disengage violence, at least in her own psyche. What would have been the result had she decided to love Addy regardless? What if it had not been about helping Addy better understand her position, but about helping them both be in relationship with each other?

WHERE DO WE GO FROM HERE

The above illustrations highlight how white supremacy creates multiple barriers to justice and equity, for and within marginalised communities in a U.S. higher educational context. The example of Mitchell and his doctoral advisor hints at an effort towards community building in response to systemic injustice. Mitchell's advisor's actions potentially engage the first step in a radical ethic of pedagogical love, which is an acknowledgement of one's limitations and the recognition that the only way to address those limitations is in community. After three academic generations, we continue to see the failures and violence that arise for non-traditional candidates and advisors in historically white spaces. However, after three generations we also articulate ways to transform that violence into productive work.

As we move into loving relationships that acknowledge limitations; address those limitations through community; engage community building through mutually interdependent humanisation; and subsequently couch all of these practices and intentions as a radical ethic of pedagogical love, we develop hope for the fourth generation. We have realised, through multiple and layered advisor/candidate (and mentor/mentee) relationships, that any response is futile if it remains bounded by the white supremacist paradigm. We would go so far as to say that humanity, community, and love cannot exist within this paradigm.

Therefore, our charge to future generations of advisors and candidates is to disengage. Disengage the current paradigm. Love radically, on purpose and pedagogically. Love with the intent to teach and learn, to model more loving ways of coexistence. The current white supremacist paradigm of doctoral education would encourage us as advisors and candidates to view individual success measures (publications, tenure, professional promotion, etc.) as our primary concern. However, we offer, as an act of resistance, the primacy of a radical ethic of pedagogical love in doctoral education. Through such resistance, we hope to dismantle the power of white supremacy – not only in schooling, but in the lives and experiences of non-traditional participants in U.S. higher education. Therefore, we propose a radical recalibration, a radical envisioning, a radical ethic of pedagogical love.

CONCLUDING WITH LOVE

We opened this chapter recognising that aspects of becoming an expert, in an academic field constituted through acts of physical and epistemic marginalisation, potentially socialise scholars, and specifically for the purposes of this chapter doctoral advisors, into an arrogance of sorts. This intellectual chauvinism, if unchecked, hampers advisors' ability to recognise the limits of their own knowledge and understanding of issues that emerge outside the academy. Our first recommendation is therefore that doctoral advisors recognise the limits of their knowledge and develop the ability to move from the expert/advisor role to the inquiring/mentee role.

We believe our particular advisor/candidate relationship, informed as it is by a radical ethic of pedagogical love, provided a conduit to develop an approach to engagement and encounter that can break free of intellectual chauvinism. A radical ethic of pedagogical love in practice is, first, non-reactionary. It is not framed in response to the white supremacist paradigm. From its inception and throughout the process of community development, participants must be committed to love. This is a love that says "before I meet you, engage you, I love you". A radical ethic of pedagogical love insists that the participant's love for the other community member, and their belief in a shared humanity, is not contingent on the other's response. There is no expectation of approved behaviour, because all desires are couched in requests. Second, the critical goal is to build mutually interdependent relationships that will enable community building as the ground where shared humanity development can begin.

A commitment to love before I know you has powerful possibilities for the way non-traditional scholars perceive of themselves in relation to white supremacist academic spaces. Instead of being trapped and paralysed, scholars can exist apart from the violence perpetuated by students and colleagues, even if only psychically. Their response ceases to cause more pain, more frustration, and ultimately more violence. A radical ethic of pedagogical love, even if unreciprocated, is fundamentally a tool of recognition, restoration, and resistance.

NOTES

[1] Supervisors are called advisors in the American PhD system.
[2] The allocation of degrees of humanity undergirds not only racism, but also multiple systems of injustice such as sexism, homophobia, ableism, classism, etc. (Erevelles, 2007).
[3] Students of colour often require a more holistic approach to advising that exceeds basic information about coursework and the dissertation process (Harding, 2008; Harper, & Quaye, 2009; Seidman, 2007).

4   Addy expected a different level of engagement from Edwards, perhaps because she was a woman and still a student herself. When Edwards did not offer it, Addy displayed personal resentment instead of professional acceptance. Edwards, in turn, felt she had failed as a teacher, student, and community member.

REFERENCES

Abedi, J., & Benkin, E. (1987). The effects of students' academic, financial, and demographic variables on time to the doctorate. *Research in Higher Education, 27*(1), 3–14.

Baird, L. L. (1990). The melancholy of anatomy: The personal and professional development of graduate and professional school students. In J. C. Smart (Ed.), *Higher education: Handbook of theory and research* (Vol. 6, pp. 361–392). New York, NY: Agathon Press.

Barker, M. (2007). Cross-cultural mentoring across institutional contexts. *Negro Educational Review. 58*(1/2), 85–103.

Bowen, W. G., & Rudenstine, N. L. (1992). *In pursuit of the Ph.D.* Princeton, NJ: Princeton University Press.

Blackmore, J. (2010). 'The Other within': Race/gender disruptions to the professional learning of white educational leaders. *International Journal of Leadership in Education, 13*(1), 45–61.

Castillo, E., & Kalionzes, J. (2008). Advising students of colour and international students. In V. N. Gordon, R. Wesley Habley, & T. J. Grites (Eds.), *Academic advising: A comprehensive handbook* (pp. 204–226). Hoboken, NJ: Wiley.

Chang, M. J. (2001). Is it more than about getting along? The broader educational relevance of reducing student racial biases. *Journal of College Student Development, 42*(2), 93–105.

Clandinin, D. J., & Murphy, M. S. (2009). Relational ontological commitments in narrative research. *Educational Researcher, 38*(8), 598–602.

Cochran-Smith, M., Albert, L., Dimattia, P., Freedman, S., Jackson, R., Mooney, J., et al. (1999). Seeking social justice: A teacher education faculty's self-study. *International Journal of Leadership in Education, 2*(3), 229–253.

Delpit, L., & Dowdy, J. (2002). *The skin that we speak: thoughts on language and culture in the classroom.* New York, NY: The New Press.

Dancy, T. E. & Brown, M. C. (2011). The mentoring and induction of educators of colour: Addressing impostor syndrome in academe. *Journal of School Leadership. 21*(4), 607–634.

Edwards, K. (2010). Incidents in the life of Kirsten T. Edwards: A personal examination of the academic in-between space. *Journal of Curriculum Theorizing, 26*(1), 113–128.

Erevelles, N. (2007). Deconstructing difference: Doing disability studies in multicultural contexts. In S. Danforth & S. Gabel (Eds.), *Vital questions facing disability studies in education* (pp. 368–378). New York, NY: Peter Lang.

Fanon, P. (2008). *Black skin, white masks* (R. Philcox, Trans.). New York, NY: Grove Press.

Freire, P. (1970). *Pedagogy of the oppressed.* New York, NY: The Continuum International Publishing Group Inc.

Fischer, B. A., & Zigmond, M. J. (1998). Survival skills for graduate school and beyond. In M. S. Anderson (Ed.), *The experience of being in graduate school: An exploration* (pp. 29–40). San Francisco, CA: Jossey-Bass.

Gallien, L., & Peterson, M. (2004). *Instructing and mentoring the African American student: Strategies for success in higher education.* New York, NY: Allyn & Bacon.

Gilbert, C. (2003). Breaking it down: performing academic advising across the colour line. *The Mentor: an Academic Advising Journal, 5*(4). Retrieved from http://www.psu.edu/dus/mentor/030303cg.htm

Goodman, D. J. (2001). *Promoting diversity and social justice: Educating people from privileged groups.* Thousand Oaks, London, England: Sage Publications, Inc.

Gregory, S. T. (2000). Strategies for improving the racial climate for students of colour in predominately White institutions. *Equity and Excellence in Education, 33*(3), 39–47.

Harding, B. (2008). Students with specific advising needs. In V. N. Gordon, W. R. Habley, & T. J. Grites (Eds.), *Academic advising: A comprehensive handbook* (pp. 189–203). Hoboken, NJ: Wiley.

Harper, S. R., & Quaye, S. J. (Eds.). (2009). *Student engagement in higher education: Theoretical perspectives and practical approaches for diverse populations.* New York, NY: Routledge.

Heisserer, D. L., & Parette, P. (2002). Advising at-risk students in college and university settings. *College Student Journal, 36*(1), 69–84.

Hill-Collins, P. (1986). Learning from the outsider within: The sociological significance of black feminist thought. *Social Problems, 33*(6), 14–32.

Hurtado, S., Milem, J. F., Clayton-Pederson, A. R., & Allen, W. R. (1998). Enhancing campus climates for racial/ethnic diversity: Educational policy and practice. *The Review of Higher Education 21*(3), 279–302.

Kirk-Kuwaye, M., & Libarios, N. (2003). Expanding the prescriptive-developmental advising continuum: Using social constructivism as an advising approach for students from high relational groups. *The Mentor: An Academic Advising Journal, 5*(4). Retrieved from http://www.psu.edu/dus/mentor/031205mk.htm

Latini, T. F. (2009). Nonviolent communication: A humanizing ecclesial and educational practice. *Journal of Education and Christian Belief, 13*(1), 19–31.

Lynn, M., & Parker, L. (2006). Critical race studies in education: Examining a decade of research in U.S. schools. *The Urban Review, 38*(4), 257–290.

Memmi, A. (1965). *The colonizer and the colonized.* New York, NY: Orion Press.

Mitchell, R., Edwards, K. (2010). Power, privilege, and pedagogy: College classrooms as sites to learn racial equity. In T. E. Dancy (Ed.) *Managing Diversity: (Re)Visioning Equity on College Campuses* (pp.45–68). Charlotte, NC: Information Age Press.

Mitchell, R., & Rosiek, J. (2005). Searching for the knowledge that enables culturally responsive academic advising. *Journal on Excellence in College Teaching, 16*(2), 87–110.

Mitchell, R., & Rosiek J. (2006). Professors as embodied racial signifier: A case study of the significance of race in a university classroom. *The Review of Education, Pedagogy, and Cultural Studies, 28*(3–4), 379–395.

Mitchell, R., Wood, G. & Witherspoon, N. (2010). Considering race and space: Mapping developmental approaches for providing culturally responsive service. *Equity Excellence in Education. 43*(3), 294–309.

Scheurich, J. J. (2002). *Anti-racist scholarship: An advocacy.* Albany, NY: State University of New York Press.

Seidman, A. (Ed.). (2007). *Minority student retention. The best of the Journal of College Student Retention: Research, theory & practice.* Amityville, NY: Baywood.

Smith, W., Altbach P., & Lomotey, K. (2002). *The racial crisis in American higher education.* New York, NY: State University of New York Press.

Smallwood, S. (2004). Doctor dropout. *The Chronicle of Higher Education, 50*(19), A10, 19.

Turner, J. L., Miller, M., & Mitchell-Kernan, C. (2002). Disciplinary cultures and graduate education. *Emergences, 12*(1), 47–70.

Wane, R., Shahjahan, R., & Wagner, A. (2004). Walking the talk: Decolonizing the politics of equity of knowledge and charting the course for an inclusive curriculum in higher education. *Canadian Journal of Development Studies. 25*(3), 499–510.

Wang, H. (2010, 27–30 April). *Unteachable moment, Kristevian revolt: Pedagogy of nonviolence.* Paper Presentation at the American Association for the Advancement of Curriculum Studies Ninth Annual Meeting, Denver, Colorado.

Watkins, W. (2001). *The white architects of black education: Ideology and power in America, 1865–1954.* New York, NY: Teachers College Press.

Wright, B. (1988). For the children of infidels?: American Indian education in the colonial colleges. *American Indian Culture and Research Journal, 12*(3), 1–14.

Yosso, T. J. (2005). Whose culture has capital? A critical race theory discussion of community cultural wealth. *Race, Ethnicity & Education, 8*(1), 69–91.

AFFILIATIONS

Roland W. Mitchell: Louisiana State University (address correspondence to: Roland W. Mitchell, Department of Educational Theory, Policy, and Practice, Louisiana State University, 121 D Peabody Hall, Baton Rouge, LA 70803. E-mail: rwmitch@lsu.edu)

Kirsten T. Edwards: The University of Oklahoma

SUSANNE MARIA WEBER

7. TRANSFORMING THE ACADEMIC FIELD

Field-Reflexivity and Access for Non-Traditional Doctoral Candidates

The doctorate is a critical and highly relevant phase for academic success. It is also a fragile and risky period (Janson et al. 2006: 572). To understand and shape the academic success of non-traditional candidates, one needs to understand the University as a cultural context, an institutional space of socialisation. Current shifts in universities towards economisation and competition in international markets are accompanied by a differentiation of academic programmes and by trends towards standardisation and homogenisation. The traditional University is changing significantly, and this has consequences for doctoral programmes. While, for instance, doctoral studies and supervisory relationships were more or less negotiated between individuals in the past, structured programmes are increasingly introduced.

Academic contexts, as contexts of knowledge and knowledge production, are full of tensions and contractions – not only at the level of formal programme designs. In her doctoral thesis, *Contesting the culture of the doctoral degree*, Judith Maxwell (2009) discusses candidates' experiences of three different doctoral degrees, Doctor of Philosophy by thesis, the Doctor of Philosophy by project and the Doctor of Education (EdD). She shows that the cultural dimension of the daily practice of cooperation between supervisors and doctoral students within different institutional settings is a highly relevant analytical perspective. In her doctoral thesis, cultural backgrounds and habitual dispositions of doctoral students, as well as the amount of their cultural capital, come into view as important factors and aspects of their experience. This perspective broadens the view of doctoral success to include the competency I call *institutional literacy*, that is, of being able to 'read' the institutional dimensions of the doctorate – and of academia in general. Beyond the obvious, formal structures of programmes and academic management structures of the University as an institution, the "hidden agendas" and cultural dimensions of disciplines and departments come into view.

To analyse these and to turn them into a reflexive, critical and transformational practice is the goal of this contribution. A question of 'cultural fit' between a candidate's habitus and the dimensions of the field – the structure of faculties, disciplinary cultures, and the given institutional rationalities – arises. If hierarchy, as a social, spatial and temporal order, is the general pattern of institutionalised power in academia – how will disciplines and departments as academic sub-fields deal with social dimensions like race, class and gender? What will their social practice look

A.-Chr. Engels-Schwarzpaul and M. A. Peters (Eds.), *Of other Thoughts: Non-Traditional Ways to the Doctorate: A Guidebook for Candidates and Supervisors*, 115–129.
© 2013 Sense Publishers. All rights reserved.

like? How will they unfold, reproduce or transform relations of hegemonic power in an unequal society?

Taking into account Bourdieu's concepts of *habitus*, *field* and *capital*, this chapter will deploy an integrated perspective on field-reflexivity in academia (Bourdieu 1988) to advance critical and transformative pedagogical and supervisory practice.[1] Following an exploration of *habitus-* and *field* theoretical perspectives (section one), the theoretical and methodological framework of academia as field and field-reflexivity (section two) is suggested as a useful tool for a better understanding of the *rules of the game*. Section three discusses three different academic cultures and power related systems of specific disciplinary fields. Approaches of a *habitus-* and *field*-transformational methodology which aim to support reflexivity and creativity are then presented – particularly during times of change within power structures in the academic field. The final section offers a methodical set of instruments for supervisors and doctoral students, but also for those responsible for programmes, departments or other academic settings.

ACADEMIA AS A FIELD OF SOCIAL POWER RELATIONS: A RELATIONAL PERSPECTIVE ON CULTURE AND INSTITUTIONS

Culture as a *root metaphor* (Morgan 1986) refers to sense making and symbolic orders, the (re)production of specific patterns of action, not only by individuals, but also by institutions as cultural agents. Practice theorists are interested in culture as *doing culture* (Bourdieu 2012; Gomez 2010); for them, differences are no longer static entities but (partly routinized and partly conflictive) effects of active interpretations of different, overlapping sense and activity modes. The French sociologist Pierre Bourdieu (1988; 1996) was particularly concerned with inequality in social practice, which is reproduced via structural categories like race, class and gender. From this point of view, PhD programmes or individual approaches to the doctorate have to be understood within the dynamics of social and biographical circumstances, as well as within institutional contexts and settings.

To Become an Academic ... to Acquire a "Sense for the Game"

Understood as *cultured space* with specific norms and values, doctoral programmes constitute a specific learning culture. They offer doctoral students, as novices in the field, various structures of opportunity which shape learning and experience. They generate opportunities for the development of academic skills and for *becoming an academic* as a corporal and bodily experience. Academia is a socialising context for its members, where doctoral students learn – or do not learn – how to adopt the *rules of the game*. To become an academic entails a gradual transformation of the original habitus. Unnoticeably for the most part, silent and invisible, the system of rules enters the body and forms an embodied structure of the institution. Whether the acquisition of an academia-specific *habitus* is easy or difficult for doctoral students depends on their social and cultural conditions prior to entering the field of the university, and their compatibility with the academic field they enter – but it also partially depends on the particular academic cultures they find there. From this perspective, the ability to create *institutional fit* and *academic belonging* depends on the acquisition of a specific habitus, and this may be close or alien to students' family contexts. Programmes may be set up to support doctoral candidates in this process, and supervisors generally will offer their assistance, too – but what 'assistance' means depends on practical experience, as something brought about and generated within the institutional sets of values, norms and interactions, and within the cultural space between institution, supervisors and doctoral students.

(Non-)Fit-Habitus in the Academic Field: Cultural Capital – A Forgotten Resource

Bourdieu (1986) captures the social and cultural preconditions of academics not only as unequally distributed, but he connects this inequality to the unequal opportunities for accumulating different kinds of capital (economic, social and cultural). Capital, in this context, is the set of resources forming the habitus as a system of dispositions acquired in the process of socialisation. Family traditions and everyday cultures are transmitted and transformed across successive generations. Families' internal social connectivity and their cultural participation in society will generate different sets of embodied cultural capital. In this sense, families not only reproduce biologically, they also reproduce the structures of their social space and social relations. Education-related everyday activities (re-)produce normalised educational strategies within each family culture. These strategies come into play even when the family members are involved in leisure activities they do not consider educationally relevant; they are 'reasonable' without being the product of deliberate decision-making; and they are not directly accessible as explicit knowledge or reflexive practice (Bourdieu 1990a).

In a qualitative research project at Philipps University of Marburg, 20 families were analysed regarding their daily practice and family trajectories. From this sample, one young participant, whom we would identify as a candidate with cultural fit to academia, comments on his life:

> When I was a little boy I already said: One day I will play that instrument. Well, then I must have been three or two years old. At that time it was … well ok, I mean everybody said something about his plans. Lots of boys like to become a fireman or a policeman. It's quite funny. And then I started at the age of …. just let me think of it … in 1992 I started with the violin. I don't know, I must have been seven, eight years old then (Richard W., 17 years in Brake 2006: 104)

Annette Lareau reveals in her book *Unequal Childhoods* (2003) that family life patterns show significant differences in the organisation of children's daily lives, language use and academic engagement. While higher-class parents promote cognitive and social skills and leisure activities, lower-class parents do not engage in such educational practices but trust in the spontaneous development of their children.

Unequally distributed access to forms of cultural capital produces unequal societal power relations. The long-lasting, although not unchangeable, dispositions of mind and body acquired in childhood will later be highly relevant for the *fit* or *non-fit* experienced by doctoral candidates in relation to the academic environment. That is because so-called *high culture* is part of the institutional and individual staging of sophistication, education and *good taste*. Moreover, these dispositions will be relevant for the acquisition of *institutional literacy*: according to Lareau (2003), parents' ways of dealing with institutions and authorities will transmit and (re)produce a *sense of entitlement* or a *sense of constraint* regarding the questioning of authorities, the right to 'take the time' of lecturers and supervisors. Similarly, the feeling of *fitting into academia* (or not), the feeling of belonging (or not) – even the feeling of being able (or not) to enter the socially and culturally rarefied space of a university building or a library will be a pertinent (but mostly forgotten) dimension of inequality. Just as the *practical sense* acquired in the family will be relevant for school trajectories, what I call *institutional literacy* will be a formative dimension of young researchers' trajectories in academia. Clearly, *institutional literacy* is a part of acquired *cultural capital,* as a resource generated by the daily processes of construction and acknowledgements in the household.

Cultural capital plays a vital role in positioning oneself in a hierarchical academic structure since one's relative capital accumulation during childhood and adolescence counts towards initiation into the academy. Aspirants enter the academic field with very different preconditions – even if candidates may share the same level in the formal hierarchy of the university. Doctoral students and supervisors differ in their habitus and are embedded in the history of their social conditions. Habitus as a structuring structure will be a pertinent dimension impacting the ways social practice takes the individual to academic paths and crossings. For instance, classifications of scholarly taxonomies, like "brilliant/dull; distinguished/vulgar; original/common; high/low", etc., structure "the hierarchy of disciplines ... and the self-image and scholastic and occupational aspirations that students nourish" (Wacquant 2005: 138).

Habitus, then, represents the collective structures entering the subjects' body and the field is the relational dimension to it (Bourdieu 1995). Both field and habitus reveal the social historicity of existing academic power structures as objectivations at the level of institutional structures and objectivations in the actors. Habitus enables one to make an institution one's own, keep it functioning and actualise it. Bourdieu sees fields as historically constituted spaces with their own laws. A field is a net of relations between single positions coming into being in the historical process,

> a field of forces within which agents occupy positions that statistically determine the positions they take with respect to the field, these position-takings being aimed either at conserving or transforming the structure of relations of forces that is constitutive of the field (Bourdieu 1995: 39).

Actors enter the game with a specific stake (*enjeu*), convinced that the stake is worth it. As Bourdieu (1988) shows, the academic field is best understood as a *space of contest* where participants fight for their relational positioning in the field or the continuance of the field itself. These power contests have a symbolic dimension. Power, brought into play to unfold a social effect in the field, works with normality, with compliance and approval, with a sub-conscious and unaware, immediate, pre-reflexive, unquestioned recognition of the given symbolic order (Bourdieu 1990b). Normality as symbolic power fails to recognise its origin and covers socially unequal distributed access to power. Symbolic power is then actualised ordinarily, non-violently, and by practice enforces its legitimacy. The structures of cultural practice will always have to be learnt, dispositions have to be developed and incorporated. Trajectories of young researchers in the academic field are created and generated by working, learning, and support structures, that is, institutional structures that may enable or hinder them.

A METHODOLOGY TO ANALYSE THE "RULES OF THE GAME": THREE LEVELS OF SCIENTIFIC REFLEXIVITY

In order to analyse the symbolic orders of different academic worlds and in order to understand the *rules of the game* (Bourdieu 1988xii; Bourdieu & Lamaison 1986), the perspective and analytical methodology of a *habitus-* and *field-reflexive* approach is suggested. If they want to transform institutional orders and practices (of the university, departments, or academic programmes), doctoral students and supervisors need to know how to reflect their own practice and how to transform the power structure of the field. To that effect, not only an individual practice of reflexivity is required: reflexivity must include the institution – certainly regarding research, but also the practice of supervising – and both at the levels of *habitus* and *field* (Elven & Weber 2012). But how can reflexivity be increased in the academic field, on the part of doctoral candidates, supervisors, departments and the university at large? As Bourdieu puts it, a dialogical approach does not suffice; the contingency of this space of experience needs to be taken into account and integrated. Bourdieu (2003, 1992) suggests a model of scientific reflexivity that can be used for the analysis of academic and institutional practice (table 1).

In change processes, supervision relationships based on mutuality enable the articulation of the positions of doctoral candidates and their supervisors – and also of the discipline and the department. In that way, various positions are granted appreciation and legitimacy, allowing alternative "sense making" (Weick 1976) to take place within the organisation. Before an institutional field (such as doctoral programmes) can undergo change through transformational practices, however, it has to be analysed at the level of practice, as a mode of reproduction of the academic field. In his book *Homo Academicus* (1988), Bourdieu aimed to analyse unspoken rules as the given historical conditions of an institutional field. The mostly unconscious exercises of power and strategic governance processes follow a "sense for the game" that rules the respective academic field. These need to be understood in order to transcend or transform them.

The *speaking positions* of doctoral candidates and their supervisors are always already permeated by power (Bourdieu 1996): their relationship is one element of the power dynamics in institutional fields (Bourdieu 2005, Maxwell 2009).

Table 1. Three levels of scientific reflexivity

STANCES	Questioning blind spots	Potential of reflexivity	Relational analysis
Social positionedness by race, class and gender	Where, when and how did I grow up? How has my social background influenced my perceptions, values, preferences, thinking?	Avoid blaming the victim or negative self-conceptions; analyse cultural differences as social bias	Social reflexivity of cultural fit or mismatch between doctoral student and supervisor
Institutional positionedness within the academic field	How is my perspective influenced by my position at centre or margin; at a mighty institution; in the hierarchy of disciplines; a specific department; an influential position, etc.?	Avoid institutional bias and pursuit of institutional normalcy in articulation, representation, and legitimation in the academic field	Institutional reflexivity of power-relations within the academic field
Epistemological positionedness of analytical practices in science and academia	How is my analytical perspective constituted? e.g.: What does the analytical category of cultural difference imply?	Avoid bias through scholastic ethnocentrism and doxic ignorance in scientific conceptualisations and academic values	Epistemological reflexivity of the social practices of drawing analytical distinctions

The mode of *matching* corresponds with the habitual dispositions, perceptual preferences and selection criteria of supervisors *and* candidates – the selection goes both ways (Bourdieu 1988: 171). Both parties choose and arrange doctoral relationships and are professionally, and thereby socially, institutionally and epistemologically, located.

ANALYZING THE SYMBOLIC ORDER OF THE ACADEMIC FIELD

From the perspective of social practice, *doing university* and *doing academia* are part of the supervision process. So, how will relations unfold between established supervisors and novice doctoral candidates? How will power relations – across gender, age and status groups – be actualised and produced in social practice? How does *non-traditional knowledge* enter the existing bodies of knowledge in the academic field? Which speaking positions are granted to the protagonists and representatives in the university? Who will be heard, with which position? What can non-traditional candidates draw on to acquire legitimacy?

These questions flag the question of representation, the possibilities of articulation, the question of legitimate speech. In contrast to positivist self-assuredness, academic reflexivity is to understand its own objectified, historically developed social structure in relation to other structures in the field. This implies not only the obedience of rules that govern an organisation, which members of the organisation can identify as *do's* and *don'ts* very soon. What also has to be taken into account are the generally pre-conscious, powerful dynamics that take on an unquestioned naturalness.

In his heretical "book for burning" (1988: 1ff), Bourdieu analyses the "hidden agendas" of the university as highly vertical, highly competitive, and highly truth claiming. As a space of social distance and differentiation, the university is the venue for the submission of dependent disciplines (Bourdieu 1988: 36ff; 84ff), a space of implementation and mediation of thinking forms, a space of mastery and masters, of "model thinkers" and "oblates", as Bourdieu calls the lower middle-class climbers who enter the academic field as foreigners (1988: xxiv). Both supervisors and doctoral candidates are entangled and woven into this social fabric and its structural constraints. The University field is an epistemically structured space, which backgrounds the relational organisation of its actors' strategies (Bourdieu 1988: 21ff). In symbolic contests, everything is about legitimate conceptualisation, the dominant standpoint, the acceptance of ruling and hegemonic positions (84ff), the doxic modality of expression, the rhetoric and fiction of science, the epistemological standpoint and stylistic positions (62). Thus, academia is first of all a social space where situated and positioned epistemic communities meet – but also fight one another. In that field, bodies of knowledge are posited as dominant and central – or marginalised and subjected. "The field of power is precisely this arena where holders of the various kinds of capital compete over which of them will prevail" (Wacquant 1996: xi) Social, institutional and epistemological biases are practised (table 2).

Cultural fit of young researchers with specific institutional settings has little to do with the principle of meritocracy. We know that gender, social status and race are significant dimensions for academic reviews (Bourdieu & Passeron 1979). As family dispositions will play into the staged social practices within academic symbolic orders, the question arises which sub-fields of academia will be open or closed, will perceive fit or non-fit of the candidate (as attractive/non-attractive), and his or her thesis contribution as worthy/unworthy of the doctoral awards. The ways in which academic fields and subfields bring about doctoral candidates' success are related to

S. M. WEBER

Table 2. Doxic field structures

Patterns and laws of the field (nomos)	Doxic knowledge	Potential of reflexivity	Heretical strategies
Nomos of verticality: social status and social-mental structures as order of distinctions	The production of nobility and elite: Consecrating those who consecrate themselves: ascetic, ideal, hierarchical, individualist, aesthetic, dominant, self-secure, elite	Analyse the logic of social domination by identifying *low* status distinctions: Hedonistic, material, egalitarian, collectivist, functional, dominated, insecure, mass	Social power analysis: reflect on social status biases and polarisation of values practiced in the social/academic field as *naturalisations* of symbolic power
Nomos in the institutional field: hierarchy, verticality, and distinction Ideology of competition: *fitting in* by *standing out*	Institutional practices of permanent symbolic contest; institutional rites of distinction by sacrifice (*making sacred*) and credentials (*giving authority*) (Wacquant 1996)	Analyse practice of ranking, e.g., specialisations in departments, hierarchically ordered research arenas, schools of thought, actors, citation-alliances	Institutional power analysis: Reflect on academic modes of domination and strategies of reproduction, the concealment of hierarchies, etc.
Epistemological illusion (*illusio*), ideology of meritocracy	Individualising success by performance measurement based on scholarly taxonomies such as: "brilliant/dull", "distinguished/vulgar", "original/common", "high/low" (Wacquant 2005; Bourdieu 1988).	Analyse collective faith in legitimate rules, analyse how social and institutional power is obscured by the illusion of "just competition" and the "cult of brilliance" (Bourdieu 1988)	Epistemological power analysis: Reflect on the circulation and concentration of the illusion of *meritocracy* as individually attributable success

the overall rules of the game – and the specific institutional and disciplinary cultures in sub-fields of academia.

HIERARCHY, EQUALITY OR MARKET? 'READING' DIFFERENT ACADEMIC (SUB-)FIELDS

The logic of the field in the University constitutes specific expectations and patterns of order one has to master if one wants to join in and succeed. The academic is portrayed as unique and doctoral students are expected to be obedient and submissive. If they want to change the rules of the game by social practice, they need to know the implicit orders of power and how symbolic power is exerted in specific ways in order to achieve obliging submission. Each disciplinary culture has its own particular ways of exerting power, according to its own position in the general academic field. Schools of Social Sciences, Medicine, Law, etc., represent different academic cultures, which are correlated with the social positions their academic staff and doctoral students occupy. It is therefore helpful to look briefly at different academic field logics in relation to disciplinary cultures.

The academic symbolic order of distinction, separation and submission relies on international and disciplinary cultures within which distinction is traditionally made and upheld by a practice of social and cultural distance. This distance to students or subordinates is (re-)enacted and refined by the separation of social worlds in the mode of distinction. Traditional and high positioned disciplines, like Law and Medicine, tend to follow a distinctively vertical academic culture, where rules are based on hierarchical practices that reproduce subtle distinctions. This academic field logic manifests, for instance, in academic conferences, where the *sense of one's own place* propels students and doctoral candidates to stay in their place, and the professors to keep their distance.

By contrast, a closer, almost family-like and egalitarian culture prevails in the Humanities, Social Sciences, Education and the agglomerating field of Visual and Performing Arts, Design and Architecture. Although the general rules of the academic field apply here, too, these academic cultures' *nomos* seems more akin to an egalitarian style. In general, social values like solidarity are legitimate dimensions of the symbolic order here, and the professor is less a person of respect and distance than of personalised authority (legitimated by knowledge, rather than position). The relationship with candidates may be more personal, in which the professor's position may exceed the limits of academic activity and include care for doctoral candidates' future. Bourdieu calls this exercise of power the strategy of *condescension* (Bourdieu 1989: 16): an actor in a higher position symbolically negates the existing social distance and secures further profits that come with the growth of appreciation. The professor, in this scenario, profits simultaneously from nearness and distance. Hence, the logic of the university field in these disciplines will tend to rely more on personal relationships between supervisors and doctoral candidates. In a more egalitarian disciplinary culture, academic leaders and doctoral candidates are legitimated not via formal attributes but through the personal and trusting articulation of individual needs. This mode of staged informal cohesion gives recognition to altruistic sacrifices for the benefit of community, research topics, and academia more widely. However, differences and social hierarchies are reconfirmed through negation *and* the consent with this negation.

A third mode of social practice in academia can be found in Management and Business Departments, where the logic of the *market* is accepted as the relevant power mode. The logic of the relation between doctoral candidates and supervisors, then, is based on a symbolic order of *meritocracy* in academic markets, a belief in rational choice and in success based on students' individual motivation. The logic of the field is based on the promotion of individual performance, increased by means of lifelong education and vocational training, incentives, and the *illusio* (Bourdieu) of individual achievement. The market type of relations pursues the productivity of successful individuals and a meritocratic ideal. It partakes in the *illusio* of the general academic field by adhering to illusions of strategic design, the selection of the best, and the credo of individualised responsibility. According to the motto "success lies within you", the locus of control is shifted into the individual, as an entrepreneurial self, and a specific type of academic. Doctoral candidates are expected to develop successful strategies of self presentation. Self-marketing becomes a structure of requests and expectations. An ethos of performance, as opposed to one of differentiated positions or of belonging, cultivates the myth of the triumph of the "better over the good". In this symbolic power order, performance oriented doctoral candidates are most susceptible to the meritocratic myth. As aspirants for social advancement, they are poised to make high investments into a change of their social position. Crucially, they require a feeling for what is 'adequate' behaviour, appearance, and speaking in this game (Bourdieu 1996).

Thus, the modes of legitimation, representation, and articulation of power in the academic (sub-)field(s) differ according to disciplinary cultures and their specific interplay of habitus and field. In particular, the subtle symbolisation of status, belonging and viability (according to the field and its strategies of distinction) creates specific relational patterns. The patterns of distance and submission, equality and community, and competition and rivalry within the logic of disciplinary and departmental reproduction and distinction are woven into the academic reproduction of elites. Both dispositions and institutional conditions are important for an open-minded analysis of social problems and solutions. To forge new paths by transcending dysfunctional logics of reproduction and to develop new competencies for dealing with given situations is the goal of transformative concepts aiming not only at individual but also social, cultural, and institutional reflexivity.

SEEING BLIND SPOTS:
TRANSFORMATIONAL STRATEGIES, METHODS, AND DESIGNS

The legitimacy of pedagogical measures depends largely on how they contribute to newness, fairness, and equality. The objective of *field reflexivity,* then, is to design processes of articulation for the not yet explicable. However, this articulation should not be carried out vicariously by powerful speakers as representatives – it needs to be engaged by doctoral candidates and supervisors themselves, as well departmental staff and representatives of the institution. Habitus- and field-reflexivity not only contribute to the consciousness raising in academic fields, it also enables participation in the collective cultivation of new cultural, academic and symbolic orders. Shared processes should then make space for diverse internal debates in polyarchic power practices.

The following section presents a range of approaches to consciousness raising and creativity at the professional and institutional level. Imaginative, verbalising and

modes of knowledge production

narrative approaches, organisationally and change oriented, can help to articulate and express underlying patterns of thought and existence. Similarly, creativity practices and whole body learning, theatrical and staging practices can be productive resources for analysis and change. These approaches and their multi-methodical integration are a flexible collection of tools in a habitus- and field-reflexive approach of academic counselling and consultancy. The suggested methods broadly resonate with Bourdieu's thoughts and, given the fact that Bourdieu himself did not suggest interventions at the level of methods, support the methodological approach of habitus- and field reflexivity developed at Philipps University of Marburg, Germany.

Adopting a concept of aesthetic transformation (Weber 2013), aesthetics, in this perspective, is not oriented towards arts or artistic expression per se. It rather follows the notion of Beuys' *"social sculpture"* (Zumdick 2001), where aesthetics is understood as a way of enhancing social democracy.

All methods described in this section can be used and integrated into the co-operation between doctoral candidates and supervisors, as well as that within doctoral peer groups. Student learning centres might also take up this opportunity to address the social, cultural and institutional dimensions of the doctorate within academic (sub-)fields. In addition, it may be helpful to use the habitus- and field-reflexive approach in specific cases of social inequalities, or in cases of conflict between supervisors and candidates. In general, it is suggested to integrate the approach of *institutional literacy* into academic programmes. In that way, institutional reflexivity could become a normal part of the doctorate – and bring reflexivity and creativity into the institutional development of academia itself.

Verbalizing approaches of reflexivity support expression by words. Since habitus structures language and speaking, though, it would be mistaken to expect a reflexive talk on habitual dispositions as such. Revealed in speaking and communication, habitus is generally an expression of social sense, internalised schemes of perception and classification. Language and styles of speaking reveal their own strategies of thinking, perception and action. For instance, verbalising approaches can be useful in group discussions seeking a collective reflection of un-reflected assumptions and positions. In this case, collective patterns of orientation become relevant as conjunctive experiential spaces (Mannheim 1997: 203ff). Cultural experiences of ethnicity, gender, or other social dimensions become relevant as orienting structures, mental framings and models. Collective orientations show best under conditions of relative homogeneity and shared experiences (regarding gender, ethnic or social background). Verbalizing approaches can be used at the level of individual or peer-reflexivity, as well as dialogical settings between students and supervisors or between supervisors. As general approach, they will be relevant as well at the level of institutional development in departmental reflexivity settings.

Narrative Approaches use story-oriented forms of expression with a beginning and an end that tell life stories and may be very useful for 'autobiographical work'. Narration can address institutional as well as individual aspects and supports hermeneutic understanding and the identification of biographical resources. A crucial dimension of narrative approaches in any setting will be trust – particularly if critical topics arise. Narrative approaches especially will be useful when focusing on solution orientation (for example, in *Appreciative Inquiry*, Cooperrider & Avital 2004). Fostering the narration of success-stories can refocus attention and may help to change perception and action. Narrative approaches can be used within different settings in which doctoral candidates, supervisors and institutional partners narrate stories of underlying organisational logics, institutional norms and the "givens" – how academia is done and realised or how it would be wished and envisioned as otherwise.

Imaginative and associative approaches organise the reflexive and creative process by connecting 'outer' and 'inner' images into highly complex associations (Weber 2013). Visual approaches to the imaginary address, on the one hand, the analytical power of images in a documentary sense and induce, on the other, a *conversion of the view* (Bourdieu 1992: 251f) through an alienation from one's own culture. They also relate to the work of symbolic representation. Visual approaches are pre-verbal or nonverbal. Projective approaches use a collection of many different images and pictures of different provenance (photos, images from magazines, postcards, art, etc.) allowing mental self-organisation and creation of meaning. In the imaginary, images are related to mental models and alternatives. Images can support reflexivity, articulation and creative practices. They may be applied within doctoral programmes to stimulate reflexivity, supported by supervisors and learning centres or departmental development workshops.

Design-Approaches aim at revealing paradigms, constructs and social innovation. Scharmer's (2007) approach "Theory U" focuses on 'personal growth' and supports the articulation of latent structures of sense. Creative and design approaches use art as a political and democratising power. Beuys' dictum, "*any human an artist*" revolutionised art and called everyone to the articulation of the self by means of art. In contrast to an art of social exclusion and differentiation, experience, articulation, and expressivity are central elements of social democratisation. These approaches can be used within systemic transformation and large group interventions (Bunker & Alban 1996).

Staging and theatrical approaches, finally, offer intense forms of expression and 'whole body learning'. Corporal representation and articulation interactively address hidden agendas in the University and academia. Especially in its critical tradition, Boal's (1995) *Theatre of the Oppressed* has become well known and is now being integrated in organisational theatre approaches. In the tradition of systemic constellations, both therapeutic and organisational analytical approaches are used in order to position the individuals in the field and its rules, analysing the potentials of transgression and alternative strategies. These approaches relate particularly well to field-analytical approaches and potentially also concern the level of the field itself. Presentational as well as representational approaches support the transformation of action sets and patterns and can be used on the level of individual and collective analysis. Theatrical approaches like the *Theatre of the Oppressed* have become an important mode of expression for those devoid of words and language, and offer potential in requesting system change. Based on whole body learning, these approaches can be applied in reflexivity workshops for doctoral students, at department level within large group interventions, or projects of institutional transformation and organisational development.

CONCLUSION:
THE CONVERSION OF THOUGHT, THE REVOLUTION OF THE GAZE

Based on Bourdieu's theoretical framework and methodology, the approach of habitus- and field-reflexivity offers a flexible set of tools for socio- and self-analysis. This methodological perspective and the methods suggested allow to relate the analysis of institutional power to the aim of consciousness and transforming the 'inner point of speaking' (Scharmer 2007) as a precondition for an ecosystem innovation approach of field transformation. As Bourdieu systematically worked with the shift of perspectives and self – as well as socio-analysis, the suggested methods supporting reflexivity, articulation and creativity can offer new perspectives for the analysis of social, institutional and epistemological power relations. Strategies of reflection and creation aim at the analysis and change of the rules of the game. Supporting and creating social reflexivity, institutional reflexivity and epistemological reflexivity will contribute to the "conversion of thought" and the "revolution of the gaze" (Bourdieu 1992: 151). Questioning and analysing the rules of the game will help to cultivate *"institutional literacy"* as competence and social practice within the relationships of young researchers and supervisors.

What is called "epistemological rupture", that is, the bracketing of ordinary preconstructions and of the principle ordinarily at work in the elaboration of these constructions, often presupposes a rupture with modes of thinking, concepts, and methods that have every appearance of *common sense*, of ordinary sense, and of good scientific sense (everything that the dominant positivist tradition honours and hallows) going for them. You will certainly understand that, when one is convinced, as I am, that the most vital task of social science and thus of the teaching of research in the social sciences is to establish as a fundamental norm of scientific practice the conversion of thought, the revolution of the gaze, the rupture with the preconstructed and with everything that buttresses it in the social order – and in the scientific order – one is doomed to be forever suspected of wielding a prophetic magisterium and of demanding personal conversion. (Bourdieu 1992: 251f).

NOTE

[1] Context and background of this contribution is a three years research project funded by the German Ministry of Research and Education (BMBF) on the topic of Habitus- and Field reflexive Counselling and Consultancy. Based on the framework of Pierre Bourdieu's sociological perspective on inequalities in society, the research project developed a theoretically grounded counselling approach. This contribution not only addresses doctoral students and their supervisors, but at the same time the transformation of the academic field and its sub-fields. An extended version of this paper will be published in the Journal "Policy Futures".

REFERENCES

Boal, A. (1995). *The Rainbow of Desire: The Boal Method of Theatre and Therapy*. London: Routledge.
Bourdieu, P. & Passeron, J.-C. (1979). *The Inheritors: French Students and their Relation to Culture*. Chicago, IL: University of Chicago Press.
Bourdieu, P. & Lamaison, P. (1986) From Rules to Strategies: An Interview with Pierre Bourdieu. *Cultural Anthropology* 1(1), 110–120.
Bourdieu, P. (1986). 'The Forms of Capital' In J. Richardson (Eds.) *The Handbook of Theory and Research for the Sociology of Education*. New York, NY: Greenwood Press, 241–258.
Bourdieu, P. (1988). *Homo Academicus*. Stanford, CA: Stanford University Press.
Bourdieu, P. (1989). Social Space and Symbolic Power. *Sociological Theory*, Vol. 7, No. 1, pp. 14–25.
Bourdieu, P. (1990b). Symbolic Power. In P. Bourdieu (1990) *Language and Symbolic Power*. Cambridge, UK: Polity Press. (original from 1977).
Bourdieu, P. (1990a). *The Logic of Practice*. Stanford, CA: Stanford University Press.
Bourdieu, P. (1992). The practice of reflexive sociology (the Paris workshop), in P. Bourdieu & L. J. D. Wacquant, *An Invitation to Reflexive Sociology*, Chicago, IL: University of Chicago Press.
Bourdieu, P. (1995). The political field, the social science field and the journalistic field. In R. Benson & E. Neveu (Eds.) *Bourdieu and the journalistic field*. Cambridge, England: Polity Press, 29–47.
Bourdieu, P. (1996). *The State Nobility. Elite Schools in the Field of Power*. Cambridge, England: Polity Press.
Bourdieu, Pierre (2003) Participant objectivation. *Journal of the Royal Anthropological Institute*, | 9, 281–294.
Bourdieu, P. (2005). From the King's House to the Reason of State: A Model of the Genesis of the Bureaucratic Field. In L. Wacquant (Ed.) *Pierre Bourdieu and Democratic Politics*. Cambridge, England: Polity Press, 9–54.
Bourdieu, P. (2012). *Outline of a Theory of Practice*. Cambridge, England: Cambridge University Press. (original from 1977).
Brake, A. (2006): Das Sichtbare und das Unsichtbare. Bildungsstrategien als Strategien des Habitus. In: Büchner, P., Brake, A. (Eds.) (2006): *Bildungsort Familie. Transmission von Bildung und Kultur im Alltag von Mehrgenerationenfamilien*. Wiesbaden, Germany: VS. S. 81–108.
Bunker, B. B. & Alban, B. T. (1996). *Large Group Interventions: Engaging the Whole System for Rapid Change*. San Francisco, CA: Jossey-Bass.
Cooperrider, D. L. & Avital, M. (Eds.) (2004). *Constructive Discourse and Human Organisation. Advances in Appreciative Inquiry*, 1. Amsterdam, Netherland: Elsevier.
Elven, J. & Weber, S. M. (2012). Organisation, Habitus und kulturelle Differenz. In M. Göhlich, S. M. Weber & N. Engel (Eds.) *Organisation und Interkulturalität. Beiträge der Kommission Organisationspädagogik*. Wiesbaden, Germany: VS.
Gomez, M.-L. (2010). A Bourdieusian perspective on strategizing. In D. Golsorkhi et al. (Eds.) *The Cambridge Handbook of Strategy as Practice*, 141–154.
Janson, K. Schomburg, H. & Teichler, U. (2006). Eher eine "gefühlte" Differenz. Karriereperspektiven von Wissenschaftlern in Deutschland und den USA. *Forschung & Lehre 13*(10), 571–573.
Lareau, A. (2003). *Unequal childhoods. Class, Race, and Family Life*. Berkeley, CA: University of California Press.
Mannheim, K.(1997). Collected Works of Karl Mannheim, Vol.10: Structures of Thinking. London, England: Routledge.
Maxwell, J (2009). *Contesting the culture of the doctoral degree: Candidates' experiences of three doctoral degrees in the School of Education*, RMIT University, PhD Thesis, School of Education, RMIT University. Retrieved from: http://researchbank.rmit.edu.au/eserv/rmit:6738/Maxwell.pdf
Morgan, G. (1986). Images of organisation. Thousand Oaks, CA: Sage.
Scharmer, C. O. (2007). *Theory U: Leading from the Future as it Emerges*. San Francisco, CA: Berrett-Koehler.
Wacquant, L. (1996): Foreword. In: P. Bourdieu (1996): *The State Nobility*. Cambridge, England: Polity Press, ix-xxii.

Wacquant, L. (2005). Symbolic Power in the Rule of the „State Nobility". In L. Wacquant (Eds.) *Pierre Bourdieu and Democratic Politics.* Cambridge, England: Polity Press, 133–150.
Weber, S. M. (2013): Partizipation und Imagination. In: Weber, Susanne Maria; Göhlich, Michael; Schröer, Andreas; Macha, Hildegard; Fahrenwald; Claudia (Hrsg.): *Organisation und Partizipation* (pp. 71 – 82) . Beiträge der Kommission Organisationspädagogik. Wiesbaden, Germany. VS.
Weick, K. E. (1976). Educational organisations as loosely coupled systems. *Administration Science Quarterly, 21*(1), 1–19.
Zumdick, W. (2001). *Der Tod hält mich wach. Joseph Beuys-Rudolf Steiner: Grundzüge ihres Denkens.* Dornach, Switzerland: Pforte.

AFFILIATION

Susanne Maria Weber
Department of Educational Science
Philipps-University of Marburg, Germany

WELBY INGS

8. QUEER AS A TWO-BOB WATCH

The Implications of Cultural Framing and Self-Declaration

INTRODUCTION

I grew up in Pukeatua. My father was a shearing contractor who worked in the sheep sheds in the back of Arohena and Ngaroma. These are places you have probably never heard of. They are small and remote. To say my origins are obscure is an understatement bordering on hyperbole. I remember as a boy hearing the men talking one day about a ram that had cost a farmer a lot of money. Purchased to sire generations of productive ewes, he proved to be completely disinterested in procreation. My uncle put down his beer bottle, leant over the pen and jeeringly

A.-Chr. Engels-Schwarzpaul and M. A. Peters (Eds.), Of other Thoughts: Non-Traditional Ways to the Doctorate: A Guidebook for Candidates and Supervisors, 131–146.
© 2013 Sense Publishers. All rights reserved.

described him as "queer as a two-bob watch". The men laughed in a strange dismissive tone I came to understand more deeply in later life.

"Queer as a two-bob watch"[1] is a vernacular insult that contains two censures. The first is against abnormality and the second against uselessness. This was the frame for gay boys who grew up in districts like mine. When I was sixteen, I was expelled from secondary school after being caught feeling one of my school mates up in the back of the German class. Outed, I nevertheless progressed on to university and discovered, along with a certain amount of rage, that what I had been told was abnormal possibly wasn't. In the following decades, as I worked as a designer and teacher, I also became politically active in the homosexual and prostitution law reforms in New Zealand. Then, in the mid-1990s, I returned as an adult to university education and, in 2004, gained a PhD in applied narratology.

My thesis, *Talking Pictures*,[2] was concerned with the design of a new form of silent film that sought to capture something of the isolation and hypocrisy of small town male prostitution. As a contributing element to the research, I conducted extensive interviews with New Zealand male sex workers. I was attempting to piece together something of the extraordinary (and largely undocumented) argot I remembered from my adolescence, and the research was instrumental in designing the unusual typographic 'monologue' that later permeated my short film, *boy*.[3] I still work in the university system, although this is balanced with a life dedicated to making films, building houses, and pursuing high levels of independent inquiry. In the last five years, I have supervised twelve queer-related theses in design or film, and fifty per cent of my current PhD candidates identify as sexual minority individuals. Even if queer as two-bob watches, I, and many of the people with whom I work, function in worlds that the men in the Arohena shearing sheds could never have imagined.

In this chapter, I would like to consider some of the implications of working as and with queer minority candidates. I will combine reflections on my own experience as a PhD candidate and something of what I have learned from the student researchers I have supervised on their respective research journeys.

RESEARCH CONTEXT

A diversity of recent writing has addressed important aspects of queer candidates' engagement with postgraduate studies. Endo & Chamness Reece-Miller (2010); Guiney-Yallop (in Shields, Novak, Marshall & Guiney-Yallop, 2011); and Gates (2010) have offered useful reflections on their experience as sexual minority candidates engaged in postgraduate research. Mizzi & Stebbins (2010) have provided an interesting discussion of autoethnological entanglements for sexual minorities in educational research, and Woods (2002) has unpacked issues around teaching Lesbian and Gay studies in higher education. In keeping with much sexual minority literature since the mid-1990s, all of these texts employ elements of personal, declarative writing.

Although, historically, there have been discernible shifts in the tone and content of academic writing about sexual minorities generally,[4] most recent material about supervision and sexual orientation has come from the disciplines of education, anthropology, psychology and social science (Halpert & Pfaller, 2001; Kumashiro, 2001, 2002; Lewin & Leap, 2002; Lovaas, Elia & Yelp, 2006; and Messinger, 2007). However, there is a significant paucity of relevant literature in technologically aligned disciplines, like Engineering, Computer Science, Business, and Design.[5] This chapter is drawn from the experiences of candidates in the fields of Design. Although not positioned paradigmatically inside the tenets of Queer theory, it is concerned with the experiences and considerations of sexual minority academics, who navigate journeys through institutions of higher learning that are superficially 'accommodating' but rarely shaped by sexual minority sensibilities (Renn, 2010).

EPISTEMOLOGY

Definition and Identity

Historically, there have been many attempts to define non-heterosexual behaviour. Terms like invert, intersexual, similisexual and homogenital, with their pseudoscientific origins, contrast with a scrambling of vernacular expressions, like Tommie, poofter, carpet muncher, AC/DC, diesel dyke, queer, and faggot; all have traditionally oppressed queer people and relayed the homophobic anxieties of their users.

I use the term *sexual minorities* here to discuss diverse groups – rather than 'non-heterosexual', which implicitly positions heterosexuality as the norm and establishes a prejudicial binary. I also tend to avoid the term *queer* because it does not always sit comfortably with many older members of sexual minorities, even though it has gained political and academic currency. Two other terms I also find problematic are *gay*, because it commonly prioritises men, and acronyms like LGBT. My difficulty with the latter is that it is often extended to unwieldy listings as complex as LGBTTTFQQ (lesbian, gay, bisexual, transgender, takataapui, two-spirited, fa'afafine, queer, or questioning). While lists like these lengthen in an attempt to become more inclusive, they can also emphasise difference rather than the distinct experiences of social marginalisation and oppression that sexual minority individuals share.

Considering Sexual Minorities

Sexual minorities have appeared in diverse cultures throughout history, and neither these minorities nor their lived identities can be adequately defined using contemporary notions of lesbian, gay, or bi-sexual (Cameron, 2005; Crompton, 2003; Driskill, Finley, Gilley, and Morgensen, 2011; Murray, 2002; Wallace, 2003; Henrickson, 2011).

In addition, recent writers have noted that minority sexual identities are not synonymous (Mizzi and Stebbins 2010; Renn, 2010). Accordingly, it is not surprising that, according to post-gay polemics, young people are no longer confined by the identity categories of their political and social forebears (Bullough, Eaklor, & Meek, 2006; Ghaziani, 2011; Green, 2002; Hammack, Thompson, & Pilecki, 2009; and Savin-Williams, 2006). However, although the post-gay analysis (as a primarily urban, Western construct) offers a possibility of integration and concord, it may not serve broader concerns with safety and social equity. Henrickson (2011) suggests that, until heteronormativity "is eliminated in every culture, the process of self-differentiation, exploration and identity redevelopment in sexual minority individuals (however defined) will continue to be both necessary and fraught, whatever language we choose to use" (3).

SEXUAL MINORITY AS A WAY OF THINKING AND A WAY OF BEING

One might usefully ask, then, how the phenomena can be framed if we no longer conceive sexual minorities in terms of causation and simultaneously recognise the need for definition? Henrickson (2011) suggests that *sexual minority status* might be usefully understood in epistemological terms. He posits that it is not sex or love that define sexual minority individuals but our way of thinking, and that this thinking is shaped by the heteronormative world in which we live. He argues that 'alienation' and 'disclosure' may be understood as two mediators of this "queer way of thinking". These mediators, he suggests, shape "the way sexual minority individuals live in the world, and encounter and process information" (8). Thus, Henrickson moves identification beyond sexual expression and attraction and argues that the related experiences of alienation and disclosure are commonly shared by sexual minorities. Let us consider these mediators for a moment.

Alienation

Henrickson (2011) notes that sexual minorities are amongst the few groups whose members are ontologically different from their parents. Often, from an early age, they encounter life differently and experience (overtly or covertly) this difference as stigmatised. Because their personal development experiences do not match those of their families and peers, they gradually learn to distrust information, in principle, until they are able to validate it. This questioning of 'givens' permeates areas of investigation as diverse as medicine, spirituality and gender.

Often, alienation leads to diverse forms of independence. This independence is driven by necessity. School situations that pose minimal threat to others, for example, are decidedly unsafe for young sexual minority individuals. Team sports, school balls, changing rooms, school bus lines, unsupervised social interaction spaces, and certain group learning activities are environments where one's difference may be recognised and reacted to. The unsafe nature of many institutional learning environments can produce a form of cultural masquing, by which sexual minority individuals strategically avoid anything intimate, comparative, or exposing. This experience of alienation often becomes a significant social bonding agent – once we are able to communicate with others who share elements of our identity. However, as Henrickson (2011) notes, the alienation can also be "one of the things that makes creating communities of sexual minorities difficult, because each person brings with them a lived experience of exclusion and mistrust" (7).

Disclosure

For sexual minorities, disclosure is a response to the constant assumptions prevalent in an environment shaped by heterosexual norms: to attain significant levels of integrity, one must eventually disabuse people, and in this process we disclose. Although often hazardous, disclosure is integral to one's self worth. Many sexual minority individuals encounter the pseudo-tolerant advice that they should live freely "but not rub other people's noses in their sexuality". This counsel generally translates as an instruction to avoid disclosure and to live a constrained life (and a public lie). As Woods (2002) notes, it also implies that sexual minority individuals have no claims on difference.

Disclosure is not a single 'coming out'. It is a lifetime process that is re-evaluated with each new encounter. Coming out criss-crosses many social interactions (with supervisors, teachers, the motel clerk, sports coaches, the guy cracking jokes at the office Christmas function); they all require decisions concerning declaration. When we consider disclosure in these situations, we weigh up safety against necessity. We also have to assess whether or not we have the emotional energy to endure reactions prompted by declaration. For, irrespective of whether we choose to disclose through language, dress, or behaviour, disclosure shapes both how we perceive the world, and how the world perceives us.

Accrued experiences of disclosure (either one's own or disclosure we observe in others) often lead to caution about assumptions others take for granted. When we remove the mask, we often experience how worlds can suddenly change, not only in respect of personal safety, but also regarding what appeared to be transparent values. Accordingly, many sexual minority individuals respect the strength evident in honest, personal declarations of being (irrespective of the issue). We live with on-going concerns about the consequences of such declarations ourselves. We often empathise with risk and understand on profound, personal levels the implications of misrepresentation, obscuration, and invisibility. As a consequence, we have developed high-level assessment processes that rely not only on cognition but also function as an integrated and necessary method of survival.

NAVIGATING THE IVORY TOWER

When PhD candidates set out on their academic journey, they also begin a crucial negotiation between their sense of self and the world they must navigate. In discussing this world in relation to sexual minority individuals' experiences (including my own), I would like to consider four issues: declaration; tokenism; marginalisation and exoticisation; and, finally, trust and responsibility.

Declaration

We have already seen how significant disclosure is to the *being* of sexual minority individuals. However, an increasing body of recent research highlights how higher learning institutions continue to be potentially unsafe environments for individuals from sexual minorities (Elia, 2005; Endo and Chamness Reece-Miller, 2010; Ewing, Stukas, & Sheehan, 2003; Henrickson, 2011; LaSala, Jenkins, Wheeler & Fredriken-Goldsen, 2008; Mizzi & Stebbins, 2010; Shields, Novak, Marshall, and Guiney Yallop; 2011, Robinson, Irwin & Ferfolja, 2002; and Woods, 2002). Despite this, many sexual minority candidates attempt to forge a connection between their research and a sense of personal wholeness. Their writing often alludes to correlations between the researcher as authentic and the research as a manifestation of this authenticity (Davies, 1992; Gates, 2010; Morrow, 2006).

Most sexual minority individuals have lived lives in which deception has been the agent binding their development. Many see admission to the university environment as a chance to begin to ask questions – not only about knowing, but also about the *being* that shapes that knowing. In discussing the risks the academic environment poses for sexual minority individuals, LaSala et al. (2008) suggest that "staying in the closet, or at least remaining unknown to colleagues and superiors, may be a reasonable choice especially for vulnerable doctoral students" (255). In contrast, Corey (1992) argues, "to be out is really to be in – inside the realm of the visible, the speakable, the culturally intelligible" (125). When sexual minority individuals weigh up life experiences of half-truth and marginalisation against issues of authenticity and wholeness, they often see the latter as integral and necessary to their status as academics. Coming out becomes a necessary personal and professional realignment of the self.

In my experience, many students move on to significant levels of discovery in research when they reach a stage of self-declaration and 'wholeness'. In the context of their inquiries, they are able to position themselves in comparatively authentic and considered ways and, in doing so, they draw upon states and narratives of being that can lead to highly complex and productive synergies. However, while personally declarative approaches can be advantageous to research, Clandinin and Connelly (1994) note that such researchers are "always speaking partially naked and [are] genuinely open to legitimate criticism from participants and from the audience" (423). This 'nakedness' can become a complex ethical and difficult emotional issue. Because theses containing significant personal disclosures draw attention to the researchers' personal features, many sexual minority candidates, especially those approaching the end of their PhD, wrestle with anxieties regarding post-doctoral employment. In contemporary academic environments, personal disclosure normally becomes public in highly accessible, online repositories.

Candidates often fear that the general availability of an essentially personal declarative document might render them vulnerable when they try to secure or maintain academic tenure or other positions (Ings, 2011; Shields et. al., 2011; Woods, 2002). In addition, those who intend to pursue a career in teaching become aware that what they reveal in their thesis may become reading material of their students.

Here we face a dilemma for which there is no simple answer. In my own case, being 'out' (and with research widely available on line) means there is no option to re-enter the closet. This 'outness' has sometimes produced distinct complications. Because my research connects me with several scholarly and creative communities, I am often asked to deliver keynote addresses to diverse organisations. When I speak on education at something like an annual New Zealand Rotary conference, I know that whoever introduces me will probably have looked up my online profile. People are likely to have come across, amongst my papers on heuristic inquiry and creativity, research into the argot and historical rituals of sexual cruising, and they may have watched film trailers on male prostitution. When I am invited to speak at overseas conferences, or when my films screen in international film festivals, I have to consider the cultural realities of my host country carefully. Traveling with an online profile that draws attention to my sexual orientation, I have serious issues to consider when the destination is a country where male homosexuality carries the death penalty (e.g., Iran, Sudan, Saudi Arabia, United Arab Emirates, or Yemen). By extension, I ask myself whether I wish to risk my personal safety to contribute to the intellectual and creative economies of over sixty other countries where my sexual orientation is illegal (including locations as diverse as Tonga, Samoa, Palestine, Malaysia, Pakistan, Sri Lanka, Egypt, Nigeria, and Uganda). Like most identifiable sexual minority travellers, my sexuality can be identified at the flick of a computer mouse, and I am forced to consider destinations in relation to both safety and survival.

Thus, when I supervise sexual minority students facing decisions about declaration, in either their thesis or research papers, I have to discuss with them what it means that they will no longer have a choice about invisibility once they have 'come out' in scholarly online environments. The old, quietly nurtured hope that one might declare one's sexuality in a thesis that will then slip into obscurity on the dusty shelves in the back of a university library is now out of step with reality. Key word searches and internationally available abstracts will pull a self-declaration into the limelight for the rest of a researcher's life. All that can be done to take control of this permanent visibility is to ensure that the integrity and quality of the work precludes disparagement. When the issue of 'outing' comes up in supervision sessions, I normally ask students to think about three questions:

1. Although your thesis is a narration arising at this moment in time, it will be unalterably preserved and represent you for the rest of your life. How do you want to be perceived?

2. What are the implications of reading your thesis for people who love you, feel neutral to you, or may intend you harm?
3. What support strategies do you have once your thesis has been lodged/ published?

These are crucial considerations concerning the impact of published theses on many sexual minority candidates' lives. They are also applicable to other candidates who choose to declare hitherto private aspects of their lives. I have learned that one cannot expect answers to these questions immediately, but their careful consideration is imperative.

Tokenism

Carefully considered declaration is important because one often encounters unpredicted expectations. Among these is the common assumption that an 'out' sexual minority individual can speak on behalf of all 'queer' culture. Organisations often recruit individuals into token positions in order to be seen to address equity issues. Simultaneously, they often limit the potential impact of dissenting paradigms (LaSala et al. 2008, and Kanter, 1977, 1980). In this situation, the role of spokesperson from the margins is problematic. One can be called upon to speak for, or provide information about, groups one is assumed to represent (even though one cannot adequately represent diverse groups). In addition, one's contributions to the organisation can become pigeonholed when one is "expected, perceived, and encouraged to be exclusively interested in LGBT issues", as one's professional development can be hindered and one's academic freedom compromised (LaSala et al., 2008, 259-260). If this limitation is problematic, so, too, is the potential loss of integrity with one's community.

I write this chapter as a gay man. While I may refer to research and experiences of other sexual minorities, I cannot speak on their behalf. Sexual minorities in universities do not comprise a monolithic, homogenous group. Diverse factors add to the complexities of alienation, disclosure and inclusion experienced by subgroups within these communities. Therefore, attempts at tokenism or spokespersonship fundamentally miss the point of one's position in, and belonging to, sexual minority communities.

If issues of representation can be problematic, so, too, can the assumption that one's disclosure of sexual preference must subsume and even cancel out the significance of other contributions. One can too easily become the gay filmmaker, the gay educator, or the gay designer, even though the vast majority of one's work is not about sexual minority individuals or issues relating to them. As Herek (1996) notes, sexual minority scholars often have to fight extremely hard to assert positions within their disciplines that are not related to the perceived significance of their sexuality.

Marginalisation & Exoticisation

An extension of tokenism is exoticisation. Herek (1996) notes that heterosexuals often define sexual minority individuals primarily in sexual terms. In addition, the latter face stereotypical expectations of hypersexual behaviour, clannishness, secrecy, orientations, moral weakness, or assumptions that individuals will not naturally engage in traditionally gendered pastimes. Often, this marked projection of otherness manifests as sudden allusions to an imagined sexual dimension of one's life, which may or may not exist, by colleagues and friends (who often want to reassure one of their support). For several years in the late 1980s, I worked in a small rural town. I was the only out man in the community. The life I lived in the stories of others was infinitely richer than anything I actually attained. In fact, the guy who preferred working on his truck and mowing the lawn was a pale ghost of the being who was assumed to have a repertoire of sexual pastimes that beggared rhetoric and personally to know every political dissident and gay man in the country.

In universities, this pattern generally plays out a little more subtly but, here too, projections frequently exoticise sexual minority individuals and what they produce. As a consequence, their scholarship can become side-lined, relegated to the realm of the self-indulgent, or treated as an amusing oddity. In addition, one often has to disabuse colleagues of an assumption that one's research about sexual minorities is automatically located within the tenets of queer theory.

It is useful to remember that the academy and the institutions that feed it are conservative, despite their rhetoric.[6] This helps to explain the challenges that the increasingly important queer paradigms of research and theorising face from within the academy. It also illuminates more subtle propensities, like the tendency of some academics to relegate sexual minority discourse into the ghettoes of special issues of journals and discrete conference strands. But there is an issue beyond this, when research dealing with marginalised material is arbitrarily dismissed. Take, for example, the research arising from my 2004 PhD thesis, which was subsequently published as papers in highly ranked international journals. These papers either dealt with the history and argot of male sex workers, or with the relationship between typography and depictions of gay male identities. Despite the status of the journals where the papers were published, I had to rapidly grow accustomed to finding my work written about as strange, humorous, or odd.

In 2007, for instance, I wrote a paper for *Public Space, The Journal of Law & Social Justice*, which examined discourses between physical, legal and linguistic frameworks impacting on the New Zealand public toilet. The article was later listed on the *Improbable Investigations* website, which describes improbable research as "research that makes people laugh and then think". The site's stated goal is "to spur people's curiosity, and to raise the question: How do you decide what's important and what's not, and what's real and what's not – in science and everywhere else?"[7] The paper, and others that surfaced from my PhD research, exhumed the history and form of a complex, undocumented language. They positioned a community of men in the social and legal history of a country that had consciously and systematically rendered them invisible. The issue, of course, was that these men were not war veterans, immigrants or sanctified minorities. They were male prostitutes. They were workers who had historically been blackmailed, beaten, imprisoned, silenced, and forced to endure compulsory 'sexual therapy'. The major portion of surviving evidence of their tenacity, strength, and social interactions had to be gathered through discreet oral history interviews. Their argot[8] was retrieved from conversations between elderly men in the kitchens of obscure, state-owned flats. Over tea and biscuits, I recorded stories in a strange language form that contained code names of beats and people since razed or forgotten. These stories told an alternative (and often frightening) history of New Zealand cities and the over ground cultures policing them.

This was not "improbable research", it was research of the marginalised. I, like many sexual minority researchers, see it as my scholarly responsibility to be a critic and conscience of society. This is not something taken lightly. It is a difficult and sometimes unpopular thing to journey into a marginalised space to retrieve and contextualise data that have been excluded because they sit uncomfortably with majority sensibilities.

As a supervisor, I am supportive of my students when they undertake such journeys. However, I am also careful to show them potential reactions to such decisions.[9] Ragins (2004) points out that lesbians, gays and bisexuals constitute one of the largest, but least studied, minority groups in institutions. As scholars, though, we often become painfully aware that our narratives and histories are marginalised for a reason. Attempts to raise them into visibility and to re-contextualise them are not always appreciated. One of the most common means institutions have for dealing with such inconvenient knowledge is dismissal.

Trust & Responsibility

If this begins to sound a little like proselytizing against engaging in sexual minority research, it's important not to lose sight of some rewarding, if byzantine, sides to the issue. Although there is a significant body of evidence that indicates supervisory relationships can become very complex when the issue of sexual orientation enters the process (Glenn & Russell, 1986; Halpert & Pfaller, 2001; Mizzi & Stebbins, 2010; Long 1996, 1997), New Zealand research suggests that sexual minority individuals are heavily represented in tertiary education.[10] As a self-disclosing gay supervisor, I often attract students with research projects from both inside and outside of the University, and I have learnt that, by demonstrating courage and integrity, and by being unafraid of including my whole self in research dialogues, I can stimulate deeper conversation and sharing of knowledge.[11] Candidates will take risks if they can see that a supervisor has a history of successfully doing the same thing. In my experience, sexual minority candidates will actively seek out institutions of higher learning (online or through social networks) in their pursuit of supervisors or environments that demonstrate informed protection, critique, empathy, and insight.

The difficulty this can pose, however, is an escalating voluntary workload resulting from the 'mentoring' of increasing numbers of researchers. Woods (2002) describes the situation graphically: "Gay students around the UK know of my existence. They get in touch with me when things go wrong. This is both gratifying and worrying. I have supervised any number of undergraduate dissertations by remote control – or by e-mail, rather – because the students in question felt they were not getting sympathetic or sufficiently well-informed supervision from tutors in their own institutions" (53).

On the other hand, theses focussing on sexual minority issues are normally rich in potential and, as LaSala *et al.* (2008) suggest, sexual minority research candidates often "have endemic perspectives that help them articulate relevant research questions" (261). Moreover, they can also activate "insider knowledge on how to gain access to information on the community and its literature, and on how to reach its members" (ibid.). In my experience, however, there are more subtle qualities one encounters with these candidates, who often have very deep levels of self-knowing. Having identities that have been shaped in (and then reshaped from) heteronormative environments, they are frequently able confidently to negotiate change. They have experienced, on very visceral levels, that knowledge and values are not absolute, and this helps them to consider new approaches to method or paradigmatic positions.

These candidates also shoulder high levels of responsibility – not only because their communities have endured generational experiences of misrepresentation and are therefore wary of being represented. As many other minority candidates in universities, they also live in and rely upon the specific communities they research. During my own PhD, I recall being questioned by a number of sex workers, who asked why I was writing up the research for the University. They had a history of reading material about themselves that was often unintelligible or (by exposing survival practices) made them unsafe. They had been studied as a problematic phenomenon and a homogenised 'other'. Their stories had been taken and re-languaged into information they could no longer understand. Their own small publications, like PUMP magazine, were forced to glean material from anecdotal accounts or overseas publications. When there was suddenly a chance of something truly home-grown, they were afraid that it would be taken from them and styled up for an already privileged world. I was told (in no uncertain terms) that I had a responsibility to 'do' the research for the community. This had a profound effect on me. As a consequence, I completely rewrote sections of my thesis, so that the 'privates' and the men working the beats could understand it. I also edited out sections of material exposing their safety rituals or 'insider business'. In articles resulting from the study, I adopted a method of writing where the argot that surfaced became incrementally more embedded in the article's mode of discourse. When one reads this work, one is increasingly spoken to in the language of the street.

On another level, the research I undertook was made even more problematic by the University's ethics requirements. Because I was conducting research with participants who might be placed at risk,[12] it was necessary to use consent forms. This was not a problem on the surface. However, an issue arose when there was a requirement that these be signed with the participant's real name: technically (under existing law), the police could ask for access to this material. Although the Prostitution Reform Act (2003) had recently come into force, these workers' safety was precarious. Not only because of existing social censure, but also because the law was considered unstable.[13] These men, who had experienced through the 1990s how the police used forced registration against them (Bennachie, 2009), would not sign forms. In the end, although the University was very supportive of the research's other dimensions, I had to conduct the oral history recordings through the New Zealand Oral History Unit. This offered a facility for signed consent where the men could use their working name and request embargos (where they felt it necessary) until the time of their death.

Not only do sexual minority researchers carry high levels of responsibility to their communities, they also bear the burden of gaining credibility within the academy. When we develop work in universities, we have considerable pressure put upon us not to reinforce negative constructions of 'queer' research, which is often perceived of as 'soft' or 'self-indulgent'. LaSala *et al.* (2008) note,

> Because openly LGBT faculty members are more than likely to stand out, they may also be more likely to be scrutinized. There might be increased pressure to perform, and also a higher likelihood that when they make mistakes, these errors will be noticed (258).

They suggest that the perception that LGBT scholarship is "overly biased and lacks rigor" can best be countered by the production of "intellectually and empirically rigorous" research (262).

The candidates with whom I work consider me a 'tough' supervisor. But that toughness is a form of protection I know emerging sexual minority researchers will need. They must be able to talk to the academy and to their communities with rigor, clarity and integrity. Their research, whether analytical or creative, must be robust and internally coherent. More importantly, (in creative work) it must *add* authentically to existing narratives of identity ,and be informed and brave enough to negotiate paths where there are few roadmaps across terrains that were formed through histories of exoticisation and distortion.

CONCLUSION

My dad died in the same year as my thesis was submitted. I dedicated it to him. While he lived in a world that made jokes about reluctant rams, he was also a good man. He and my mum raised (unwittingly) three confident, socially active, queer children.

Children like us make educational journeys that sometimes navigate the corridors of ivory towers. Historically, these institutions expelled students caught, or suspected of, engaging in same sex activities (Dilley, 2002; MacKay, 1992; Renn, 2010), even if the expulsions were generally kept away from public records. Today, many of the same institutions have policies and practices that protect the rights and safety of sexual minority individuals. Some of them have been sites of significant research into issues that directly impact on our lives as sexual minority researchers. A few have historically even formed part of a vanguard for political activism, documentation and change. Nevertheless, significant evidence indicates that institutions of higher learning are not experienced as safe, but that their internal tensions compromise both learning and research for sexual minority candidates.

Accordingly, this chapter has not focused on explaining 'how to' address these problems. There are no generic solutions that will rectify candidates' complex and interlacing experiences of problems and issues. Rather, assuming that individual experience might cast light on parallel situations, it presents a story. Within that story, it outlines some issues that might be overlooked if we were to take a cursory glance at the implications of scholarly sexual minority identification and disclosure. I hope that in thinking through these experiences, we might also think more broadly about supervision and the experiences of sexual minority researchers – across the rich spectrum of disciplines available in institutions of higher learning.

In so doing, we potentially enrich both our own lives and the lives of those with whom we work.

NOTES

1. The term refers to a period before 1967, when New Zealand still dealt in pounds, shillings and pence. 'Two bob' was a slang term for two shillings. A watch bought for such a price was considered junk.
2. The thesis is accessible at: http://aut.researchgateway.ac.nz/handle/10292/346.
3. The short film *boy* can be viewed at http://www.nzonscreen.com/title/boy-2004.
4. In her overview of LGBT and queer research in higher education, Renn traces a trajectory of discussions about sexual minority identity and expression from paradigms of deviance and disease (prior to 1974), through normalcy and visibility (post 1970), to narratives of experience (the 1990s and early 2000s), to the emerging uses of queer theory to examine policies and systems of knowledge beyond sexual minority issues.
5. This unevenness has contributed to a somewhat distorted view of the realms in which sexual minority research candidates site their academic engagement.
6. Renn (2010) reminds us that, although certain histories suggest a significant role for universities in generating social change for sexual minorities, many leaders of gay and lesbian rights, transgendered visibilities, and prostitution law reforms were not university educated or aligned with institutions of higher learning. Although universities may have helped to theorise and chronicle changes, they cannot necessarily assume the mantle of initiation.
7. http://www.improbable.com/about/
8. For a discussion of this argot see Ings (2010).
9. Wood's (2002) article, outlining the reaction of the press to his appointment as the first professor of lesbian and gay studies in the United Kingdom, offers a good example.

[10] A significant research project, undertaken by Henrickson, Neville, Jordan & Donaghey in 2007, found that, relative to the general population, sexual minorities in New Zealand are significantly better educated: 51% of their sample of sexual minority participants held at least an undergraduate degree, compared to approximately 11% of the general population (Henrickson, 2011). Interestingly, the research also identified that three-quarters of men and two thirds of women in the sample had been verbally assaulted because of their sexuality, and that 18% of men and 9% of women had experienced physical assault for the same reason (ibid.).

[11] According to Lannutti and Strauman (2006), self-disclosure is perceived by tertiary level students to reflect greater integrity and depth, and Punyanunt-Carter's (2006) research found that accurate, positive self-disclosure was a quality students felt was indicative of 'good' teachers.

[12] Male street working was formally criminalised in New Zealand in 1981, when the Summary Offences Act altered the charge of soliciting to include men. Until this time, male workers could not be arrested for soliciting, but were often charged with vagrancy, loitering or indecency. For a period of twelve years, from 1981 until the passing of the 2003 New Zealand Prostitution Reform Act, a charge of soliciting could be brought against a male prostitute. In addition, male sex workers seeking to advertise their services were required to be registered with the Police.

[13] The Prostitution Reform Act passed its third reading with a fractional majority on 25 June, 2003. Of 120 MPs, 60 voted in favour, 59 against, and one politician abstained. Following the passage of the Act, a number of conservative Christian organisations attempted to organise signatures for a citizens' initiated referendum to overturn the Act, but they fell short of gaining the required number. Legislation and management of prostitution remain contested issues in New Zealand at both national and local government levels.

REFERENCES

Abrahams, M. (2010). *Improbable investigators: News about research*. Retrieved from http://www.improbable.com/2010/02/21/ings-on-public-toilets/

Bennachie, C. (2009). Oral history recording: *Male prostitution in New Zealand*, MS-Papers OHInt-0956–02. Wellington, New Zealand: Alexander Turnbull Library.

Bullough, V., Eaklor, V., and Meek, R. (2006). *Bringing lesbian and gay rights into the mainstream: Twenty years of progress*. New York, NY: Routledge.

Burghardt, S. (1982). The not so hidden realities of race, class, and sex. In S. Burghardt (Ed.), *The other side of organizing* (pp.109–135). Cambridge, MA: Shenkman.

Cameron, M. (2005). Two-spirited Aboriginal people: Continuing cultural appropriation by non-Aboriginal society. *Canadian Women Studies, 2*(2/3), 123–127.

Clandinin, D.J. and Connelly, F.M. (1994). Personal experience methods. In Denzin, N.K. and Lincoln, Y. (Eds.), *The Sage handbook of qualitative research* (pp. 413–427). Thousand Oaks, CA: Sage.

Corey, F. (1992). Gay life/ queer art. In A. Kroker & M. Kroker (Eds.), *The last sex: Feminisms and outlaw bodies (*pp. 121–132). New York, NY: St. Martin's Press.

Crompton, L. (2003). *Homosexuality and civilization*. Cambridge, MA: Harvard University Press.

Davies, P. (1992). The role of disclosure in coming out among gay men. In K. Plummer (Ed.), *Modern homosexualities: Fragments of gay and lesbian experience* (pp. 75–83). London, England: Routledge.

Dilley, P. (2002). 20th Century post-secondary practices and policies to control gay students. *Review of Higher Education, 25*, 409–431.

Driskill, Q., Finley, C., Gilley, B., and Morgensen, S. (Eds.). (2011). *Queer indigenous studies: Critical interventions in theory, politics, and literature*. Tucson, AZ: University of Arizona Press.

Elia, J. (2005). Homophobia. In J. Sears (Ed.), *Youth, education, and sexualities: An international encyclopedia* (pp. 413–417). Westport, CT: Greenwood Press.

Endo, H., and Chamness Reece-Miller, P. (2010). Retracing queer moments: Drawing a comparison between past and present LGBTQ issues. *International Journal of Critical Pedagogy, 3*(1), 134–147.

Ewing, V., Stukas, A., & Sheehan, E. (2003). Student prejudice against gay male and lesbian lecturers. *The Journal of Social Psychology, 145*(5), 569–576.

Gates, T. G. (2011). Coming out in the social work classroom: Reclaiming wholeness and finding the teacher within. *Social Work Education 30*(1), 70–82.
Green, A. (2002). Gay but not queer: Toward a post-queer study of sexuality. *Theory and Society 31*(4), 521–545.
Ghaziani, A. (2011). Post-gay collective identity construction. *Social Problems 58*(1) 99–125.
Glenn, A. A., & Russell, R. K. (1986). Heterosexual bias among counselor trainees. *Counselor Education and Supervision*, 25, 222–229.
Halpert, S. & Pfaller, J. (2001). Sexual orientation and supervision. *Journal of Gay and Lesbian Social Services, 13*(3) 23–40.
Henrickson, M., Neville, S., Jordan, C., & Donaghey, S. (2007). Lavender Islands: The New Zealand study. *Journal of Homosexuality, 53*(4), 223–248.
Henrickson, M. (2011, 29 November). *Surviving education: Sexual minorities and a queer way of thinking.* Keynote address, Equal Opportunity Practitioners in Higher Education Australasia conference, *Nga reo mo te tika: Voices for equity*. AUT University, Auckland, New Zealand.
Herek, G.M. (1996). Why tell if you're not asked? Self-disclosure, intergroup contact, and heterosexuals' attitudes towards lesbians and gay men. In G.M. Herek, J. B. Jobe, and R.M. Carney (Eds.), *Out in force: Sexual orientation and the military* (pp. 197–225). Chicago, IL: University of Chicago Press.
Ings, W. (2011, 25 May). *The internal pathway of the self: Supervisory implications of autobiographical, practice-led PhD design theses*. Paper presented at the Doctoral Education in Design Conference: Practice, Knowledge, Vision. Hong Kong.
Retrieved from http://www.sd.polyu.edu.hk/docedudesign2011/doc/papers/308.pdf
Ings, W. (2010). Trolling the beat to working the soob: Changes in the language of the male sex worker in New Zealand. *International Journal of Lexicography, 23*(1), 55–82.
Ings, W. (2007). A convenient exchange: Discourses between physical, legal and linguistic frameworks impacting on the New Zealand public toilet. *Public Space, The Journal of Law & Social Justice, 1*(1), 1–44.
Ings, W. (2004). *Talking pictures: The creative utilisation of structural and aesthetic profiles from narrative music videos and television commercials in non-spoken film texts.* (Doctoral thesis). Auckland University of Technology, Auckland, New Zealand.
Retrieved from http://aut.researchgateway.ac.nz/handle/10292/346
Kanter, R. (1977). *Men and women of the corporation.* New York, NY: Basic Books.
Kanter, R. (1980). *A tale of "O": On being different in an organization.* New York, NY: Harper.
Kumashiro, K. K. (Ed.) (2001). *Troubling intersections of race and sexuality: Queer students of color and anti-oppressive education.* Lanham, MD: Rowan & Littlefield.
Kumashiro, K. K. (2002). *Troubling education: Queer activism and anti-oppressive education.* New York, NY: Routledge.
Lannutti, P. & Strauman, E. (2006). Classroom communication: The influence of instructor self-disclosure on student evaluations. *Communication Quarterly, 54*(1), 89–99.
LaSala, M., Jenkins, D., Wheeler, D & Fredriksen-Goldsen, K. (2008). LGBT faculty, research, and researchers: Risks and rewards. *Journal of Gay & Lesbian Social Services, 20*(3), 253–267.
Lewin, E., & Leap, W. L. (2002). *Out in theory: The emergence of gay and lesbian anthropology.* Urbana, IL: University of Illinois Press.
Long, J. K. (1996). Working with lesbians, gays, and bisexuals: Addressing heterosexism in supervision. *Family Process, 35*, 377–388.
Long, J. K. (1997). Sexual orientation: Implications for the supervisory process. In T. C. Todd & C. L. Storm (Eds.), *The complete systemic supervisor: Context, philosophy, and pragmatics* (pp. 59–71). Boston, MA: Allyn & Bacon.
Lovaas, K., Elia, J. P., & Yelp, G, A. (2006). *LGBT studies and queer theory: New conflicts, collaboration, and contested terrain.* Binghamton, NY: Harrington Park Press.
MacKay, A. (Ed.). (1992). *Wolf girls at Vassar: Lesbian and gay experiences.* New York, NY: St. Martins.
Messinger, L. (2007). Supervision of lesbian, gay and bisexual social work students by heterosexual field instructors. *The Clinical Supervisor, 26*(1–2), 195–222.

Mizzi, R., Stebbins, A. (2010). Walking the thin line: White, queer (auto)ethnographic entanglements in educational research. *New Horizons in Adult Education and Human Resource Development, 24*(2–4), 18–29.

Morrow, D. (2006). Coming out as gay, lesbian, bisexual, and transgender. In D. Morrow & L. Messinger (Eds.), *Sexual orientation & gender expression in social work practice: Working with gay, lesbian, bisexual, and transgender people* (pp. 129–149). New York, NY: Columbia University Press.

Murray, S. (2002). *Pacific homosexualities*. San José, CA: Writer's Club Press.

Phillips, K. M., & Reay, B. (2011). *Sex before sexuality: A premodern history*. Cambridge, England: Polity Press.

Punyanunt-Carter, N. M. (2006). College students' perceptions of what teaching assistants are self-disclosing in the classroom. *College Student Journal, 40*(1), 3–10.

Ragins, B. R. (2004). Sexual orientation in the workplace: The unique work and career experiences of gay, lesbian and bisexual workers. *Research in Personnel and Human Resources Management, 1*(23), 35–120.

Renn, K. (2010). LGBT and queer research in higher education: The state and status of the field. *Educational Researcher, 39*(2), 132–141.

Robinson, K.H., Irwin, J. and Ferfolja. (2002). *From here to diversity: The social impact of lesbian and gay issues in education in Australia and New Zealand*. Binghamton, NY: Harrington Park Press.

Savin-Williams, R. (2006) *The new gay teenager*. Cambridge, MA: Harvard University Press.

Shields, C., Novak, N., Marshall, B., & Yallop, J. J. G. (2011). Providing visions of a different life: Self-study narrative inquiry as an instrument for seeing ourselves in previously-unimagined places. *Narrative Works: Issues, Investigations, & Interventions, 1*(1), 63–77.

Wallace, L. (2003). *Sexual encounters: Pacific texts, modern sexualities*. Ithaca, NY: Cornell University Press.

Woods, G. (2002). Educationally queer: Teaching lesbian and gay studies in higher education. *Changing English, 9*(1), 47–58.

AFFILIATION

Welby Ings
School of Art and Design
AUT University, Auckland

MICHAEL A. PETERS

9. ANXIETIES OF KNOWING

Renegade Knowledges – of Choice and Necessity

We don't know ourselves, we knowledgeable people – we are personally ignorant about ourselves. And there's good reason for that. We've never tried to find out who we are – how could it happen that one day we'd discover ourselves? (Nietzsche, 1887)

INTRODUCTION TOWARD A THEORY OF ACADEMIC COLLABORATION

(All resemblances to living people unless otherwise specified is fictional and used to develop a 'philosophy of advising'.)[1]

I choose the American terminology here because the term *supervision* sounds factory-like, with an emphasis on control and administration, rather than joint knowledge production, co-development, co-creation, and co-evaluation within a collegial relationship that carries an ethic of responsibility on both sides. A traditional model of collaboration is wide spread in the physical sciences, medicine and engineering: doctoral candidates work in teams on a common problem and are inducted into science cultures and into team publishing. Doctoral work in the human sciences has traditionally been dominated by the model of the lone scholar, 'supervised' by a professor with subject expertise. However, as the neoliberal University has gradually come under the sway of administrative reason (which regulates and administers often at the expense of academic reason), older models of PhD research arrangements give way to other forms that are premised on the *innovative university*. The latter has a strong orientation toward commercialisation and immediate market pay-offs for applied knowledge, which is directed at and appropriated by business.

The shifts in university knowledge cultures, from the traditional liberal University to the neoliberal and innovative universities, recode and reformat doctoral study to accord more with the demands of the State and the market. Having recently returned from the US, I am surprised at the extent to which financial and administrative reason dominates New Zealand universities which are, at the same time, experimenting with a variety of new entrepreneurial forms. This is in response to diminishing budgets and other forms of direct government support and requests for public-private partnerships and new forms of transnational and export education.

A.-Chr. Engels-Schwarzpaul and M. A. Peters (Eds.), *Of other Thoughts: Non-Traditional Ways to the Doctorate: A Guidebook for Candidates and Supervisors*, 147–162.
© 2013 Sense Publishers. All rights reserved.

In my experience of advising doctoral students at the Universities of Canterbury, Auckland and Waikato in New Zealand, the University of Glasgow in Scotland (UK) and the University of Illinois (US), the doctoral relationship is of overwhelming significance. While there are a range of important legal, evaluative and international protocols, norms and standards to be observed, the aspect that outweighs all others is an ethical approach to knowledge that puts the doctoral candidate first and makes the student experience a priority. I think that this ethical aspect may be best unpacked in a collegial relationship of collaboration, where both partners are engaged in similar kinds of tasks and sometimes study and write together. I should say that this was my own experience when I completed a PhD with Prof. Jim Marshall at the University of Auckland. There was one-to-one engagement, often around a paper, a chapter, or around the word processor. I wrote a couple of papers with Jim while a Masters student. He was 'captain' (with Navy experience) and he steered the process. This was an excellent form of mentoring. Sometimes, he would respond directly to a draft of a chapter; sometimes (especially during the doctoral years) we would write papers, and later books, together. I wrote something like nine books and thirty-five papers with Jim Marshall. Our relationship was based on a friendship and a shared understanding and exploration of the philosophical tradition. It was a unique experience and the very best form of mentoring that I could possibly have gained anywhere in the world. Jim enjoyed the Oxford model of close questioning, and he was widely read and a scholar of considerable repute. When I mentioned this to him in a recent meeting, he responded: "You taught me how to teach you" – a dialogical philosophy that aims at the highest educational ideal.[2]

I learned the beginnings of a theory of collaboration from Jim and then put it to practice with other colleagues – male and female, young and old, Western and non-Western – all around the world. Together with journal editing, this experience really began to expand my horizons. The collaboration with doctoral students came a little later, especially as I began actively to explore theories of mentoring at Glasgow and Illinois. At Illinois, knowledge production involved me in doctoral course work. I taught an advanced doctoral seminar with a group of international students, who negotiated with me the course outline according to their interests. These courses became the basis for collaborative writing projects. Some years, I would organise a project where everyone contributed. At other times, I would work with one or two students to edit a collection around the doctoral theme.

My theory of collaboration is simple: first, the imperative to work with as many different people as possible – irrespective of age, gender, class or culture; second, to understand ethically that the writing or knowledge producing relationship is fundamental (it is usually task oriented); third, the collaboration is only as strong as the quality of the 'link' (this third condition is the basis for the network, as in net 'work'. The notion of a 'link' points to a performative epistemology that transcribes Wittgenstein's "now I know how to go on" into the digital age. We might even think this as an aspect of the digital epistemology of research networks). Collaboration is based on the trust in a collegial relationship and demands an almost brutal honesty, the ability to give and take constructive criticism that is the essence of the Kantian University.

Condensed in this last sentence is the theme for an entire book. How does one develop knowledge cultures in which argumentation is accepted, and in which criticism is expected and given in the best spirit? Certainly, trust is a condition of the right kind of relationship. It requires clear professional boundaries but also a recognition of power relations as they are constructed administratively, legally, and psychologically. It is easy to say, with power comes responsibility. The ethic of responsibility acts as a counter to power, as does 'truth" (speaking truth to power). Yet in all these relationships there are anxieties of knowledge on the side of the 'supervisor' *and* the doctoral candidate. Anxieties of knowing are part of the academic pathologies that are produced out of power relationships.

MICHELLE'S ANXIETIES. MY RESPONSIBILITIES

Michelle[3] came into the room and sat down in the chair opposite me. I had already read the chapter she had supplied me much earlier. It concerned Derrida's discussion on drugs, "Rhétorique de la drogue", where he maintains: "Already one must conclude that the concept of drugs is a non-scientific concept, that it is instituted on the basis of moral or political evaluations" (Derrida, 1995: 229). I had actually given this piece to Michelle while she was in prison on heroin drug charges. In retrospect, I am not sure whether this was because I felt a responsibility to help unmask the socio-cultural mystifications of the current discourse. For Derrida, the notion of pharmakon *(both poison and beneficial drug) shows that the concept of* drugs *is an institutional one.*

Michelle had been caught at immigration, coming back into New Zealand from Penang, with one of the largest stashes of heroin hidden on her body. When the incident happed I was in Mexico visiting friends at the Autonomous University of Mexico. At the time, I had acted as one of Michelle's 'supervisors' for several years. Her thinking and work on Nietzsche was sophisticated, but I was wary of her because I never knew what she was on: often her pupils were dilated when she came to see me. Almost all sessions followed the same pattern: when Michelle came in, I would start by asking how she was. Invariably, she would begin a conversation about her father and her body: she would always refer to her body in unflattering terms. Frustrated with her repetition I remember saying to her one day: "Look Michelle I'm not your father, I'm not your lover, I'm not your psychiatrist, I'm your supervisor!"

When she went to prison I went to see her. She came into the visitor's room sporting a huge black eye. Otherwise, she didn't look or sound depressed. In fact, she was positively sparking. I arranged to help her finish her thesis, and we both agreed that a term in prison allowed her to do this. I scrambled around to get her thesis typed as a computer file and would take copies for her to proof. Later, I was asked to act as a character witness when her case came to court. I testified to her potential, dragging out the liberal rhetoric of the University, and what a great person and student she was. She was indeed an excellent student and had one of the most curious minds I had the pleasure of advising. Partly as a result, she was allowed to get treatment in a half-way house and no longer had to experience the privations of the cell.

During this process, some friends alerted me to a Sunday paper. One reporter quoted her as saying that she had gone up to Penang to meet Michael Peters. This was totally untrue. I had been in Mexico during the episode and never been involved in the heroin trade, nor taken heroin myself. When she was allowed out to meet me over a cup of coffee, I finally confronted her about the front-page story. She had been quite sombre up to the point when I mentioned the story, but then, slowly, a smile crept across her face and she said: "I wondered if you would find out about that!" I was very angry with her for trying to implicate me in her addiction and her crime. She had been less than honest with me. She said to me with a smile on her face: "I had no intention of ever giving up the drug." I remember saying to her: "Michelle you have lied to me and used the university and your supervisors to support your heroin habit. I can't support you anymore. Please don't contact or attempt to see me again." I got up and walked away without further comment. The matter was further complicated, though, by the fact that she seemed to have designs on me. She used to ring me at home. Since I was alerted to her feelings, I tried to manage them by keeping a discrete 'professional distance'. When Michelle finished her prison term, she decided not to continue with her PhD. That was strange because she was almost ready to submit. She told me that her father, an engineer, had ridiculed her PhD efforts. She went cold on the idea. Some time later she was caught for a second time in a heroin bust! Another two years later, I got a call from Michelle, who said, "Michael, I want to complete my PhD". I declined to be involved in any way.

I mention this case because Michelle was an intelligent woman. She had almost finished her thesis, which could have been excellent. And she was the only PhD student of mine who did not complete.

"Subjectivity as Truth": Notes on the Philosophy of Advising

I had supervised my first thesis students at Canterbury University before I was appointed as senior lecturer at Auckland University in 1992. I received a personal chair in 2000, the year I left to take up a new position as research professor at the University of Glasgow. I continued to hold the personal chair at Auckland for five years on a 0.2 appointment, working mainly with PhD students. In 2001, I had five PhD students all graduate together. They were all women: one from Germany, three from New Zealand, and one from Taiwan. They were an extraordinary group of self-supporting scholars, all of whom went on to do very fine work in their respective areas of study.

Michelle was my failure. I wanted her to complete, even though she was in prison, but it was her decision to halt her studies so close to submission. After the second heroin bust I no longer had a shred of trust left in her. I thought there were elements of betrayal. The experience made me understand how important trust is in the relationship between a student and advisor. It also brought home the significance of the subterranean strata of consciousness in the relationship. I found myself in the position of a counsellor, who had to understand and analyse the deeper layers of repetitious behaviour. Every time we met, we talked about Michelle's fixation with her father and her body (and, by implication, her bulimia). Of course we talked about structure and the administrative requirements, but every supervision meeting was dominated by her anxieties about her father. I think that I became a father-analyst substitute and that Michelle consciously took on the role of someone who was confessing, who indeed had to confess in order to clear her conscience. The whole experience was further complicated by the fact that Michelle's thesis focused on the educational philosophy of the subject: it was all about subjectivity and drew on the work of Nietzsche, but also of Derrida and Foucault and their French antecedents – Canguilhem, Bachelard, Sartre and others.

There were other candidates who also exemplified what I shall call the *anxieties of knowing* and *subjectivity as truth*. During the course of exploring ideas and topics for their PhD study, they found that the process was at least equally about themselves and their own inner transformation or development. And if this was true for the PhD students I had the privilege of advising, then equally it was true of me (maybe even more so). For me, the process was revealing. First, to sustain a relationship for several years is in itself a remarkable thing. Expectations, obligations, and motivations are not necessarily transparent in normal relationships. Why would they be? Why would we want them to be? At one level, the process of learning in such a relationship is easily spelled out in manuals and PhD handbooks. Yet these regulations can, by themselves, only provide some ethical guidelines to protect the student from exploitation. They cannot go far in specifying the 'ideal relationship', because each relationship is different. Regulations can state expectations: hold regular meetings; provide useful feedback; be nice to each other, etc. PhD regulations are as much about indemnifying the institution as about offering advice about advising; they imply little that is useful about learning processes within such a relationship. Is this even a kind of knowledge that can be usefully generalised or theorised? Is it idiosyncratic and unique and can be acquired only through example and experience? I suspect that, beyond a few ethical guidelines, the attempt to specify rules or processes is really a waste of time. Sometimes, over-regulation actually even gets in the way, especially when the regulations also serve as gatekeeping mechanisms.

This account of my experience is based on my relationships with doctoral candidates in five universities in three countries and on others as adjunct or visiting faculty. I had a range of different relationships with doctoral candidates from different and sometimes minority cultures, both men and women, young and mature candidates. Some were already very highly qualified in a related field when they tackled a PhD late in life. I can really only talk about individual cases, individual personalities. And I have to be careful not to identify individuals, especially with students with whom I have an on-going advisory relationship at the Universities of Illinois and Waikato.

Relational Knowing: Anxieties of Understanding

I need to reflect on the advisory relationship: for me, the processes of knowledge acquisition, of reading and writing, of analysis, and of reflection ought to be relational – based on co-constructions, co-evaluations, co-directions. The advisor brings to the relationship some expert skills regarding a literature, method, academic writing and publishing. But there is something more important than skills: understandings that come from a different place, that are more to do with the empathetic understanding of a scholar who has himself experienced the process of studying for a doctorate. This empathy characteristic of *Verstehen* (understanding), it seems to me, is a philosophical orientation towards a deeper existential level that recognises the struggles and anxieties of people who are coming to learn how to know.

My position is that *most* of the important events of understanding occur at the existential level of a person. The term *anxieties of knowing* suggests that knowledge based on insight is often sporadic. It comes to us at the strangest times – at night when we are asleep, or when we are doing unrelated things, and mostly after much reading and thinking and attempts to give form to inchoate thoughts and feelings. *Anxieties of knowing* is an expression that gives recognition to emotions and the feeling-side of coming to know: coming to know involves self-doubt and self-reflection, and it is often transformative of the self. In this existential line of argument one might say also (given its relational basis, experienced in often intense and very 'thick' episodes) that it is fundamentally dialogical. Dialogical all the way through, in fact, in the sense that many existential philosophers give this term, from Søren Kierkegaard to Paulo Freire and Mikhail Bakhtin. This is dialogical orientation is my preference for theorising *learning*, and by extension *advising*. My understanding (gleaned from Marx, Wittgenstein and Heidegger) is that all knowledge is rooted in social relations, and that advising is a special, intensified dialogical form of relationship. (And we need to reinvent this term again and again – dialogue as the philosophical form of pedagogy, of the form of philosophy itself).

If this is accepted, then the anxieties in relation to knowing are both personal and public: there are some recognised public processes and resources – reading, writing and speaking – and also highly personal and idiosyncratic processes that spring from forms of reflection, the unconscious, and our spontaneous emotions, dreams, desires, feelings and struggles. I *know* this mainly because I try to be aware of my own inner life. I work best through the non-conscious: I used to dream in full sentences and paragraphs. In the morning, almost as a form of automatic writing, I would do the word processing. Dream processing followed by word processing – followed by thought processing. And for me to write is to think, so I encourage my students to write.

WHITE PHILOSOPHY AND THE BLACK SUBJECT: THE DECONSTRUCTION OF A DISCIPLINE

Melvin Armstrong Jr. is an African-American scholar who commands excellent oral skills and has read widely on the philosophy of Black consciousness and American pragmatism.[4] Melvin has always gone to church and, in hindsight, it is fairly obvious that what made him a *philosophically oriented individual* (Lewis Gordon)[5] was nurtured in the Black Church or, more specifically, in the prophetic Black Baptist tradition. A very large fellow, Melvin fills the room with his presence.[6] He is from the "Dirty South",[7] deeply religious and committed to the Baptist Church's Black emancipatory theology.[8] He expresses his thoughts articulately, though unstructured (it appears to me), and he often rambles.[9] He is full of knowledge. He came to me after being advised by three others in the department. I want Melvin to write the first Black philosophy of education. He sends me everything he writes, including past essays – all written in the dialogue form. He calls me "Sir". I say, "please don't do this, I am a New Zealander and I can't stand being call Sir". "OK, Sir, Professor" he says. It's his upbringing and Southern Baptist training, he explains. I sent this paragraph to Melvin, who restyled it and added footnotes. He wrote the thesis description below.

White Philosophy and the Black Subject: The Deconstruction of a Discipline

This thesis is located at the cross-section of philosophy and African American Studies. The study moves between the discipline of philosophy and the actual historical narrative on and about black practitioners of philosophy. It is the most earnest attempt to keep the intellectual unity of both enterprises. In my view, much of the discourse on the profession of philosophy and its social implications is too abstract, insufficiently located in a historical context. By this, I mean I will attempt to tie, as concretely as possible, the theoretical underpinnings of philosophy and professional theory to the historical reality of those blacks who have dared to undertake the philosophical enterprise. The narrative framework of which this text is derived is constituted from a comprehensive survey and in-depth reading of the sociology of professional occupations, philosophy, etc., as well as a critical reading of all available literature using critical race theory as a methodology. It is with this in mind that I propose that this study differs from existing research; its primary value is the attention to a discourse of what it is to be black and a philosopher. In my estimation, critical race theory best embodies a theoretical basis by which to both critique and reconfigure philosophical discourse with respect to race. I have a commitment to qualitative social change. As we shall see, critical race theory is the progeny of critical theory as luminary Angela Davis asserts:

> Critical theory envisions philosophy not so much as an abstract or general engagement with questions of human existence; rather, it envisions a productive relationship between philosophy and other disciplines – for example, sociology, cultural studies, feminist theory, African American studies – and the use of

this knowledge in projects to radically transform society. Critical theory, as formulated and founded by the Frankfurt School – which included Horkheimer and Marcuse – has as its goal the transformation of society, not simply the transformation of ideas, but social transformation and thus reduction and elimination of human misery. It was on the basis of this insistence on the social implementation of critical ideas that I was able to envision a relationship between philosophy and Black liberation. (Davis in Yancy, 1998: 22)

Advising Melvin

Melvin approached me to act as his advisor. He worked as a graduate assistant on a Masters course on Global Citizenship, which focused on slavery and the Black civil rights struggles. Melvin had strong opinions. Immediately, he took it upon himself to educate me by providing reading material on the rise of Black consciousness and the absence of Black philosophy in the US, at least until quite recently. Melvin spent a lot of time talking, and we discussed his work and ideas. My need to assert my own views led to a paper called "White Philosophy in/of America" (2011). This paper, based on some of the resources that Melvin made available to me, forced me to reflect on the *white* philosophy of American pragmatism. I focused on the work of Richard Rorty and Stanley Cavell, two post-Wittgensteinian thinkers, who somehow avoided the central fact of American life: that *race* that dominates US institutions. I was aware that Cornel West commented that Wittgenstein and Heidegger made philosophy relevant to Black thought because they historicised philosophy: both admitted a kind of thinking that could acknowledge Black theology and existentialism growing out of Black culture, and especially Black churches.

Every PhD relationship is a kind of intertextuality, in which thinking springs from conversation and agency involves the writing and ownership of ideas. This seems to me the case for all *work* – thought or thinking. It is a labour born of sociality that takes place at different times – sometimes with someone or many, sometimes on one's own – but it always implies a textual sociality. Yet the trick is for the 'student' finally to display author competence, to write the words that comprise the thesis, to become an author. And the role of the advisor is to assist this process. How difficult it is to assist another to become an 'author', if that word is taken in its fullest meanings! Word and concept have literary, philosophical and legal significance. For me, the emergence of an author is central to the advisory relationship, and so I place an emphasis on writing and learning to write.

When I left the University of Illinois, advising Melvin officially passed to another member of the doctoral committee, as a matter of regulation. One thing I learned from the advising relationship with Melvin is how important an aspect the *subjectivity as truth* is, especially for someone like Melvin, who grew up in a cultural environment so different from mine that I could hardly ever imagine it (even at my best moments of imaginative empathetic understanding). The existential reality of Melvin's life is something I cannot feel, but only witness. I am pleased to say that Melvin passed his preliminary exam recently with flying colours and now intends to submit his dissertation by the end of the year (2013).

EXCURSUS: THE WILL TO KNOWLEDGE AND EPISTEMOLOGICAL ANARCHY

I was once told to supervise an older male. In fact, it happened on more than one occasion. In this case, a School Inspector came to me to write a thesis on teacher competences. I met this man over the course of a year and spent most of the time listening to him. Each time he came to see me, he would start talking. After an hour or two, I would 'guide' him to 'come down' and he would finish, we would exchange pleasantries and he would wander off. This happened for over a year. He talked and I listened. Eventually, after a year, he ran out of talk and was prepared to listen to my suggestions on how he should proceed. He ended up completing an excellent thesis, but he felt considerable anxiety about presenting any of his work – even though he had talked in my office with considerable authority.

The case illustrates an interesting problem at the centre of advanced one-to-one pedagogy. Psychologists usefully call it *readiness*, but the concept I'm after is much larger and points to a fundamental problem: it is not possible to teach anybody anything against their will. More precisely, this is more than a matter of will, it involves the emotions.

The will to knowledge (1998, originally published in 1976) is the title of the first volume of Foucault's *History of Sexuality*, in which he details the development of a science of sex, devoted to the analysis of desire rather than the increase of pleasure. In *Leçons sur la volonté de savoir 1970-71*, Foucault proposes an investigation of the history of truth using Nietzsche's texts. Nietzsche opens *Beyond Good and Evil* (1966, orig. 1886) with the suggestion that our knowledge relies on a simplification of the truth, a necessary simplification to make it expressible in language and understandable to everyone. It follows that our will to knowledge is built upon, and is even a refinement of, our will to ignorance. Nietzsche argues that philosophers, most of all, should not pose as defenders of truth or knowledge. The 'truths' of philosophers are just their prejudices, and no philosopher has been proved right. Philosophers are at their best when they question themselves and free their spirits from their prejudices. Nietzsche extols the *free spirit* who faces a difficult life because she risks not being understood and constantly exposes herself to danger.

> And here I again touch on my problem, on our problem, my *unknown* friends (– for as yet I *know* of no friends): what meaning would *our* entire being have if not this, that in us the will to truth has come to a consciousness of itself *as a problem*? (Nietzsche, Clark, & Swensen, 1998: 177)

I do not have enough space here to discuss in more detail Nietzsche's understanding of different forms of nihilism, or Heidegger's famous discussion of it. Let me circumvent this by adverting to Peter Sloterdijk's *Critique of cynical reason* (1987) where he beautifully describes the way in which the will to knowledge is nourished by the will to power:

> The urge to go beyond the limit remains stronger than the insight into the limitations of our knowledge. In Faust we can already see what Nietzsche and, later, pragmatism will emphasize: that the will to knowledge is always nourished by a will to power. For this reason, the will to knowledge can never come to rest in knowledge itself; its urge, according to its roots, is immeasurable because, behind every knowledge, new puzzles mount up: A priori, knowledge wants to know more. 'What one does not know, that is precisely what is needed. / And what one knows, cannot be used.' Wanting-to-know is an offspring of the desire for power, the striving for expansion, existence, sexuality, pleasure, enjoyment of the self, and for anesthesizing the necessity of dying. Whatever presents itself as theoretical enlightenment and research, in the nature of things, can never reach its alleged goals because these do not belong to the theoretical sphere. (179)

For Nietzsche, the will to power is the basic animating principle of life. As he says in *The Will to Power*: "This world is the will to power – and nothing besides! And you yourselves are also this will to power – and nothing besides!" (Nietzsche, 1968, para 1067). (Oh! the problem of the will!)

In the PhD project, knowledge involves volition but also a trust that the advisor can somehow *make things happen*, guide the process (Socratically, with irony and questions, help give birth to the idea). However, if there is no commitment, there is no progress. I do favour argumentation, and I like to retrace the structure of argumentation. It is impossible to *teach* anybody, as Ivan Illich would argue; it is only possible to encourage learning. The problem is only compounded by trying to *teach* teachers, or trying to *teach* teachers of teachers. Those who know too much are already full. Some are already *full*, others are *bloated*. And so, *unlearning* must occur: there has to be a ritual disgorging or purification by purging: a kind of vomiting of disguised, disused old knowledge-as-custom.[10]

On the other hand, when dealing with the Other (itself a result of years-and-years of institutional de-legitimating forms of learning, culture and language) it seems a matter of insurrection of renegade knowledges. This was Foucault's problem: how do we *un*-subjugate knowledges? How do we release the counter-memory, how do we develop the counter-language? How do we provide the language to release subjugated memories? Part of the solution is to introduce 'students' to a body of literature and methods. I like the expression *body of literature* because it reminds me of *body politic* and introduces the idea that one can become part of the social body that is literature. Method is a different story: so many courses on method, the magic bullet, are sterile. They make a travesty of methods, without any awareness of the process of rational reconstruction or indeed the history of method. I like Paul Feyerabend's *Against Method* (1993), which seems like the complete knockdown of all rational reconstructions. The reference to epistemological anarchy in the subtitle indicates that there are no certain methodological rules that would ensure the progress of science.

Taken beyond a methodological pluralism, this idea encourages an experimental attitude to knowledge sources, processes and creation. I think it also encourages a critique of the ideology of the self that is similar to unlearning. If there are (*pace* Feyerabend) no useful and exception-less methodological rules governing the progress of science or the growth of knowledge in the history of science, then how can we give guidance in the form of a *handbook* about the progress of a single scholar – except by inducting her into the academic conventions that we all pay too much lip-service too (uttering the pious liberal 'truths' about peer review)? *Progress* is also an administrative fiction. The path of PhD scholars is a fundamental will to power and an attempt to impose an order on the world, or to give their description an inflection that makes it, at least, *interesting*. While there are conventions to be mastered and literatures to be read (sometimes only a mere selection is acceptable), and methods or approaches to be understood, it is the PhD scholar who marshals all her resources and imagination to give coherence to an argument or description. Foucault noted in his inaugural lecture at the Collège de France in 1970 that

> in every society the production of discourse is at once controlled, selected, organised and redistributed according to a certain number of procedures, whose role is to avert its power and its dangers, to cope with chance events, to evade its ponderous, awesome materiality (1971: 8)

Reading Foucault on discourse we understand that the *discourse of the thesis* has changed. Today, new forces shape this discourse; they are a combination of administrative and commercial reason that not only outlaws certain suppressed knowledges but also produce the thesis subject. We desperately need a critique and genealogy of the discourse of the thesis in the digital age of the neoliberal university that aims to produce 'useful' knowledges and docile, but innovative subjects. To be made elsewhere …

FINALLY: THE DIALOGUE ABOUT 'SUPERVISION'

This chapter seemed to require some concluding section. I wanted to return to the philosophy of advising and to an actual case and suggested to Tina that I complete the chapter by engaging in a dialogue with her about the nature of supervision focused on her own thesis. Tina offered her comments on my chapter and I responded to her:

TES: I was surprised by your chapter, which I think is a very desirable reader reaction, and I like it! It needs some compositional work done on it, I think, but that should be easy. Do you want me to make suggestions or do you want to have another go before I do my 'hands-on'?

M. A. PETERS

MP: I really want this chapter to be kind of free-flow consciousness that comes off the top of my head and I know there will be unevenness but it is important that these are thoughts shared without too much self-editing or reflection. I am thinking of giving it the title Anxieties of Knowing and Renegade Knowledges. *I would like to conclude by having a conversation with you about our 'supervision' relationship. You ok with this? Risky?*

TES: OK. But how are we going to represent this?

MP: I am starting this conversation about 'supervision' by saying that when I offered to act as your advisor I knew very little about ornament, the theory of ornament, versus a kind of structural purism one finds in the play of form or structure and content. I only became aware of these dimensions as a kind of post-PhD reflection on your work. Now I realise that your struggle had a kind of philosophical depth between what we might call grammar and words. (This is just to get started. Response?)
…. (weeks pass)

TES: I seem to remember an email from you to the effect that we should continue the conversation via email cos you are travelling in Asia somewhere. Can't find the darn thing … anyway, I think we need to talk before I can go any further, the uncertainty about direction paralyses me at the moment. When could we do that? If not face-to-face, then at least skype or telephone?

For me as a designer, there are lots of open questions about the character of our exchange in the middle chapters, and how that could be represented on a page, given that we are severely limited by black and white printing and a very tight page layout. I have done a test but didn't get very far. … I would like to discuss this with you before we go further.

BTW, a scene I still remember from our supervisory relationship is an incident after one of the coffee/lunch breaks in a café we often went to for supervisions sessions. On the way back, you said to me, almost casually, something like: "every time things start moving you throw a spanner in the works". I protested but wondered whom you were referring to with that 'you' … I wasn't aware of any spanners I had thrown but, after all, I was aware that my ego was not the mistress in her own house. Still wondering today …

[MP: In hindsight, I pondered hard and long why I decided to supervise Tina, especially given that I did not have the content knowledge required. My easy position was to say to myself – "philosophy equips you for everything because you are only looking at structure and argument and you can tell when that's astray whatever discipline it is". What attracted me to Tina was her German intensity: the fact that she cared so deeply about what she was doing (and it was something that eluded me!). I wanted to know why she cared so deeply. I liked her passion and also found her very attractive.][11]

TES: [... passion/attraction ...] *When I began my PhD, I was old enough to be aware of a condition that had afflicted me for what seemed like ages, and which I had ironically come to call the* attraction of white coats: *obviously dentists and doctors, but also lecturers, bosses, tour guides. Aware of the condition, I always resisted it (though I did act out once, but only after the fact, as it were – and I was conscious then that it was also about changing the power balance). This attraction to white coats might have continued in the relationship with you-as-supervisor, had not an event taken place that unhinged normal power relationships between supervisor and candidate: we both lost our mothers at the same time. When we met in a café for the first time afterwards, I felt a fundamental equality between us: no matter how different our experiences, knowledges and skills, positions and responsibilities – in this one respect, we both were humans who found themselves changed by the experience of their mothers' death. Somehow, this undermined the principal difference between candidates and supervisors: the power (and lack thereof) created by the authorisation of the academic system.*

This has no direct relationship with what you wrote ... so many possible starts ... as an English supervisor of architectural PhDs said in an interview last year, there's got to be a fair amount of splashing around at the beginning ... ;)

MP: I think we can run with this. Not everything has to follow on, and having multiple starting points is an interesting gambit. Often the starting points are different. We come to situations and relationships with different perspectives and expectations. My idea is to publish this conversation in the raw, so to speak, to preserve something of its immediacy and authenticity. – So one of the things that you remind me of is our mothers' deaths ... how strange how those facts impacted on our relationship and especially the power dimension. I am pleased to hear this because I never thought that power per se was an issue at any stage, certainly not institutional power that defines the responsibilities of the relationship between supervisor and student. I have to say incidentally I was not close to my mother so I probably did not feel traumatised by the event of her death in the way that you clearly were about yours.

What your comments make clear is that we started from very different places ... Neither death not sex were on my mind. My motives were more cerebral: I wondered where this beautiful German woman was going to take me and wondered whether I had the background to be able to assist in this journey. (I dislike the metaphor of journey*: it sounds to me like Tolkien's* Hobbit *and boy's own adventure stories). Now I am glad to hear about the white coat (it seems like a result of an institutionalisation that takes place with professionalism. I am thinking of Illich's* Disabling Professions*). I am anti-institutional by force of class habit – a renegade, often at my own expense.*

The lack of power is an interesting starting point: "a fundamental equality", yes, except I felt I was venturing into unknown waters with your work on theory of ornament.

TES: *You did? Well, if so, you seemed to venture into unknown water with confidence. And that might be important. When I, more than a decade later, was somewhat nervously monitoring the progress of a PhD candidate, I took heed of a piece of advice that one should not project one's anxieties onto the candidate. ... thank goodness! It all worked out really well in the end.*

MP: *This is the thing about supervision, about advising; sometimes one never gets beyond the first step and one returns again and again to the same starting point. (I feel that I am quoting T.S. Eliot's* Little Gidding *but nothing quite as profound as Hegelian). However, much of the supervision relationship is regulated, and I accept that there has to be some institutional guidance, some rules, some routines, some rituals. (It is important to have some mutual protections always in in a relationship involving relations of power). In a way, it comes down to* ethics *and* subjectivity, *and I am taken with the figure of Socrates who vehemently denies he is a teacher, not only to distinguish himself from the Sophists (whom I would appraise differently from Plato); he sees the essential job as a philosopher to help others to confront their assumptions, especially those they hold about themselves and the world – while professing ignorance himself. This is very much the ancient model of philosophy as a way of life that can only be experienced not taught. So we have only scratched the surface of what our relationship was. I say "was" because it has now changed; it was always collegial but now there is a radical equality about it. So ethics and subjectivity. Socrates and Nietzsche. As Nietzsche puts it:*

> "Who are we really?" Then, as I've mentioned, we count – after the fact – all the twelve trembling strokes of the clock of our experience, of our lives, of our being – alas! in the process we keep losing the count ... So we remain simply and necessarily strangers to ourselves, we do not understand ourselves, we must be confused about ourselves. For us this law holds for all eternity: "Each man is furthest from himself" – where we ourselves are concerned, we are not "knowledgeable people" ... (Nietzsche, 1887)

NOTES

[1] In all cases, the identity of Master or doctoral students has been rendered anonymous and fictionalised to protect their privacy. In some cases, I have tried to obtain the consent of the person involved and also asked for their own contribution. The issue of identity is an ethical, epistemological, and methodological problem intrinsic to this kind of (auto)biographical reflection.

[2] I have been privileged to have a close and ongoing writing relationship with Jim Marshall and with a number of other partners and colleagues including, Colin Lankshear, Tina Besley, Peter Roberts, Mark Olssen, Simon Marginson, Peter Murphy, Susanne Weber, Alicia de Alba, Dan Araya, Rodrigo Britez, Ergin Bulut, Garret Gietzen, Ruyu Hung, and many others. These collegial relationships have been quite different (why wouldn't they be?). I should mention that working with Tina Besley, who is also my life partner, has been an expansive experience with many co-presentations, books and papers. I have an implicit theory of collaboration that guides my practice, which aims to work with as many people different from me as possible.

[3] The ethical issue of anonymity here is a difficult one. I have changed Michelle's name, but from aspects of the profile I render it would not be difficult to identify her, even though our collaboration is now over a decade ago. I have to some extent fictionalised the case in order to disguise her identity but without some specific information, the case would not be enlightening. I did my best to locate her, in order to gain comments about my depiction. The events are complex and difficult to compress.

[4] In a chapter entitled "The dilemma of the Black intellectual", West articulates that the two greatest institutions of Black intellectual achievements are products of the Black Church: the Black tradition of gospel music and the prophetic tradition of preaching (West, 1997). In his key work, *The Signifying Monkey* (1988), Professor Gates argues that, despite beliefs to the contrary, there is a silent blackness of tongue through signifying. In "The Blackness of Blackness: A Critique on the Sign and the Signifying Monkey" (1983), Gates defines two types of literary signifying: oppositional (motivated) and cooperative (unmotivated) signifying.

[5] To this end Gordon suggests to consider that a "place where you'd find most Black people who do philosophy, but are not listed as philosophers, will be in religion. Another place would be education. Black studies, American studies, and Political theory (rather reluctantly) are next. Philosophy departments are near, if not at, the bottom of this list ... There are however, [Black] people who have Ph.D's in philosophy of education who do philosophy, but are not recognized as philosophers" (in Yancy, 1998: 111).

[6] See the transcript of *Race, the floating signifier – featuring Stuart Hall* (Jhally & Hall, 1997).

[7] The term *Dirty South* was coined by Goodie Mob on his album *Soul Food* in 1995. This is the same dirty South that produced James Cone (Bearden, Arkansas) Cornel West (Tulsa Oklahoma), Richard Wright (Jackson Mississippi), Maya Angelou, (Stamps, Arkansas) Angela Davis, (Birmingham, Alabama) and Martin Luther King Jr. (Atlanta, Georgia). This region and its Black inhabitants created the only truly American music form, the blues.

[8] I would like to mention that this is not out of a blind sense of racial nationalism but out of a commitment to qualitative social change. Melvin ardently believes that, if the social issues of Blacks are solved, the world will be qualitatively different.

[9] Though it could be argued, following Geneva Smitherman in *Talkin That Talk: language, culture and education in African America* (2000), that Melvin is practicing Black linguistic coda. Smitherman argues that it is important to understand that students (not only Black students) see Black English as a true language with its own beauty. She wants to stress that Black English is powerful and comes with its own set of rules. It should therefore be respected for its rich historical value. Additionally, knowing Melvin has heightened my awareness of *code-switching* in the academy. Melvin would argue that Black academics are required to know both the Western philosophy canon *and* their own – something that is not expected of White thinkers.

[10] See my essay on Wittgenstein and unlearning in Peters, Burbules & Smeythers (2008).

[11] Parts in square brackets are not part of the original email conversation but were inserted later, for instance as parts of drafts of our chapters or hindsight reflections.

REFERENCES

Derrida, J. (1995). The Rhetoric of Drugs (P. Kamuf, Trans.). In E. Weber (Ed.), *Points . . : Interviews, 1974–1994* (pp. 228–254). Stanford, CA: Standford University Press.

Feyerabend, P. (1993). *Against Method: Outline of an Anarchistic Theory of Knowledge*. London, England: Verso.

Foucault, M. (1971). Orders of discourse. *Social Science Information, 10*(2), 7–30.

Foucault, M. (1998). *The will to knowledge*. London, England: Penguin Books Limited.

Gates Jr., H. L. (1983). The Blackness of Blackness: A Critique on the Sign and the Signifying Monkey. *Critical Inquiry, 9*(Literary Theory: An Anthology), 685–693.

Gates Jr., H. L. (1988). *The Signifying Monkey: A Theory of African-American Literary Criticism*. New York, NY: Oxford University Press.

Gordon, Lewis (1998) *African-American Philosophers: 17 Conversations*, 95–119. New York, NY: Routledge.

Jhally, S., & Hall, S. (1997). *Race, the floating signifier featuring Stuart Hall [Transcript]*. Retrieved from http://www.mediaed.org/assets/products/407/transcript_407.pdf

Nietzsche, F. W., Clark, M., & Swensen, A. J. (1998). *On the genealogy of morality: a polemic*. Indianapolis, IN: Hackett Publishing Company Incorporated.

Nietzsche, F. (1887) Prologue, *Genealogy of Morals*. Translated into English by Ian Johnston of Malaspina University-College, Nanaimo, BC. Online edition at
http://records.viu.ca/~johnstoi/Nietzsche/genealogytofc.htm

Nietzsche, F. (1966) *Beyond Good and Evil*, translated by Walter Kaufmann, New York: Random House, (Orig.1866).

Nietzsche, F. (1968) *The Will to Power*, trans. Walter Kaufmann and R. J. Hollingdale. New York: Vintage Books.Peters, M. A. (2011). White philosophy in/of America. *Linguistic and Philosophical Investigation*(10), 144–154.

Peters, M. A. (2010) Philosophy, therapy, and unlearning. In Peters, M., Burbules, N. & Smeyers, P. *Showing and Doing: Wittgenstein as a pedagogical philosopher*. Boulder, CO: Paradigm.

Peters, M. A. (2011). White philosophy in/of America. *Linguistic and Philosophical Investigations* (10), 7–22.

Sloterdijk, P. (1987). *Critique of cynical reason* (M. Eldred, Trans.). Minneapolis, MN: University of Minnesota Press.

Smitherman, G. (2000). *Talkin that talk: Language, culture, and education in African America*. New York, NY: Routledge.

West, C. (1997). *The Cornel West Reader*. New York, NY: Basic Civatas Books.

Yancy, G. (1998). *African-American philosophers: 17 conversations*. New York, NY: Routledge.

AFFILIATION

Michael A. Peters
Wilf Malcolm Institute of Educational Research,
Policy, Cultural and Social Studies in Education
University of Waikato

A.-CHR. ENGELS-SCHWARZPAUL

10. EMERGING KNOWLEDGE, TRANSLATION OF THOUGHT

[P]aradigmatic controversies are often taking place at the edges ... Those edges are where the border work is occurring, and accordingly, they are the places that show the most promise for projecting where qualitative methods will be in the near and far future. (Denzin & Lincoln, 2011: 121)

The PhD [through visual arts practice] provides an opportunity for – and indeed makes necessary – a critically reflexive pedagogy. The on-going interrogation of the supervisor's role is the precondition – or at the very least the corollary condition – of developing the reflexive doctoral practitioner. (Wilson, 2009: 65)

... no one knows how to supervise these degrees. ... (Elkins, 2009a: xii, 65)

It was sometimes incredibly strange to edit my ex-PhD supervisor's text – the previous chapter in particular. I believe we maintained good communication during my candidature, but there were some issues we obviously never talked about. During the editing and the email exchanges, seemingly idiosyncratic moments from the past became part of a larger picture – I started to wonder whether, I, too, had talked at Michael about my father/mother, my knowledge, my inadequacies ... and made him listen. When was I ready to learn? Or, for how long had I been anxious because no advice seemed to be coming? What had I not heard? I do remember getting anxious about not receiving what I would have considered good, solid critical feedback and wondering whether this was just cultural difference (Germans are great criticisers while New Zealanders seem to abhor critique). Alternatively, Michael might have been a particularly hands-off supervisor (this anxiety was allayed when I happened to overhear a conversation with another candidate and realised that he can actually be quite hands-on).

But I had also known, from the beginning, what not to expect. We had become a supervisory team more or less by chance: my PhD proposal was located so far outside of the then current habits and fashions in my disciplinary area that there were very few potential supervisors at The University of Auckland. Michael's field was the philosophy of education, there was no obvious connection with my project, but at the time he was working on the politic of space and he had already taken on another candidature in the creative sector. We were aware that our disciplinary backgrounds were clearly different: I knew I could not expect an understanding of what matters to

A.-Chr. Engels-Schwarzpaul and M. A. Peters (Eds.), Of other Thoughts: Non-Traditional Ways to the Doctorate: A Guidebook for Candidates and Supervisors, 163–179.
© 2013 Sense Publishers. All rights reserved.

designers from Michael. He, in turn, did not expect me to be a philosopher, though he still expected me to think 'philosophically'. Importantly, Michael respected the set of autodidactic habits I had built up over time (as a very young mother in my undergraduate studies, I had had to learn to find alternative ways of learning). He also accepted my strong opinions, but he had many questions for me.

In the acknowledgements prefacing my PhD thesis, I wrote that he was "continuously empathetic and encouraging, never directly steering me but providing me with possibilities and choices". This supervisory practice was part of the conditions of possibility that made my PhD life changing and opened up a totally different way of understanding the world. I still use it as a reference point and model in my own PhD supervisions.

In the first part of this book, several authors have referred to various degrees of distance and closeness in the relationship between candidates and supervisors. However great or small the distance may be in different constellations and at different times, it is a principal condition in PhD supervisions. Difficult to articulate, it precedes every single supervision relationship, even in seemingly mainstream projects: it results from the power (and lack thereof) bestowed by the authorisation of the academic system (see Weber, chapter 7).

The distance arises from difference and, in the best case, affords an opening: one's location in the common world is principally different from all others' (see Arendt p. 5, above). It is this difference that generates potentially productive geographical, geo-political, social, cultural, or disciplinary encounters. While the principal distance between a candidate and a supervisor certainly poses a challenge to be addressed, different in each particular situation (see p. 311, below) as a space-between (separating and relating at the same time, see Arendt, 1958/1998: 52), it also allows for diverse and divergent perspectives. From that perspective, the sense of distance from mainstream paradigms and procedures expressed by several contributors in the first part may also indicate a space of potentiality in which something new might arise (see Nepia p. 21, above).

There is a generative connection between non-traditional candidates' approaches and emerging knowledge fields that are opened up by new research engagements. Non-traditional candidates are often very familiar with the uncertainty and marginality of knowledge, so typical of emerging research fields and disciplines. Indeed, they have often learned to question apparent givens long before they arrive in the academy (see Edwards p. 61 and Ings p. 134, above). Often, an extended experience with alienation has helped them develop an independence that allows them to bring to their projects ways of knowing that are novel in the academy. Literally and/or metaphorically bi- and multilingual; inter- and transdisciplinary; idiosyncratic and collaborative; individual and community based; reflective and activist; analytical and creative; practical and theoretical; participatory and experiential; material and embodied; art- and technology-based ... non-traditional candidates *and* new research fields are poised to jettison binaries of positive/speculative, text/image, universal/particular and so on. The challenge they issue may be quite different from those we know already. At its best, it may not involve the familiar dynamics of routinely turning the tables and replacing the prevailing with something else. Rather, some of these new researchers already creatively reconfigure the prevailing and the something-else in unexpected constellations – "betwixt and between theory and theatricality, paradigms and practices, critical reflection and creative accomplishment" (Conquergood, 2002: 152). In established *and* marginal modes of inquiry, divided knowledges begin to criss-cross and intersect. Layered connections "between creativity, critique, and civic engagement" become "mutually replenishing, and pedagogically powerful" (153).

However, lest an unwarranted and absurd sanguinity obscure real and severe problems, a word of caution is in order. Despite the overlap between the ontological, epistemological and methodological positions assumed by candidates and supervisors in the first part of this book, there are also significant differences. Aspects of a shared marginality (which in many ways apply also to the emergent fields of knowledge practices in the second part) arise from a disaffection with the urge, predominant in the academy and particularly in positivist and instrumental sciences, to control and to exploit the world (manifest in research cultures that objectify and rationalise and research applications that amount to the conquest and exploitation of natural and cultural resources). Paradoxically, the sources of a shared sense of alienation can also be divisive, as they cut very differently into the fabric of knowing for different candidates.

In Settler societies, for instance, the term *post-colonial* – which many associate with a research direction that seeks to address the history and outcomes of colonisation – is a misnomer. It obscures continuing colonialism, albeit in a different form. In Aotearoa/New Zealand, the impact of hegemonic Western knowledge traditions has been destructive for those considered non-Western. Western research as global *discovery* (as "[h]unting, racing, and gathering", Smith, 2005: 85) has always been a competitive effort to secure advantages, usually at the expense of others. Thus, the Social Darwinist myth of Empire assumed an entitlement of the winners in its self-defined race to claim their colonial subjects' territories and knowledge as bounty. In its milder version, this myth assumed that "Māori would survive only as a 'slight golden tinge' on the skins – and in the cultural symbols – of the Pākehā" (Belich, 1996: 248).[1] In Canada, Peter Cole makes a connection between genocide ("not just something that happens during warfare in Canada") and Western research and the suppression of Indigenous knowledge: "'Other' is to be eliminated one way or another" (Cole & O'Riley, 2010: 331).[2] Many Indigenous doctoral candidates belong to communities that have been subjected to intensive research since the imperial age of discoveries. Even today, research projects sometimes amount to "rampant prospecting", particularly in the fields of biodiversity and pharmaceuticals. Globalised "open-cast mining approaches to research (see, take and destroy)" (Smith, 1999: 118-9) often differ only marginally from those under colonial regimes.

Indigenous communities are still vulnerable to exploitative research, but they have also defined their own research agendas, based on their living memory of other ways of being in and knowing the world (Smith, 2005: 86). Research that contributes to the survival, recovery and development of Māori communities, governance structures and institutions is urgently needed (117). Obviously, questions about who does the research, for what, and for whom are crucially important here. They shape the aims, methods and conditions of Indigenous research agendas, which sometimes clash with established Western ideas of hierarchies and purposes of knowledge. Knowledge is not seen as an end in itself, not as unambiguously good and desirable in all situations. There is sometimes a palpable gap between the research that academic committees are used to and that undertaken and endorsed by Indigenous researchers and their communities. This gap – like the distance between PhD supervisors and non-traditional candidates, perhaps – can be regarded as one to be closed or filled (under the guidance of those who know best what research is and how to do it). It can also be left as an open and productive space in which new positions can be generated for Western *and* non-Western researchers, supervisors *and* candidates. From it can arise a "common world of thinking and speaking beings who all enter distances that cannot be suppressed but must continually expand" (Whittaker, 2011: 50). Meredith Whittaker suggests that both candidates and supervisors are translators and countertranslators on expeditions during which they prize open the distances and the gaps they traverse to generate spaces in which equality can be staged.

TRANSLATION OF THOUGHT

'[I]nternational' tends to code to 'non-Western' or even 'Asian' when referring to students, but to western, high-prestige northern-hemisphere when it comes to publications […]. And what about Māori students and the knowledges that they can generate? If they stand for local knowledges (including of course the global importance of such knowledges), can non-Māori New Zealanders make some kind of related stand? (Jones, 2007: 87)

Deborah Jones' remarks point to a peculiar condition of a country that often sees itself as at the margins of the world. There is a direct relationship between this geo-politically and culturally marginal position and the positions of several groups participating in Aotearoa/New Zealand's academic knowledge economies. Jones evokes a distance from "high-prestige northern-hemisphere" research, but paradoxically also from non-Western knowledge practices. This constellation implies a constant moving of knowledge "from one place to another", a turning "from one language into another": the etymologies of *translation* preserve the sense of a spatial distance to be overcome, and of the extraction and re-embedding of meaning in the transfer between two languages (*The Concise Oxford Dictionary of English Etymology*, 1996). In such transmissions, the inflections of words change.

Translation, then, adds new dimensions to words – in an interplay between kinship and mutual foreignness between languages (Benjamin, 1923/1969: 74-5, 80). Conflictual *and* solicitous, translation helps unfold the strange that is always already implicit in the familiar (Baecker, 2012: 16). As a creative act, an act of imagination, it goes beyond an understanding how other people "either construct the world or are constructed by the world" (Smith, 1999: 37): if the translator's language is "powerfully affected by the foreign tongue" (Benjamin, 1923/1969: 81), translation can be "a way of sharing the world" (Smith, 1999: 37). Paul Ricoeur calls translation ("a correspondence without adequacy") *linguistic hospitality* towards "the peculiar and the foreign" (2006: 10); an "act of inhabiting the word of the Other paralleled by the act of receiving the word of the Other into one's own home, one's own dwelling" (xvi, see also p. 10, above). Or, as Richard Kearney puts it, "we are called to make our language put on the stranger's clothes at the same time as we invite the stranger to step into the fabric of our own speech" (2007: 151). Kearney highlights the welcoming of difference implicit in *dialogue* (*dia-legein*), and the inherent exposure to strangeness in translation, where attentiveness "to stories other than our own" thrives alongside "the virtue of detachment vis-à-vis one's own obsessive attachment to what is 'mine' and 'ours'" (155-6).

This detachment is akin to Immanuel Kant's notion of an "*enlarged* thought", which arises from "putting ourselves in the place of any other man" (Kant, 1914) through the force of imagination. In Arendt's interpretation, this move opens up a space for thinking that is "open to all sides" (Arendt, 1992: 43). She adds that to think with the enlarged mentality of a world citizen, "means that one trains one's imagination to go visiting" (43). Leaving one's familiar location to spend some time in someone else's – provisionally and perhaps tentatively to begin with – leads to a better understanding of other standpoints, of "the place where they stand, the conditions they are subject to" (43) – their conditions of possibility. The distance to the familiar and to self-interest allows us not only to recognise our pre-judice (Gadamer) but to extend the reach of our thought to an open in which our particular conditions can stand next to those of our hosts – never becoming the same and always maintaining their distance. To "look upon the same world from one another's standpoint, to see the same in very different and frequently opposing aspects" (The Concept of History, in Arendt, 1961: 51) changes not only the way in which one looks at an object, *seeing anew*, but ultimately also the object itself. And so the common world arises in our conversations across distances: it is "not a given but produced as a result of visiting" (Peng, 2008: 74).

The last decades have seen not only Indigenous peoples, but also "women, gay and lesbian communities, ethnic minorities, and other marginalized communities" (Smith, 2005: 88) taking charge of the translations concerning their research engagements. They have challenged "the epistemic basis of the dominant scientific paradigm of research" (88) and developed new approaches to knowledge and getting-to-know. Such acts of translation, relocation and recounting contribute to the emergence of new fields and types of research (which is the concern of the second part of this book).

The translation of thoughts, their carrying-over on visits, between researchers' different standpoints is often a very important part of the conversations between candidates and supervisors, and it can be traced in the growing development of the thesis project in its various stages and forms (see Nepia, Bredies, Mika, Refiti, McGann & Milech, and Ho). Increasingly, the body of writing or creative work then begins to serve as an example, an object that is "presented to be looked upon" (Peng, 2008: 74). As a supervisor might suggest terms from the field of his knowledge, the candidate weighs and checks them to test their applicability and usefulness for his research (see Jenner, p. 214, below). In the weighing and conversing, disparate but also corresponding elements are brought together, assuming the possibility of a cohesive field of meanings and "a shared desire to arrive at the same result" (Callon, 1980: 211). While translation "recognises the existence of divergences and differences that cannot be smoothed out" it also "involves creating convergences and homologies by relating things that were previously different" (211).[3]

The principal distance between candidates and supervisors implies successive acts of translation on both sides. The creation of convergences between previously separate aspects of knowledge specific to Aotearoa/New Zealand (Māori and non-Māori) can lead to important contributions to global knowledge cultures from what is perceived by many as marginal. Doing good translations of the foreign into one's own repertoire of thought, experience and research practice, and creating a common language in the process, is – as some contributors have already explained – certainly a challenge in the supervisory relations of non-traditional doctoral researchers and their supervisors, particularly in non-traditional disciplines and emerging research fields.

The juxtaposition of diverse perspectives in the first part shows some common patterns of needs, interests, and passions. In this sense, the contributions in this book map some of the ground on which effective joint initiatives could grow and alliances be formed – an important consideration in a hegemonic field like the University. When all parts of the supervisory team recognise a need to be educated, the greater ontological epistemological, personal and political challenges, which non-traditional candidates all face in one way or another, can turn into a potential to develop new, transcultural spaces of thought, in which problematic assumptions about the 'other' are recognised, acknowledged and rendered productive. The desire for equity so prominent in some of the contributions to the first part (notably Nepia, Heraud, Tulloch, Edwards, Manathunga, Mitchell & Edwards, Weber and Ings), paired with an interest in areas of knowledge and ways of getting to know that were out of bounds of academic research until quite recently, is a strong motor for change in the way we produce and distribute knowledge.

EMERGENCE OF KNOWLEDGE

Above all, new values concerning knowledge, new approaches, new interest, new methods and new practices arise in the interfaces of these diverse perspectives. They have affinity, I think, to shifts in the distribution of the learning economy, which Palle

Rasmussen, Edward Lorenz and Bengt-Åke Lundvall argue are required in Europe, to accommodate better types of knowledge that are at present underrepresented. Institutional pedagogies are currently dominated by "mode 1 learning", which situates learning in traditional school and university environments and methods (Rasmussen, Lorenz, & Lundvall, 2008: 695). Two types of knowledge are integral parts of both secondary and tertiary curricula here: *Know-what* (factual knowledge that can be broken down, packaged and communicated as data) and *know-why* (knowledge of causality and conceptual connections). "Mode 2 learning" occurs in more open contexts and normally includes practical training or experience in the curriculum. Curricula are typically interdisciplinary, encourage problem-based and collaborative learning and crucially integrate two other forms of knowledge, *know-how* and *know-who*. "Know-how refers to the ability to do something. It may be related to the skills of artisans and workers" but also plays important roles in post-industrial societies. "Know-who involves information about who knows what and who knows what to do as well as the social ability to cooperate and communicate with different kinds of people and experts." (Rasmussen et al., 2008: 683). Both forms of knowledge tend to comprise greater or smaller components of tacit and embodied knowledge, where the links between "theoretical universe to practical problems" are constituted in different ways from the more codified types of know-what and know-why. Experience fosters "a more coherent understanding of theory and practice" (684) gained in an in-depth engagement with specific (often real-world) problems or challenges, frequently requiring collaboration, participation and initiative as part of know-how (694-5).

Know-how and know-who are arguably important types of knowledge for project-based and practice-led PhD thesis research, which is growing exponentially. In the UK, for example, where creative practice-led PhDs were first vigorously promoted, the number of PhD completions in Art and Design rose from 100 between 1976 and 1985, to 181 between 1986 and 1995, and then to 406 between 1996 and the first part of 2005 (Mottram, 2009: 12, 15). This surge in numbers is an indication of a policy interest in creative industries; it also implies a growing influence of *mode 2* type knowledge production. In Aotearoa/New Zealand, the development practice-led PhDs was connected to the establishment of University faculties or departments dedicated to "creative industries" or "creative technologies". These had been promoted in the 2002 Labour government's agenda of innovative, "Better by Design"-led export economies. Internationally, the terms "cultural" and, subsequently, "creative industries" were mobilised in response to the demands of the knowledge economy and the increasing importance of symbolic and cultural production in market economies (Garnham, 2005: 15-6, 21). This policy shift combined with a growing tendency to regard education as a contributing factor in the development of human capital and national productivity, and this consequently led to a marketization of PhD level creative practice-led research.

The inherent link between the degree creation and the 'markets' is not often discussed. It is, however, a strong factor in the organisation and implementation of creative practice-led research at PhD level and has implications for the funding and control of outcomes, in particular (see Halse & Mowbray, 2011: 520). The now common term *communities* in mode 2 research, for example, has acquired new inflections. They refer, more often than not, to commercial enterprises and business ventures (Halse & Mowbray, 2011: 515), rather than to civil and cultural communities in need of, and deserving, support.[4] Over the same period, however, the number of non-traditional candidates in Aotearoa/New Zealand increased, certainly in my field of art and design, due to an increase of funding for postgraduate, particularly PhD, degrees. As a direct consequence, tertiary institutions directed their energies towards increasing postgraduate enrolments. Domestic funding attracted larger numbers of Māori and Pacific students,[5] while, at the same time, the income generated from international students' fees became increasingly important for the universities' households, given an overall shortening of educational funding (see Halse & Mowbray, 2011: 520).[6] Changing governmental funding regimes influence definitions, standards and processes in PhD research and supervision. In my observation, they shape our definitions of research and practice indirectly and mostly unacknowledged. This development may impact, too, on the relationship between theory and creativity, and their perceived manifestations in *written* and *creative* components. The binary implies that writing is not creative – whereas creative components naturally are. This was perhaps an understandable conception as long as, for instance, an object was the expected outcome of design processes. Today, as systems design, service design and other forms of process oriented design areas gain more and more recognition and importance, such polarities disregard less understandably the designed-ness of all research, all research tools, and all modes of fabrication. They miss a great potential of creativity in all forms knowledge production (see Preston & Thomassen, 2010, and Jonas and Chow in this volume). Dwight Conquergood makes the point that performance studies bring to the academy a "rare hybridity", "a commingling of analytical and artistic ways of knowing that unsettles the institutional organization of knowledge and disciplines" (2002: 152). Performance studies' constitutive liminality translates into a "capacity to bridge segregated and differently valued knowledges, drawing together legitimated as well as subjugated modes of inquiry" (153).

Where the interests of artists, engineers and physicists commingle, as in a "'network' of associations between ideas, things, people and resources", "translation processes are enacted", things "made new", and associations formed and distorted (Brown, 2002: 6, see also Wölfel p. 43, above). Steven Brown draws attention to Michel Serres' account of Turner's painting in the 1830s and 1840s: Turner "blends rather than calculates", but he "directly confronts the changes in how matter and force are understood", even before the science of thermodynamics fully matured (Brown, 2002: 6). Thus, Turner contributed through his creative practice "to the development of a model that is at that moment cultural *and* scientific, practical *and* theoretical". He effects a translation in "an act of invention brought about through combining and mixing varied elements", such as "issues of technical composition in art with the emerging model of work and matter accompanying the industrial revolution" (6). Between different cultures, but even in the interstices of the same, decisions already made are unsettled and translated into decisions still to be made (Baecker, 2012: 157). The conjuncture of mode 1 and mode 2 types of knowledge in many new and emerging fields opens the field of academic knowledge production to new research questions, methods, and ethics.

There is, perhaps, a significant difference between conventional research modes and arts-based and creative practice-led research. The latter often tends "to work at the edge of possibility", as it attempts to address different questions from those posed in traditional research, and aims towards the creation of new worlds rather than the discovery of facts. In this situation, knowing "takes on the attributes of a verb" – it is "a process rather than an object or product that is fixed and definitely knowable" (25). Tom Barone therefore advocates epistemological modesty (2008: 35) and a greater social engagement than one would normally see in academia. This is to be achieved through practices poised on the edge, often disturbing conventional, accepted politics of representation and narratives. The aim is to change the current conversation and foster the appreciation of "an array of diverse, complex, nuanced images and partial, local portraits of human growth and possibility" (39).

The appeal to epistemological modesty concerns PhD supervisors in particular. An awareness of her lack of knowledge, or at least the limitations of her knowledge, is palpable, for instance, when Barbara Grant professes her ignorance. She still has, as she writes, to supervise a PhD project to completion and is not fluent in the knowledge systems some of her Māori candidates are embedded in, and engaged with. Grant goes further and pleads for the suspension of the type of knowledge supervisors were taught as part of their normal training. Instead, she proposes to foreground "the generative value of the difficult condition of ignorance". This requires courage and a *negative capability* to tolerate (pedagogical) uncertainties,[7] since a lack of understanding of the concepts that drive a candidate's work is likely to be frightening for a supervisor. The supervision of PhD research candidates is "a pedagogy under pressure" (Grant, 2005: iii).[8]

But does it have to be? Or is the figure of the knowing supervisor not only a fiction but a calamity? Rancière would claim the latter. For him, the supervisor's explication first constitutes the candidate as not-knowing (1991: 6, 7, 21, 70-1). Martin Heidegger proposed that *letting-learn* is more difficult than learning: "Teaching is more difficult than learning because what teaching calls for is this: to let learn. The real teacher, in fact, lets nothing else be learned than – learning" (Heidegger, 1968: 15, see also Ross Jenner in this volume). This is easier to approach by taking into account yet another side to not knowing and knowing: the partial nature of all knowledge. Both Kenneth Burke, who noted that every mode of seeing (knowing) is a mode of not-knowing (not seeing) (1984: 49), and Martin Heidegger, who observed that unconcealing is always accompanied by the withdrawal of Being (Heidegger, 1972: 52), amongst many others, highlight the condition of knowledge in its intimate relation to not-knowing. More recently, Dirk Baecker (who considers the possibility that design is a practice of not-knowing, 2000: 162) argues that, while modern science is based on the "systematic comparison of one knowledge with another for the sake of gaining a third", each comparison is contingent on "a particular, historically and regionally bounded culture" which permits certain questions and not others. Even comparison, it turns out, is "bound up with specific preliminary decisions, which are themselves not subjected to comparison" (2012: 70). Baecker claims elsewhere that universities increasingly aim to enable their graduates to deal with not-knowing methodologically, theoretically and practically (2007: 107).[9] Knowledge, in this model, is distributed (see Jonas, Chow and Grand in chapter 11) – its production no longer involves just supervisors and candidates, as individual members of the academy, but various networks of different intelligences in which they partake. These networks – inside and outside of the academy – are concerned with diverse forms of knowledge, and participants have to be able to respond to unregulated, wild circumstances and events. PhD supervision (like research), insofar as it is implicated in the "production of original, independent academic work", is "as much a practice of improvisation as it is of regularity" (Grant, 2005).[10]

New fields of knowledge production will, in turn, change PhD pedagogies, and new doctoral degrees provide opportunities to review the supervisor's role. Mick Wilson even regards such reflexive interrogation of supervisory practice as "the precondition – or at the very least the corollary condition – of developing the reflexive doctoral practitioner" (Wilson, 2009: 65). The uncertainty about appropriate questions, methods and standards at PhD levels, as well as the roles and responsibilities of supervisors and candidates, in multi-disciplinary, professional, hybrid and practice-led PhDs (Taylor & Beasley, 2005: 41) can be perceived as threat *and* opportunity, disconcerting or exciting. While supervisors and candidates may initially have to sort out standards and procedures for new types of PhD theses "on the hoof" (Taylor & Beasley, 2005: 41-2), and while, in every PhD project, there will be "inevitably a kind of splashing around at the start, where various things are being tried and tested" (Dorrian, Jenner, & Engels-Schwarzpaul, 2012), efforts to theorise, test and define, for instance, the relationship between an artefact and a written submission are underway (Crouch & Pearce, 2012; Milech & Schilo, 2004; O'Brien, 2007; Scrivener, 2002; Thomassen & Oudheusden, 2004).[11] In the meantime, however, supervisors, candidates, and examiners still have to negotiate volatile terrains, subject to changing policies – even concerning doctorates that are already under way. Candidates and supervisors need high levels of *negative capability,* an ability to endure in "a psychically open process" (Jemstedt, 2000: 128), yet to remain coherent in changing circumstances (Bonz & Struve, 2006: 152). Negative capability permits an open and creative engagement with unexpected and surprising aspects – the more so, the greater candidates and supervisors' trust and confidence (Winnicott, 1967: 372). Supervisors who find it difficult to deal with uncertainty, particularly when faced with intensifying accountability regimes (see Halse & Mowbray, 2011), may become "very directive in shaping and guiding students' work" and discourage them from "intellectual risk-taking". They may also blur "the boundaries between reviewing and writing students' theses" by providing excessive feedback (Halse, 2011: 562). As one of the supervisors interviewed by Christine Halse put it:

I think one thing that we may be in danger of is too much spoon feeding. We're wanting the student to get through – we're wanting completions – [so if the student is] a bit deficient in this area, we'll just fill it up with 'spakfilla' [a commercial brand of plaster] ... but, in the long run, that doesn't work. We're sending out people who find that the 'spakfilla' dries and falls off and they don't have the skills. (Science Professor, in Halse, 2011: 563)

While the first part of this book set out from Aotearoa/New Zealand, the second part starts in its Antipodes, with a contribution about design doctorates in Germany by Wolfgang Jonas, Rosan Chow and Simon Grand: "Alternative design doctorates as drivers for new forms of research, or: Knowing and Not-Knowing in Design". In their historic and systematic narrative, they show how Sciences and Art, still integrated in the Renaissance, were increasingly separated from the seventeenth century onward so that, today, Science is supposed to produce theoretical knowledge which Design then applies in practice. They argue that a new "trans-domain" explores not-knowing and knowledge gaps to integrate different knowledge domains by articulating strong relationships between forms of scientific and artistic knowledge production. The chapter aims to support PhD candidates and supervisors working in these new areas.

Similarly, in chapter 12, Ross Jenner explores two different, but related, sets of issues arising in the supervision of architecture theses. The first relates to project-led PhDs which, more than a century after the discipline's acceptance into universities, now examine what architects actually do. Design and making were traditionally out of bounds of PhD level research. How then to frame design as itself a mode of thinking, to let it think in and from its own place? How to return the excluded to the core? Also out of bounds were until recently many candidates' first languages, cultures and epistemological frameworks – a problematic exclusion, given the growing numbers of non-Western PhD candidates. How then to let become visible and open to conceptualisation what cannot be translated or thought outside of their cultures? How to admit modes of thought, art and practice that seem incompatible with the academy? Jenner suggests that certain conditions of boundlessness and boundary breaking provide fruitful encounters and reversals and allow what was discounted in traditional doctorates to happen: the very things closest to the discipline and to the hearts of the candidates.

Thinking through moving image and performance, Sarah O'Brien discusses in chapter 13 the need to generate methodologies for non-traditional projects that are adequate to the research subject matter and consistent with its guiding frameworks. She addresses ways of articulating differences within the continuing debates concerning the dissemination of PhD theses in the field of performance. O'Brien suggests that methodology in a practice-led PhD is always ideologically loaded. Consequently, divergent positions between supervisor and candidate may require mediating procedures and comparisons with other practitioners' and researchers' practices and reflections. O'Brien puts forward her own experience of a practice-led PhD as one possible example of a methodology. She claims that her practice was not designed as an investigation to uncover an imminent 'truth', but as the realisation of theoretical schemas (performance ideas) that would allow new knowledge to emerge through both the failure to realise these ideas fully *and* the alternative brought about by the realisation. This methodology interrogates the relationship between written and performance work and demonstrates how the writing process can be integral to a creative research project.

In Barbara Milech and Ann Schilo's consideration of the collaborative process of PhD supervision in chapter 14, writing also plays a significant part. They propose that it is a process in which both supervisor and candidate learn, and in which there is a subtle crossover of 'authority': the supervisor begins as teacher, learns along the way, and ends as editor/mentor/hand-holder as the student takes the next large step toward publication/practice. In the context of creative practice-led research, this basic proposition takes on specific relevance. In "Generating thought through text" Milech and Schilo draw on their 'research-question' model for creative-production theses and on vignettes provided by students to suggest options that support supervisors' and candidates' collaborations. The research-question model assumes that the two components of a creative-production thesis – practice-led research (creative production) and exegesis – are cognate research modalities, complementary ways of exploring a question that matters; and that some questions are best answered when not limited to a discursive (exegetical) modality. They argue that understanding the relationship between these two modes of inquiry can temper anxieties many creative-production research students feel, and that doing so is key to the success of practice-led postgraduate research.

Treahna Hamm and Laura Brearley went through a doctorate together as an Indigenous candidate and a non-Indigenous supervisor. In chapter 15, they reflect on the development of their relationship, which was underpinned by the Indigenous concept of Deep Listening. In her PhD, Hamm explored ways of reconnecting with her family through individual and community narrative. Deep Listening involves listening not only with your ears, but with your eyes and with all of the senses. It is connected to something bigger than our individual selves. Hamm and Brearley's chapter makes a significant contribution to the understanding of the doctoral experience: beyond the cognitive domain, in ways which can ultimately enrich the practice of both doctoral candidates and supervisors.

Barbara Grant finds, in chapter 16, that "Not all academics can do it" – 'it' being doctoral supervision in the haunted spaces of post-colonialism. Between 1998 and 2006, the number of Māori doctoral student enrolments in Aotearoa/New Zealand grew by 79%. Given the current under-representation of Māori academics in the academy (to varying degrees in different disciplines), there is a clear need for non-Māori academics to take on the supervision of Māori students, even when their projects traverse unfamiliar epistemologies. Grant draws on her research into the experiences of Pākehā supervisors who undertake this work and passes on the advice these colleagues have for others. In a post-colonial context of sometimes fraught, certainly haunted, relations between Pākehā and Māori, meeting the obligation to supervise Māori candidates may offer Pākehā supervisors unexpected and welcome rewards.

Finally, in chapter 17, Bob Jahnke speaks in an interview about his experiences of creative practice-led research in a uniquely Māori context, at Te Pūtahi a Toi (School of Māori Studies, Massey University). Its visual arts programmes are unique in that te reo Māori (Māori language) is spoken at all levels. Exegeses written in te reo Māori are common at Masters' level at Te Pūtahi a Toi and are expected soon at doctoral level. These theses require examiners who are fluent in te reo Māori, which raises interesting questions regarding the accreditation of different types of knowledge and the status of the knowledge bearers. Jahnke also broaches the conceptual difference between creative practice-led research that is kaupapa-driven (grounded in issues related to the candidate's socio-economic or cultural reality) and research that is process-driven (experimentation and exploration of media, perception, and form). However, his supervision practice is about being Māori first and foremost – a context in which knowledge sources and knowledge production are always collectively held – so that the search for knowledge can continue.

James Elkins' observation about PhDs in fine arts, namely that "no one knows how to supervise these degrees", applies to a greater or lesser extent to a range of doctorate level qualifications. This lack of certain knowledge is, if appropriately engaged, one of the most interesting aspects of non-traditional PhDs: it affords a rare opportunity "to rethink the supervisor's role" (Elkins, 2009b: xii). This rethinking might privilege a currently rare scholarly identity for both supervisors and candidates, which involves collaboration, interdependence in supervisory relations, and an appreciation of each other's specific capacities. This scholarly identity, today often found on the margins and engaged with with paradigmatic controversies (Denzin & Lincoln, 2011: 121), is likely to correlate the production of knowledge with specific contexts (Halse & Bansel, 2012: 388); to regard knowledge as resolutely open, multidimensional, contextual, dialogical, and distributed across boundaries (Volckmann & Nicolescu, 2007); and to view its production as co-operative or co-creative (see Thomassen & Bradford, 2009).

NOTES

[1] Bicultural relationships in Aotearoa/New Zealand are presumed to be better than in most settler societies, yet a newspaper editor advocated less than 150 years ago that certain "natives" who "rendered colonization impossible" should be "treated as wild beasts – hunted down and slain" ("The patea campaign," 1868:5). In the 1930s, it was thought that Māori were a dying race (Belich, 1996: 174) and many of today's PhD candidates will have heard elders talk about the punishment they received for speaking Māori at School (Waitangi Tribunal - Te Rōpū Whakamana i te Tiriti o Waitangi, 1986: paras 3.2.4 -3.2.8). In the mid-1980s, I was the recipient of comments by academics that overtly discounted Māori language and knowledge as obsolete and irrelevant. Even today, the experience of being the only Māori in a class is not uncommon, and the air often gets thinner as students move into postgraduate studies. It is in this context that Linda Tuhiwai Smith wrote in 1999 about an emerging field of Indigenous research "which privileges indigenous concerns, indigenous practices and indigenous participation as researchers and researched". (1999: 107)

A.-CHR. ENGELS-SCHWARZPAUL

2. "Australian Aborigines have consistently challenged the doctrine of terra nullius or 'empty land' which has been used to deny the advancement of any claims to territory." (Smith, 1999: 111) They gained substantive citizenship rights only in 1967 (109).

3. This process of translation is significantly helped or hindered by the configuration of the wider research environment. As this book is nearing completion, I am deeply affected by news of the imminent death of a person who has been an excellent translator as the Head of Research at the School of Art and Design. Aukje Thomassen understands these issues better than many and has thoughtfully and determinately opened up spaces for non-traditional researchers. Aukje was to contribute a chapter to this book in which she wanted to discuss "how the current educational climate in Aotearoa/New Zealand (and elsewhere) influences the supervision of creative practice-led PhDs" and the importance of understanding not only "the current candidates, but also the industries they come from and the nature and conditions of open innovation". Her chapter was to "establish a common ground on which it is possible and productive to engage with the tensions between economic growth, fluid creative supervision and technology enhanced design learning." Aukje's deteriorating health prevented her from writing her chapter. Her insightful initiatives at our school, however, have already left their mark and will not be forgotten.

4. Similarly, the "neo-liberal discourse of participation – organised through the conceptual practices of the market, social capital, and participatory development – continues to appropriate and reconstitute" participatory action research methodology "in ways that are antithetical to both its founding principles and traditions" (Jordan, 2003: 195).

5. In New Zealand, the Tertiary Education Commission's policy provision for twice the amount of funding for Māori and Pacific postgraduate completions, and four times for completions in te reo Māori (2013:31), is perhaps an acknowledgement of an implicit, but fundamental incompatibility of its overall funding regime with the principles of the Treaty of Waitangi (*Te Tiriti o Waitangi. The Treaty of Waitangi*, 1840).

6. These strategic interventions by government agencies have shaped postgraduate education in art and design to such an extent that we have become used to calling research what before the early 2000s would have been called design exploration (because papers with substantial research components were funded better). Initially, the question of what constitutes research (and how funding is related to research criteria and outcomes) was a matter for collegial discussion and debate with students but gradually this issue dropped from visibility. A reclassification of activities took place, from *practical and theoretical investigations in studio* to *creative practice-led research*. Yet, some candidates resisted, as Mottram observes (2009: 4), the request to engage with a review of knowledge – which clearly and explicitly included a review of precedents in their particular field – be that paintings, videos, performances, buildings, design objects or other notable and relevant works. It would seem that some candidates' primary motivation may not be about "finding out a lot" (8), nor to develop knowledge and aptitude regarding processes, research methods and conceptual agility to address a particular question and to generate "some new perspective, understanding or knowledge of interest or useful to that subject field" (9). Some candidates' decision to enrol in a PhD may be driven largely by the lack of funding in the creative sector outside of universities.

In this context, statistics from the USA about the growth of aid recipients with postgraduate degrees are alarming: in the three years between 2007 and 2010, the number of recipients with Masters degrees almost tripled from 101,682 to 293,029 and the number of recipients with PhDs more than tripled from 9,776 to 33,655 (published by The Chronicle of Higher Education in May 2012, "The Ph.D. Now Comes With Food Stamps", http://chronicle.com/article/From-Graduate-School-to/131795/).

7. "Negative capability" is a term used by John Keats to mean the ability "of being in uncertainties, mysteries, doubts, without any irritable reaching after fact and reason" (quoted in Bion, 1970: 125).

8. Under such pressure, it is easily forgotten, for instance, that a discipline is "always much more than an ensemble of procedures which permit the thought of a given territory of objects"; it is, first of all, "the constitution of this territory itself, and therefore the establishment of a certain distribution of the thinkable" (Rancière, 2006: 8). When words, images and objects circulate outside of the control of a master or a discipline, disciplinary thought "must ceaselessly hinder this haemorrhage in order to

establish stable relations" and claim back its territory, its objects and its methods to stabilise always uncertain boundaries (9, 11).

[9] The core social function of research is to produce and increase uncertainty in a controlled manner (128). In this way, research provides society with a space of potentialities in which researchers, together with other members of society, can examine the factual (128).

[10] This does not deny the fact, however, that greater transparency regarding standards and procedures, and the provision of different positions and perspectives for negotiation, will foster relationships of equality between candidates and supervisors.

[11] See also the comprehensive list of resources at the University of Roehampton's Centre for Research in Creative and Professional Writing, particularly the section "Thesis writing, research training and postgraduate study" (Centre for Research in Creative and Professional Writing).

REFERENCES

Arendt, H. (1961). *Between past and future: Six exercises in political thought*. New York, N.Y.: The Viking Press, Inc.

Arendt, H. (1992). *Lectures on Kant's Political Philosophy. Edited and with an interpretive essay by Ronald Beiner*. Chicago, IL: The University of Chicago Press.

Arendt, H. (1998). *The human condition* (2nd ed.). Chicago, IL: University of Chicago Press. (1958)

Baecker, D. (2000). Wie steht es mit dem Willen Allahs? *Zeitschrift für Rechtssoziologie, 21*(1), 145–176.

Baecker, D. (2007). *Studien zur nächsten Gesellschaft*. Frankfurt a.M., Germany: Suhrkamp.

Baecker, D. (2012). *Wozu Kultur?* Berlin: Kadmos.

Barone, T. (2008). How arts-based research can change minds. In M. Cahnmann-Taylor & R. Siegesmund (Eds.), *Arts-based research in education: Foundations for practice* (pp. 28–49). New York, NY: Routledge.

Belich, J. (1996). *Making peoples*. Auckland, New Zealand: Allen Lane, The Penguin Press.

Benjamin, W. (1969). The task of the translator. In H. Arendt (Ed.), *Illuminations* (pp. 69–82). New York, NY: Schocken. (1923)

Bonz, J., & Struve, K. (2006). Homi K. Bhabha: Auf der Innenseite kultureller Differenz: "In the middle of differences". In S. Moebius & D. Quadflieg (Eds.), *Kultur. Theorien der Gegenwart* (pp. 140–153). Wiesbaden, Germany: VS Verlag für Sozialwissenschaften.

Brown, S. D. (2002). Michel Serres: Science, translation and the logic of the parasite. *Theory, Culture & Society, 19*(3), 1–27.

Burke, K. (1984). *Permanence and change: An anatomy of purpose*. Berkeley, CA: University of California Press.

Callon, M. (1980). Struggles and negotiations to define what is problematic and what is not: The socio-logic of translation. *The social process of scientific investigation, 4*, 197–219.

Centre for Research in Creative and Professional Writing. *Practice-based research: A selective bibliography*. Retrieved from http://www.roehampton.ac.uk/Research-Centres/Centre-for-Research-in-Creative-and-Professional-Writing/Practice-based-research/

Cole, P., & O'Riley, P. (2010). Coyote and Raven talk about equivalency of other/ed knowledges in research. In P. Thomson & M. Walker (Eds.), *The Routledge doctoral student's companion: Getting to grips with research in education and the social sciences* (pp. 323–334). Milton Park, England: Routledge.

The concise Oxford dictionary of English etymology. (1996). Retrieved from http://www.oxfordreference.com/view/10.1093/acref/9780192830982.001.0001/acref-9780192830982

Conquergood, D. (2002). Performance Studies: Interventions and radical research 1. *TDR/The Drama Review, 46*(2), 145–156.

Crouch, C., & Pearce, J. (2012). *Doing research in design*. London, UK: Berg.

Denzin, N. K., & Lincoln, Y. S. (2011). *The SAGE handbook of qualitative research*. Los Angeles, CA: Sage Publications, Incorporated.

Dorrian, M., Jenner, R., & Engels-Schwarzpaul, A.-C. (2012). *Interview with Mark Dorrian in Newcastle*. University of Auckland and AUT University. Auckland, New Zealand.

Elkins, J. (2009a). *Artists with PhDs: On the new doctoral degree in studio art*. Washington, DC: New Academia Publishing.

Elkins, J. (2009b). Introduction. In J. Elkins (Ed.), *Artists with PhDs: On the new doctoral degree in studio art* (pp. vii-xiii). Washington, DC: New Academia Publishing.

Garnham, N. (2005). From cultural to creative industries. *International Journal of Cultural Policy, 11*(1), 15–29.

Grant, B. M. (2005). *The pedagogy of graduate supervision: Figuring the relations between supervisor and student* (PhD thesis). The University of Auckland, Auckland.

Halse, C. (2011). 'Becoming a supervisor': the impact of doctoral supervision on supervisors' learning. *Studies in higher education, 36*(5), 557–570.

Halse, C., & Bansel, P. (2012). The learning alliance: ethics in doctoral supervision. *Oxford Review of Education, 38*(4), 377–392.

Halse, C., & Mowbray, S. (2011). The impact of the doctorate. *Studies in higher education, 36*(5), 513–525.

Heidegger, M. (1968). *What is called thinking?* (F. D. Wieck & J. G. Gray, Trans., Vol. 21). New York, NY: Harper & Row.

Heidegger, M. (1972). *On Time and Being* (J. Stambaugh, Trans.). New York, NY: Harper Colophon Books.

Jemstedt, A. (2000). Potential Space – The place of encounter between inner and outer reality. *International Forum of Psychoanalysis, 9*, 124–131.

Jones, D. (2007, 16 February 2007). Management PhDs in Aotearoa/New Zealand: The trick of standing upright here. In C. Prichard, D. Jones, & R. Jacques (Chair), Symposium *Organization, Identity, Locality III. Organizing the Postcolonial in Aotearoa/New Zealand: A one day symposium on being a critical organisational scholar in Aotearoa/New Zealand*, Auckland: Massey University Albany Campus.

Jordan, S. (2003). Who stole my methodology? Co-opting PAR. *Globalisation, Societies and Education, 1*(2), 185–200.

Kant, I. (1914). *The critique of judgement. Translated with introduction and notes by J.H. Bernard*. Retrieved from http://ebooks.adelaide.edu.au/k/kant/immanuel/k16ju/chapter19.html

Kearney, R. (2007). Paul Ricoeur and the hermeneutics of translation. *Research in Phenomenology, 37*(2), 147–159. doi:10.1163/156916407x185610

Milech, B. H., & Schilo, A. (2004). "Exit Jesus": Relating the Exegesis and Creative/Production Components of a Research Thesis. *TEXT*(3 - Special Issue). Retrieved from http://www.textjournal.com.au/speciss/issue3/milechschilo.htm

Mottram, J. (2009). Researching research in art and design. In J. Elkins (Ed.), *Artists with PhDs: On the new doctoral degree in studio art* (pp. 3–30). Washington, DC: New Academia Publishing.

O'Brien, S. (2007). Practice-as-research in performance: A response to reflective judgement. *Studies in theatre and performance,* (1), 73–81.

The patea campaign. (1868, 16 September 1868). *New Zealand Herald*. Retrieved from http://paperspast.natlib.govt.nz/

Peng, Y. (2008). *A U-turn in the desert: Figures and motifs of the Chinese Nineteen Eighties* (PhD). University of Minnesota, Minneapolis. Retrieved from http://proquest.umi.com/pqdweb?did=1537472881&sid=1&Fmt=2&clientId=79356&RQT=309&VName=PQD

Preston, J., & Thomassen, A. (2010). Writing through design, an active practice. *Journal of Writing in Creative Practice, 3*(1), 45–62.

Quinn, M. (2011). Committing (to) ignorance. In E. Malewski & N. E. Jaramillo (Eds.), *Epistemologies of ignorance in education* (pp. 31–52). Charlotte, NC: Information Age Publishing.

Rancière, J. (1991). *The ignorant schoolmaster: Five lessons in intellectual emancipation* (K. Ross, Trans.). Stanford, CA: Stanford University Press.

Rancière, J. (2006). Thinking between disciplines: An aesthetics of knowledge. *PARRHESIA*(1), 1–12.

Rasmussen, P., Lorenz, E., & Lundvall, B.-Å. (2008). Education in the learning economy: a European perspective. *Policy Futures in Education, 6*(6), 681–700.

Ricœur, P. (2006). *On translation*. Abingdon, England: Routledge.

Scrivener, S. (2002). Characterising creative-production doctoral projects in art and design. *International Journal of Design Sciences and Technology, 10*(2), 25–44.
Smith, L. T. (1999). *Decolonizing methodologies. Research and Indigenous peoples.* Dunedin, New Zealand: University of Otago Press.
Smith, L. T. (2005). On tricky ground: Researching the native in the age of uncertainty. In N. K. Denzin & Y. S. Lincoln (Eds.), *The Sage handbook of qualitative research* (pp. 85–107). London, England: Sage Publications.
Taylor, S., & Beasley, N. (2005). *A handbook for doctoral supervisors.* Milton Park, England: Routledge.
Tertiary Education Commission - Te Amorangi Mātauranga Matua. (2013). Performance-based research fund (PBRF) annual report for 2010. Wellington, Aoteraoa/New Zealand: Tertiary Education Commission - Te Amorangi Mātauranga Matua. Retrieved from http://www.tec.govt.nz/About-us/News/TEC-Now/PBRF-Annual-Report-2010-Published/
Te Tiriti o Waitangi. The Treaty of Waitangi. (1840). Retrieved from http://www.govt.nz/en/aboutnz/?id=a32f7d70e71e9632aad1016cb343f900#E2
Thomassen, A., & Bradford, M. (2009). Beyond the individual: The complex interplay of creativity, synthesis and rigor in design led research processes. Paper presented at the *IASDR Conference, Korea.* Retrieved from http://muir.massey.ac.nz/bitstream/handle/10179/2475/IASDR2009_ThomassenBradford.pdf
Thomassen, A., & Oudheusden, M. v. (2004). Knowledge creation and exchange within research: The exegesis approach. *Working Papers in Art and Design, 3.* Retrieved from http://sitem.herts.ac.uk/artdes_research/papers/wpades/vol3/atfull.html
Volckmann, R., & Nicolescu, B. (2007). Transdisciplinarity: Basarab Nicolescu talks with Russ Volckmann. *Integral Review*(4), 73–90.
Waitangi Tribunal - Te Rōpū Whakamana i te Tiriti o Waitangi. (1986). *Report of the Waitangi Tribunal on the Te Reo Māori Claim (Wai 11).* Wellington, New Zealand: Waitangi Tribunal. Department of Justice. Retrieved from http://www.waitangi-tribunal.govt.nz/scripts/reports/reports/11/2580F91B-5D6F-46F4-ADE0-BC27CA535C01.pdf
Whittaker, M. (2011). *Restaging Rancière: New scenes of equality and democracy in education* (PhD dissertation). The Ohio State University.
Wilson, M. (2009). Four theses attempting to revise the terms of a debate. In J. Elkins (Ed.), *Artists with PhDs: On the new doctoral degree in studio art* (pp. 57–70). Washington, DC: New Academia Publishing.
Winnicott, D. W. (1967). The Location of Cultural Experience. *International Journal of Psycho-Analysis*(48), 368–372.

AFFILIATION

A.-Chr. Engels-Schwarzpaul
AUT University, Auckland

PART II

EMERGING FIELDS OF RESEARCH

WOLFGANG JONAS, ROSAN CHOW & SIMON GRAND

11. ALTERNATIVE DESIGN DOCTORATES AS DRIVERS FOR NEW FORMS OF RESEARCH

Or: Knowing and Not-Knowing in Design

INTRODUCTION

We currently observe an interesting paradox: on the one hand, a narrow and determined preoccupation with the world we actually live in, away from the multiple pasts and futures in which we are embedded. On the other hand, we note a recurrent appeal to transcend the present towards the future – without reference, however, to the questions, perspectives, value propositions and investments that might define the necessary steps for 'moving forward' in important areas of social, cultural and economic life. This situation presents new challenges, opportunities and responsibilities for designers, both in their practice and in their research. It thus has substantial implications for design education, and particularly for the future of design doctorates.

Design doctorates are controversial when they claim to follow their own, 'designerly' paradigm of inquiry (practice-led, project-grounded, research through design, etc.). Not least, because they deviate from the taken-for-granted epistemological traditions, methodological guidelines and academic standards of more established disciplines. Nonetheless, these disciplines are themselves undergoing changes, as does their relationship with practice. Non-traditional epistemological approaches are gaining importance, and the relation between facts and values, or rigour and relevance in inquiry is increasingly delicate. A strong convergence between the Sciences and Design is emerging, which creates a new *trans-domain*. It stands to reason that all these changes necessitate the exploration of new forms of doctorates.

We approach this exploration by means of a historic and systematic narrative: The academic cultures of Sciences and Art, still very much integrated in the Renaissance, were increasingly separated from the seventeenth century onward and eventually became what we know as "traditional Science" and "traditional Design". In this constellation, Science is supposed to produce theoretical knowledge, which Design then applies in practice. Many arguments and efforts, mainly on the side of designers, have been extended to overcome this opposition: For example, the Bauhaus, the New Bauhaus and the Ulm School of Design have all attempted to reconcile the split. Their practical influence has been limited until recently and the binary still underpins today's debates about design.

A survey of current discourses in Science and Technology Studies (e.g. Knorr-Cetina, 1999, Nowotny, Scott & Gibbons, 2001, Bammé 2009) and Design Research (e.g. Telier, 2011, Koskinen et.al., 2011, Grand & Jonas, 2012, Tröndle & Warmers, 2011) show that scientists have come to reflect on the social relevance and the context-dependency of their knowledge production; while designers have realised the knowledge-intensity of their working processes, and they have begun to develop their own research questions, concepts, methods and standards. Even though there are clear distinctions regarding the character of the outcomes, we are more interested in the convergence of scientific and designerly approaches than the split between them, as the latter mostly implies a deficiency in designerly research. We create a narrative that sets out to reveal the common core of *both* scientific *and* designerly approaches to knowledge generation. Evolutionary theories of experiential learning, which strongly correspond to the basic patterns of design processes, seem to be the generic mechanisms of knowledge generation. In a projected new *trans-domain*, we propose that design might provide a valuable model for research. The fundamental contradiction between facts and values is reconciled in this approach.

By analysing an on-going exemplary PhD thesis, this chapter will not only provide theoretical argument and conceptual comparison but also the case study of an alternative approach, which will support PhD candidates and their supervisors working within new frameworks in design research: in her doctoral thesis project *Seltsame Sachen. Experimentelles Interfacedesign und Design-im-Gebrauch (Not Ready for Use. Experimental Design of Interfaces and Design-in-Use)*, Katharina Bredies adopts a *Research Through Design* (*RTD*) approach that places issues of not-knowing, transdisciplinarity and research ethics at the centre. Bredies challenges user study practices, which are considered successful and almost taken for granted in *User-Centred Design (UCD)*, and argues that established *UCD* standards may actually impede innovation in product development. Rather than simply critiquing *UCD's* limitations, she aims to contribute to *Design-in-Use (DiU)* as an emerging design paradigm by inventing and examining different interface design strategies. Drawing on the traditions of social scientific research as well as design practice, she describes, constructs, analyses, projects, theorises, designs, writes and makes – all in an effort to integrate science and design to achieve both rigour and relevance. Dealing with the unknown within a transdisciplinary research framework, Bredies involves ordinary people in the research-cum-design process as active participants. She seeks to understand their understanding of her designed objects in order to derive principles that are pertinent for *DiU*.

We will discuss Bredies' project in greater detail in the final section, but first we want to look at some important changes within the University and propose changes to doctoral design research in response.

THE NEXT UNIVERSITY

The present dramatic changes of economic, social, cultural and technological structures and processes and their implications for knowledge production present serious challenges for universities and, consequently, for the form of doctorates. Yet the types and forms of knowledge currently imparted by universities are mostly of limited relevance to these challenges; they are predominantly descriptive rather than projective, and generated for academic peers rather than the public. Most socially and economically *relevant* knowledge is currently conveyed outside the university (Scharmer & Käufer, 2000).

From our perspective, University education can no longer be concerned merely with the transfer of established knowledge and know-how, or the socialisation into already established institutional and societal norms. It must rather provide spaces and opportunities for experimental actions; examine possible, desirable and promising futures; and transcend the present world towards a utopian space of exploration, improvisation and controversial sense making. In this context, Scharmer and Käufer's perspective on the development of the University (as mapped in table 1) can be discomforting or even threatening for some, but it also offers opportunities for re-inventing the university. It helps re-articulate the relationship between science and the public, between knowledge and research, and between academic and non-academic practices. In our opinion, design doctorates are particularly promising for creating and discussing such challenges and opportunities.

Table 1. Three phases of university evolution (Scharmer & Käufer, 2000: 7)

Concept of University	Teaching	Research	Practice
Scholastic middle age university: *Unity of teaching*	Study by lecture: *co-listening, co-thinking*		
Humboldt classical university: *Unity of Research and Teaching*	As above, plus seminar-style studies: *co-speaking*	The individual researcher *in solitude and freedom*, Institutes	
C21 university: *Unity of Praxis, Research and Teaching*	As above, plus infrastructures for *co-initiating, co-creating* and *co-entrepreneuring*	Action research; research consortia, clinical research, community action	Strategic co-creation with companies, consortia, venture capitalists, business incubators

The Scholastic University was focussed on *teaching* a given canon of knowledge in a limited set of disciplines. The Modern University was and is grounded on Humboldt's ideal of the unity of *teaching and research*, in a growing number of academic disciplines and fields. Increasingly, its focus was the generation of knowledge, clearly separated from the rest of the society (in the 'ivory tower'). The limits of this model are obvious today. In response to increased societal complexity, the University is now renewing its conceptual core, beyond mere structural and procedural reform. Humboldt's *Unity of Research and Teaching*, which underpins the classic idea of the University, expands and is re-founded on a new basis.

In the emerging *Next University* (Baecker, 2007), the strict separation from society is eroded and the focus shifts towards the *Unity of Practice, Research and Teaching*. Researchers and teachers abandon their positions as external observers to become active, committed co-designers of social, cultural and economic realities. Research (producing knowledge), teaching (disseminating knowledge) and practice (using knowledge to guide action) can no longer exist separately, nor can technology, design and art. Like it or not, the best we can do is to examine and reflect the dynamics of these developments. For Dirk Baecker, the *Next University* is about empowering students and teachers to deal with a complex society, in which all conceivable knowledge exists in close proximity to its own non-knowledge.

> The competencies the universities are beginning to foster, and the talents that industry, political organisations, the military, churches and cultures are looking for, are competencies and talents that draw their expertise from the fact that they have learned – methodically, theoretically and practically – to deal with not-knowing. Those who cannot do this cannot do anything. But those who can will – on this basis – be able to acquire all conceivable knowledge, without ever confusing it with certainty, and thus running the risk of immediately losing their competence and talents again. (Baecker, 2007: 106-107; our translation)

In a similar vein, Helmut Willke (2002) analyses a perceived crisis of knowledge in many societies and argues that, as in all operations producing or marking distinctions, we have to consider what it is distinguished from in order to understand a concept. This conception of knowledge denotes the unity of knowledge and not-knowledge, if not-knowledge is the counter-concept of knowledge. And if knowledge was opposed to faith in traditional societies, and to power in industrial societies, we are now

> exposed to the cruelty of a concept of knowledge that finds its opposite in neither faith nor fabrication, but in not-knowing itself. This concept of knowledge no longer permits a deportation of not-knowing into the distant realms of transcendental symbolism or the immediacy of forced fabrication. (Willke, 2002: 19; our translation)

Baecker (2000) applies this view to design. He extends Luhmann's (1996) social systems theory, in which humans/persons are conceived as combinations of two closed but connected, *autopoietic* systems, namely bodies and consciousnesses (see Maturana & Varela, 1987). The social is created by a third autopoietic system, which is communication. The autopoietic closure of these three system types means that they cannot control but only perturb each other. They are causally de-coupled, because each of them operates according to its own internal structure and organisation. Thus Baecker argues that design necessarily has to deal with knowledge gaps between these causally de-coupled systems.

ALTERNATIVE DESIGN DOCTORATES AS DRIVERS FOR NEW FORMS OF RESEARCH

> Design as a practice of not-knowing may be read in reference to diverse interfaces, but the interfaces between technology, body, psyche and communication are probably dominant. If these 'worlds', each described by a more or less elaborate knowledge, are brought into a relationship of difference, this knowledge disappears and makes room for experiments, which are the experiments of design. ... Not to take anything for granted here anymore, but to see potential of dissolution and recombination everywhere, becomes the playground of a design that eventually reaches into pedagogy, therapy, and medicine. (Baecker, 2000: 163; our translation)

The idea of the *Next University* and its concomitant perspectives has substantial implications for education and research, on all levels and in all fields of study. Compared to other educational settings and other disciplinary constellations, though, Design doctorates are particularly well positioned to engage with and realise these novel perspectives. Not only are design doctorates methodologically less well defined, and therefore more amenable to experiments and new approaches, there are also several recent intellectual developments in design that help prepare for new approaches.

Internationally, the number of design doctorates has increased over the last decade. However, there is much controversy regarding their form, at least if they claim to follow their own, designerly paradigm of inquiry (e.g., *practice-led, project-grounded, research through design*; for a comparison of these different approaches, see Chow, 2010). In Germany, for instance, traditional academic norms from the Humanities and Sciences are mostly still taken for granted and determine the general procedural and epistemological standards of a PhD in Design. However, the controversy over research paradigms is not specific to Design – it is part and parcel of a larger shift toward the *Next University*, where the new and the conservative collide. Specifically, the concepts of *Mode 2 Knowledge Production* and *Transdisciplinarity* impact alternative design doctorates in the mode of *Research Through Design (RTD)* or *Design Fiction*. As we see it, the latter are associated with a convergence of Science and Design and with an emergence of a *trans-domain*.

SIGNS OF CONVERGENCE BETWEEN SCIENCE AND DESIGN

The academic cultures of the Sciences and the Arts were still very much integrated in the Renaissance. Their separation from the seventeenth century onward finally led to what we know paradigmatically as 'nineteenth century Science' and 'Art School Design'. According to popular opinion, Science produces theoretical knowledge. Design – at best – applies it in practice. Despite many arguments advanced to challenge this black-and-white dualism (and various past efforts to overcome it: e.g., the Bauhaus, the New Bauhaus, the Ulm School, the Design Methods Movement), it still underpins today's prejudices against designerly paradigms of inquiry. Sometimes, the contrast between 'scientific' and 'art school' approaches to design research is even emphasised in order to promote one or the other. Yet, these debates seem rather idle when considering some of the recent intellectual movements in both Science and Design.

Table 2. Convergences of science and design, listed in approximate chronological order

Science → Indications or evidence of the shift of Science towards designerly processes of socially relevant innovation.	← Design Indications or evidence of the shift of Design towards socially robust knowledge creation.
The forgotten controversy at the beginning: Cartesian rationalism vs. Montaigne's scepticism (Toulmin, 1992)	The concept of the *Sciences of the Artificial* (Simon, 1969)
The concept of *problems of organised complexity* (Weaver, 1948)	The strong definition of scientific research as design activity (Glanville, 1980)
The increasing importance of generative and synthetic forms of research in the sciences, for example in engineering, nano- and genetic design (e.g., Pfeifer & Bongard, 2007)	The de-mystification of the creative process as evolutionary (Michl, 2002)
	The importance of design beyond the product: services, systems, organisations, scenarios, social design (e.g., Vezzoli & Manzini, 2008)
Grounded theory building as creative action in the social sciences (Glaser & Strauss, 1967)	The concept of the *trajectories of artificiality* (Krippendorff, 2006)
Evidence generated by empirical laboratory studies (e.g., Knorr-Cetina, 1999, Rheinberger, 2006)	The concepts of *Practice-led Research*, *Project-grounded Research*, and *Research Through Design* (e.g., Jonas, 2007, Findeli, 2008)
STS (Science, Technology and Society) and ANT (Actor-Network Theory): "We have never been modern" (Latour, 1993)	The concept of *Design Thinking* (Brown, 2009)
The emerging concept of *Mode 2 Science* and *Transdisciplinarity Studies* (Nowotny et.al., 2001, Nowotny, 2006)	The approaches of *Design Fiction* (Bleecker 2010, Lukic & Katz, 2010) and *Critical Design* (Dunne & Raby, 2001)
Design-based research in pedagogy, nursing, management, etc. (e.g., Boland & Collopy, 2004)	The exploration of the concept *abduction* in design (Chow & Jonas, 2010b)

On the one hand, the social embeddedness and context-dependency of scientific knowledge production have been widely acknowledged, and there are indications of Science gearing toward a designerly process of innovation and change. On the other hand, the intensity of knowledge production in design has been recognised, and there are signs that Design is moving toward deliberately producing socially robust knowledge. To us, these developments are an indication of a convergence between Design and Science toward a *trans-domain*. Trans-domain is a tentative term for a social and intellectual space and mind set which accommodates trans-disciplinary projects and develops facilities and networks. There is no space here to elaborate all of these tendencies, but we sketch an outline of the theories and concepts in table 2. Furthermore, we will discuss some salient aspects in the following sections: *Research Through Design* and *Design Fiction*, and *Mode 2 Science* and *Transdisciplinarity*. The above table suggests that both Science and Design create socially robust knowledge, though in different ways, and that the two different traditions and cultures converge toward this common goal. The notion of convergence arises from our observation that both traditions share the same underlying process pattern, which might be called *experiential evolutionary learning*.

Experiential Evolutionary Learning as Process Pattern in Design and Sciences

Above we have introduced the notion of *knowledge gaps* between systems and contexts. Herbert Simon (1969) and Christopher Alexander (1964) consider design an appropriate mechanism to build interfaces for bridging these gaps. Furthermore, Baecker (2000) characterised design as the "practice of not-knowing", which tries to bridge the gaps between causally de-coupled systems by means of artefacts. In Bruno Latour's terminology (1993), design creates the *mediators* as active interface agents. There would be no need for design without these gaps, there would be just causal/ functional links or *intermediaries*. These hybrid subject matters, well known to design, are increasingly being dealt with by Science, although Science tends to disregard the specific character of the interfaces between the knowledge gaps. To these different characterisations, we add the temporality of not-knowing, or knowledge gaps between causally de-coupled process phases. With this temporal dimension, socio-cultural developments, including science and design, become visible as evolutionary processes. Or, more precisely, they are a co-evolution of systems in interaction with their contexts. Evolution theory relieves us from the need to assume an Intelligent Artificer at some mysterious point of origin. Utter un-designed-ness, pure chaos was the starting point; no longer are conditions, foundations or final goals required for explanation. We adopt here a generic three-phase pattern of variation-selection-re-stabilisation (Jonas & Meyer-Veden, 2004) and argue that the conscious design process is merely the *variation* phase of an evolutionary trial-and-error process. Design interventions are episodes in the process of evolution. Most of them disappear, and a few are integrated into further systemic development. Failures as well as successes are part of the socio-cultural archive of humankind. By means of research, design and science we try desperately to achieve control of the causally de-coupled *selection-* and *re-stabilisation* phases. This denotes a further set of knowledge gaps, which are shared by design and science. And this is another reason for re-thinking scientific processes from a design perspective.

The evolutionary model of knowledge production assumes far-reaching correspondences between biological, cognitive and cultural structures (Riedl, 2000). These correspondences between basic structures reveal a circular process of trial (based upon expectation) and experience (success or failure, confirmation or refutation), or of action and reflection. The aim of these knowledge production processes cannot be a final, 'true' representation of some external reality, but rather a process of *(re-)construction*, for the purpose of appropriate *(re-)action*. Starting with past cases, an inductive/heuristic semi-cycle leads from the purposeful learning from experience to hypotheses, theories and prognoses about how the world works. It is followed by a deductive/logical semi-circle that leads to actions and interventions, which result in new experiences that confirm or refute existing experiences or theories, etc. Internal or external perturbations (called ideas, creativity, accidents, environmental changes, etc.) influence the cycle, leading to stabilisations (negative feedback) or amplifications and evolutionary developments (positive feedback). One of the most prominent process patterns of this type is Kolb's (1984) experiential learning model, which also conceives of an inductive and a deductive semi-cycle. The pattern finds application in various fields, especially in design methods (see, for example Owen, 1998). Yet, these models have a severe deficit: they do not account for the essential step of *creating the new*. They neglect abduction, which we take to be the central mechanism of knowledge generation in everyday life, design, and science. There is, therefore, a need for models that explicitly acknowledge the creative phase and provide a theoretical framework for *Research Through Design* *(RTD)*. Table 3 below illustrates this claim.

Another strand of argument emphasises the importance of empirical processes in the generation of knowledge. The pragmatist John Dewey (1986) argues that the separation of thinking, as pure contemplation, and acting, as bodily intervention into the world, is obsolete: thinking depends on real world situations that have to be met. The active, intentional improvement of an unsatisfactory, problematic situation is the primary motivation for thinking, designing, and, finally – in a more refined, purified, quantitative manner – for scientific knowledge production. The achievement of expected consequences is the measurement of success. According to Dewey, knowing is a manner of acting and "truth" is better called "warranted assertibility" (Dewey, 1941: 169-186). Dewey's perspectives come close to what we argue to be emerging forms of design research and a convergence of design and science.

Research through Design (RTD) & Design Fiction: Designerly
Manifestation of Convergence

Design Research, like Design, is intended to improve the probability of good fit between co-evolving systems. We propose *Research Through Design* (*RTD*, Frayling 1993, Jonas, 2007) as a typical methodological model for this project. Similar to *Mode 2 Science* and *Transdisciplinarity Studies*, *RTD* is a situated/contextualised, transdisciplinary three-stage process aiming to improve problematic situations through knowledge generation.

In table 3, which juxtaposes some related concepts, the argument for convergence is implicit: various "Sciences of the Artificial", such as Design (Jones, 1970, Archer, 1981, Nelson & Stolterman, 2003, Jonas, 2007), Management Studies (Weick, 1969, Simon, 1969), and Human-Computer Interaction (Fallman, 2008) reveal the same pattern.

Table 3. Triadic concepts of experiential learning processes in design research, especially providing the framework for Research Through Design and Transdisciplinarity Studies

Authors	Phases / components / domains of knowing in design research		
Jones (1970)	Divergence	Transformation	Convergence
Archer (1981)	Science	Design	Arts
Simon (1969) Weick (1969)	Intelligence	Design	Choice
Jonas (2007)	*Analysis*	*Projection*	*Synthesis*
Fallman (2008)	Design Studies	Design Exploration	Design Practice
Brown (2009)	Inspiration	Ideation	Implementation
Nicolescu (2002) Transdisciplinarity	System knowledge	Target knowledge	Transformation knowledge

In designerly methodological terms, we speak of *Analysis*, *Projection* and *Synthesis*, which articulate the *RTD* process. The essentially 'designerly' competences are located in the middle column. The overall process of *RTD* integrates *Analysis* (science) and *Synthesis* ('normal design') by means of *Projection*, which is underpinned by abductive reasoning (Chow & Jonas, 2010a and b). There is a striking structural resemblance of *RTD* to the basic processes in *Transdisciplinarity Studies* (Nicolescu, 2002), which integrate system knowledge, target knowledge and transformation knowledge. Bredies, whose doctoral thesis we will elaborate below, employs an *RTD* approach.

Projection and transdisciplinarity are key elements in *Design Fiction*, though they are conceptualised in different terms. *Design Fiction* (Bleecker, 2010) presumes that design is to re-think and re-imagine what can be possible. *Design Fiction* bundles, assembles, relates and integrates the qualities of multiple disciplines; it questions assumptions about what the present and the future are about, what they contain, and what counts as an advancement toward a better, more habitable future world. *Design Fiction* thus tells stories through design.

It creates material artefacts that start conversations and suspend one's disbelief in what could be. It's a way of imagining a different kind of world by outlining the contours, rendering the artifacts as story props, using them to imagine new possibilities ... (Bleecker, 2010: 62).

In this perspective, "science and design and fact and fiction collapse together. They all wonder what a world would be like, if …" (63). *Design Fiction* approaches have recently been implemented in design education at Masters level (for example at the Royal College of Art in London), or they are about to be implemented in future programmes (for example at the HGK Basel), which are typically located in the area of design & interaction. The design of 'interactions' implies a focus on interfaces between humans and machines, disciplines, knowledge domains, societal interests, or epistemic cultures. At PhD level, these programmes have the potential to cultivate transdisciplinary competences, drawing on in-depth knowledge of several knowledge domains. They can stimulate discussion of and reflection on multiple methodological, epistemological and theoretical premises; develop effective transdisciplinary projects; and establish specific initiatives at the interfaces of different actors (human and non-human) requiring intense relationship building.

Mode 2 Science and Transdisciplinarity: Scientific Manifestation of Convergence

Helga Nowotny (2006) emphasises transdisciplinarity as a central feature of *Mode 2 Science*. *Mode 2* denotes a new form of knowledge production, which started to emerge in the mid-twentieth century (Scott et.al., 1994). It involves the assembly of multidisciplinary teams to address specific real-world problems. While *Mode 1* knowledge production is academic, investigator-initiated and disciplinary-based, *Mode 2* is problem-focused, context-driven and interdisciplinary. *Transdisciplinarity* concerns that which is at the same time between the disciplines, across the disciplines, and beyond each individual discipline. According to Häberli et.al., "The core idea of transdisciplinarity is different academic disciplines working jointly with practitioners to solve a real-world problem. It can be applied in a great variety of fields." (2001, p.4) Like in *Mode 2 Science*, the goal is to understand and change the present world. When the very nature of a problem is under dispute, transdisciplinarity can help generate relevant problems and research questions. In our schema of *Analysis*, *Projection* and *Synthesis*, the first type of question might address the causes of present problems and their future development (system knowledge/*Analysis*). The second type concerns the values and norms that define the goals of problem-solving processes (target knowledge/*Projection*). The third type relates to the potential transformations and improvements of a problematic situation (transformation knowledge/*Synthesis*). When addressing the fundamental gaps between knowledge types, transdisciplinarity strives to deal adequately with the complexity of problems by integrating diverse and often contradictory perceptions without destroying them. Furthermore, it utilises and links general and case-specific knowledge.

So far, we have not distinguished clearly between *Mode 2* and *Transdisciplinarity* – which perhaps reflects a typical German use of the concept of transdisciplinarity, as it is represented by Nowotny (2006). Yet, there are more comprehensive and more radical conceptions. Basarab Nicolescu (2008), for example, suggests three *Axioms* of *Transdisciplinarity*, which explicitly address the knowledge gaps between the different levels of reality and the perceiving subject:

- The *ontological axiom*: in nature and society, as well as in our perception of and knowledge about them, there are *different levels of reality* for the subject, which correspond to different levels of the object.
- The *logical axiom*: the transition from one level of reality to another is vouchsafed by the *logic of the included* third.
- The *epistemological axiom*: the structure of the totality of all levels of reality is *complex*; each level is determined by the simultaneous existence of all other levels.

Open Transdisciplinarity, as suggested by Valerie Brown (2010), goes a step further and implies the equal practice of various heterogeneous knowledge cultures in a collective learning/designing process. Here, specialised (scientific) knowledge is just one of several possible types:

- *Individual knowledge*: Own lived experience, lifestyle choices, learning style, identity. Content: identity, reflections, ideas.
- *Local community knowledge*: Shared lived experience of individuals, families, businesses, communities. Content: stories, events, histories.
- *Specialised knowledge*: Environment and health science, finance, engineering, law, philosophy, etc. Content: case studies, experiments.
- *Organisational knowledge*: Organisational governance, policy development, legislation, market. Content: agendas, alliances, planning.
- *Holistic knowledge*: Core of the matter, vision of the future, a common purpose, aim of sustainability. Content: symbol, vision, ideal.

In addition to these aspects, *trans-domain* thinking also suggests a conceptual shift from thinking in ontologically fixed *categories* to epistemologically more flexible *topics*. This is a radical shift that we do not expect 'normal' Science to follow. It has no need to do so. Furthermore, the concept is controversial. For example, John Ziman (2010) concurs with the diagnosis of an emerging *Mode 2* Science but warns of the deterioration of scientific standards.

Trans-Domain

The convergence of Science and Design does not mean that two original components merge into one and disappear in the process. Rather, a *trans-domain* emerges, a new intellectual mind-set, which allows a multitude of approaches in-between – the beauty of grey between the fundamentalist poles of pure black and pure white. Individual sub-domains will undoubtedly include elements of *Mode 1 Science* and traditional disciplines.

We introduce the concept *trans-domain* to create an experimental space for discussions of transdisciplinarity, research through design, not-knowing and other, not yet solidified or substantiated aspects of a new intellectual tendency. The provisional character of this *trans-domain* allows for a multitude of alternative approaches, including the preservation of traditional disciplines and their interactions. In line with this perspective, Ranulph Glanville, in his farsighted, classical paper "Why design research?" (1980), conceives of *research as a design activity* and regarded scientific research as a sub-discipline of design research. This conception lends support to our hypothesis that design research will be the principal paradigm of the *trans-domain*:

> Under these circumstances, the beautiful activity that is science will no longer be seen as mechanistic, except in retrospect. It will truly be understood honestly, as a great creative and social design activity, one of the true social arts. And its paradigm will be recognised as being design (Glanville, 1980: 93).

In our *trans-domain*, it is imperative for design researchers to develop and reflect on their own specific knowledge production processes, rather than fetishizing Science. Design and Science may then produce fruitful interconnections that have the potential of leading to new, appropriate structures and processes in various fields. In this process, we argue that it is *Projection* that integrates science and design and is thus instrumental to establishing the *Mode 2 Science* model.

Table 4. The topology of the trans-domain. Mode 2 Science and Transdisciplinarity link Design and Science by means of Projection.

	Analysis *Induction*	*Projection* *Abduction*	*Synthesis* *Deduction*
Design Practice or *Normal Design*			… just address a given brief
Scientific Research or *Mode 1 Science*	… does not aim at change		
Mode 2 Science Transdisciplinarity, RTD, Design Fiction	System knowledge	Target knowledge	Transformation knowledge

FACTS AND VALUES – ETHICS AND *TRANS-DOMAIN*

Our proposal of a *trans-domain* is bound up with issue of facts and values since ethics is implicit in the practice of *trans-domain*: the processing of target knowledge immediately implies the question of values. Critics query whether this is 'proper' research. De Zeeuw (2010), who argues in favour of the 'trans-' concept, points out that approaches such as action and evidence-based research, or those involving soft-systems, *Mode 2* form of knowledge or *RTD*, are criticised because they permit observations as well as judgements. In this regard, Chad Lykins suggests that a more direct link between social science and societal progress could be forged if "the relationship between facts and values" was better understood.

Experts and laypersons will deal with each other in one way or another. Matters will be left private or managed publically. And these interactions will produce consequences, some pleasing and others not. The more we can know about these consequences and how to control them, the more we can speak intelligently about them. (2009)

At this point, it is worth recalling three major positions on the relations between facts and values, which render visible the historical and artificial character of their separation. The distinction between facts and values was prominently proposed by Max Weber (1864-1920), who conceived of sociology as a science that was given the task of understanding and causally explaining social action and its conditions and effects. Weber conceded that social inquiry arises from concrete needs and values, yet he argued that sociology cannot tell us what should be. For another founding father of sociology, Émile Durkheim (1858-1917), social facts and structures determine human action and establish matters of fact. They can be discovered by the sociologist by using methods and epistemic standards of natural science. Science can provide a way of evaluating value-claims objectively.

In contrast to both Weber and Durkheim, the pragmatist philosopher John Dewey (1859-1952) argued that facts (means) und values (ends) are interdependent and that they are different only in degree:

> One involves taking things as they are, the other involves taking things in their relations to antecedents and consequences. ... The difference between the scientific study of natural as opposed to social questions is due to the degree of complexity of the relations under investigation ... (Lykins, 2009).

Dewey's position is relevant to ours insofar as we want to overcome the facts-values separation that creates a rift between social sciences and the public. Transdisciplinarity, at least in its strong interpretation, includes non-experts in research and in the design of social transformation. If, as Dewey argued, the standards for judging means cannot be furnished from outside, and if the criteria for evaluating ends comes *from within* the *situation itself*, epistemic heterogeneity has to be taken as the essential condition for any socially relevant inquiry. Accordingly, Anderson (2006) argues for the epistemic benefits of democracy, for example, even though she clearly realises the problems of a public trying to understand and respond to its own problems.

Dewey contended already in 1916 that the lay/expert question is best posed as an educational and social problem of enabling a citizenry to conduct their own social inquiry, involving heterogeneous *knowledges* that integrate facts and values. Today, Latour (2003, 2004) claims that scientific and political debate should take place in a common space. He discusses "collective socio-scientific experiments" that are no longer conducted in an isolated laboratory but involve wider communities, and in some cases the whole world population. And he proposes specific protocols of conduct for each individual problem. Similarly, Gerard de Zeeuw suggests a "hybrid" form of research for social intervention that makes use of observations as well as judgement, without ignoring the distinctions between them. This new form of research should "include the dilemma as part of its knowledge production" (De Zeeuw, 2010: 8). To incorporate judgements in research, though,

> would require the ability to create judgement systems that resemble recognition systems. One example would be a collective whose members decide which values to assign and which values to include in order to maintain and defend their decisions (13).

Research that includes judgemental contributions is often processual and evolutionary. In this process, *autopoietic closure* can create a collective that is an observing and acting system (Luhmann, 1990). Judgement then becomes an integral part of the knowledge-producing system, and the research problems, aims, ethics, etc., need not be stated externally. This means a shift from satisfying needs that have been observed and diagnosed by outside experts and/or authorities (including designers and scientists) towards enabling people/groups/nations to become social actors who define their own preferred states. Alexander Christakis (1996) suggests a "people science", which performs a "'shift' from an individual-centred conception of knowledge and understanding to one that is socially-based". Similarly, John Chris Jones introduces the internet-based notion of "creative democracy",

> a vision of the future in which the controlling roles and functions of Modern life could be shared with everyone ... a virtual planet earth ... an expanded version of the internet through which 'universal despecialisation' and 'creative democracy' and other such unexpected conditions are already implicit if not active (Jones, 1999: 407).

In this context, *Research Through Design* as a concept can be the methodological basis for *Social Transformation Design* processes and even a model of designerly inquiry that supports "epistemic democracy" (Anderson, 2006). The generation of knowledge by collectives, and the inclusion of various knowledge types including judgement, results in more complex research situations and therefore implies the necessity of increased reflection and carefulness in meeting the standards of research.

STRANGE SHAPES AND UNEXPECTED FORMS

We now return to Bredies' doctoral research, which might be presented as a manifestation of the core issues of our theoretical discussion. The separation of science from design, research from practice, and facts from values are bridged in her thesis through *RTD*; overcoming the centuries-old dualistic worldview toward a new intellectual posture – what we have called *trans-domain*.

ALTERNATIVE DESIGN DOCTORATES AS DRIVERS FOR NEW FORMS OF RESEARCH

Doctoral design research is relatively young and, until recently, most design dissertations have tended to follow either sciences or humanities approaches and methodologies to explain or interpret existing phenomena. Although Bredies also draws on social science theory, namely Niklas Luhmann's systems theory to conceptualise innovative design as systemic irritation, she does so not to verify the validity of Luhmann's theory, as social scientists would do. Rather, she tests it for its potential to open new ways of thinking or perceiving the idea of *Design-in-Use (DiU)*. In other words, she mainly uses it for projection rather than analysis.

Following Luhmann, she takes artefacts to be perturbations for closed and causally de-coupled autopoietic systems. Human reactions are regarded as unpredictable in Luhmann's theory, because bodies, consciousnesses and communications proceed according to their own internal structure and dynamics. Adopting this knowledge (or hypothesis), Bredies proposes to view interface de-familiarisation as irritation, or a source of innovative design. Her principal research question is: which kinds of design irritation (in the form of interface strategies) make an artefact suitable for creative appropriation in use.

It is important to note that her research question is fundamentally a design question in that it seeks new relations, rather than describing or explaining existing relations between two variables. In order to answer her research question, she must therefore invent and design different kinds of interface strategies that 'perturb' people. At this juncture, Bredies leaves social scientific theoretical discussion behind and returns to design. To conceptualise different 'irritating' interface strategies, she first draws on design theories to create meaningful distinctions – formal, contextual, structural and processual. Based on these distinctions, she experiments with electronic textiles, a new technological materiality, to design and make experimental products that embody these distinctions (see figure 1). It must be mentioned that, without former design training on her part, this part of the research would have been very difficult to achieve. Imagination, aesthetic sensibility, and the ability to think through materials are essential, not to mention other practical skills like sewing and weaving. It should be obvious by now that her project places design knowing and practical knowledge on par with scientific theory, and that the integration of these types of knowledge is a key characteristic of her approach.

With these experimental objects in place, Bredies once again draws on social scientific methodology to conduct 'meaning reconstruction sessions' with ordinary people in a studio or at their home. As in *Participatory Action Research*, the research participants are actively involved as they step out of their normal life to 'play' with the experimental objects and to create new meanings. Bredies relies on their capacity and imagination, without which no new insights can arise. In contrast to traditional research, participants not only describe the known here, but also venture into the unknown, together with the researcher. Bredies is now in the process of analysing the research results and developing principles for designing for *DiU*.

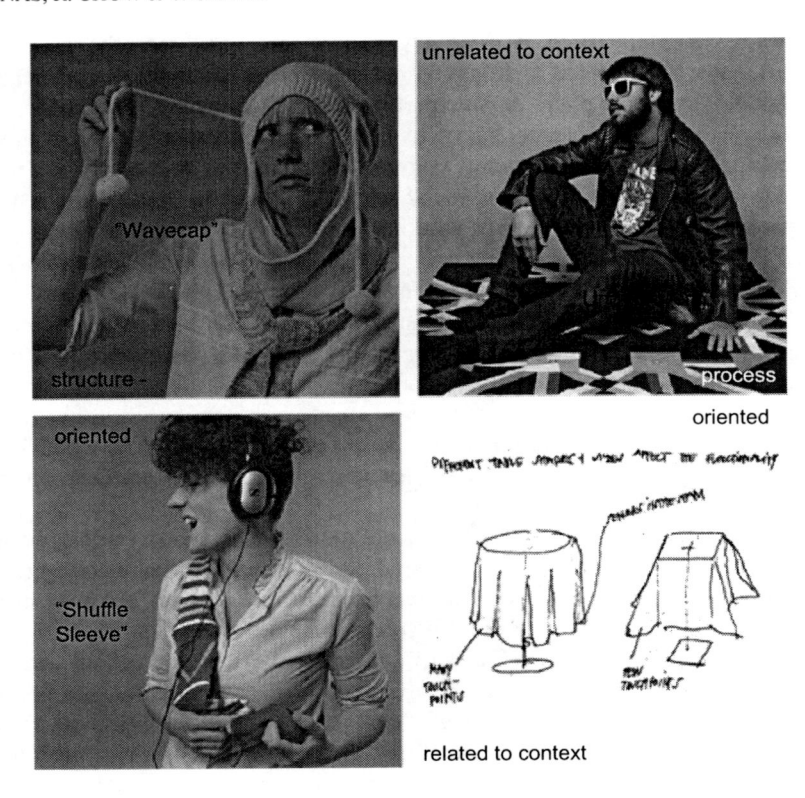

Figure 1. Matrix of 'irritating' interfaces (Bredies).

CONCLUSIONS AND IMPLICATIONS

The current development of design research is not only an opportunity to re-invent scientific research in relation to design, but also to re-invent our understanding of design in relation to scientific research and designerly practices. It provides the great chance and the potential of bridging the chasm between theory and practice. Accordingly, non-traditional epistemological approaches gain importance. The relation to practice is changing. Laboratory studies in the Natural and Engineering Sciences reveal design-like processes in these fields and the relationship between rigour and relevance of inquiry becomes increasingly delicate. Furthermore, the debates concerning the conceptualisation of 'design' are manifold, thus opening up new possibilities – not only for design study but also design practise – for instance by identifying artefacts *and* activities as design objectives. Particularly in the German context, with its relatively short history of Design PhDs, we are open to actively challenge the limits that are posed by too rigid and inappropriate standards adopted uncritically from the Sciences.

Yet, these changes require new standards and procedures that go beyond the established, traditional ones. New forms of research have to be explored. These challenges are essentially design tasks. In view of the emerging *trans-domain*, we suggest, it is imperative for design researchers to develop, test and reflect on their own specific processes of knowledge production, in order to contribute – from their perspective and expertise – to new, productive interconnections with scientific research.

The most important implication of this paradigm shift for doctoral supervisors and students is that they ought to invent new theoretical frameworks, strategies, approaches and methods. In other words, we suggest that they need to practice in research what they preach in practice. Inventing new doctorates should be treated as a design process with the following objectives:

Dealing with not-knowing: In contrast to the idealised model of the laboratory, which simplifies or neglects the messiness of the condition of inquiry, we have to establish experiential settings that allow productive interactions among diverse participants and positions in the process of inquiry. This would preserve the complexity that calls for original, rich and dynamic solutions. By implication, questions would not be finally formulated at the beginning of research, but rather be iteratively developed through a series of reflection and action, in some ways similar to Grounded Theory inquiries.

Transdisciplinarity: We need to overcome taken-for-granted dualisms and value hierarchies to facilitate the interaction of multiple or even contradictory perspectives and approaches. That way, we would provide the conditions for describing complex situations and problems adequately. For example, lay people would collaborate with experts; practice would be blended with theory, 'soft' sciences with 'hard' sciences, making with thinking, iconic with symbolic signs, projection with analysis; there would be greater integration in research of body and mind, Indigenous and Western knowledge, material and cognitive thinking, and old and new media.

Research ethics: Ethical considerations need to be integral and essential parts of all research processes, and facts and values have to be appropriately integrated. This implies reflecting on and making explicit research participants' involvement in the process, i.e., in the design and implementation of research. Rigour and relevance will be combined in new ways to exploit designerly ways of inquiry by representing, visualising and documenting the design process to enable diverse communities to trace and ground research results. These results need to be couched in a language that is inclusive and encourages the participation of the public.

These aspects are not to be confused with criteria for the judgment of the quality of doctoral theses. Rather, they are offered here as an encouragement for pursuing alterative doctorates.

NOTE

[1] Since only recently the COST programme of the European Union invites "Trans-Domain Proposals", see http://www.cost.eu/domains_actions/TDP.

REFERENCES

Alexander, C. (1964). *Notes on the Synthesis of Form*. Cambridge, MA: Harvard University Press.
Anderson, E. (2006). The Epistemology of Democracy. *Episteme*, *3*(1–2), 8–22.
Archer, B. (1981). A View of the Nature of Design Research. In R. Jacques & and J. Powell (Eds.), *Design:Science:Method* (pp. 30–47). Guildford, England: Westbury House.
Baecker, D. (2000). Wie steht es mit dem Willen Allahs? *Zeitschrift für Rechtssoziologie*, *21*(1), 145–176.
Baecker, D. (2007). Die nächste Universität. In *Studien zur nächsten Gesellschaft* (pp. 98–115). Frankfurt a.M., Germany: Suhrkamp.
Bammé, A. (2009). *Science and Technology Studies. Ein* Überblick. Marburg, Germany: Metropolis-Verlag.
Bleecker, J. (2010). Design Fiction: From Props to Prototypes. In Swiss Design Network (Ed.), *Negotiating Futures – Design Fiction* (pp. 58–67). Basel, Switzerland: HBK Basel.
Boland, R. & Collopy, F. (Eds.). (2004). *Managing as Designing*. Stanford, CA: Stanford Business Books.
Lukic, B. & Katz, B. M. (2010). *Nonobject*. Cambridge, MA: MIT Press.
Brown, T. (2009). *Change by design: How design thinking transforms organizations and inspires innovation*. New York, NY: Harper Business.
Brown, V. A. (2010). Collective inquiry and its wicked problems. In V. A Brown, J.A. Harris, & J.Y. Russell (Eds.), *Tackling wicked problems through the transdisciplinary imagination* (pp. 61–83). London, England: Earthscan.
Chow, R. (2010). What should be done with the different versions of Research Through Design. In C. Mareis, G. Joost, & K. Kimpel (Eds.), *Entwerfen. Wissen. Produzieren. Designforschung im Anwendungskontext* (pp. 145–158). Bielefeld, Germany: Transcript Verlag.
Chow, R. & Jonas, W. (2010a). Far beyond dualisms in methodology – an integrative design research medium 'MAPS'. In: *Proceedings of DRS conference Design&Complexity*. Montréal, Canada, 2010.
Chow, R. & Jonas, W. (2010b) Case transfer: A design approach by artefacts and projection. In: *Design Issues*: Volume 26, Number 4 Autumn 2010, 9–19.
Christakis, A. N. (1996). A people science: The CogniScope™ systems approach. In: *SYSTEMS*, *1*(1), Retrieved from http://sunsite.utk.edu/FINS/loversofdemocracy/PeopleScience.htm.
Dewey, J. (1916). *Democracy and education*. New York, NY: The Macmillan Company.
Dewey, J. (1941) Propositions, Warranted Assertibility, and Truth. In: *The Journal of Philosophy*, Vol. 38, No. 7 (Mar. 27, 1941), 169–186
Dewey, J. (1986). *Logic: The theory of inquiry*. Carbondale, IL: Southern Illinois University Press.
De Zeeuw, G. (2010). Research to support social interventions. *Journal of Social Intervention: Theory and Practice*, *19*(2), 4–24.
Dunne, A. & Raby, F. (2001). *Design noir: The secret life of electronic objects*. Basel, Switzerland: Birkhäuser Verlag.
Fallman, D. (2008). The interaction design research triangle of design practice, design studies, and design exploration. *Design Issues*, *24*(3), 4–18.
Findeli, A. (2008). Research through design and transdisciplinarity: A tentative contribution to the methodology of design research. In: *Proceedings of Focused, Swiss Design Network Symposium* (pp. 67–91). Berne, Switzerland.
Frayling, C. (1993). Research in art and design. London, England: Royal College of Art.
Glanville, R. (1980). Why design research? In: R. Jacques & A. Powell (Eds.), *Design: Science: Method* (pp. 86–94). Guildford, England: Westbury House.
Glaser, B. G. & Strauss, A. L. (1967). *The discovery of grounded theory. Strategies for qualitative research*. New York, NY: Aldine de Gruyter.
Grand, S. & Jonas, W. (Eds.). (2012). *Mapping design research*. Basel, Switzerland: Birkhäuser Verlag.

Häberli, R., Grossenbacher-Mansui, W. & Klein, J.T. (2001). Summary. In: J.T. Klein et al. (Eds.), *Transdisciplinarity: Joint problem solving among science, technology and society* (p. 4). Basel, Switzerland: Birkhäuser.
Jonas, W. & Meyer-Veden, J. (2004). *Mind the gap! – On knowing and not-knowing in design*. Bremen, Germany: Hauschild Verlag.
Jonas, W. (2007). Research through DESIGN through research – A cybernetic model of designing design foundations. In: *Kybernetes*, 36(9/10 - special issue on cybernetics and design), 1362–1380.
Jones, J. C. (1970). *Design Methods: seeds of human futures*. London, England: John Wiley & Sons.
Jones, J. C. (1999). The internet and everyone. London, England: Ellipsis.
Knorr-Cetina, K. (1999). Epistemic *cultures. How the sciences make knowledge*. Cambridge, MA: Harvard University Press.
Kolb, D. A. (1984). *Experiential learning: experience as the source of learning and development*. New York, NY: Prentice-Hall.
Koskinen, I., Zimmerman, J., Binder, T., Redstrom, J., & Wensveen, S. (2011). *Design research through practice. From the lab, field and showroom*. Waltham, MA: Morgan Kaufmann.
Krippendorff, K. (2006). *The semantic turn*. Boca Raton, FL: Taylor & Francis Group.
Latour, B. (1993). *We have never been modern*. Cambridge, MA: Harvard University Press. (French: 1991)
Latour, B. (2003, 17 November). Assembly or assemblage? Politics and polytechnics. A lecture at Politecnico di Milano. Retrieved from http://www.fondazionebassetti.org/06/argomenti/2004_01.htm#000203
Latour, B. (2004). *Politics of nature. How to bring the sciences into democracy*. Cambridge, MA: Harvard University Press.
Luhmann, N. (1990). Essays on Self-Reference. New York, NY: Columbia University Press.
Luhmann, N. (1996). Social Systems. Stanford, CA: Stanford University Press.
Lukic, B. & Katz, B.M. (2010) Nonobject, Cambridge, MA: The MIT Press.
Lykins, C. (2009). Social science and the moral life. In *Society for the Advancement of American Philosophy Annual Conference*. Retrieved from http://www.philosophy.uncc.edu/mleldrid/SAAP/TAMU/P39G.htm
Maturana, H. R., & Varela, F. J. (1987). *The tree of knowledge: The biological roots of human understanding* (R. Paolucci, Trans.). Boston, MA: Shambhala.
Michl, J. (2002). On Seeing Design as Redesign. An Exploration of a Neglected Problem in Design Education. Dept of Industrial Design, Oslo School of Architecture, Norway, http://www.designaddict.com/essais/michl.html, retrieved 10 December 2012.
Nelson, H. G. & Stolterman, E. (2003). *The design way. Intentional change in an unpredictable world*. Englewood Cliffs, NJ: Educational Technology Publications.
Nicolescu, B. (2002). *Manifesto of transdisciplinarity*. Albany, NY: State University of New York Press.
Nicolescu, B. (2008). *Transdisciplinarity: Theory and practice*. New York, NY: Hampton Press.
Nowotny, H. (2006). The potential of transdisciplinarity. *interdisciplines* (May).
Nowotny, H., Scott, P. & Gibbons, M. (2001). *Re-thinking science. Knowledge and the public in the age of uncertainty*. Cambridge, UK: Polity Press.
Pfeifer, R. & Bongard, J. (2007). *How the body shapes the way we think*. Cambridge, MA: MIT Press.
Owen, C. (1998) Design research: Building the knowledge base. *Design Studies, 19*, 9–20.
Rheinberger, H. J. (2006). *Experimentalsysteme und epistemische Dinge. Die Geschichte der Proteinsynthese im Reagenzglas*. Frankfurt a.M., Germany: Suhrkamp.
Riedl, R. (2000). *Strukturen der Komplexität. Eine Morphologie des Erkennens und Erklärens*. Berlin, Germany: Springer.
Scharmer, O. & Käufer, K. (2000). *Universities as the birthplace for the entrepreneuring human being*. Retrieved from http://ottoscharmer.com/docs/articles/2000_Uni21us.pdf
Scott, P., Gibbons, M., Nowotny, H., Limoges, C., Trow, M., & Schwartzman, S. (1994). *The new production of knowledge: The dynamics of science and research in contemporary societies*. London, England: Sage.
Simon, H. A. (1969). *The sciences of the artificial*. Cambridge, MA: MIT Press.

Weick, K. (1969). *Social psychology of organizing*. Reading, MA: Addison Wesley.
Telier, A. (2011). *Design Things*. Cambridge, MA: The MIT Press.
Toulmin, S. (1992). *Cosmopolis: Hidden agenda of modernity*. Chicago, IL: Chicago University Press.
Tröndle, M. & Warmers, J. (Eds.). (2011). *Kunstforschung als ästhetische Wissenschaft. Beiträge zur transdisziplinären Hybridisierung von Wissenschaft und Kunst*. Bielefeld, Germany: Transcript Verlag.
Vezzoli, C. & Manzini, E. (2008). *Design for Environmental Sustainability*. London, England: Springer.
Weaver, W. (1948). Science and Complexity. *American Scientist, 36*, 536–544.
Willke, H. (2002). *Dystopia. Studien zur Krisis des Wissens in der modernen Gesellschaft*. Frankfurt a.M., Germany: Suhrkamp.
Ziman, J. (2000). *Real science. What it is, and what it means*. Cambridge, England: Cambridge University Press.

AFFILIATIONS

Wolfgang Jonas, HBK (University of Arts) Braunschweig, Germany
Rosan Chow, HdK (University of Arts) Berlin, Germany
Simon Grand, University of St. Gallen, Switzerland

ROSS JENNER

12. THOUGHT OUT OF BOUNDS

Theory and Practice in Architecture Doctorates

INTRODUCTION

Two different, but not unrelated, sets of issues are worthy of question in architecture supervision today. Firstly, non-traditional research, particularly creative practice- or project-led PhDs, which flush out the question of the very core of the discipline: acts of design and making. Since acceptance into universities well over a century ago, architecture has not been articulated at the PhD level, except via the disciplines of science, engineering, construction, fabrication, history and theory or, generally, what is termed *research for practice*. In a sense, this means that the core of what architects actually do has traditionally been precluded, isolated or put out of bounds as a field capable, and even worthy, of being treated in the manner appropriate to a PhD. How then to frame design as itself a mode of thinking? How to return the excluded to the core, to turn the outside in? How, in other words, to let design think in and from its own place?

Secondly, students' first languages, cultures and epistemological frameworks increasingly derive not from the Western world, but apart from and often quite outside it. Hence arises another set of questions, which are not easily assimilated to 'traditional' thinking and research practices. How to let students admit modes of thought, art and practice that are so intimately part of themselves but often seem incompatible with the academy? Even prior to this, however, is the issue of letting become visible and open to conceptualisation that which cannot be translated or thought outside of their cultures.

Both these sets of questions involve letting happen what has previously been out of bounds in traditional doctorates: the very things closest to the discipline and to the heart of the student. In the process, they provide fruitful encounters and reversals.

DOES PROJECT-LED RESEARCH IN ARCHITECTURE REALLY CONSTITUTE A NON-TRADITIONAL DOCTORATE?

It might be thought that, since project-led and practice-based PhDs in architecture have been in existence for a decade, they might now be regarded as traditional approaches to the doctorate. The field, is however, still contested – even in the UK, and Scandinavia, whence it sprang. Further, most discussion remains only

A.-Chr. Engels-Schwarzpaul and M. A. Peters (Eds.), Of other Thoughts: Non-Traditional Ways to the Doctorate: A Guidebook for Candidates and Supervisors, 203–220.
© *2013 Sense Publishers. All rights reserved.*

descriptive and prescriptive.[1] Little, it might be suggested, has been done to argue or shape the degree in theoretical or pedagogical terms. The move to project-led and practice-based PhDs has been accompanied mostly by business plans and institutional self-promotion. Almost as a consequence, discussions of the relation between practice and theory in the Fine Arts and other disciplines quickly become bogged down in questions of the legitimacy of practice-led research (Groat, 2002; Gray, 2004). Architecture, however, has had a long-standing tradition of design theses as the conclusion of professional degrees, usually accompanied by a report, and often, theoretical writing. Following the Bologna agreement, this now takes place at the Master of Architecture (MArch Professional) level, which in Australasia has been shaped largely by academic requirements that the thesis be presented as research – even though the degree is subject to accreditation by the profession. And yet, in many institutions the regulations governing the new PhD provide guidelines for the written part by little more than word count.[2]

Arguing against moving architectural design into the realm of research degrees, Stanford Anderson distinguishes between *discipline* and *practice*. He poses the MArch as the graduating professional degree, beyond which the Ph.D. must remain purely a research degree (Anderson, 2001). For Anderson, architectural practice and the discipline of architecture intersect but cannot become one. This dichotomy still rules the prescription of the new doctorate – design *plus* writing – and governs most discussion on creative PhD supervision. I would suggest it dates back to the practice/theory split that occurred at the beginning of Greek philosophy in the separation of *tekhné* and *poiésis* from *épistémé*. More precisely, it is manifested in the philosopher's accusation in Plato's *Sophist* regarding the instrumentalisation of the *logos* as rhetoric: instrument of power and renunciation of knowledge. Since this conflict, Bernard Stiegler, for one, argues all technical/artistic knowledge has been devalued (1998: 1). Another consequence, via Plato's theory of Ideas, is that an intelligible sphere extracted – or purified – from the milieu of the sensible holds sway. How then to admit, or might it even be said to restore, questions of skill, craft, play, invention, imagination, making, design and art to academia without simply splitting off everything that conforms with ratiocination by discarding the poetics of making and creativity, which must themselves be held to be forms of thought?

One of the principal forces behind the academicization of artistic and architectural practices in the UK was the legal incorporation of polytechnics as universities, resulting in both the need and opportunity to compare the creative arts with other university disciplines. Little more than a decade ago, there was scarcely mention of research in the creative arts, and it was the subject of discourse in only a limited number of countries: the UK, Australia and Scandinavia. By and large, art and design were ahead of architecture. Practice-based and project-led PhD theses in architecture were accepted into the fold of academia perhaps last of all. By the late 1990s, the concept that design itself might constitute research had not yet entered into Holt's *Guide* (1998).[3]

WHAT IS ARCHITECTURAL RESEARCH?

In the seventeenth century *research* meant "a strict enquiry"; the word deriving from the Old French *recerche*, "a diligent search", which derives, in turn, from the Latin *circare*, to circulate, go around, go about (see Skeat, 1888: 504 and Partridge, 2006: 515). The *re-* of research does not necessarily imply repetition, and certainly not scientific repeatability, rather, *intensification*: systematicity and thoroughness. This does not necessarily exclude, however, a lot of wandering around in circles. Research aims at the discovery or creation of something new, hence, changing and resituating knowledge. What is new is evaluated by proof: literature review, exhibition or display, all of which must be made publicly available, rendering newness identifiable and subject to authorial claim. Research must demonstrate an originality and make some contribution to knowledge such as would be recognizable in other disciplines (see Biggs & Büchler, 2007: 66-67).

If there is a separate category of research, which goes by the name of *architectural research*, it can only be guided by the conceptions and questions that arise from its discipline. Yet, traditionally, architectural theses approach topics by methods derived from science, technics, history, aesthetics, philosophy, etc. Already in the earliest extant treatise on architecture, Vitruvius argued that the architect must be skilled in many areas of knowledge, all of which in today's terms require the observation and taking account of their respective research criteria (1970: I.J.3). These are researches *for* design, which are required in order to design, but they leave untouched the whole issue of research *by* and *as* design, which may or may not be seen as separate categories. If designing, that is, practising, is *not* a separate category of research in general, then the normal criterion of research: question(s) posed and answered – here *in* and *by* designing – would apply. By this step, practice becomes a mode and method of research, and research and practice might thereby become one and the same. Can a work of art, design or architecture ever be simply the answer to a question anyway? But, then, is the aim of a PhD to produce a work of art? What *is* the aim of a PhD? Further, does the formulation of the project arise from a question, i.e., is the thesis about the formulation of a question, or a project or both?

THE QUESTION OF THE QUESTION

Hans-Georg Gadamer argues that we need to know the question to which something is an answer in order to understand it. Texts, artworks, and buildings ask a question of the interpreter when they become the object of interpretation. What is to be recognised is "the horizon of the question within which the sense of the text is determined". "A work of art", he continues, "can be understood only if we assume its adequacy as an expression of the artistic idea. Here we also have to discover the question that it answers, if we are to understand it as an answer" (1975: 333-34). "[T]he reconstruction of the question, from which the meaning of the text is to be understood as an answer passes into our own questioning" (337). Thus, might it not in turn be argued that, if texts and works can be interpreted as responses to questions, the author, artist or designer should have a question, even if only at the back of the mind? In a PhD, this would be brought out, made manifest.

On quite different grounds, Michael Biggs and Daniela Büchler rule that "the peers must judge the merit of the solution, not as a creative contribution, but as an answer to a question" (2007: 68).[4] Practice is inherently devoted to creative contributions but not simply solutions. Even in the era of High Modernism, when to America was attributed the tag of seeking 'the engineering solution to a building problem,' any simple 'solution' alone was never enough. Rather, the design was to spring from the unexpected: invention, the shedding of new light, something not necessarily authorized by a set of conventions. Four years later, in accounting for the split between an "academic community" and a "practice community", Biggs and Büchler modify their stance. Noting that in most disciplines *question and answer* forms the core of academic research activities, they argue that

> this can present a stumbling block in areas of creative practice because the creative practice community values 'the event' which promotes direct encounter with the artefact. The direct encounter, in turn precipitates a plurality of experiences and, because these experiences are all different, a single unified answer does not emerge. (2011: 91)

As regards architecture, unfortunately, there is very rarely any direct encounter with an artefact until a work is realised – only with its representations. Since design is always separate from production until realisation, imagination is required on the part of both architect and audience. Architecture differs from the other plastic arts (and the performing arts), where inception and realisation are concurrent – indistinguishable, even. In architectural practice, the production of experience and the encounter with the artefact is mediated and rarely central. Moreover, because students are familiar with question and answer since undergraduate studio critiques, the advance into the formulation of a central research question does not necessarily "sound somewhat final and relate to the idealised world of facts" or "of cause and effect" (91). They argue,

> In areas of creative practice, both questions and answers, both issues and how they are addressed, are more volatile. They are 'culturally determined': as the culture changes certain issues become pressing and certain other issues fall away from the field of view or interest. (91)

Nevertheless, whilst architecture is also subject to the vicissitudes of cultural changes, questions in it, as in most other art forms, are never *finally* answered but tend to recur over and over again, usually with the result of reframing or overturning the issues themselves. There is a place for the large body of architectural theory in contemporary thinking, but only insofar as it provides unlimited questions about modes of living, technics, aesthetics and ethics, in an on-going process of critique and conservation. "Could it be", asks David Leatherbarrow accordingly, "that these texts have survived precisely because they have raised and tried to answer questions that were vitally important to the person questioning them – questions that are still with us?" (2001: 94)

Might his question of open questions asked and/or answered not also be extended to works, built or otherwise, contemporary or historical?

Biggs and Büchler's notion of "event" surfaces in the oral defence, which would presumably coincide with the exhibition of project-led or practice-based work. The exhibition and explication of plans, sections, elevations, details, Building Information Modelling, etc., each being cross-referenced to everything else, might make such an "event" in a performative demonstration of how a mutually dependent matrix of individual figures come together. An exhibition, however, does not guarantee that any event of thought or aesthetic creation take place. What happens in this way is not necessarily an original work but may well be something authorized only by a set of conventions agreed upon by an institutional community behaving *as if* it had reliable concepts at its disposal, which, in effect, inconspicuously reinforce subtle bounds and horizons.

Moreover, the fictive or creative character of a project-led thesis, being *conspicuously* outside the theoretical and constative order of utterances found in 'traditional' theses, though they ought to belong to that order (hence the need for an accompanying text, exegesis, statement, argument or suchlike) which, however, perfectly calls attention to the very same difficulty at the core of discourse in general (Derrida, 2001: 39). What, then, would an event be? Can such a question be asked, even? It might be said that the event can only spring from the unexpected, surprising constative and propositional modes of knowledge. As long as the production and determination of an event can be guaranteed in a performative act by conventions, legitimate fictions, what happens remains controllable and programmable within a horizon of anticipation being both possible and able to be mastered: "As I have often tried to demonstrate", writes Derrida, "only the impossible can arrive" (54). The event is an irruption puncturing any preconceived bounds.

Processes of argumentation, nevertheless, are needed in formulating the project, developing the question to be posed, and in deriving the answer from it – be this by words, diagrams or drawings. The architectural thesis is a negotiation between project and text in which the logic of the supplement works each way. Hence, it is useful that each part proceeds apace, with the student devoting alternatively half a day, a day or a week to each. The most successful students both write *and* draw from day one. Similarly, some parts of the research will be hypothesis-led, some discovery-led. Answers *and* questions can be offered without the intervention of text-based language, for instance by the use of diagrams (see van Berkel & Bos, 1999). However, it must be recognised that, even with diagrams, the design process does not necessarily share the linear structure of language or argumentation. In fact, anything that attempts this linearity risks becoming 'academic' in the worst sense of that word.

Torsten Kälvemark cites Henk Borgdorff on a tension between artistic research and academia that "could be productive" (Kälvemark, 2011: 21). As Borgdorff puts it, "these specific 'border violations' can spark a good deal of tension" (Borgdorff, 2011: 44). Such tension can also occur productively *within* a project-led thesis. Uniting with academic research, practice moves out of its former bounds, with the intent of contributing to modes of thinking and understanding that are imbricated in practices. The fact that a large proportion of a project may be non-discursive, heuristic, fuzzy, or messy need not mean that questions should be lost to sight. In line with Theodore Schatzki (2001), Borgdorff also notes "[k]nowledge and experience are constituted only in and through practices, actions and interactions. In the context of discovery, pre-reflexive artistic actions embody knowledge in a form that is not directly accessible for justification" (2011: 47).

To persist with the question and questioning is to recognise that there are wider questions that can and must be asked. Ultimately, the connection between the discursive and the poetic rises to visibility, as St-John Perse states in his 1960 Nobel Prize acceptance speech, in recognising that the scientist and poet "[b]oth put the same question to the same abyss: they differ only in their methods of investigation" (1971: 5).

> Indeed, in in its beginnings every creative act of the spirit is 'poetic' in the proper sense of the word. In giving equal value to sensory and mental forms, the same activity serves, initially, the enterprises of the scientist and the poet alike. Which has travelled, which will travel, a longer way – discursive thinking or poetic ellipsis? From that primal abyss where two blind figures, blind from birth are groping, one equipped with all the apparatus of science, the other assisted only by flashes of intuition – which comes to the surface sooner and more highly charged with a brief phosphorescence? How we answer this question is of no importance. All that matters is the mystery in which both share. (5-7)

So, anterior to the question is the *incentive* - the state of wonder. Whereas Socrates remarked on wonder as the beginning of philosophy, Perse (taking from Plato, who most mistrusted artists) makes *poiésis* instead begin in wonder. The word that Plato puts into the mouths of Socrates and Theaetetus is *thaumazein* (Plato, 1924: 155c-d), which means in Greek to be in a state of *aporia*, dilemma, quandary, perplexity, but also of awe, marvel and wonder. Much has been written on this passage, not the least by Martin Heidegger (1994: 133-150). The spark of a doctoral project could do a lot worse than begin with (and continue to consider) the whole gamut of these states.

SITUATED AND EMBODIED KNOWLEDGE

Representations – be they in writing or drawing – are inherently mobile and can be circulated in the form of plans, models or files and applied to almost any situation and location. Globalised architectural practice would otherwise not be possible. The architectural works and practices, by contrast, are not – they are situated. Through them, knowledge emerges from particular contexts of application, with and within their own theoretical frameworks, methods of research and practice. One of the great opportunities creative practice–led PhD research might have to offer could be the production and uncovering of situated knowledge which practice necessarily involves. In this practice, the meaning of a building arises from the interactions with relevant *milieus* – some of which might suffer less from the theory/practice split in the academy and have continued to pursue traditions of embodied knowledge in architecture. Thus, the third candidate whose project I discuss (on p. 214, below), endeavours to theorise the situated knowledge of Samoan space, building and builders' traditions (*tufuga*) in his (fully written) PhD thesis. The context in which architectural research takes place is moulded by both practice, social and professional, *and* academic theory: while research derives from and enlarges the discipline, it is also situated in a practising community. The relation between the two is reciprocal and iterative.

Designs are embodiments of the experiences and insights delivered by research as design. The material outcomes of such research, including the ways of arriving at them, are, as Borgdorff suggests,

> non-conceptual and non-discursive, and their persuasive quality lies in the performative power through which they broaden our aesthetic experience, invite us to fundamentally unfinished thinking, and prompt us towards a critical perspective on what there is. (2011: 47)

To reveal and articulate the tacit knowledge situated and embodied in specific works and processes, the experimental and hermeneutic methods employed are documented and disseminated to the research community and wider public (Borgdorff, 2006). But, Borgdorff questions, what is the epistemological status of these embodied forms of experience and knowledge? How to relate the material-performative to the rational-discursive and the engaged-critical in the research? He notes that "[i]n the debate on artistic research, these ontological, methodological, contextual and epistemological issues are still the subject of extensive discussion" (2011: 48).

I find it difficult to see the need to await a distinctive architectural worldview and the development of appropriate architectural research models, as Biggs and Büchler do. They already exist and have for some time. Architecture is, and has been for centuries, a discipline with its own body of knowledge. Within the contemporary university, master's theses by design have existed for at least 50 years. Nonetheless, Biggs & Büchler provide a useful model in which they locate architectural research within a triadic overlap of research cultures (Humanities & Human, Applied & Social and Natural & Technological), even if the specific nature of architectural research still remains somewhat vague in that model (2011: 69-73). While I certainly agree that practice alone, without research questions and theorisation, is insufficient (see Büchler et al., 2008), it also seems to me that some graduates take part neither in science nor scholarship, nor even in architectural practice, but are practitioners of a particular mode of research – confined only to the academy.

In any art form one of the most difficult aspects (if not impossible to objectify) of making (*poiésis*), being quasi magical, is the "extreme level of complicity where reality seems to shape itself within the poem" (Perse, 1971: 7). In any form of making, the world is caught in the act of making itself, where the maker is an amazed observer/participant. Art and architecture are not a matter of simple representation, but of something transformed into reality: poetic reality. This is something that no longer follows reality, even if configured and founded in reality.

DESIGN AND PROJECT

One of the main things architects do is to make drawings and other representations. This must surely be regarded as lying at the core of practice- and project-based research – the very means whereby architecture entered the academy was by the promotion of drawing. In 1563, Giorgio Vasari founded the *Accademia delle Arti del Disegno* in Florence, which became a model for art and architecture schools. On the assumption that architecture, painting and sculpture were concerned with ideas, they were elevated to the level of liberal arts, since *disegno* linked form and concept. In a neo-Platonic understanding, a form is an *Idea*, the word he used to designate intelligible models of the real (Nancy, 2007: 15-16). Drawing as *disegno* came to designate the form or idea, on the premise that ideas are superior to matter and intellectual work superior to manual labour. Drawing and geometry – forms of thinking – replaced workshop instruction. Thus, architecture performed another version of the theory/practice split already perpetuated since Antiquity. In affirmation of their new status, architects began to theorise and published not only drawings, but also books. In the seventeenth century, the French term for drawing (*dessein*) was derived from *disegno*: "project, enterprise, intention. It is also the thinking one has in the imagination of order, issue (*distribution*) and the construction of a painting, a poem, a book, a building" (Furetière, 1690). *Dessein*, as project or intention, implies a certain manner of thinking drawing, as always the realisation of an intellectual project.[5] Today, the Italian word for design, *progettare* (to project) lacks etymological relation to the act of drawing or representation.

What distinguishes representations in design and architecture from those in other arts is that they are *projective*, they have an intention or purpose. It is this intentionality that connects the project to drawing and design. A project, as its etymology implies, is inevitably something *thrown forward*, involving a form of representation awaiting existence. Hence, drawing is a statement of intention towards some artefact other than itself. It is also a form of translation:

> Such intention involves a transition from the capture of a thought or a sight by drawing a line or lines "around" it, as it were, so as to transpose it onto the more corporeal business of other [building] techniques – essentially speaking, in a kind of translation. (Rykwert, 2005: 2)

THOUGHT OUT OF BOUNDS

The notion of *disegno* calls attention to the need to rethink the greatly underestimated potentialities of drawing today – as a mode of thought. This operates at a different level from the many current usages of digital design and rendering, which are devoted to bringing to perfection a long Western tradition of verisimilitude. In our infant knowledge of digital reproduction we have still to learn other modes, besides the demonstration of an accomplished fact, such as the suspension that would allow thinking drawing through, or thinking through drawing.[6]

Here, for example, it remains to think Jean-Luc Nancy's proposition that "drawing is the opening of form: *Le dessin est l'ouverture de la forme*" (Nancy, 2007: 13), rather than a foreclosure by preconceived logic or algorithm.

PROJECT AND THESIS

If the project heads towards a future, the thesis places something in the Now. In "The Origin of the Work of Art", Heidegger argued that even things "outlined, admitted-into the boundary (*peras*), brought into the contour" are never rigidly fixed, motionless, and secure, "[b]oundary sets free into the unconcealed" (1975: 83). In discussing the idea of the figure, *Gestalt*, as a setting in place of truth, he argues that this is to be thought of in terms of a particular placing or framework.[7] He recalls the Greek sense of setting and placing – *thesis* – which he translates as "to let lie forth in its radiance and presence" (82). His understanding is far from that of a thesis in modernity – where it is a statement or proposition (placed, posited, proposed or set down) to be argued or maintained;[8] a definition going back to Plato and Aristotle, nevertheless. A design *project* is already, in a sense, a proposal and a thesis – though not necessarily as a making present or as something requiring proof (even if both argumentation and disclosure are required in an architectural thesis, in representations *and* texts). Heidegger is not explicit what this truth is that is brought into being and held in place in the work of art. Rather, he tells us what it does and how it happens by adopting the sense of the Greek word for truth -*alétheia* -which means uncovering or unconcealing. This truth is not about propositions or attributes of factual things - the most dominant ways of thinking truth in Western philosophy. It is a truth which offers profound disturbance and undoing:

> The nature of art, on which both the art work and the artist depend, is the setting itself-into-work of truth. It is due to art's poetic nature that, in the midst of what is, art breaks open an open place, in whose openness everything is other than usual. By virtue of the projected sketch set into the work of the unconcealedness of what is, which casts itself toward us, everything ordinary and hitherto existing becomes an unbeing. (72)

In both project-based and scholarly PhDs, the interactions of supervisor and candidate in formulating the project (in locating or translating concepts from one position to another) set up a conversation, in which a common language is established. Gadamer puts this so:

[I]n a successful conversation they come under the influence of the truth of the object and are thus bound to one another in a new community. To reach an understanding with one's partner in a dialogue is not merely a matter of self expression and the successful assertion of one's own point of view, but a transformation into a communion, in which we do not remain what we were. (1975: 371)

GLOBALISATION AND THE SITUATEDNESS OF KNOWLEDGE

The second set of issues I raised at the beginning revolves around the question of place and site: global or local. Increasingly, architects practise and students learn in countries far apart from their origins, at times travelling further still (and even home!) on high level design research. Students' first languages, cultures and knowledge systems derive more and more often from places other than the context of their university. Both PhD supervisors and candidates seem short of guidelines in this situation. Non-Western students (Indigenous, Pacific Island, Asian, Middle Eastern, for example) are required to become adept in *Western* protocols, when their own ways of approaching architectural, artistic and design issues, without respect for Western distinctions between *techné* and *poiésis* from *épistémé*, could potentially heal that very rift and open other thoughts.

In essence, the question here is framed by an architectural phenomenon: thinking happens within and without particular places. The issues raised by this condition can only be left open as questions to be pondered here. But, if architects increasingly build in other countries and students from other countries study abroad, how then can they locate themselves and their practice in another culture? Reciprocally, how can they locate foreign cultures in their own? Should the foreign knowledge be seamlessly integrated into the local, or could a certain friction or traction between cultures, modes of thinking and languages prove fruitful? That is, how can architectural thought be out of bounds, yet in contact with specific local/native thought and practice of thought? How can knowledge generated under this condition contribute to knowledge or research more widely? How do non-English students encounter their PhD experience and supervision? What are specific aspects that make their situation different, and what can their supervisors do to respond? How can they deal with epistemic potentialities that relate practice and theory, native and new cultures in different ways? These are all questions that arise from the challenges of non-traditional candidates concerning the supervision process and relationship. They await more questioning and partial answers in conversations between candidates and supervisors – they need the development of a common language that transforms all participants.

A. He Might Have...

Most international students coming to do PhDs in Western universities are leaving something they would rather not work on. They come to work on something else; at the same time, they come for the authorisation and certification of a Western degree, which will be of value on return or for a future in the West.

'A.' was one of my candidates who had come from Hong Kong, wishing to work on Walter Benjamin's thoughts on the contemporary city. The main thrust of A.'s project was to discover as much about Benjamin as possible by analysing his writing and the secondary literature, to condense the literature into an account of Benjamin's concept of the city, and then to relate it to today's cities. His thesis examined, in particular, Benjamin's notion of a *new barbarism* as a form of resistance, capable of proposing an alternative culture against the contemporary, which A. saw (as Benjamin did for his time) as an overwhelming aestheticization of politics. Much of A.'s work was devoted to analysing Benjamin's thought, particularly his *new barbarism*, which was intended as a decisive intervention into what is repressed by the world of appearance. The resulting culture of integral actuality would embody a new humanity, organised by a tradition that passes down not finished treasures, but unfulfilled tasks. From here, A. examined Benjamin's suggestions for a different mode of experience, which Benjamin conceived in terms of active translation in the city, as a site of *rencontre*, meeting, encounter.

The world's greatest conurbation – Pearl River Delta Mega City, reaching from Guangzhou to Macau, with around 40 million people – was in the background of A's mind but this connection was never articulated. Thus, a possible encounter between Chinese conceptions of the city and aestheticization did not occur. The research was *not situated in relation to his experience*. A. conceived of his thesis as a European project but even in that context, he did not arrive at the point where he could relate his research to any contemporary city, with any degree of specificity.

Despite that, the thesis was successful. At the time of supervision it did not occur to either of us that anything was missing. Only in retrospect do the lost potentialities become evident to me. It is a pity, because the thesis could have been all the stronger for making it relevant to contemporary questions, *and* to his own experience. Benjamin's key terms: "repressed", "unfulfilled tasks", "active translation", "*rencontre*", etc., employed self-critically, might have entered into his own approach and given rise to a mode of research practice that produced new understanding by embracing his own experience.

But, as my editor comments, "you can't finish something you haven't started". Fortunately, A. is now embarking on a second doctorate in Canada – on life politics in the time of global network existence. He now has a chance to finish the first thesis.

B. Globalisation Objectified

My next example is 'B.', a candidate who researched the impact of globalisation on the role of architecture, and how this might be interpreted ethically. Thence arose the question of how to link this ethical evaluation to architecture's ability to maintain connections with the culture from which it derives. In modernity, cultural identity is closely linked to national identity. B. focused on four trajectories affecting architecture's ability to relate to national-cultural identity: the physical nature of the region, materials and methods of construction, belief systems, and memory. In her terms, all four trajectories are challenged and severely undermined by the impact of social and cultural diversity, technology, industry and forgetfulness. B. examined how global culture dynamically advances its version of homogeneity, which is, however, challenged by the need for change and the dynamic nature of modern nations. The iconic architecture of celebrity architects, for example, leads to innovation/transformation processes, whereas the tendency of contemporary architectural theory is to advance the interpretation-reinterpretation dynamic in architecture. The latter destabilises meaning in architectural language, which, when transformed into real world buildings, can result in alienating human settings.

The thesis was, again, successful and has been published subsequently, but if I were to consider things observed, thought and learnt here, I believe that perhaps the work might have been stronger had it been more situated in local cultures and their commitments. As an Iraqi, B. had lived through three wars, fourteen years of international sanctions, two US invasions and two years of US occupation. She has experience in practice *and* as an architecture faculty member at two Iraqi universities. It could be that, in the interests of universality, what she might have brought to the topic from her personal experience, circumstances and engagement was pushed under the surface; as a consequence, immediacy and local colour were not as evident. One learns in hindsight. The other side of her leaning towards the systematic and objective, I hasten to add, was her very powerful diagrammatic thinking, for which her examiners complimented her. The diagram, something between word and image, more like a theorem and non-lingual, enabled formulation and summarisation of her argumentation with great succinctness.

C. Meeting but Not Knowing

Diagrams also feature convincingly in the thesis of 'C.', a Samoan candidate, trained and practised in architecture, perfectly suited to working back and forth between Polynesian and Western frameworks. C. is widely read in Western philosophy, architectural theory and anthropology, which he brings to a doctorate devoted to the traditional meeting-house, *faletele*, as exemplification of the Samoan experience and understanding of what we call 'space'. His doctorate is an excavation of origins, a way of navigating across the oceans between the South Seas, Europe and its colonies, between today and the times before written history.

Non-traditional students bring with them, and develop further, many and various kinds of scholarly questioning. Mark Dorrian, whom I interviewed on this subject, presents the difficulties connected with such research approaches:

> It's quite hard to formulate because it really happens through dialogue and I don't think there's a linear process or formula one can put in place – PhDs are inevitably a kind of splashing around at the start, where various things are

being tried and tested – there's a testing of the field, what's been done and what hasn't been done and inevitably an attempt to begin to write or to drill into particular lines of approach to the subject matter in more detail, to test how productive it could be to take the approach. (Dorrian, 2012)

When I took over as primary supervisor during the leave of a colleague, our meetings became more dialogical, an encounter, a discovery of and discourse on fundamental terms, where nothing could be taken for granted and everything became a source of quandary, wonder and contestation. Since I am not a speaker of Samoan, we were faced with the task of finding a conversation in which we could establish a common language.

Without intending to, we probed unanswerable questions such as: what is space?, what is time?, what is material? ... Western or otherwise. That I am not an expert seems to prove fruitful to the extent that it leads to interchanges and questioning, as I try to locate my knowledge of Western antiquity against his of the same, and of Samoa. "Is it like this?" I ask, filtering the Samoan cosmogony, divinities and mythologies through Homer, Hesiod and current accounts of antiquity. C. would contemplate my suggestion and reply: "Yes, something like that", or, "No – not at all, it's rather like ...". Establishing links between anthropological understandings of material culture and specifically architectural understandings, we explored and linked theories in order to find common ground. Thus, Gottfried Semper (who relied on the anthropologist Gustav Klemm) led us to examine concepts of place, social interaction, time-space, making and materiality, especially the theorisation of Semper's "Four Elements": weaving, cutting, stacking and moulding. Semper linked material culture and praxis to cosmogony and symbolism, and grouped craftspeople around these categories. We discussed how Semper's concepts might relate to the Samoan guild of builders, *tufuga*, and how they might, in turn, relate to Austronesian, Polynesian and Samoan culture. We established ties through theorists linking architecture to anthropology, like Joseph Rykwert, or anthropology to architecture, like Tim Ingold – useful models for treating the topic from an architectural perspective. Thus, embodied and local knowledge could be connected with architectural knowledge, situating it to an extent at least, I hope, for the candidate.

Perhaps it is only when a candidate has a foot and an existence in both cultures that opportunities of tapping the 'between' arise and the most interesting cross-cultural encounters. Reflective questioning of this situation is rare and overshadowed by the desire for cultural fit. C. has a back-up team of local experts in language, history and anthropology, but not in architecture. As supervisor, I try to take the position of critical respondent, rather than speaking from a position of expertise in his field. The discussion of process, the logic of the approach, the rationale and comparisons with other cultures, I trust, allow us both to come to grips with the concepts and practices that feature in his thesis, to imagine what they were over the course of Samoan history and what they might mean today. Essential from my point of view is to render an architectural account, even as, at times, the research appears to stitch together various disciplines.

I had previously supervised two Tongan research masters students on Tongan topics. For this I was castigated by a dean of graduate studies, who informed me that such students should gain traditional Western master's degrees, to be followed by an Oxbridge PhD. Only then would they be capable of researching their own culture. I am very pleased to add that both received first class honours from external examiners and one was even offered a scholarship to work in the field of Tongan art and architecture at Cambridge University. Thus, the question arises as to how an indoctrination into received thought might help students understand their culture, particularly if that culture has things worthy of thought that are not immediately accessible to, expressed by, or integrated into traditional Western doctorates. Above all, how can anyone trained purely within another culture be expected to become adept in his or her own when finally let loose on it?

CONCLUSION

The tradition of placing candidates in an on-going research project may be productive for some, if their contribution is to be no more than a small part of research which has remained unexamined in detail. This can then be integrated into a larger, on-going project in a positive way. Candidates in such situations are likely to align themselves with a particular scholarly position. For the supervisors, it has the great advantage of being located right in the centre of their on-going research engagement, which presumably they know very well. Nevertheless, a position of unknowing can also be fruitful: it may lead to a situation where one's teaching comes into question entailing risk, courage, and a certain amount of trust. When concepts and practices from outside challenge Western research, the Socratic paradox (*The Apology*) of the principle of not knowing, "I do not suppose that I know" (Plato, 2008) leads to an attentiveness and responsibility to the matter at hand. Benefits can arise from *not* being bound into pre-established frameworks, topics or disciplineships (since experts never have sovereignty over the field within which they claim expertise). Here, the unusual is more likely to happen, as Mark Dorrian notes.

> From my point of view, the benefit of studying with someone who has experience in research methodology or approaches to cultural and critical research – but is not necessarily an expert on the particular subject – is that it has the possibility of opening up a different kind of approach to the subject matter which is less likely whenever one is positioned in terms of a much more dominant position, which you get when you're working with a recognized expert in the field. (Dorrian, 2012)

Not everything can be translated from one culture to another. What is important then is the cultivation of a point of intersection, encounter or meeting. On the one hand, the historical *fale*, on the other, the metaphorical, or maybe even, true *fale*, still existing, which sets up an in-between realm or potential space for the search. For a thought that seeks its place, seeks for its basis, while working from that conjectured ground up.

Implied in practice-based knowledge, particularly in the embodied skills of guilds (such as the Samoan *tufuga*), but also in thought passing across cultures is the idea of a localised knowledge. Thinking which relates to the local, the specific or vernacular craft, as opposed to any theory applied from without, relates and responds to the matter at hand, "with all the hidden riches of its nature" as Heidegger puts it, linking the craft of teaching to craft itself:

> A cabinetmaker's apprentice, someone who is learning to build cabinets and the like, will serve as an example. His learning is not mere practice, to gain facility in the use of tools. Nor does he merely gather knowledge about the customary forms of the things he is to build. If he is to become a true cabinetmaker, he makes himself answer and respond above all to the different kinds of wood and to the shapes slumbering within wood – to wood as it enters into man's dwelling with all the hidden riches of its nature. In fact, this relatedness to wood is what maintains the whole craft. Without that relatedness, the craft will never be anything but empty busywork, any occupation with it will be determined exclusively by business concerns. Every handicraft, all human dealings are constantly in that danger. The writing of poetry is no more exempt from it than is thinking. (Heidegger, 1968: 14-15)

Matter, here, be it material or content, is nothing fixed. Rather, it is a site of potentiality and questioning. This can happen only when teachers can impart the specific relatedness to the subject matter being learned. For Heidegger, teaching is a craft whose purpose is to let learn.

> The real teacher, in fact, lets nothing else be learned than – learning. His conduct, therefore, often produces the impression that we properly learn nothing from him, if by 'learning' we now suddenly understand merely the procurement of useful information. The teacher is ahead of his apprentices in this alone, that he has still far more to learn than they – he has to learn to let them learn. The teacher must be capable of being more teachable than the apprentices. The teacher is far less assured of his ground than those who learn are of theirs. If the relation between the teacher and the taught is genuine, therefore, there is never a place in it for the authority of the know-it-all or the authoritative sway of the official. (15)

Non-traditional candidates' approaches can and often should be sited in their situation, however much that may seem a tautology. It is important that candidates not simply end up writing the supervisor's thesis. This is the lesson of learning to unlearn and learning to let learn. It is crucial that both thesis topic and approach come from the student. Motivation is all. Students must answer and respond to the questions and theses they formulate, fully owning and inhabiting them.

In both project-based and scholarly PhDs, the interactions of the supervisor and the candidate in formulating the project (in arriving at it, in locating or translating concepts from one position to another) a conversation, a common language is established where, as Gadamer puts it,

> in a successful conversation they come under the influence of the truth of the object and are thus bound to one another in a new community. To reach an understanding with one's partner in a dialogue is not merely a matter of self expression and the successful assertion of one's own point of view, but a transformation into a communion, in which we do not remain what we were. (Gadamer, 1975: 371)

Both varieties of non-traditional supervisions I have endeavoured to treat here – the endless probing of the discipline in search of its core (applicable equally to theory and design, both being modes of thinking) and the continual rediscovery of one's culture in encounter with others' – involve some meeting in the form of a conversation. Unfortunately, in the contemporary university, accountability to knowledge management rather than any risky encounter with the discipline, its possible future and other cultures seems to predominate. Fully to accept an absence of knowledge either as *aporia* or awe in this setup presents only a 'liability'. The truly creative, however, can never be prescribed, least of all as 'innovation.' New communities can take place only under "the influence of the truth of the object" or, as the case may be, of the truth of its space.

NOTES

[1] "Today in Europe there are collections of self-professed practice-based PhDs and research that are financed by research funding bodies. However, even in the UK where PbR has been recognized for longer, there is still considerable disagreement about what constitutes PbR as well as what constitutes indicators of excellence in academic research in general. Evidence of this situation can be seen in the disagreements amongst peer groups in the quinquenial British Research Assessment Exercise (RAE) in art and design about the role of design practice and in the various debates on academic discussion lists such as PhD Design and Practice-led Research". (Büchler, Biggs, Sandin, & Ståhl, 2008)

[2] Kälvemark (2011) provides a comprehensive account of the emergence and rapid development of practice-based arts research, the integration of art schools into the university structure and hence the need to gain access to university funding.

[3] Only in 2007 did the UK Arts and Humanities Research Council produce its review of practice-led research in art, design and architecture (see Rust, Mottram, & Till, 2007). Ultimately, the debates concerning what constitutes research in design practice arose from this academicization of art, design and architectural practices (Biggs & Büchler, 2011; Biggs, 2000; Biggs & Büchler, 2007: 62–63; Büchler et al., 2008; Kälvemark, 2011).

[4] The specificity of architectural communal values arises, at least partly, from the disciplinary conventions that determine issues, questions, methods and responses as relevant and acceptable (see Biggs & Büchler, 2011: 66).

[5] The word *dessin*, which would be substituted a century later, has a much a much narrower sense: only drawing. The English *design* corresponds to the French *dessein* and was introduced into English art theory by Shaftsbury (see also Frascari, 2011: 129–150).

[6] "Drawing is designing, presenting, showing or ostensive thought" writes Jean-Luc Nancy. But it is not the demonstration of an accomplished fact. "'The accomplished fact (*fait accompli*)' of drawing is not simply that of a display of the thing, it is that of a display of form, of the idea, of thought. Of the thing as much as it is thought or thinkable." (Nancy, 2007: 15)

[7] "What is called *Gestalt*, is always to be thought in terms of the particular placing (*Stellen*) and framing or framework (*Ge-stell*) as which the work occurs when it sets itself up and sets itself forth" (Heidegger, 1975: 64).

[8] On this distinction see Allpress & Barnacle (2009).

REFERENCES

Allpress, B., & Barnacle, R. (2009). Projecting the PhD Architectural design research by and through projects. In D. Boud & A. Lee (Eds.), *Changing Practices of Doctoral Education* (pp. 157–170). London, England: Routledge.

Anderson, S. (2001). The Profession and Discipline of Architecture: Practice and Education. In A. Piotrowski (Ed.), *The Discipline of Architecture* (pp. 292–305). Minneapolis, MN: University of Minnesota Press.

Biggs, M., & Büchler, D. (2011). Communities, values, conventions and actions. In M. Biggs & H. Karlsson (Eds.), *The Routledge companion to research in the arts* (pp. 82–98). London, England: Routledge.

Biggs, M., & Büchler, D. (2011). Some Consequences of the academicization of design practice. *Design Philosopy Papers,* (1). Retrieved from http://www.desphilosophy.com.ezproxy.auckland.ac.nz/dpp/dpp_journal/back_issues/paper3_BiggsBuch/dpp_paper3.html

Biggs, M., & Büchler, D. (2011). Transdisciplinarity and New Paradigm Research. In I. Doucet & N. Janssens (Ed.), *Transdisciplinary knowledge production in architecture and urbanism: Towards hybrid modes of inquiry* (pp. 63–78). Dordrecht, Holland: Springer.

Biggs, M. A. R. (2000). Editorial: the foundations of practice-based research. *Working Papers in Art and Design 1*. Retrieved from http://sitem.herts.ac.uk/artdes_research/papers/wpades/vol1/vol1intro.html

Biggs, M. A. R., & Büchler, D. (2007). Rigor and practice-based research. *Design issues, 23*(3), 62–69.

Borgdorff, H. (2006). *The debate on research in the arts (Sensuous knowledge 2)*. Bergen, Norway: Bergen National Academy of the Arts.

Borgdorff, H. (2011). The production of knowledge in artistic research. In M. Biggs & H. Karlsson (Eds.), *The Routledge companion to research in the arts* (pp. 44–63). London, England: Routledge.

Büchler, D., Biggs, M., Sandin, G., & Ståhl, L.-H. (2008). Architectural design and the problem of practice-based research. *Cadernos de Pós-graduação em Arquitetura e Urbanismo, 2,* 1–16.

Derrida, J. (2001). "The future of the profession or the university without condition (Thanks to the 'Humanities,' what could take place tomorrow)". In Cohen, T. (Ed.), *Jacques Derrida and the Humanities: A critical reader,* Cambridge, England: CUP. 24–57.

Dorrian, M., Jenner, R. & Engels-Schwarzpaul, A.-Chr. (2012). Interview with Mark Dorrian in Newcastle.

Furetière, A. (1690). *Dictionnaire universel, contenant generalement tous les mots François, tant vieux que modernes & les termes de toutes les science et des arts.* archive.org/stream/DictionnaireUniversel/furetiere#page/n1/mode/2up

Frascari, M. (2011). *Eleven Exercises in the Art of Architectural Drawing: Slow Food for the Architect's Imagination.* London and New York: Routledge.

Gadamer, H.-G. (1975). *Truth and method.* London: Sheed and Ward.

Gray, C. & Malins, J. (2004). *Visualizing research: A guide to the research process in art and design.* Burlington, VT: Ashgate Publishing.

Groat, L. & Wang, D. (2002). New York, NY: John Wiley and Sons Inc.

Heidegger, M. (1968). *What is called thinking?* (F. D. Wieck & J. G. Gray, Trans., Vol. 21). New York, NY: Harper & Row.

Heidegger, M. (1975). The origin of the work of art (A. Hofstädter, Trans.) *Poetry, Language, Thought* (pp. 17–81). New York, NY: Harper and Row.

Heidegger, M. (1977). *Holzwege. GA I. Abteilung: Veröffentlichte Schriften 1914–1970* (Vol. 5). Frankfurt am Main, Germany: Vittorio Klostermann.

Heidegger, M. (1994). *Basic questions of philosophy* (R. Rojcewicz & A. Schuwer, Trans.). Bloomington, IN: Indiana University Press.

Heidegger, M. (2002 (1951–1952)). *Was heisst denken? GA I. Abteilung: Veröffentlichte Schriften 1910–1976* (Vol. 8). Frankfurt am Main, Germany: Vittorio Klostermann.

Holt, G.D. (1998). *A guide to successful dissertation study for students of the built environment.* Wolverhampton, England: Built Environment Research Unit, University of Wolverhampton.

Kälvemark, T. (2011). University politics and practice-based research. In M. Biggs & H. Karlsson (Eds.), *The Routledge companion to research in the arts* (pp. 3–23). London, England: Routledge.

Leatherbarrow, D. (2001). Architecture is its own discipline. In A. Piotrowski (Ed.), *The discipline of architecture* (pp. 83–102). Minneapolis, MN: University of Minnesota Press.

Nancy, J.-L. (2007). *Le plaisir au dessin.* Paris, France: Éditions Hazan.

Partridge, E. (2006). *Origins: A short etymological dictionary of modern English.* London, England: Routledge.

Perse, St.-J. (1971). *Collected Poems.* Princeton, NJ: Princeton University Press.

Plato. (1924, 2009). *Theaetatus* (Benjamin Jowett, Trans.) Retrieved from http://classics.mit.edu/Plato/theatu.html

Plato. (2008). *Apology* (Trans. Benjamin Jowett). Retrieved from http://www.gutenberg.org/files/1656/1656-h/1656-h.htm.

Rust, C., Mottram, J., & Till, J. (2007). *AHRC research review: Practice-led research in art, design and architecture.* Arts and Humanities Research Council, England.

Rykwert, J. (2005). Translation and/or representation. Retrieved from http://www2.cca.qc.ca/pages/Niveau3.asp?page=mellon_rykwert&lang=eng website

Schatzki, T. R., Cetina, K. K., & Savigny, E. v. (2001). *The practice turn in contemporary theory.* London, England: Routledge.

Skeat, W. (1888). *An etymological dictionary of the English language.* Oxford, England: Clarindon Press.

Stiegler, B. (1998). *Technics and Time, 1: The fault of Epimetheus.* Stanford, CA: Stanford University Press.

van Berkel, B., & Bos, C. (1999). *Move* (Vol. Volume 2: Techniques). Amsterdam, Netherlands: UN Studio and Goose Press.

Vitruvius. (1970). *Vitruvius on Architecture* (F. Granger, Trans.). Cambridge, MA: Harvard University Press.

AFFILIATION

Ross Jenner
School of Architecture and Planning
The University of Auckland

SARAH O'BRIEN

13. THINKING THROUGH MOVING IMAGE AND PERFORMANCE

BETWEEN A MAKER AND A SCHOLAR

What is the difference between making performance work within the academy and making work outside of it? How can I situate my performance event within the field of knowledge? Those were amongst the key questions when embarking on my PhD. This chapter outlines the journey of my experience as a Research Council funded practice-led PhD candidate in the Creative and Performing Arts in the UK.

The answer to the questions above may initially seem self-evident: some academic writers in Performance Studies see knowledge, in terms of performance, as explicated by critical writing. Historically in the UK, academic knowledge in drama, performance and theatre studies grew out of English Literature (Kleiman, 2012: 131) and now commonly dealt with the performance event from a critical and analytical perspective alone. In this position, the tools of analysis come not from the field of performance making itself, but from historical and theoretical fields (e.g. semiotics, phenomenology, cultural and post-structural theory). Academic writing has changed now, following the onset of practice-led research where analysis of work is undertaken by the makers, but during this process of change the majority of critical writing in performance still situates the writer as a critic, distanced from the performance to be analysed.

It is therefore easy to understand how new candidates undertaking practice-led PhD research may have some mislaid assumptions regarding what is expected of them, and how their work can make the transition from 'professional' to 'academic-professional'. Initially, a new candidate may struggle to understand how to contextualise their performance work in academia and may be confused at how historical, social/cultural or critical theory may be important to their own practice. New candidates may default to critical writing and offer detailed historical backgrounds to their specific field and/or complex readings of their work *via* high theory. If these backgrounds and analyses have had no influence on the actual making of the performance work, then how, indeed, could the writing of new practice-led researchers be any different from that of the traditional researcher? On the other hand, it may not be clear to them how the process of creation, or the witnessing of performance work, can produce new knowledge that influences the writing. The word *influence* here conceals a lot of complex issues, as it marks one of the possible 'meetings' between performance creation and new knowledge. It is these *meeting points* that often remain mysterious to the new researcher.

A.-Chr. Engels-Schwarzpaul and M. A. Peters (Eds.), *Of other Thoughts: Non-Traditional Ways to the Doctorate: A Guidebook for Candidates and Supervisors*, 221–238.
© 2013 Sense Publishers. All rights reserved.

Throughout this chapter, I will endeavour to demystify these meeting points by outlining the way in which I approached the difficulty of performance creation in the pursuit of new knowledge; putting forward reasons for the importance of this pursuit to my own work and to the field of performance in general. I will align my own experiences with common concerns that PhD candidates and/or supervisors might face when embarking upon practice-led research in the performing arts, including:

- *The area of knowledge*: how do your selected theories, practices and research questions engage with the debates surrounding knowledge production in performance research?
- *The circumstances*: with whom are you working (supervisor/s, associates, company members, funding bodies)? And what is their role in the work? Are their views consistent with your own in terms of the area of knowledge, knowledge production and the practice you intend to engage with?
- *The creative process*: How can you move from creative intention to knowledge production? What is the role of writing in this process? How do you demystify its connection to practice?

I hope that putting forward my own ideas, experiences, and methods within this context will contribute to a framework in which new researchers can situate their decisions.

I shall begin by outlining some of the current debates that address methodology, outcomes, documentation and the nature (or worth) of thesis writing. These debates begin to illustrate how and why every practice-led PhD in performance can potentially bring with it new methods, new forms of submission, and new ways of situating the event within a body of knowledge. Decisions about methods and forms of submission not only depend on the candidate's response to these debates, but also on the circumstances of the candidature. A discussion of my own PhD journey, therefore, cannot be a 'how-to' guide; but it can serve to clarify how I answered key questions and how I dealt with some stages of the process that are pertinent to all practice-led performance research candidatures.

THE AREA OF KNOWLEDGE

Knowledge production in all academic research must endeavour to first clarify the area of knowledge with which it engages, explain the method of research, and then clarify how the work submitted contributes to this area of knowledge. In practice-led research, however, the method and the form of the final submission are complicated by current debates regarding what constitutes new knowledge in performance. PhD candidates, with the support of their supervisor(s), need to be able to engage with these debates, to be able to identify and articulate the meeting points between writing, performance and new knowledge. When I began my research, my understanding of these relationships was quite 'traditional': knowledge was to be made known through writing alone. I presupposed that a theory (or a knowledge base) gives justification for the method, which then prompts the practice, from which the 'raw' data can be collected; *raw*, because (like performance) data is initially undisciplined and unordered, much like a qualitative interview (not everything that is said by the interviewee will be relevant to the 'new' knowledge outcome). Subsequently, the process of analysis disciplines and orders the raw data; and this ordering is expressed by the *writing*, which renews the theory/produces new knowledge.

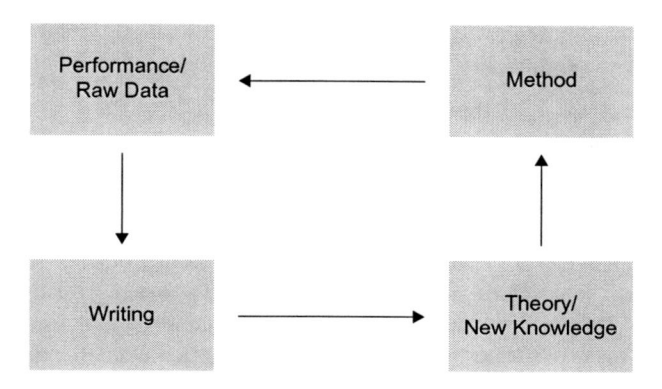

Figure 1. Traditional approach.

In this traditional approach, writing appears to have a unique link to new knowledge (see figure 1), whereas any knowledge gained from the performance experience is limited to the undisciplined and chaotic field of the ephemeral moment; it can only be channelled and disciplined by the written word.

Critical writing in performance studies and the wider academic field can give the impression that it stands in for the witnessing of the performance event – a replacement that puts into words what the event could not utter. In my experience as a teacher, many students often feel that, after reading a critical piece of writing that analyses a performance, there is no need to see (or have seen) the actual event. This misunderstanding subordinates the performance event to the writing that is to define it, as it implies that the only knowledge that can be gained from witnessing the event is its interpretation expressed in writing. In undergraduate studies, writing is thus presented to the students as separate from what they engage with in the studio, or what they experience when attending professional performances. Some see this approach as antithetical to the values performance practice as a discipline can bring as to the production of knowledge.

In her pioneering book, *Unmarked* (1993), Peggy Phelan asserts that "[p]erformance's only life is in the present. Performance cannot be saved, recorded, documented, or otherwise participate in the circulation of representations" for "once it does so, it becomes something other than performance" (146). Phelan's statement captures a cultural shift in performance studies, where the value of performance lies in its resistance to representation, particularly that of patriarchy. Following this, Simon Jones believes that the strength of performance, as knowledge production, is its non-reproducible form. The subordination of performance to reproducible forms that fit into a commodity culture is therefore problematic:

> Unlike the good experiment, which can be written up, then endlessly reproduced globally, performance as a play of weakness troubles the strong logics of so called disciplines: its very here-nowness resists the ubiquity of the commodity and offers us a glimpse of another way of knowing. (Jones, 2009: 25)

Jones argues that, throughout the history of the academy, "abstractors [have been] favoured over applicators as the primary knowledge formulators" (2009: 23) because abstract knowledge is infinitely repeatable and therefore compliant in the "operation of commoditization" (25). Consequently, Jones demands a shift in the conception of what constitutes research and knowledge. For Jones, Practice-as-Research (PaR) in performance[1] is a political manoeuvre to readdress this balance. PaR can provide a *new* context for performance; it can demonstrate how the prioritisation of text as a source of knowledge not only limits the production of new knowledge; it also betrays the value of the performance event in its implicit claim to represent it (Jones, 2009: 27).

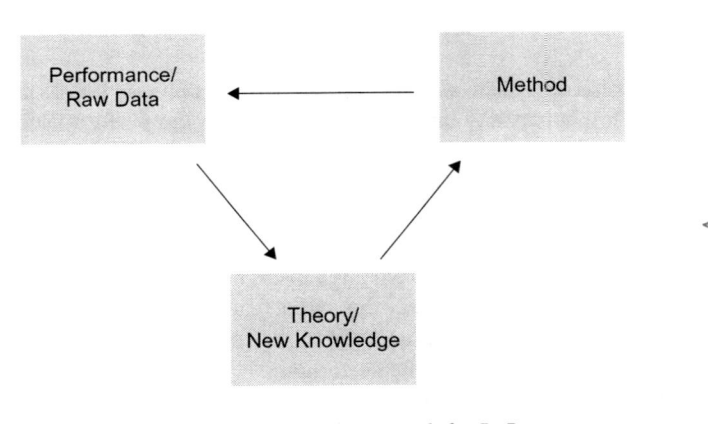

Figure 2. Proposed approach for PaR.

So, if we remove *writing* from the diagram, giving performance a direct link to new knowledge (see figure 2), then how are we expected to interpret the 'weak' or 'raw data' that performance generates? Jones appears to have great difficulty to put forward a way in which to make this new form of knowledge 'work' in the current system of higher education institutions in the UK. It seems that performance is also 'weak' because its knowledge value, as a stand-alone event, is also hotly debated within the academic spheres of theatre and performance. Thus, Jones proposes that, in place of judgement (in the form of the traditional and "abstract" "writing alongside") there should be an "extension of dialogue" amongst the research community members (2009: 28). The value of the work as research will then accrue through the on-going responsive dialogue within the practice-as-research community. Such a community, however, is very small and its exclusivity threatens to undermine the transparency of the criteria in which the doctoral award is given. Kershaw and Piccini concede, on the one hand, that there may be some occasions where the production of work within the academic community is "enough" for the final submission of the PhD (2003: 121). On the other hand, even if an expert panel of peer reviewers judged a performance in this way, it could not be critiqued on the global stage of academia due to its restricted circulation.

Robin Nelson, too, acknowledges that an "artwork may stand alone as evidence of a research outcome" when "judged by those in a position to make such judgements, namely peer reviewers" (2009: 125), but he fervently demands more traditional methods of assessing, nevertheless. Nelson maintains that it would be difficult to identify the knowledge value in such artwork without some contextual guidance. Even though the research imperative may be "in play", the reviewer may need context in order to identify the performance work's complexities: "However an artefact may be disseminated, the context(s) of its showing may not be transferrable" (125). Nelson also asserts that "... merely to expose something is not to argue it": while artwork can produce ideas and even reflect arguments, it is independent of *developing* those arguments (116). This view was, and is currently, shared by funders in the UK.

Therefore, a 100% submission of performance events was not an option when I was a PhD candidate, nor is it currently available for any funded practice-led researcher in the UK. Although the Arts and Humanities Research Board's (AHRB) requirements (then and now) do not specify either form or volume of the written support for the practice component of a thesis, a report was and is formally requested.[2] Furthermore, my institution's (Lancaster University) academic regulations include an expectation of a written submission of between 40,000 to 60,000 words. Thus, the idea of thinking through performance alone was not something that I was ever in the position to consider.

However, the theoretical assertion that performance can carry knowledge, coupled with the demand for writing (from both funders and the academy), prompts a new approach to thinking about the relationships between performance, theory, writing and new knowledge. In this way of thinking about the relationships, the performance practice does not rely on the writing, simply to justify its link to new knowledge. In chapter 14, Barbara Milech and Ann Schilo refer to a similar structure, a "research-question model" (2013: 10), where the journeys of written practice and performance practice run in parallel, emanating from the same research question(s). In performance, if judgement through a scheme of peer reviewing is tenable, this would account for the arrow between performance practice and new knowledge (see figure 3).

```
        ┌──────────────┐                    ┌──────────────┐
        │ Performance/ │◄───────────────────│   Writing    │
        │   Practice   │                    │   Practice   │
        └──────┬───────┘                    └──────┬───────┘
               │                                   │
               └───────────────┐   ┌───────────────┘
                               ▼   ▼
                        ┌──────────────┐
                        │   Theory/    │
                        │ New Knowledge│
                        └──────────────┘
```

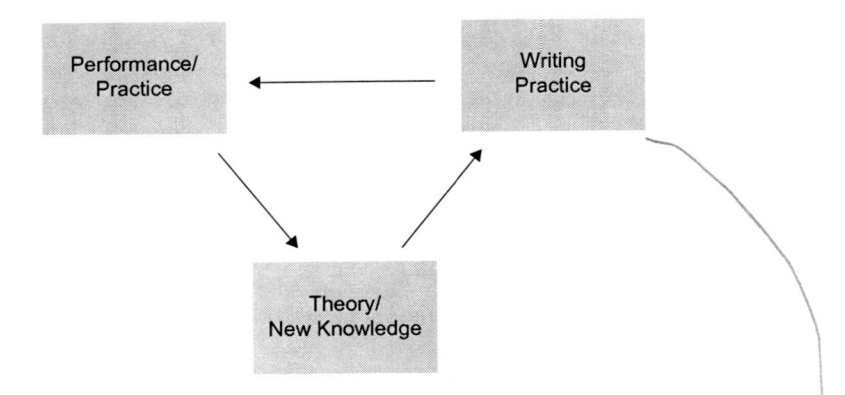

Figure 3. New approach.

However, there is an important omission in this new approach, which needs explaining. When compared to the *Traditional Approach* (in figure 1), *Method* is missing in the *New Approach* diagram. In the new approach, writing is recognised as a practice; an alternative but equal practice to the practice of performance. There is a method to creating performance, just as there is a method to creating writing. The method of creating writing, however, is not usually discussed in written submissions, unless it is specifically relevant to the knowledge outcomes of the submission. If performance is considered as a different but equal expression to writing, it could be argued that there should be no obligation for the performance to outline or justify its method or process if it is not considered to be relevant to the knowledge outcomes. Method in arts practices (including writing) has a different relation to knowledge from that which it has in most academic research (I'm thinking here of scientific methods in particular), where it is usually imperative that the method for the practical component is outlined, explained and justified. A candidate is not expected to include the process of writing and re-writing in the final written thesis; nor are they expected to present or discuss the thesis structure alongside the actual discussion. The same should apply, in principle, to the performance practice. The inclusion of this 'messy' and chaotic practice that is traditionally hidden from, and often subordinated to, the final PhD submission should be a *choice* in the same way it always has been for the written component. If this messy practice does not work for the thesis, then its relevance is limited. To include (or highlight) the messy and chaotic method of making creative work must be a decision made by the candidate; a decision that works together with how he or she chooses the particular approach for situating his or her work.

In figure 3, there is also a new link (or meeting point) between performance practice and writing practice that needs to be explained. The link represents an area that can be unique to each PhD, and I shall therefore discuss it in more detail in the section titled *The Creative Process*. In any event, whether a candidate should actually follow the *New Approach* (rather than the *Traditional Approach*) is a decision that could depend on the theories with which the thesis engages. In the following section, I outline the particular circumstances that shaped my own journey and reasoning behind my approach, and the ways in which I made the connection between knowledge and creative practice.

THE CIRCUMSTANCES

Working on my own, I felt that I had actually too much freedom, which prompted anxiety and doubts about the starting point for my creative practice. In 2001, I had secured funding from AHRB with an application outlining the general area of my research and the initial research questions. From there, no clear direction presented itself. In retrospect, though, I realise that I did not have as much freedom as I had anticipated. First, funding from the AHRB was granted on condition that I adhered to their quality assurance and guidelines. Second, in initially following a traditional approach – by default – I discovered that this choice did not support the theories and research questions I was to engage with. Third, my creative method and style had already developed well before the PhD, so to consider the PhD as a blank piece of paper was naïve.

The AHRB guidelines for the initiation and framing of performance work dictated, to some extent, the initial form of knowledge production in my thesis. Before starting the creative process, I was to generate "Research Questions":

> [F]rom the start, for virtually all of its grants schemes, the AHRB required applicants at all levels of experience to formulate a "research question or questions" that their projects would address. ... a move that, of course, significantly restricts the exploratory quality of research as all questions imply a limit to their potential answers. (Kershaw, 2009: 111)

This was certainly a limitation that I perceived at the outset of my research: putting forward a series of questions, for me, placed the event of performance into a traditional context. But how was I to expect the performance practice to answer my questions? Was the performance to be understood as 'raw' data? That is, could I really expect a performance (or a series of performance workshops or rehearsals) created by me to answer questions that I had put forward? Subsequently, and I will discuss this in more detail later, I realised that the problem lay in my assumption about what a research question was (or could be) in relation to the practice. However, my thoughts at the time were that, surely, what I intended to happen as the artistic creator/director, *would* happen – therefore, how would this open up the space for unintentional, unforeseen occurrences that could answer my research questions? Even if unintentional occurrences did occur, then what was their place if they did not answer my research questions? How was I to value these occurrences within the context of the research?

These were the questions that I asked my supervisor in the early stages of the research. As a dancer and phenomenologist, he had a very clear view about how to research through practice; and this view accommodated the AHRB's demand for research questions. Accordingly, my early research questions were born from critical and philosophical theory and concerned the experience of an event, agency, power and responsibility when confronted with a video/live image. They arose in response to academic writings about media and authenticity, and often quite specific reactions to writers such as Walter Benjamin, Jean Baudrillard and Philip Auslander. Some other questions responded to various arts practices, including the work of Bill Viola, Gary Hill and Tony Oursler. After producing these questions, though, I was at a loss as to how I could progress to the next stage. My supervisor suggested that I use the research questions to develop a series of drama workshops that would actively investigate them. He also suggested that everything in the workshop plan must be justified: the method and reasoning behind the creative method must be transparent and clearly related to the journey of the thesis, which was to be explained in the written component of my thesis. In that way, there would be a sound, transparent logic that was 'carried' from the questions through to the practical tasks in the workshop.

However, this approach proved to be exceptionally difficult. I found that there was usually a significant leap between a question regarding perception, on the one hand, and an actual practical suggestion for a workshop, on the other. I found myself writing and writing, for the sake of moving from one question to another; on to a question that might move towards a specific practical workshop suggestion. I started to get frustrated with the process, feeling that it was moving further and further away from the works that had inspired my initial questions. Nevertheless, my supervisor was convinced that this way was the only 'true' method of using performance practice to generate new knowledge. Although I was beginning to have my doubts (and felt quite insecure about being able to fully justify the workshop outline I put forward), I therefore completed the task for the first workshop.

The workshop consisted of drama based exercises with a video camera, with five invited undergraduate student performers. I set the performers tasks, such as to copy the actions of a live performer and then to copy the actions of a pre-recorded videoed performer; to anticipate these actions, and to develop them/respond to them. Afterwards, I interviewed all of the student performers on their thoughts about their experiences. When attempting to analyse the 'raw data' in order to develop the next workshop (but possibly also thinking about working towards a performance), I reached a difficult question: what exactly counted as 'data'? The only tangible result was the qualitative feedback from the performers. I felt the creative process closing down and mutating into a social or psychological study that positioned performance within a traditional approach as in figure1. I felt that this particular approach to understanding and deploying the research questions was taking me away from the performances, art and literature that had inspired the questions and was therefore not a productive methodology for my research project. It could not take full advantage of the "openness and excess" of creative performance Kershaw writes about (2009: 112).

I took these thoughts back to my supervisor who still suggested that I stick with this process. A difference in our theoretical commitments began to become apparent at this time. In his own academic work as a PaR researcher, my supervisor's method was to notate his movement "in response to what he had witnessed ... according to a method derived from the descriptive phenomenology of Edmund Husserl and the hermeneutic ontology of Martin Heidegger" (Stewart, 2005: 363). On the other hand, much of the reading I was engaged with, and which had inspired my original questions, critiqued the possibility of 'essence', a concept that lies at the heart of phenomenological understanding. At this time, I became quite distressed about the fact that I had no faith in the only method available to me, and I started to look into the possibility of changing supervisor. As it turned out, a change of supervisor was not as traumatic as I had anticipated: it was amicably dealt with by all concerned. It is therefore worth noting that, due to the possible resistance this new approach to research might trigger in supervisors committed to more traditional approaches, debates over how to precede might test and highlight theoretical differences between candidate and supervisor at quite an early stage.

Under the guidance of a new supervisor, I began to put forward an alternate idea for a methodology. I was encouraged to develop my questions further through the practice of reading and writing, in order to clarify the theoretical framework within which the questions tentatively existed. Several new clusters of theoretical concerns developed, each of which provided temporary platforms from which to frame my research questions. In psychoanalytical writings, for instance, there are many historical references to technology, such as Sigmund Freud's analogy of the 'Mystic Writing Pad' (1925) or Jacques Lacan's writing on anamorphism in Holbein's *Ambassadors* (1977).[3]

Figure 4. Voice.

Inspired by these references, I decided to use the video image as an active metaphor through which to develop my research questions.[4] These questions concerned neither the actor's craft, nor psychology, nor human experience in phenomenological, sociological or psychological terms; rather, they grew, with the help of my supervisor, from a very specific combination of cultural, aesthetic and philosophical theory and psychoanalytic practice. A clear theoretical framework now enabled me to determine how key historical and contemporary arts practices could be situated, and therefore understood. While my reading helped me analyse the artwork of others, it also led me to practices that were to inspire my own. I tried to identify specific ideas in art that were said to achieve particular aesthetic effects, and then reworked these ideas within the context of my own making. For example, following a lead by Josette Fèral (1992), I began to look at 1960s Minimalist work. I discovered how the sheer dynamic of an object could fill the environment with a presence that resonated beyond its 'objectness'. This discovery inspired the twenty, six metre high white muslin strips that provided the walls of my first video performance installation, *Voice*.

This starting point generated another idea for how I might, on the one hand, frame a live body in a way that makes its aesthetic quality similar to that of a video image; and, on the other, how to frame the video image of a body in a way that gives it the aesthetic quality of a live body. This meant that my research questions would help to identify what Robin Nelson (my external examiner) would later call the "research dimension" of the project: the research questions offered a focus or context to my ideas (Nelson, 2004:125). I realised that, rather than expecting performance to answer research questions directly, each question was a *creative response* to what I had read and subsequently furthered the reading and contextualised *performance ideas*. The questions were *not distinct* from the ideas I had for the performance work; they, too, were a response to the same writings and artworks. However, whereas the performance ideas tended to be prompted by other performances and art, the research questions led to further reading (as well as helping frame the performance practice). I no longer had to justify every step between a question and an action: the questions, rather than directly developing performance practice, continually contextualised it within an identified theoretical framework. Now, I no longer felt that my initial written questions had to take precedence (come before) my performance ideas. So, the meeting points between the theory (knowledge) and the performance creation were becoming clear – I had started to gain some kind of direction about how I could begin to bring ideas forward into practice in a way that could begin a working method. But I still was not clear on the exact form of the written component; nor was I clear in how my performance ideas could be generative and investigative.

THE CREATIVE PROCESS

There is a paradox connected with the question of *intention* in PaR. On the one hand, intention (in the form of research questions, performance ideas, contextual framework etc.) is often seen as fundamental in defining the piece of work as a PaR project, rather than a piece that exists outside of the academy (Nelson, 2009: 125). On the other hand, when the question is "what constitutes research for assessment purposes, the key factor is not what is intended or produced as research, but what is received as research" (Chamberlain in Mock, 2004: 131). I was concerned with the real possibility that, once I had followed through with my ideas for performance, I would nevertheless end up simply using the written component to justify and contextualise the decisions I had made, rather than really thinking through performance itself. How could I divorce myself from my intentions when working through performance? Was I to assume that putting these performance ideas into a context of my own making would necessarily produce an event that was PhD worthy?

In response to work presented at the PARIP[5] conference in 2003, Franc Chamberlain articulates this anxiety well:

> I didn't get a sense of the theory being used either as a perspective on the work, or as an articulation of the making of this specific piece of performance, but more as a general justification for the work. I didn't get a sense, for example, that a particular performance was engaged in testing a claim by a specific theorist, or in using a resonant remark as a stimulus for investigation. Without this connection, any theory can be applied to the work by any audience member. How can we, in these circumstances, privilege the maker of the performance over any receiver of it? (in Mock, 2004: 131)

Chamberlain's remarks fit quite neatly into the *Traditional Approach* of how knowledge can work in PaR: the understanding of "theory" as the (I assume, written) "articulation of the making" reminds me of the time I was asked to write to justify the link between the research question and the workshop idea. However, Chamberlain's words do point towards one key issue: that the "connection" between writing practice and performance practice remains 'mysterious' for him as a 'receiver' of the work. This appears to be the case because no information is provided that enables the receiver to identify the investigative journey between the first *intention* of the artist (the "stimulus" or the "claim") to what is received as a knowledge output. In other words, the process of development is not transparent.

So, how can you mark a process of development in creative arts research? My original attempts at a methodology following a *Traditional Approach* aimed to make transparent the link between my research questions and the performance outcome. However, this meant that, for me, the methodology began to take over the creative process. It produced qualitative outcomes that I could not locate within an arts context. However, if there is no transparent and direct (reproducible) link between the research questions and the thesis outcome, then how can the thesis be understood as PaR? Furthermore, if writing is no longer seen to represent the knowledge lost in the moment of performance, then how are these two practices related to each other?

Roberta Mock claims: "Too much analysis by practitioner-scholars of their own work seems to me to be justification rather than *reflection*" (Mock, 2004: 137-138.

Emphasis added). Reflection refers to the artist's personal, as well as objective, response to the work, and this is of vital importance when responding to artistic work. In chapter 14, Milech and Schilo write about a "hollow" at the heart of an artwork:

> [W]hen art does more than recapitulate generic conventions, it paradoxically speaks the not-sayable, and so forms a space for the reader to draw on her thinking and feeling to make a meaning that makes sense of things in her world. (Milech&Schilo, 2013: 237)

Crucially, this attempt to make meaning can take place in either further artistic practice *or* written practice. First, I wish to outline how this process can be seen to occur through artistic practice.

Figure 5. Voice.

Marcel Duchamp articulates this essential "hollow" (or what he calls "gap" in the work) and, interestingly, relates his experience directly to a *loss of intention* in the creative process:

> In the creative act, the artist goes from intention to realisation through a chain of totally subjective reactions. His struggle toward the realisation is a series of efforts, pains, satisfaction, refusals, decisions, which also cannot and must not be fully self-conscious, at least on the aesthetic plane. The result of this struggle is a difference between the intention and its realisation, a difference which the artist is not aware of. Consequently, in the chain of *reactions* accompanying the creative act, a link is missing. This gap, representing the inability of the artist to express fully his intention, this difference between what he intended to realise and did realise, is the personal 'art coefficient' contained in the work. In other words, the personal 'art coefficient' is like an arithmetical relation between the unexpressed but intended and the unintentionally expressed. (Duchamp, [1957] 1959: 77-78. Emphasis added).

The not-sayable is seen here from the perspective of the maker of the work, in terms of the distance between what was originally intended and what was actually produced. The not-sayable here is double: the artist's failure to articulate herself through the object, as well as the object's expression of something *other* to what the artist wanted to 'say'. These expressions of failure and unintended realisation index the work's digression from original intentions. The failure of the work, and its unintended expression, form "spaces" that provoke the practice-led researcher to attempt to 'fill' these spaces in order to make meaning.

Susan Melrose asserts that this process is also implicit within the practical process of making performance, and it is within this process that the development of the theory can be identified. Following Umberto Eco (who discusses Immanuel Kant's notion of *schemata*), Melrose argues that the practitioner must put forward schemata before being able to make a discovery:

> On the operations of reflective judgement, Eco notes that "the reflective judgement produces schemata to be able to observe, and to experiment". My suggestion here is that devising practices, in the mainstream (e.g. in the recent work of Lepage, together with Complicité and DV8) operate through the (experimental) schemata of reflective judgment – that is, they "produce schemata [in the devising workshop] to be able to observe..."With this schematism", Eco adds, "the intellect does not construct the simple determination of a possible object, but makes the object, constructs it, and in the course of this activity (problematic in itself) it proceeds by [a crucial] trial and error". (2002: np)

So, the aim of the artist is to construct a particular object (schema) in order to see (through trial and error) how it manifests itself in actuality (through the course of an activity). However, if this gap, necessary for development and therefore the possibility of the 'new', always occurs in the creation of art (art that "does more than recapitulate generic conventions" or produces something more than what can be determined by the intellect), then one could ask, as Melrose does, what would be the point of the practitioner's attempt to outline this process in written words?

From the perspective of an academic researcher, the attempt amounts to regaining some control over a process that, says Duchamp, eludes conscious activity. Melissa Trimingham shows how the researcher can acknowledge this elusive activity in a process commensurate with Melrose's articulation of schemata. Trimingham describes a "hermeneutic" methodology that she believes may have a "wide application" for those in PaR (2002: 55). Following a concept by Gestalt theorist Kurt Lewin (further developed in Action Research), she articulates a spiral process, during which we are returned to our original point of entry, but with renewed understanding:

> What I am suggesting here is that setting tasks ... guided by very clear aims and objectives keeps the research on course and maintains control over a very disparate and unpredictable process. When linked to the spiral model the researcher is not bound by such tasks; it is perfectly possible to abandon the original intent in the heat of creative work. ... however, I suggest that the very process of later evaluating such work, ... then formulating and articulating new aims and objectives and *new* tasks ... is a necessary discipline for keeping the research process under control. (2002: 56-57).

Here intention, in the form of research aims, is not that which should be attempted to be realised but, instead, that which can be abandoned in the "heat" of the creative process. In this "heat", alternative aims or aspirations presumably emerge from the artist's interaction with the object/environment. It is this shift from the original aims to the evaluation of the work that marks the "gap" that separates intention from reflection. What is brought forward by Trimingham is a further articulation of "intention", and how it can be understood in terms of research. Here, the process of development becomes evident in the contrast between the original tasks and the new ones.

Writing and discussions about the performance(s) with peers and my supervisor initially provided the reflection I needed to distance myself from my original intentions for the piece. It is not uncommon in the UK that a PaR candidate belongs to a theatre company, where such discussions can provide a much needed support work for the candidate. In this situation, there are other people in the group who could have alternative ideas to put forward, though, and may take the process in a different way to that planned by the candidate. Moreover, a company may have other priorities alongside a thesis, such as certain commitments to funders or producing houses. When speaking to other PaR candidates at the time, it seemed to me that the solution might be to carefully locate and define the 'object' in play, within the process and/or performance, and take full artistic responsibility for that (e.g., the narrative, or the scenography). In this way, the candidate can keep clear focus on her aims for the thesis and the meeting points between the performance, the writing and the new knowledge.

For me, the practice of writing brought its own momentum to the creative process. As stated earlier, the non-sayable forms a space that provokes the practice-led researcher to fill it in order to make meaning. The writing can attempt to make sense of the work in terms of a) what the work does not 'say' (how it has shifted away from the aims put forward, and b) what it does express in terms of the artists personal reflection and where these reflections might be resituated in the theoretical framework.

In the case of my thesis research, all workshops and rehearsals were undertaken alone. I had no intention to experiment; I simply aimed to 'carry out' performance ideas or 'rules' for performance in the space. For me, it was artistically liberating not to have to expect that the performance practice should, would or could produce 'the new'. I felt that to aim for the 'new' at the point of entering the studio would be to place the wrong kind of pressure and expectation on what was essentially an artistic process of trial and error. Aiming to uncover the 'new' would divert from the creative or aesthetic agenda of realising the performance ideas and/or the 'rules'. In the studio, I put up the muslin sheets; I manipulated them so that I could see the video and the shadows together; I positioned objects like a set of standing dominoes ready to be triggered by, for instance, the 'play' button on the DVD; or triggered by the presence of an audience. There was therefore little reflection during this time of 'setting up'. The work had to be complete before I could begin to reflect on it within the context of the theoretical framework from which it had emerged. This is not to say, however, that I did *not* discover the 'new' during this process (only that I did not set up a workshop expecting it). Indeed, unexpected outcomes relevant to my thesis did occur on occasion. For example, the video image that was projected onto the uneven surface of muslin sheets brought with it a quality that gave the impression that the figure projected was 'more' than a video projection. Its weight during movement seemed heavier and it appeared to be able to 'hide' behind the muslin cloth at will. This quality was not to be found amongst my ideas for performance. Yet this quality spoke quite clearly to the themes concerning my thesis and, on reflection, developed into 'rules' for an expression of the 'uncanny'.

Figure 6. Voice.

The performance practice therefore provokes the practice-led researcher to make meaning. Due to its personal nature, this meaning seems to run parallel to the 'not sayable' form of meaning brought about by the performance work. It is in this way that writing, as a *reflection* on the space that opens up in performance, can be part of the research process and part of the research methodology. My own PhD thesis (including performance events and a written analysis and reflection) mapped onto Trimingham's hermeneutic circle of understanding. 'Tasks' were initially put forward as performance ideas (discussed above) and later as 'rules', which I arrived at by reframing my reflections through writing. The rules identified patterns in the application of the video image in performance from both architectural set design and dramatic engagement. In order to identify these rules, I had to pare down, simplify and generalise the complexities of performance practice. For this reason, the analysis of my practice that takes place in the written practice would be exceptionally limited if it were to be considered a 'justification' of the performance submission. The decisions about how the complexity of the performance should be pared down were not informed by my experience of making performance, but by my experience of academic reading. In *Absorption and Theatricality* (1980), Michael Fried categorises artistic practices into those that have a high dramatic engagement with the viewer and those that have an architecturally immersive one. Based on these very general notions (derived from similar theoretical ideas in other academic sources), I produced the rules[6] that were to initiate each next phase of performance practice. The production of the rules therefore marked both the completion and the limitation of the writing at that stage.

The writing process was absolutely central to the development of my methodology, as well as to my early career as a teacher and academic.[7] The theoretical framework provided me with a kind of lens through which to 'see' the work. In writing about the performance through this lens, I could (re)situate the performance.[8] The written component and the creation of performance were mutually necessary for the production. Under such conditions, writing can be an essential part of a process of reflective judgement, in which the relationship between the performance and the writing is complimentary, rather than supplementary. Although there were still moments of performance analysis in the final written component, the thesis itself did not stand as a justification for each performance. Rather, it brought together rules for categorising arts practices; its initiative was therefore very different to simply interpreting each performance; and also very different from the performance ideas that drove each performance.

So, it might be helpful for a new artist academic to consider that, when thinking about writing, there are different ways to understand how writing can work within a thesis — and that this 'work' depends on the research approach. The traditional approach may demand a critical viewpoint that can only be identified and expressed through writing; or a report or a document that attempts to recall or justify a past event in terms of the research questions. Here, writing is understood as translating knowledge inherent in the artwork or creative process to make it accessible to a wider audience. Or, writing can be seen as an essential element of the methodlogy, where its course runs parallel to the performance practice, with playful interjections a reader can recognise as inspirational to the process in some way. Instead of doing the work of justifying, it can offer alternative 'lenses' through which the performance practice can be understood; it can offer insights into the failure to meet with ideas or with reflection on, and analysis of, the unexpected or unintended. In that way, its connection with the arts practice can be both playful and contextualising. So, although there can be no rules to the relation between writing practice and performance practice, especially if each is to be considered a creative act, it is important for both candidates and supervisors to understand exactly how each is being put to work, and how each functions toward the production if the thesis.

NOTES

[1] There are many terms surrounding research in this area, but practice constitutes part or all of them. My use of the term practice-as-research refers to "research into performance practice, [that] determine[s] how that practice may be developing new insights into or knowledge about the forms, genres, uses, etc., of performance itself" (Kershaw, 2000:138).

[2] The AHRB is now known as the Arts and Humanities Research Council (AHRC)."We expect all of our research projects to have some form of documentation of the research process, which usually takes the form of textual analysis or explanation to support the research's position and to demonstrate critical reflection." (AHRC, May 2012)

[3] I must stress that actually settling on and developing one particular theoretical framework in conjunction with my performance ideas actually took years, and I eventually put forward Lacanian psychoanalysis in order to simplify and draw some order from what was a very fragmented process.

[4] The research questions at the time were as follows: In an environment where technology (the object) represents the human subject, when does the subject lead/act/make decisions/dominate their immediate perception of events; when does the subject follow/when is the subject dominated through choice/no choice/when does the subject make themselves invisible; when does the subject negotiate or manage/reflectively readdress/respond to this environment?

[5] Practice As Research In Performance. A five-year project funded by the Arts and Humanities Research Board, UK, led by Baz Kershaw, University of Bristol (2001–2006). http://www.bris.ac.uk/parip/introduction.htm

[6] Specifically, the rules were as follows: 1) The body or architectural space physically changes or disrupts the video image. 2) The materiality of the audio sound and video light is emphasised over, or equally expressed alongside, its representational features. 3) The a-synchronisation of the technologies whose usual synchronisation serve the technologically produced subject position. 4) The video image as absorptive object makes a direct reference to the physical space/absorptive subject.

[7] A side issue to be considered here is that 100% practice theses at PhD level could produce successful candidates who lack essential writing skills. The whole academic system is currently based on the ability to write well; researchers without those skills would be under qualified, disempowered and disadvantaged in the academic community. I embarked on the PhD immediately after completing my MA and, before it, the BA. Once I had completed my PhD, I realised that I was not experienced enough in the 'professional world' to apply for an artist's residency. I could have gained experience, but I knew that in doing so I would risk missing out on a university position. After studying for eight years, I was also deeply in debt and so felt under pressure to gain financial stability. However, professionally I had concerns with following a career in University: when thinking about publishing my written thesis, I knew that it was far too focussed on a singular practice and not broad enough to be of general relevance (as a lecturer at Lancaster University commented, PaR theses have an inherently narrow focus, which makes it difficult to get them published). However, I was qualified to teach, write and produce performance in HE and so have been successful in gaining posts in HE institutions that are 'industry facing' and value 'professional' teaching. In these posts, I have had to follow my written research as there are no resources for the practice-as-researcher in my position, other than to practice through teaching.

[8] In the earlier stages of the work, before I had even developed a theoretical framework, the process was more or less the same, but the lens was a little more 'long distance'. For example, the writing would answer such questions as where is the work situated historically? Culturally? What aspects of the performance can be identified elsewhere, in other arts practices? Who has written about those practices? The writing that developed from such analyses served to inspire the next set of performance ideas.

REFERENCES

Arts and Humanities Research Council, UK (2012). Retrieved from:http://www.ahrc.ac.uk/FundingOpportunities/Documents/RGPLA%20Pamphlet.pdf

Duchamp, M. ([1957] 1959).The creative act. Transcript of Duchamp's talk at the session on the creative act, Convention of the American Federation of Arts, Houston, Texas, April 1957.In R. Lebel, *Marcel Duchamp*(pp. 77–78). New York, NY: Grove Press.

Féral, J (1992). What is left of performance art? Autopsy of function, birth of a genre. In *Discourse, 14*, 142–62.

Freeman, J. (2009). *Blood,sweat and theory: Research through practice in performance*. Faringdon, England: Libri Publishing.

Freud, S. (1961). A note upon the 'mystic writing-pad'. In *The Standard Edition of the Complete Psychological Works of Sigmund Freud, Volume XIX (1923–1925): The Ego and the Id and Other Works* (pp. 225–232). London: Hogarth Press.

Fried, M. (1980). *Absorption and theatricality: painting and beholder in the age of Diderot*. Berkeley, CA: University of California Press.

Jones, S. (2009). The courage of complementarity: Practice-as-Research as a paradigm shift. In L. Allegue, S. Jones, B. Kershaw & A. Piccini (Eds.), *Practice-as-research in performance and screen*. Basingstoke, England: Palgrave Macmillan.

Kershaw, B. (2009). Practice as Research through Performance. In H. Smith & R.T. Dean (Eds.), *Practice-led research, research-led practice in the creative arts* (pp. 104 - 125). Edinburgh, Scotland: Edinburgh University Press.

Kleiman, P. (2012). Scene changes and key changes: Disciplines and identities in HE dance, drama and music. In *Tribes and territories in the twenty first century: Rethinking the significance of disciplines in higher education*. New York, NY: Routledge.

Lacan, J. (1977). *Four Fundamental Concepts of Psychoanalysis*. London, England: Hogarth Press.

Melrose, S. (2002).*Entertaining other options: Restaging 'theory' in the age of practice as research*. Retrieved from: http://www.sfmelrose.u-net.com/inaugural/

Mock, R. (2004). Reflections on practice as research following the PARIP conference, 2003. *Studies in Theatre and Performance, 24*(2), 129–141.

Nelson, R. (2009). Modes of Practice-as-Research knowledge and their place in the academy. In L. Allegue, S. Jones, B. Kershaw & A. Piccini (Eds.), *Practice-as-research in performance and screen*. Basingstoke, England: Palgrave Macmillan.

O'Brien, S. (2006). *Creating the subject: Towards a psychoanalytical framework for the use of video in performance art* (PhD thesis). Lancaster: Lancaster University.

O'Brien, S. (2007). Practice as research in performance: A response to reflective judgement. *Studies in Theatre and Performance, 27*(1), 73–81.

Phelan, P. (1993). *Unmarked: The Politics of Performance*. London, England: Routledge.

Stewart, N. (2005). Dancing the time of place: Fieldwork, phenomenology and nature's choreography. In *Performing nature: Explorations in ecology and the arts*. Bern, Switzerland: Peter Lang.

Trimingham, M. (2002). A methodology for practice as research. In *Studies in theatre and performance*. Volume 22, No. 1, pp54–60

AFFILIATION

Sarah O'Brien
Teesside University
United Kingdom

BARBARA MILECH & ANN SCHILO

14. THINKING THROUGH ART, CREATING THROUGH TEXT

"I Think I May Be Finding My Own Voice"

On meeting in the corridor, a colleague commented, "Ann, you're looking happy!"
  "Just returning from a supervisory meeting", I responded.
  "Ahhh," she nodded, "real work"!
Back at my desk, confronted by a pile of spread sheets for the next Excellence in Research Assessment exercise, a box full of emails, and the usual start-of-semester paperwork, I paused to reflect on contemporary academic life and my "real work".

Seventeen years ago, I was thrown in at the deep end of supervision. I had just completed my own PhD, the first staff member in my School of Art to hold one, and so deemed qualified to supervise our School's first doctoral applicant. At that time, creative doctorates were new to our university, and I still recall the feedback on my first student's initial candidacy proposal: one reviewer questioned why she bothered to undertake a PhD when clearly she couldn't write and would be much better served going back to the studio and to painting, a skill in which she was well qualified. We were incensed, but, through her determination and my on-going belief in her, she was awarded her doctorate with a Vice Chancellor's Commendation for an exceptional thesis in 1999. Since then much has changed. (*Ann*)

* * *

Early in the 1990s, a colleague and I proposed that an applicant in our area – literature, creative writing and cultural studies – enrol in our university's doctoral programme and that his thesis should take the form of a novel. His proposal was rejected, with advice that the applicant should resubmit, showing that the thesis would include a theoretical piece; he did, but even then his proposal was denied, because university regulations then didn't allow for a research thesis pursued even in part through a creative component. We were incensed (as was the student, who withdrew), but failure was motivating. We worked with colleagues from creative-arts disciplines in Humanities and research administrators at university level to establish pathways for research students working in fields of creative production. And we had success: in 1997 Curtin University established a Masters of Creative Arts; in 1998 it established a Doctor of Creative Arts – indeed, university regulations were adjusted to enable a wide range of exegesis-plus-production forms of doctoral

---

A.-Chr. Engels-Schwarzpaul and M. A. Peters (Eds.), Of other Thoughts: Non-Traditional Ways to the Doctorate: A Guidebook for Candidates and Supervisors, 239–257.
© *2013 Sense Publishers. All rights reserved.*

theses across the university. In this way, Curtin was typical of the development of creative-production research degrees in Australian universities during the 1990s (see Baker and Buckley, 2009, 27). (*Barbara*)

* * *

As we look back to that time a generation ago, when proposals for studio-based doctoral study or for a doctoral project that included writing a novel were rejected, we see clearly that then (as now) the central question is "how can a work of art/ design/journalism/architecture/film/creative-writing, etc. be a piece of research?" We understand research as posing a question about something of significance to more than oneself, and providing an idea that forms an answer to that question. And we believe research needs to be disciplined – that it entails not only pursuing an answer to a formulated question, but also knowing the fields of practice, criticism and social life from which that question emerges, understanding what others in those domains have made and said in regard to the prevailing question, and then trying to add a further perspective. What we did not see then, or now, is why university research defined in this way cannot be pursued and expressed in ways that embrace imaginative as well as rational ways of knowing.

* * *

A poem should not mean, but be. (Archibald MacLeish, "Ars Poetica", 106)

In his poem "Ars Poetica" (1926), Archibald MacLeish, poet, playwright, lawyer, and critic in the tradition of high modernism, suggests that there are at least two ways of knowing the world and our place in it: one attached to "meaning" and another to "being". In doing so, he recurs to a long-standing Western tradition that opposes philosophy and science to art, but he defends the way of knowing provided by a poem, a dance, a painting, a sculpture, or even, though not in his experience, a digital installation.

It is a tradition whose bedrock is Plato, for whom art is that which feeds and waters the emotions, permissible in an ideal republic only if it functions in the service of philosophy, of reason. That tradition carries on through Aristotle, who sought to defend the value of art as an independent way of knowing through explicating its nature as imitation and its function as catharsis; through Horace, whose *Ars Poetica* is alluded to in the title of MacLeish's poem; through European Renaissance and Neo-classicist theorists who argued that the value of poetry/art is that it teaches through delighting; through European Romantics who insisted that Imagination is a way of knowing, different and superior to wit or reason or science (with its devotion to 'truth' built on an edifice of 'facts'); and through twentieth-century debates which define art either as meaningful in-and-of-itself or as a response to human experience that finds completion through its reception.

Michael Polayni — tacit knowledge

Our purpose here, as we think about creative-arts research, is not to detail this tradition of Western aesthetic debate, nor even to probe its presiding binaries in any detail (though we observe that current debates about creative-production research enact them apace). Rather, it is to underscore what is implicit in such a long tradition: there are at least two ways of knowing, and one belongs to what we call art.

When MacLeish concludes "Ars Poetica" with a couplet that says a poem should be, not mean, he rather violates his premise by telling us something outright, in the language of philosophy or theory, thus undercutting the lovely metaphors of the couplets leading to his concluding statement. Still, he helps us to understand something about *how* art means as opposed to philosophy or science (hard or soft), how there are (at least) two ways of meaning. One operates by metaphor and imitation, by indirection; the other through statement, by direction. At the heart of a work of art there is a hollow shaped by the specifics of the work; at the heart of the treatise there is an idea proposed at the outset. Both are highly structured artefacts, both propose ideas for living – but differently.

Art provides a structure of words or movements or bronze or sounds or moving images whose 'meaning' inheres in the shape of its details and materials. Such a structure, when more than mere recapitulation of generic conventions, captures a space in which something tacit is 'said' about human living, its terrors and joys, something that cannot be said in any other way, something that escapes the networks of scientific or philosophical discourse. That is, when art does more than recapitulate generic conventions, it paradoxically speaks the not-sayable, and so forms a space for the reader to draw on her thinking and feeling to make a meaning that makes sense of things in her world. In some frameworks (for example, Romanticism) this 'not-sayable' is conceived as transcendent or spiritual; in others (for example, Existentialism) it confronts a constituent loss, a nothingness at the heart of living. Either way, art means differently to philosophy and science – a point explored in detail in *Practice as research: Approaches to creative arts enquiry* (Barrett and Bolt, 2010), where, for example, Paul Carter speaks of "material thinking", Estelle Barrett invokes Martin Heidegger's notion of "handlability" and Michael Polanyi's notion of "tacit knowledge", and Barbara Bolt argues for "material productivity".

*tacit knowledge

But what happens when this way of knowing asks to be part of the academy, not just where art practice or art appreciation is taught, but as a form of academic research?

* * *

As Picasso once said to the shocked surprise of those around him, I do not seek, I find. (Jacques Lacan, *Four Fundamentals of Psychoanalysis*, 7)

Picasso made works of art – paintings, sculpture, collages, found objects (bicycle handles) turned into art… Lacan reread Freud to develop a theory to underpin a renewed psychoanalytic practice that can help people who suffer. He looks to an artist to define the purpose and direction of his theoretical work, and so tells us something about research when he argues that one should not "seek" but rather, like the artist, "find". In saying this, he plays on the word "research" – opposing his work to those *re*-searchers who recapitulate what is already known in order to add another piece of information, just as, say, popular fiction or film recapitulates generic forms and meanings in order to add another instance. That is, Lacan opposes the normative idea of research as seeking/replicating to significant research as finding/creating. He claims his own work is different to normative research in that its purpose is to "find" a new idea, an interpretation of what is known in order to provide a new understanding. In this, Lacan (albeit he would protest against this comparison) is allied to university protocols which require that doctoral research, as Michael Biggs says, citing one such protocol in his incisive contribution to the debate about non-traditional research degrees, "must 'advance knowledge, understanding and insight'" (2003).

This is a dictum which, in our supervisory experience, somewhat terrifies doctoral candidates, whether they work as traditional or non-traditional researchers. When we supervise, we tend to address the terror by talking about "interpretation"; we suggest that interpretation includes not only the critical process of considering a human situation or problem by searching closely what has been said of it through works of art, theory, literature, and criticism, but also the creative process of "finding" a new understanding of that situation or problem – an understanding that is singular, if only because it belongs to the researched understanding of one engaged writer/maker, in this case, the doctoral candidate.

This idea of interpretation bridges oppositions between reason and imagination, theory and art, thinking and making, and so on and on. It suggests that *both* traditional and non-traditional forms of doctoral research can be (should be) creative: that, at their best, both, in the words often used to describe research through art (be it conceived of as practice-led research or research-led practice), are "messy", *bricolage*, "bowerbird" and "fuzzy". For both are iterative processes of making/writing, reflection/reading, remaking/rewriting. That is, both are processes that spring from and probe an initial research question in order to find a fresh interpretation of human experience. When the traditional and non-traditional come together in creative-art research, the "messy" business of research entails what Cora Marshall describes as a "helical" process, in which the research question, as it is investigated across two ways of knowing, is "posed, re-posed, refined, and posed again" (2010, 80). In other words, when significant, both traditional and non-traditional research are creative and, when they come together, they are specially so.

What *is* different is the 'language' or form, the way of knowing, in which each sort of research is conducted and expressed; and so what is different is the nature of reading/interpreting required when reading each form of research – something critical both to conceptualising the relationship between the exegetical and creative components of a creative-production research thesis, and to the practice of examining such theses.

* * *

[C]reation can find its fulfilment only in reading, since the artist must entrust to another the job of carrying out what he has begun.... (Jean-Paul Sartre, "Why Write?", 32)

When Sartre speaks of "creation" here, he is not concerned with the creativity inherent in the best theoretical or empirical research, but rather with that which belongs to the aesthetic object. His elegant essay argues that the meaning found in an aesthetic object resides not in the work itself (the formalist's position), but rather in a dialectic between maker and reader. The artist shapes an artefact that implicitly expresses skill, passion, understanding, insight – in Sartre's words, it is an "appeal" to the passion and understanding (the "freedom") of the one who interprets it (1948/1950, 32). Before that moment of releasing a work to another reader, it is a provisional set of marks on the page, collection of paint strokes on canvas, combination of movements in dance, sequence of orchestral sounds, flow of moving images. Before that moment, it is a purely subjective object, an expression of self, tied to the maker/performer – for, however much she 'reads' the work being made or rehearsed, she cannot complete it because she can always alter it. Thus, the work as an *object* comes into being only through another's reading of it, an act of interpretation. Put another way, the aesthetic work is an object whose meaning is tacit, residing in the hollow shaped by its structure (whether a permanent form like a canvas or a transient form like a performance), and realised only in an act of reception, each time it is 'read'. As Barbara Bolt argues in *Art beyond representation* (2004) and in "Material thinking and the agency of matter" (2007), art is a dynamic relationship of materialities, bodily engagements and mental activities, in which the creation of a work relies not only on the artist's performativity but also upon the reader's performance (guided by the work) of the work's meaning. In Sartre's metaphor it is a "gift" given by writer/artist/performer and reader/viewer/listener to one another (36).

This position – that the meaning of a work of art results from a *way of knowing* that is other to the protocols of reason and explicit statement, a way of knowing that requires a reciprocity between making and apprehending – is an antidote to Plato's strictures, an echo of Aristotle (in an existentialist mode), a refutation of Neo-classicist and Platonic notions of teaching-by-delighting, a correction to formalist notions of art as encapsulated meaning, and (in Sartre's argument that aesthetic works appeal to an individual's freedom) a contemporary version of what Romantics meant by Imagination. And it is also a challenge to the assumptions that inform both university protocols regarding what constitutes a "new contribution to knowledge" and university norms for examining theses.

Creative-arts research degrees have been admitted into the academy only on the condition that the aesthetic component of such a degree be companioned by a discursive work, usually called an exegesis, and variously described as a piece of theory or history or explanation. Again, Michael Biggs is instructive. He forcibly argues that the formalist position (meaning is inherent in an aesthetic object) is untenable, since incontrovertibly meaning is realised variously, depending on the work's reception in a particular time and place, that is, upon a reader's socio-historically inflected position. So far, so good. But then Biggs argues for the "instrumentalism" of the exegesis, for "a critical exegesis that describes *how* [the aesthetic object] advances knowledge, understanding and insight", because we "expect the researcher to be unambiguous about both the evidence and argument, and the conclusions" (2003, original emphasis). And so, working through the questions of what research means in the university, how creative production can be an important part of that enterprise, and how creative-production theses can be examined, Biggs retreats to a Platonic/Neo-classicist/institutional position that undercuts the knowledge, understanding and insight provided by aesthetic objects: in effect, he argues that the exegesis serves to explain the work of art. In doing so, he overlooks that "the appearance of a work of art is a new event which cannot *be explained* by anterior data" (Sartre, 1948/1950, 32, original emphasis), and so he misses the main opportunity provided by creative-production research. As Sartre might say, requiring an exegesis to interpret a work of art is a failure of freedom…

THINKING ABOUT THE EXEGESIS

> But the supplement supplements. It adds only to replace. It intervenes or insinuates itself in-the-place-of; if it fills, it is as if one fills a void. (Jacques Derrida, *Of Grammatology*, 145)

Given the history of western universities, in which rational knowing is prioritised, it may be understandable that they admit creative-art research on the basis that a creative-production thesis takes the form of a text that embodies one way of knowing (aesthetic) on condition that it is accompanied by a text that embodies another way of knowing (rational). The usual term for this second text, "exegesis", derives from ancient traditions of religious commentary on holy texts and clearly positions the exegesis as an 'explanation' of the aesthetic object. We may be stuck with the term, but we do not need to accept such positioning. For to do so is to ignore profoundly the dual ways of knowing provided by such research – to ignore that the modes of knowing provided by aesthetic and discursive objects are different, that the ways of making them are different (however much both can be messily creative), and that the reading or examination of each component requires a specific mode of understanding – understandings that might be called apprehension in the one case, and comprehension in the other.

Put another way, to define the exegetical component of a creative-production research thesis as the interpretation of the aesthetic work is to become mired in the sort of binary logic (reason/imagination, science/art, theory/making, etc.) that Derrida describes as the endless logic of supplementarity, wherein the exegesis completes the work of art, but the exegesis itself is incomplete without that work, and so on and on. In the event, willy-nilly, creative-arts students often find this logic of supplementarity productive, either when they resist it and/or when they discover that researching the archive and engaging in critical debates enhances their creative practice. Nonetheless, put politically rather than pedagogically, when the exegesis is defined as "contextualising" or "explaining" the work of art, it becomes an insurance policy for the candidate and a reassurance policy for the university – insurance for the candidate who wants academic recognition, assurance for the academy which wants its largely traditional notion of research to be observed. In Ian Grieg's words, the exegesis (lamentably) becomes a "managerial exercise" whose function is to "legitimate" the work of art (2009).

Most research students know when this is happening, however intuitively, and often resist such positioning of their art practice with a reciprocal denigration of the exegetical component, giving it nicknames like the "extra jesus" or "exit jesus." They sense they are being required to compose two separate theses – an apprehension (in both senses of the word) sometimes reinforced by the practice of assigning separate supervisors for each component. As a result, research students often struggle with allocating time to each component and rarely feel compensated by the usual lesser word limits for the exegesis: they feel trapped in the logic of supplementarity. In an attempt to address these and like issues in our supervision – to be neither mired nor trapped – we work from the "research question model" for creative-arts higher degree research that we developed early on (see Milech and Schilo, 2004). The model could be seen as a response to what Derrida called "the violence of hierarchies" residing in dominant binaries (where one term is given value and the other devalued; 1972/1981, 41), if only because we experienced such "violence" (as opposed to theorising it) as we first guided students through university protocols. J. Hillis Miller argued that recourse to a "third term" is needed when confronting violent hierarchies, that the two parts of conflict-producing oppositions can become productive when related by something "across which they meet" (1977, 444). So we ask our students to imagine their projects in terms of a central research question that guides the iterative/helical process of research as it relates to *both* its exegetical *and* aesthetic components, that informs and relates both but does not make one subordinate to the other. We intend the model to be useful, and so provide a simple diagram:

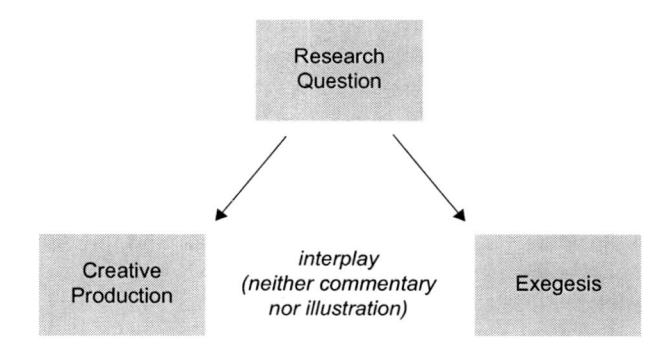

Research Question

Creative Production

interplay (neither commentary nor illustration)

Exegesis

We find the model works in more than one way: politically, it addresses current university requirements; theoretically, it honours our understanding that aesthetic and discursive ways of knowing are different in kind, and that the exegesis should not (cannot) 'replace' the aesthetic component of a creative-production thesis by 'explaining' it through contextualisation or commentary; and, perhaps best of all, it provides a framework that not only directs students in the first instance but also provides an intense learning experience in the last. To these ends, we emphasise that a creative-arts researcher works in two 'languages', aesthetic and discursive; that each language (and consequent mode of research) is independent, but that a productive synergy pertains when both modes arise from a shared research question. This is the synergy Cora Marshall describes above in her "helical" methodology for creative-production research, and Ross Gibson imagines when he speaks of "the chain of actions, reactions and outcomes that must be managed well in any productive research process" (2010).

Conceptualising the exegesis as part of a whole thesis flowing from a central research question enables a researcher to make connections between doing/making and thinking/writing – to "find," as Lacan urges, an insight that emerges from the interplay between them. The model encourages researchers to explore understandings outside their usual frameworks and practice by working between their practice and ideas drawn from the work of other artists and from theory and criticism. For example, Angela Stewart, a respected portrait painter, created a doctoral exegesis that took the form of an imagined epistolary discussion of portraiture with a Renaissance painter, Sofonisba Anguisola. The exegesis, *Unlacing carnal margins* (2010), offers an analysis of the practice of portraiture (together with insights into the works of both Anguisola and Stewart) generated from an artist's engagement in a "finding" that springs from companioning the 'doing' of art alongside intensive archival research. Stewart performs meanings in two modes, in the portraiture that comprises the aesthetic component of her thesis and in the dialogue that comprises her exegesis. These meanings become available to readers/viewers/examiners in two modes when they apprehend the art work and comprehend the exegesis, when they re-perform the reciprocal knowings achieved through the interrelated forms of a creative-production thesis.

Commentary and contextualising models of the exegesis (see Milech and Schilo, 2004) also offer an opportunity for learning and developing skills in both practice/performance and theory/history (never mind that they provide a form of exegesis that neatly conforms to university paradigms). But our experience is that, though research students working within these models may well learn something about why they prefer working in a particular way in their creative practice, or something about how their work fits into the historical archive, or something about how it may relate to presiding – nonetheless such approaches tend to reinforce dominant (debilitating) distinctions between two forms of knowledge. And so they are likely to encourage tendentious recapitulations of theory and simple descriptions of art practice: the exegetical work can lack rigour, the creative work can become an illustration of theory, and the artist-researcher can find herself in the invidious position of having to explain/evaluate what she has made. The larger opportunity is missed – an opportunity that has specific value not only to the researcher, but also to the university. What is needed, then, is a way of fostering creative-arts researchers who, in Barbara Bolt's words, can begin "working hot" (2000) between two forms of knowing (and reception). The research question model tries to find that space, a space that, even as it makes good on current university definitions of doctoral research, imagines a form of production that extends knowledge beyond the confines of one field, through the making of a thesis that integrates imaginative and reasoned articulation.

Some research students, like Vahri McKenzie, find the research-question model too canted toward university requirements, an "evasion" of the essentially paradoxical nature of creative-arts theses, a refusal to "embrace the paradox" of researching within and between two modes of knowing (2008, 24). Others, like Sally Berridge, find it helpful in balancing the uncertain risks of creative-production research with the more structured approaches involved in academic analysis: "I gathered information and then looked at ways in which that information can be used visually and textually to tell my story, so both forms of expression pivoted on the same basis, the research question. It fitted my action research procedure, the spiral framework of observing, reflecting, imagining, making, writing, observing, reflecting, imagining and so on. It overcame the need for a split personality" (2008). Both responses reflect pivotal issues in the now generation-long debate surrounding the arrival of non-traditional research programmes in contemporary universities.

In his survey of the last fifteen years of debate in Australia, "Not quite theorist, not quite artist", Ian Greig begins by saying (as we do) that the pivotal questions are "what constitutes creative research and how it is to be evaluated" (2009). He notes that the normative positioning of the exegesis is as an 'explanation' of the creative work, and argues (as we do) that this deleteriously leads to "the exegesis becom[ing] the prism through which the examiners assess the project". He then concludes by imagining a "third model" for the relationship of the two components of a creative-arts thesis, a model in which the exegesis serves neither to contextualise nor comment. He provides two alternatives: either dispense with the exegesis altogether and let the work of art speak for itself; or, alternatively, set aside the creative-production as non-examinable and situate the exegesis as the examinable component of a creative-production, because, like a literature review or research report, it meets the criteria of generating new knowledge. This "third model" (in either variant) has a Damoclean appeal, but, as Greig himself observes, it can carry the danger that "candidates can become disenfranchised from their own practice" (Vella 2005, p. 2) and so lose the "balance between making and writing that is conducive both to the capacity of the candidates' studio project ... as well as to their ability to recognise and articulate how their project sits within and negotiates this terrain" (Greig 2009). Also, one might add, "a literature review" or "research report" may not quite meet university criteria for "advanc[ing] knowledge, understanding and insight". The research-question model seeks to circumvent such dangers by imagining the exegesis as more than Greig's "useful supplement", that is, by imagining it as integral to a form of thesis that is "hybrid" – not as Jeri Kroll suggests when she says creative-production theses are "schizophrenic [in] nature" (2004), but rather in the sense of being a new breed of thesis possessed of heterosis or hybrid vigour.

Similarly, Jillian Hamilton and Luke Jaaniste provide an overview of current debates on exegetical writing in "Content, structure and orientations of the practice-led exegesis" (2009) and propose another sort of "third model". They note that the exegeses archived at Queensland University of Technology mostly deal with three aspects: situating concepts, precedents of practice, and the researcher's creative practice. And they conclude that the exegesis has developed as a hybrid, insofar as it reconciles "the traditional, external, objective and disinterested situation of the observer with the internal, invested position of the maker". Hamilton and Jaaniste call this hybrid form of the exegesis "the connective model", arguing that it integrates "the context and commentary models", "offsets the problems and deficits that arise when either is used alone", and "provides the opportunity to situate the creative practice as research". Unlike Greig's suggestions for a "third model" the "connective model" imagines a connection between aesthetic and discursive parts of a creative-arts thesis. But, as they argue it, the connection occurs within the exegesis only; that is, the "connective model" does not *integrate* the two parts of a creative-production thesis, either theoretically or practically – and so creative-production students across all areas in which non-traditional theses are practiced can be left still wondering if they are writing two theses named as one. The research question model (another "third" model) seeks to obviate this and allied concerns with its argument that aesthetic and discursive ways of knowing are equally potent, that the products of both are eminently examinable, and that students thrive best when they see how the two components of their project are reciprocal.

Canvassing these and like contributions to the debate about creative-arts research degrees in the contemporary university leads us to a range of inter-related conclusions: a generation on, art students no longer have to model their research interests in terms of the traditional framework of a solely written thesis; the creative-arts doctorate still needs to engage with university research cultures by making strong claims for the distinctive way of knowing provided by an aesthetic work; and there is a large population of practitioner-academics (and fellow-traveller academics) who fully understand that a work of art cannot be 'explained' by an exegesis – who understand, as Ross Gibson observes in "The known world" (2010), the dual consciousness required when creative-production and scholarly traditions are drawn together. Having argued that "linguistic explication" cannot "decode" the art work, he emphasises that hybrid (in the best sense of the word) arts-based research entails a special, doubled mentality, proffered both in the aesthetic object and in the linguistic account, *and* that such research is important to the academy as a special response to the complexity of contemporary culture. In a passage that echoes Archibald MacLeish's point, he remarks:

[given] most experts agree that complexity can be understood only by *experiencing it directly*, by imbibing and appreciating it from inside the systematics of its always-unfolding occurrence, then it follows logically that artists are specialists in this major aspect of contemporary life.... (2010, original emphasis)

And, in a phrase we would like to have written, he continues: "as the world blooms in the artist's consciousness, the mutual commitment of the two modes can abide and provide". Our hope is that the research-question model gives the artist-researcher a method for embracing the paradox of working through two modes of knowing in the process of making a single work (the thesis), one that can provide a form of insight that can abide and provide.

In "Modelling Best Practice in Supervision of Research Higher Degrees in Writing" (2008), Rosemary Williamson, Donna Lee Brien and Jen Webb note that numerous university policy documents, guidelines and handbooks provide assistance with traditional theses, but that most give little effective advice in regard to non-traditional research programmes, even though they present special problems that impact on supervisory relationships. Among the special problems they note are: negotiating institutional frameworks and research policies grounded in traditional forms of knowledge-production; uneven power relationships between supervisor and student (in particular, when a supervisor and student may exhibit through the same venues); and the trickiness of offering career advice when supervisor and student are competitors in the same market or cultural space. When we work with our students in supervision sessions and workshops and on papers following their graduation, they sometimes (usually late, rather than early) remark on power differentials in the supervision but mostly on what they hoped from it. Even more, they comment, early and late, on how academic forms of knowing and expression can feel alien and inimical.

BECOMING A "'THINKING' ARTIST"

[A] 'thinking' artist [is] one who expresses himself with his brush marks *and* -- with his 'own' voice... (S. Chandrasekaran, personal communication, August 2004, emphasis added)

Shortly after our university inaugurated creative-production research degrees, we initiated a series of research-skills workshops. At one such workshop, we invited a professional artist enrolled in a doctoral programme, Chandrasekaran, to join a panel discussing non-traditional forms of research. An artist with years of professional experience, Chandra struggled with the institutional demands of a creative-arts doctorate. During the discussion, he was asked, "why would an artist want to undertake a higher degree by research?", and found himself saying:

Preparing the Candidacy Proposal Application (and resubmissions!), as well as attending the seminars organised by my Faculty, helped me not only develop

> my personal academic skills and knowledge, but also to develop as a 'thinking' artist – who expresses himself with his brush marks and with his 'own' voice, a 'voice' that provides a personal identity for both disciplines – writing and painting. Having my 'own voice' not only allows me to confront the reflections of others (such as art critics, audiences) but also to challenge their personal opinions, agenda or writing styles with a critical stance. (2004)

At this moment, Chandra saw more clearly than before the reciprocity involved between his endeavours in the studio and those in the academy. It was a turning point: he came to know what he knew, and identify himself as a "thinking artist", someone who recognises his role in creating a link between creative arts and academic research.

His remarks highlight the distinctions between different sorts of research: research people undertake as part of professional practice (as artists and writers, or in adjunct professional roles as journalists, public servants or policy-makers) and research undertaken within the context of a university research programme. It is a difference between a focus, on the one hand, on "express[ing]" oneself "with brush marks" and, on the other, on a "critical stance" that engages with "the reflections of others" in the process of developing an aesthetic object and exegesis as companioned forms of creativity. In essence, Chandra's insight was that he could reconcile two modes of knowing, could connect imagination and reason, making and thinking.

The distinction between professional practitioner and critical artist is echoed by another doctorate candidate, who, on hearing the gallery where she exhibited was to close (a gallery which played a key role in the development of her growing national profile), remarked:

> You know, in a way, I am glad that Gallery E. is closing. It now gives me the freedom to focus on my PhD, to take greater risks and do things that I may not have done before. I can't imagine them allowing me to cover their floors with mud and dirt and that sort of thing. I'm no longer constrained by commercial interests. (S., personal communication, 2012)

The "freedom to focus on [a] PhD" suggests that working within a doctoral or Masters research programme affords the liberty to research through practice in ways that are not available or even considered when the artist has to maintain a professional profile by exhibiting or publishing commercially successful work. Within the framework of a research programme, the work can move in and between spheres of practice and academia, and so engage with ideas gleaned from both in a serendipitous reciprocity between imaginative play and reasoned opinion.

Such engagement is not always easy. It involves challenges like those sketched by Chandra: a testing of one's own practice and an adopting of "a critical stance" toward the "personal opinions, agenda or writing styles" of others. In turn, that sometimes entails working through preconceptions about the academy…

* * *

I came to this University because I wanted to do a doctorate with creative-production. I suppose ... a PhD is something very serious, a heavy written thesis. I enjoy art history, but it is the studio practice I want to pursue. I keep forgetting I am allowed to do that for my doctoral research. (Kelsey Giambazi, personal communication, 2012)

Following enrolment in a research programme, students normally have a six-month period in which to develop a confirmation of candidature (or candidacy proposal), which, once approved, authorises continuation in that programme. In effect, the candidacy proposal is an institutional protocol intended both as a research-training exercise and as a 'gatekeeper'. Generally, the format of the document is standardised and, no matter what Faculty the student is enrolled in, she must articulate her proposed research within prescribed sections such as "abstract", "objectives", "background", "significance", "methods", "ethics", and "facilities" and "resources". Most prospective candidates working in Humanities disciplines struggle to fit their ideas into such specified sections, but this protocol presents particular problems for candidates enrolled in non-traditional research programmes: they find the candidacy-proposal framework inflexible; its headings at odds with the types of research they plan; and the writing of it confronting because of a mismatch between their expectations and the institutional contexts in which they have chosen to work.

Kelsey Giambazi, a new-to-course student with a background in professional design practice, expresses this mismatch when she talks about the idea of a doctoral thesis she brought with her when enrolling: "something very serious", a "heavy written" tome. She experienced the initial stumbling blocks many creative-production research students face: a presumption about the type of research expected of them and a misapprehension about what constitutes a creative-production thesis. Presumption and misapprehension played out in Giambazi's draft candidacy proposal, which focused entirely on the theoretical and historical frameworks which informed her study. What was largely missing was a discussion of its creative component – she wrote a document she expected to fit the gravitas she associated with the university. Similarly, many new-to-programme creative-production research students, having spent long hours reviewing the literature in order to develop a candidacy proposal, somehow overlook the studio, film-set, stage or creative-writing page as they try to fit a description of their projects into the typical candidacy framework. Assumptions, misapprehension and just plain apprehension can lead to a kind of 'forgetting' of whole fields of knowledge with which candidacy applicants are familiar and in which they have competence – they proceed, in effect, with one arm tied behind their backs.

Still other applicants tend to limit early drafts of their candidacy proposal to a discussion of creative practice, barely mentioning the theoretical, historical, methodological or aesthetic domains from which their project emerges. Typically, such applicants confidently locate their ideas in terms of a progression from Honours activities or professional practice, and describe in detail various examples of their work. The proposal then reads like an artist's statement for an exhibition catalogue, or a proposal for a publisher of creative writing, or a pitch to a producer of film, theatre or music: it omits core issues or conceptual frameworks which ground the proposed research. In either case – whether their draft candidacy proposal is canted almost wholly toward the exegesis or almost wholly toward the art work – candidates have yet to find a balance between the theoretical- and practice-based processes that together should inform their research; they have yet to find the reciprocity between both parts of their research that Chandra discovered through the struggle of writing his candidacy proposal.

* * *

> I polarised academia into preconceived adjectives, such as cold, conservative, predictable, rational, disinterested, closed, intellectual. I loved ideas but bucked at the thought of having to present them in a way I thought academia expected. (Anna Sabadini, personal communication, 2007)

When reflecting on her study, Anna Sabadini, now a graduate with a Doctorate of Creative Arts, draws attention to another way in which preconceptions sometimes inhibit the progress of creative-arts research students. She entered the university thinking:

> Art is wild and unknown and mysterious and messy.... It aligns truth in all sorts of strange ways that allows it to escape from itself. It cannot be contained.... The requirements of the university are external to the impetus of the work, impose an untruthfulness, an untruthful state on what I do. And how many stupid exegeses sit there? Unread, because they don't touch people. (2007)

Imagining academia as a place which demands "cold" objective-truth statements, Sabadini not only instantiates all the binaries that characterise the debates about creative-production research degrees, but also describes the tension students often feel when grappling with creative-arts doctoral research – the tension between the perceived messiness and free play of making an aesthetic object ("the strange ways that allow it to escape from itself") and the seemingly cold order of archival work and verbal articulation of ideas that feel "external to the impetus of the work".

Tess Brady offers a keen insight into how she negotiated such tension when a doctoral student:

> I was combining in my process both the creative and the academic. I was writing a novel and I was writing a PhD. The academic became the creative; the creative became the academic. My desk was covered with the trappings of the academy, with filing cards, photocopies, Manila folders marked "bibliography".... My desk was also covered with the trappings of the novelist, with photographs and pictures, yellow stick-ons, a feather, a smooth black

pebble, a list of characters, a bent and twisted paperclip, red, blue, black pens, marked-up manuscripts. But I could not maintain the division as one slid into the other and the academic and the creative processes blurred. (2006, 2)

In her account, Brady invokes the reciprocity involved in the best creative-production research, how the "academic became the creative" and vice versa. The combination of the "trappings of the academy" and the "trappings of the novelist" play out on her desktop to the point that the boundaries between the two research processes become blurred. This stage of research generates a thesis that is not so much schizophrenic as a vital hybrid, a single whole produced and articulated through two modes of knowing.

Still, it is easy to become disoriented by the intensities of this form of thesis, to lose oneself in one or other component, and then to forget that getting lost is part of everyone's research experience, even for those involved in more traditional forms. Creative-production students need to negotiate research activity in ways appropriate to their own sense of things, their own manner of working. They may find their best way of working is a period of two months engaged in studio-work, filming, staging or writing poetry, followed by two months devoted to library research and writing the exegesis. Or they may develop a discipline of working on one aspect in the mornings and the other in the afternoons. Similarly, they need to find the form of the final thesis – it may be a 'two-hander', where the exegesis and creative work stand separately, even as they spring from a shared research question; or it may be an integrated form where exegetical and creative components 'speak' together across one text, something like the model provided by Julia Kristeva's essay "Stabat Mater" (1997/1987). The important thing is to find a way to work iteratively in relation both to the creative work and the exegesis, and to work between them – not always an easy task. Here, the research-question model can help to maintain or regain focus and re/combine the two components of the research in meaningful ways by returning to the motivating intention that underpins the research.

Even so, many creative-arts research students often face still another hurdle – working in a medium that seems alien, working with words...

**

In my childhood I learned to play with visuals not with words. Words were indeed fixed. Once they were said or written they remained. How strange that something so immaterial could seem so monolithic.... (Brian Doherty, personal communication, 2009)

While Brady found a way to work with apparent ease between two research processes to produce a coherent thesis (aided, perhaps, by both modes of her project being word-based), non-traditional research students unaccustomed to working in a verbal medium sometimes have particular difficulty. Brian Doherty, a practicing designer, alludes to something that plagues many such research students – 'word phobia'. Such phobia can reflect previous learning experiences. For instance, students enrolled in Visual Arts in undergraduate and Honours programmes typically spend most of their time in the studio, with little time devoted to developing theoretical arguments or honing writing skills. And often undergraduate programme structures collude with student inclinations by focusing on visual rather than verbal literacies. It becomes important, then, early on in a research programme, that students develop confidence and fluency in written forms; to paraphrase Chicago's Mayor Daley advice to voters to vote early and often, it becomes important that they write early and often. And, even more, it becomes important that creative-production research students come to know that (exegetical) words are simply materials for making meaningful structures: just as the artist works her materials to shape an aesthetic structure whose meaning is implicit, so too, the writer of an exegesis works words (hers and others') to shape a structure whose meaning is stated.

That discovery relates to Chandra's struggle to find his "own voice" – a struggle echoed by Sabadini:

> I am stuck in my writing: everything comes out halting, fake, contrary to my nature. I seek ... to just write, to find the way like I do with painting.... I want to make and break off arguments, to connect bits to other bits, to weave an overall fabric that feels like being in the bush.... I seek to write in an authentic voice. It is so hard to find. (Personal communication, 2007)

The search for an authentic voice dogs most research students, no matter what form their theses may take, traditional or non-traditional. For creative-production research students, however, the quest has a particular dynamic. Like Sabadini, they may feel at ease in 'speaking' through their aesthetic practice, but "stuck in [their] writing" and worried that "everything comes out halting, fake". Stuck in this way, research students (even those working within traditional modes of research) often feel compelled to use polysyllabic words and complex sentences to legitimate their place within the institution. They may also feel a need to defer to and emulate the voices of theorists and critics relevant to their field of study.

When this happens – when the researcher feels burdened by the weight of historical and theoretical precedents, somehow "stuck" in words and "inauthentic" because struck dumb by the words of others – a kind of 'forgetting' of creative practice can occur. The antidote is to work within and between art-making and word-making, to find a balance between the different creative processes that comprise a creative-production research project. That is, the escape from word phobia and the discomfort of inauthenticity requires a full engagement with both spheres of knowing as they flow from the research question – a finding of a path between vision and writing, a coming to write "like I do with painting", to "weave an overall fabric that feels like being in the bush".

In those exciting moments, when a researcher feels a synergy between practice and exegetical work, 'knows' that the making and the writing are not necessarily opposed, she can work to provide a specific mode of understanding available only through creative-arts research.

***

As you know, writing has never been in my comfort zone. I have always seen it as fixed and fixing. Now I am more able to see it as unfinished and fluid. I am seeing how I can bend it and create the correct discursive connections, tone, length, urgency for each location.... I think I may be finding my voice. (Brian Doherty, personal communication, 2009)

All doctoral research challenges candidates to step outside their "comfort zone", whether that involves dealing with the latest models of statistical data analysis, with unexpected encounters in field work, with unexplained phenomena in the laboratory, or exposure to theoretical frameworks not previously considered. But when Doherty speaks of writing as being outside his comfort zone, he exhibits the discomfort that can relate to prior training or to assumptions related to conventional oppositions between imagination and reason, to a sense that making is "wild and mysterious" but writing is ordered and constrained. When writing is positioned as "fixed and fixing", academic, "serious", "conservative", and "disinterested", as something that 'others' creative production (and when that perception is reinforced by an assumption that 'making' offers unconstrained access to understanding), research students can come asunder. They can fail to progress beyond such polarisations and to develop as a "thinking artist" who, expressing herself in dual modes, finds authentic voice.

Visual arts students delight in the flexibility afforded by the studio, the push and pull of clay, the layering of brush marks on canvas; they are comfortable with the possibility that a line needs to be erased, or a plane of colour reduced in tone, or that a glaze may turn the wrong shade in the kiln. The film maker knows it will require several takes before the scene is right, and the performer is well aware of the dynamic shifts that occur in the rehearsal room. These are the hazards, the mishaps and trials of practice, recognised as necessary parts of the process of refinement that goes into creating art works. Still, creative-production researchers (other than, perhaps, those engaged in creative-writing) may not 'have a process for writing', may not understand that writing is a *process*, an art. When they do discover that writing an exegesis is an act of word-making, in much the same way as the aesthetic component is an act of art-making, they find the ability to take risks with words, to deal with them as they would with the materials of their practice.

At that point, they can come to finesse bifurcations like making *vs* writing, imagination *vs* reason, and all the rest. That moment is not instantly arrived at; it requires an on-going iterative cycle of practices. But when it comes – when, in Barbara Bolt's phrase, a researcher begins "working hot" or, in Cora Marshall's words, becomes engaged in a helical process of discovery through shaping a thesis composed of both a written document and an aesthetic object – a non-traditional researcher finds, in Gibson's lovely phrase, a way of research that entails an understanding that "the mutual commitment of the two modes can abide and provide".

REFERENCES

Baker, S. & Buckley, B. (2009). *CreativeArtsPhd: Future-proofing the creative arts in higher education—Scoping for quality in creative arts doctoral programs*. Project Final Report. Retrieved from http://www.creativeartsphd.com

Barrett, E. (2010). Introduction. In E. Barrett & B. Bolt (Eds.), *Practice as research: Approaches to creative arts enquiry* (pp. 1–14). London, England: Tauris.

Berridge, S. (2007). Arts-based research and the creative PhD. The *and is* papers. In *Refereed proceedings of the 12th conference of the Australian Association of Writing Programs*, Canberra, Nov. 2007. Retrieved from http://www.aawp.org.au/and-papers-proceedings-12th-conference-aawp

Berridge, S. (2008). What does it take? Auto/biography as performative PhD thesis. *Forum: Qualitative Social Research, 9*(2).
Retrieved from http://www.qualitative-research.net/index.php/fqs/article/view/379/825

Biggs, M. A. R. (2003). The role of 'the work' in research. In *Papers from the PARIP (Practice as Research in Performance) National Conference*. University of Bristol, 11–14 September 2003. Retrieved from http:/www.bris.ac.uk/parip/bi.htm

Bolt, B. (2000). Working Hot: Materialising Practices. In P. Florence and N. Foster (Eds.) *Differential aesthetics: Art practices and philosophies: Towards new feminist understandings* (pp. 315–332). London, England: Ashgate Press.

Bolt, B. (2004). *Art beyond representation: The performative power of the image*. London, England: Taurus.

Bolt, B. (2007). Material thinking and the agency of matter. *Studies in Material Thinking, 1*(1). Retrieved from http://www.materialthinking.org

Bolt, B. (2010). The magic is in handling. In E. Barrett & B. Bolt (Eds.), *Practice as research: Approaches to creative arts enquiry* (pp. 27–34). London, England: Tauris.

Brady, T. (2000). A question of genre: De-mystifying the exegesis. *TEXT 4*(1). Retrieved from http://www.textjournal.com.au/april100/brady.htm

Carter, P. (2010). Interest: The ethics of invention. In E. Barrett & B. Bolt (Eds.), *Practice as research: Approaches to creative arts enquiry* (pp. 15–26). London, England: Tauris.

Derrida, J. (1974). *Of Grammatology*. (G. C. Spivak, Trans.). Baltimore, MD: Johns Hopkins University Press. (First published in French 1967.)

Derrida, J. (1981). *Positions* (A. Bass, Trans.). Chicago, IL: University of Chicago Press. (First published in French 1972.)

Gibson, R. (2010). The known world. *TEXT* (8), Special Issue: Creative and practice-led research – Current status, future plans. Retrieved from http://www.textjournal.com.au/speciss/issue8/Gibson.pdf

Greig, I. (2009). Not quite theorist, not quite artist: The place of the exegesis in studio-based research higher degrees. Proceedings of *ACUADS (Australian Council of University Art and Design Schools) Conference*, Griffith University, 30 September – 2 October, 2009. Retrieved from http://kali.qca.gu.edu.au/ACUADS/acuads2009-web/pdf/greig.pdf

Hamilton, J. & Jaaniste, L. (2009). Content, structure and orientations of the practice-led exegesis. Proceedings of *Art.Media.Design: Writing Intersections. Conference and workshop*, Swinburne University, 18 - 19 November. Retrieved from http://eprints.qut.edu.au/29703/1/c29703.pdf

Hamilton, J. & Jaaniste, L. (2010). A connective model for the practice-led research exegesis: An analysis of content and structure. *Journal of Writing in Creative Practice, 3*(1), 31–44.

Kristeva, J. (1987). Stabat mater (L. S. Roudiez, Trans.). In *Tales of love* (pp. 234–263). New York, NY: Columbia University Press. (Essay first published as *Hérethique de l'amour* in *Tel Quel* Winter 1977).

Kroll, J. (2004). The exegesis and the gentle reader/writer. *TEXT* (3), Special Issue: Illuminating the exegesis. Retrieved from http://www.textjournal.com.au/speciss/issue3/kroll.htm

Lacan, J. (1977). *The four fundamental concepts of psycho-analysis* (A. Sheridan, Trans., J-A. Miller, Ed.). Harmondsworth, Middlesex: Penguin. (First published in French 1973.)

MacLeish, A. (1985). Ars Poetica. *Collected poems 1917–1982*. Boston, MA: Houghton Mifflin, 106. (First published in *Poetry*, June 1926.)

McKensie, V. (2008). *As the owl discreet: Essays towards a conversation* and *Carly's dance: A novel*. Unpublished doctoral thesis, Edith Cowan University, Perth WA. Retrieved from http://ro.ecu.edu.au/theses/24 Marshall, C. (2010). A research design for studio-based research in art. *Teaching Artist Journal, 8*(2), 77–87.

Milech, B. & Schilo, A. (2004). "Exit Jesus": Relating the exegesis and creative/production components of a research thesis. *TEXT* (3), Special Issue: Illuminating the exegesis. Retrieved from http://www.textjournal.com.au/speciss/issue3/milechschilo.htm

Miller, J. H. (1977). The critic as host. *Critical Inquiry, 3*(3), 439–447.

Sartre, J.-P. (1950). "Why write?" (B. Frechtman, Trans.). In *What is Literature?* (pp. 26–48). Bristol, England: Methuen. (First published in French 1948.)

Stewart, A. (2010). *Unlacing carnal margins: portraits by Angela Stewart*. Unpublished doctoral thesis, Curtin University, Perth WA.

Vella, R. (2005). Postgrad [R]evolution: Supervision. Keeping the degree creative, *RealTime 68*(Aug/Sep). Retrieved from http://www.realtimearts.net/article/68/7916

Williamson, R., Brien, D. L., & Webb, J. (2008). Modelling best practice in supervision of research higher degrees in writing. The creativity and uncertainty papers: Refereed proceedings of the *13th conference of the Australian Association of Writing Programs*. Retrieved from http://www.aawp.org.au/creativity-and-uncertainty-pa

AFFILIATIONS

Barbara Milech
School of Media, Culture and Creative Arts
Curtin University

Ann Schilo
School of Design and Art
Curtin University

LAURA BREARLEY & TREAHNA HAMM

15. SPACES BETWEEN INDIGENOUS AND NON-INDIGENOUS KNOWLEDGE SYSTEMS

Deep Listening to Research in a Creative Form

INTRODUCTION

There are multiple ways of experiencing, knowing and communicating. In our shared doctoral experience as an Indigenous candidate and a non-Indigenous supervisor, Treahna and I developed a relationship which was underpinned by the Indigenous concept of Deep Listening. Deep Listening is a concept which appears in many Aboriginal languages in Australia. In the Ngangikurungkurr language of the Daly River in the Northern Territory, the word for Deep Listening is *Dadirri* and in the Yorta Yorta language of the Murray River in Victoria where Treahna Hamm comes from, it is *Gulpa Ngawal*.

The Indigenous concept of Deep Listening describes a way of learning, working and being together. It is informed by the concepts of community and reciprocity. Deep Listening involves listening respectfully in ways which build community. It draws on every sense and every part of our being. Deep Listening involves taking the time to develop relationships and to listen respectfully and responsibly. It involves reframing how we learn, how we come to know and what we value as knowledge.

Treahna describes it like this:

> Aboriginal people don't give information easily
> You have to really listen
>
> Not only listen with your ears but with your heart
> Deep Listening is about listening with your heart

As a research methodology, the practice of Deep Listening is an invitation into culturally congruent ways of learning and knowing. It incorporates multiple ways of knowing and multi-vocal texts such as narrative, digital story-telling, poetic text, theatre and music.

In her PhD, Treahna found that it bridged her research experience creatively and culturally. In representing our experience in this chapter, we interweave narrative, theory, artwork and poetic text. Through the use of multiple voices, we hope to stimulate critical reflection by stretching and dissolving boundaries, in both content

---

A.-Chr. Engels-Schwarzpaul and M. A. Peters (Eds.), *Of other Thoughts: Non-Traditional Ways to the Doctorate: A Guidebook for Candidates and Supervisors*, 259–278.
© 2013 Sense Publishers. All rights reserved.

and form. We have structured this chapter by using our own voices to introduce ourselves and describe our experiences as supervisor and candidate. The voice used in the conclusion is collaborative. Our intention is to contribute to an understanding of the doctoral experience, beyond the cognitive domain, in ways which can ultimately enrich the practice of doctoral candidates and supervisors and then extend beyond the life of the doctorate.

LAURA'S INTRODUCTION

This chapter is our invitation to you to engage with stories of risk-taking and becoming. Treahna and I came together as a non-Indigenous PhD supervisor and an Indigenous PhD candidate. In partnership, we challenged what those roles could mean and what a university could be.

I have always been drawn to artists, musicians and researchers who work on the edge of their own becoming. Their work feels inspired, alive and brave. Treahna is such a person. She is a highly regarded Aboriginal artist who works in many media and who uses her art to facilitate cultural regeneration. Treahna played a significant role in helping establish the groups of Indigenous research students, at both RMIT University and Monash University. Together, we challenged the boundaries of knowledge within the university system.

Treahna was one of the first candidates in the Koori Cohort of Researchers to collaborate with jazz musicians interested in improvising to artworks and stories. This work blossomed into The Deep Listening Project, a framework which facilitates research-based cultural regeneration, language revival and cross-cultural exchange. Treahna and I have worked together in this way for many years now. We have co-facilitated Deep Listening Circles in the community and made joint presentations in the corridors of power. We continue to work together today, both within and beyond the academic world, drawing on the knowledge we gained from those years.

HOW IT BEGAN (LAURA)

As I searched for meaning in my own PhD, I also searched for myself. In my PhD, I came to see myself and the world in new ways. When it was over, I felt profoundly tired. I did not think I would get so lost along the way and I did not expect to find what I did.

> It began with me with me straining for respectability
> As I learned the trade of academic writing
>
> I wanted to do well
> But my early writing was derivative and dull
>
> The research was so rich and multi-layered
> Full of emotion

The data spoke in its own creative voice
And my early writing squeezed the life out of it

The research participants were happy to talk to me
They needed it even

Their stories were intense and alive
And their images rich with metaphors and symbols

I felt privileged to be told these stories
I wanted to do them honour

So I began exploring their stories through the voices of
Poetry, songs and multi-media

I was introduced to the academic literature
About alternative forms of representation

I'd had no idea others were experimenting too
It was exciting, permission-giving, liberating

Another question emerged
The 'so what' question

How might this work be used?
How might this work be useful?

I began experimenting with different ways
Of giving voice to our shared humanity

Research as an invitation to become more human
Now there's a creative trail to follow

EMERGENCE OF CREATIVE APPROACHES TO RESEARCH (LAURA)

Creative approaches to research have emerged from post-modern theories of reflexivity, multiplicity and complexity, as well as the doubt that any single method or theory has a universal claim of authoritative knowledge (Richardson 2011). They are supported by an epistemological premise that there are multiple ways of experiencing, knowing and communicating (Jipson & Paley 1997). There is no single, correct way to have an experience or transmit knowledge of that experience (Lather 1991; Lather & Smithies 1997).

Challenging the shape and appearance of research opens the door to issues of authority, legitimacy, responsibility and power, which go to the very core of how we view the world and what we value. Creative approaches to research often embrace the Freirean ontological view, which entails the task of interpreting the world so that we can become more fully human (Kincheloe & McLaren 2011). Creative approaches acknowledge our own humanness as researchers and research participants and invite levels of engagement which we hope will connect with the humanity in others.

After I finished my PhD, I undertook a project in which I worked with twenty-two researchers who had undertaken or were undertaking doctoral research. I needed to do the research to make meaning of the ways my own experience had changed me. The data from this project revealed a great deal about the emotional and existential dimensions of the research experience: the creative tension of 'both/and' was a recurring theme as researchers searched for their voices within their projects. Here are some examples of poetic text co-created in partnership by research participants and myself. They reveal the complexities of the research experience through dialectics such as:

Fear and Authenticity
> The risk of not being ourselves is real
> The fear is not about going public
> It's about discovering what might be within
>
> The opportunity of my dissertation
> Is to work right on the edge
> Of creating myself
>
> Some people say I take risks
> I would say I'm just becoming myself
> I don't see the risk in that

Powerlessness and Agency
> I am a work in progress
> I've learned to sit with myself and my flaws
>
> And to have patience
> With my stuckness at times
>
> I cannot tell where my research ends and I begin
> It has shaped me more than I have shaped it
>
> Initially I was overwhelmed by it
> Flattened and consumed
>
> Now it is allowing me
> To become who I am

Lostness and Discovery
> You die to your old self during the research process
> I think unless you do
> You don't find life

It's important to get lost and confused
You're supposed to be
You've got to go into the deserts and be blown away

It's important that they're there
You should see some of the deserts
They're amazing

Be brave

Confusion and Understanding
I came into research so I could make some changes
The research has given me a way to understand
The conflicts and confusions in the world
And in me

Having been through the experience
I feel both brighter and greyer
So many shades of grey
Have hints of rainbows in them

It's a struggle at times
I often go to the edge
It has been so difficult at times
And so beautiful

THEORETICAL PERSPECTIVES ON THE RESEARCH EXPERIENCE (LAURA)

Some authors exploring the experience of research and advising candidates on how to complete successful academic research recognise the diversity of methodological, theoretical, ontological and epistemological approaches from which candidates can choose (Glesne, 1999; Mauch & Birch, 1998; Lewins, 1993; Nickerson, 1993; Denzin & Lincoln, 2011. This work typically encompasses cross-cultural (Geertz, 1988, Kalantzis & Cope, 2000), feminist (Maynard & Purvis, 1995, systems theory (Bateson, 1972), critical theory (Habermas, 1987) and deconstructive approaches (Derrida, 1981). However, some texts in this genre do not acknowledge the existence of multiple paradigms and are written from a scientific empirical orientation: "Keep values out … Objectivity is essential in research writing. Be factual" (van Wagenen, 1991: 133).

Another body of literature explores the experience of research from a subjective rather than a procedural perspective. This includes texts on issues of voice and identity (Richardson, 2011; Brew, 2001; Meloy, 2002; Rhedding-Jones, 1997; Leonard, 2001) and on the relational dimensions of the research (Lee & Green, 1999). Some writers explore the emotional nature of the experience of qualitative research from ethnographic, phenomenological or feminist perspectives (Richardson, 2007, 2001; Ellis & Bochner, 2002; Ellis, 2004; Gilbert, 2001; Jaggar, 1992, 1994; Rosenblatt, 2001; Harris & Huntington, 2001). They contend that our understanding of the world is enriched by integrating emotional and cognitive dimensions in research.

Theories of learning and knowledge creation provide another perspective on the experience of undertaking research. This includes literature which explores the transformation of experience into knowledge (Merriam & Clark, 1991; Merriam 2001; Jarvis, 1987; Habermas, 1987); the inter-relationship of learning to the construction of self (Rogers, 1951; Mezirow, 1981, 1990); the range of potential responses to experience, such as non-learning, reflective learning (Usher, 1996; Jarvis, 1987), problem solving approaches (Dewey, 1938, Kolb, 1984), instrumental and expressive responses (Houle, 1961); and the learning experience as a transformation of meaning (Mezirow, 1981, 1990; Gould, 1980).

LEARNING ABOUT DEEP LISTENING (LAURA)

The emotional and existential aspects of the research experience were in the forefront of my awareness after completing my own PhD and investigating the experiences of other doctoral students. I had come to recognise that research can be both transformative and traumatic, and I knew that its multi-layered nature requires knowledge, sensitivity and self-awareness. I recognised the need to acknowledge and manage complexity and paradox in order to be able to support and challenge, to be present and leave space. I thought it was important to develop collaborative communities of practice, in which we, as supervisors, could learn to listen deeply and respectfully as we walked alongside our doctoral research students.

Not long after my own doctoral completion, I was introduced to my first Indigenous doctoral student, Mark Rose. He was almost out of time. The demands on him were enormous and it looked like he would never make it. Mark wanted the doctorate though. He recognised its symbolic and practical power. He also wanted to contribute to the community and to be a role model for Indigenous youth. He told me stories of his Aboriginal father's abduction from the mission when he was eight years old, lured into the government car with a jar of lollies. His father, a deeply troubled man, spent his life passing as Spanish. The story of Mark's father's abduction is a common one in Aboriginal communities in Australia. It has become known as the Stolen Generation.

Mark also told stories of his own long struggle to reclaim his identity, the process of making his peace with his father and how Uncle Banjo Clarke had helped with the unification with his Gunditjmara family. Mark and I found a way of working together that felt like a partnership, a bridge that we could both cross. We bent and stretched and trust between us grew. He taught me about the Indigenous Standpoint Theory of Professor Errol West (Japanangka) which reflected the multi-dimensional nature of experience through an integrated model of eight voices; cultural, spiritual, secular, intellectual, political, practical, personal and public (West 2002). I shared with him the literature of narrative enquiry and the theorisation of creative forms

SPACES BETWEEN INDIGENOUS AND NON-INDIGENOUS KNOWLEDGE SYSTEMS

of representation in research. We struggled with questions of form and content and confronted some of the inherent absurdities of a system based on exclusion. We explored the ethical complexities and sensitivities of research. Who owns this knowledge? Who is it for? How might knowledge be shared and still protected? Who has the authority to determine this? Together we questioned and challenged the power relationships of the academic system.

There was a big celebration on the night of his graduation. The Senior Elder at his graduation ceremony told me she could feel the ancestors very close and they were dancing. Word got around of Mark's successful completion. Other Indigenous candidates wanted to join the research programme. They had heard there was a way of doing research in which there was room for Indigenous voices and multiple ways of knowing. They were artists, musicians and educators, well-known in their community as leaders. They were interested in developing new models of culturally-inclusive research practice.

Culturally Inclusive Research Practice

Cultural Translation — Interstitial — Multi-vocal — Creative Interpretation

Inter-generational — Collaborative

Relational — Respectful

Deep Listening

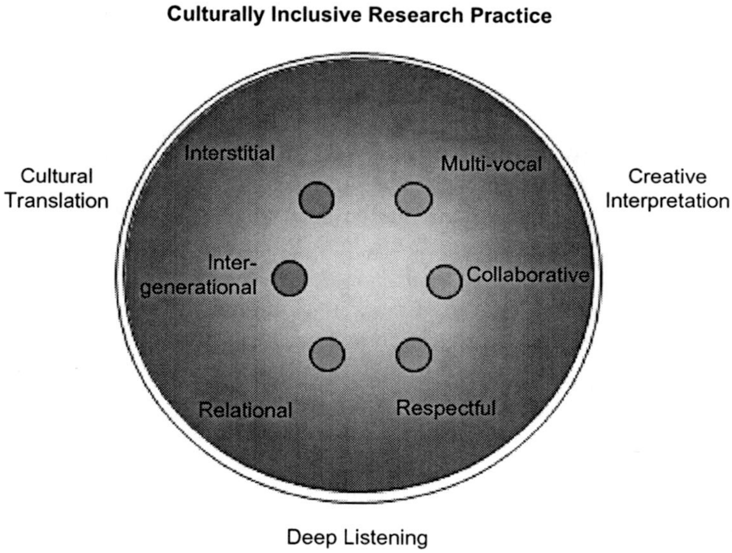

Figure 1. Culturally inclusive research practice (Brearley 2012).

The model Treahna is using in this chapter describes culturally-inclusive research practice through three interrelated concepts:

1. *Cultural Translation* – What has been our experience of working between systems?
2. *Deep Listening* – In what ways can Deep Listening enrich research practice?
3. *Creative Representation* – How is knowledge revealed through art work?

265

Treahna's experience is told here through stories and artworks, which illuminate this analytic frame.

TREAHNA'S INTRODUCTION

My name is Treahna Hamm. I'm a Yorta Yorta woman. In my research and in my artwork, I use the concept of Deep Listening as a way of bringing together my experiences, creatively and culturally. In my PhD, I looked at reconnecting with family through individual and community narrative.

When I first began my PhD, I met with Dr Laura Brearley, and I spoke about my connection to family, culture and land through my art. At the meeting I highlighted the importance of the timing of my PhD and that it needed to be right culturally. For two decades I had learnt from my Elders in the Australian bush and wanted to honour their voices. I wanted to pass on the stories of the Elders through the Arts, a medium through which, I believe, our Elders' stories were best told. I was determined to portray my connections using my own voice as an Indigenous woman. In previous study, my sense of identity had been diluted within the dominant discourse of mainstream study.

I felt a sense of urgency to gain knowledge and stories that were on the brink of extinction within my own tribe, the Yorta Yorta, in relation to my people's connection to the history of South Eastern Australia. For too long, a void had existed in relation to Indigenous history and culture in the Australian education system whereby English history had replaced the voice of Indigenous experience and its oral history. As I saw it, our old people were vitally important in saving cultural knowledge and nurturing strong cultural links to our past. I could not put this aside. I hoped my study would affirm my deep connection to land, identity and community and to the stories of the Elders.

Family Totems (figure 2) highlights the connection between family and tribal homelands. The patterns on the turtle totems link to the panels of possum skin cloaks. The totem for the Yorta Yorta people is the long necked turtle, which we cannot harm or eat. The turtles represent our tribe and also represent the resilience of our environment. The turtles each represent family clans which make up my family line within the Yorta Yorta tribe.

CULTURAL TRANSLATION (TREAHNA)

Part of my motivation in wanting to do a PhD was the importance of keeping my family stories alive. I also wanted others to benefit from what I had learned along the way. Most importantly, I wanted to create a document for my community, one which I could take out to the bush, sit down with the Elders and show them. Photos and pictures were important, to represent Elders' stories in a more traditional format, without obscure university words.

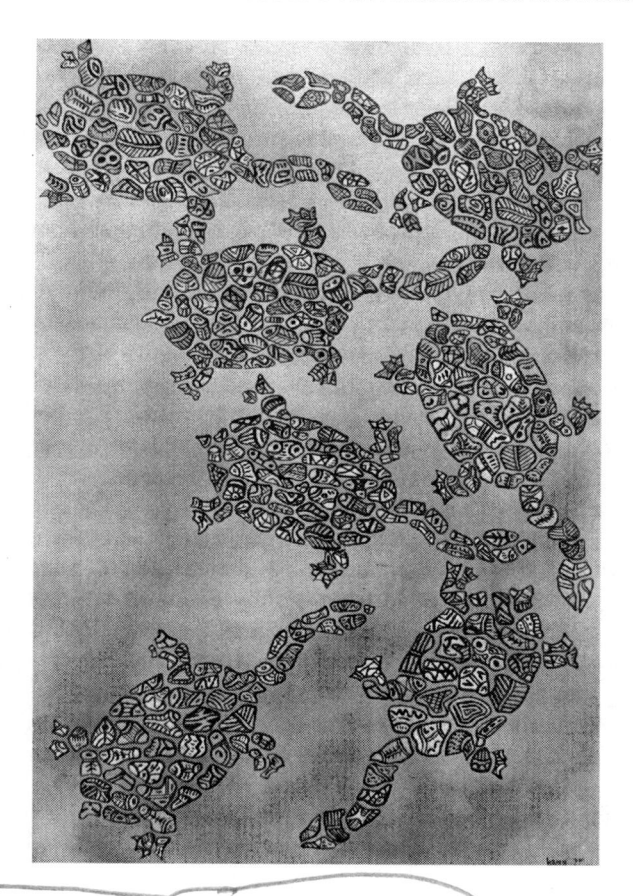

Figure 2. Family Totems.

I felt that my PhD would give me the opportunity to save some of the Elders' stories within my family's Indigenous communities in South Eastern Australia. The continuing generations of Elders are so important. They lived through the impact of colonisation (since 1770), Stolen Generations (1909–1969), Mission life, the Great Depression (1930's), decades of protest, about land rights in particular. The term Stolen Generations refers to generations of Aboriginal people who were, usually forcibly, removed from their family under the Government assimilation policy. They were to be raised in a non-Aboriginal environment, where Aboriginal identity and culture, by and large, were discouraged and non-existent. It is a testament to the strength of Elders that our culture did survive. I felt it was my role, with their permission, to gather information and to create lasting and memorable legacies for younger generations.

Early on in my PhD, I remember showing Laura a series of images of my mother's maternal line, which depicted six generations of women. This was Laura's introduction to the members of my family who had shaped my Indigenous identity. It was important for me to share these inter-generational stories with Laura at the very beginning of my PhD. Laura understood my constant referral to my family, and that keeping family stories and histories alive was important to my identity. Indigenous cultural knowledge lived within me, through my extensive links with family which could, at times, be complex. I was raised in a non-Indigenous family: my parents adopted three Aboriginal children. We were, in fact, cousins and so, from a young age, I inherited four families – all of whom I was to meet further on in my life's journey. I first met my birth mother in Sydney in 1992. My experience of Indigenous cultural knowledge is embedded in my experience as a Yorta Yorta woman, separated at birth from my Indigenous mother and family. It was a twenty-year journey back to my family. Indigenous cultural knowledge brings with it many responsibilities. I cannot say I am Aboriginal without practicing my culture.

Elders, who attain and live their cultural knowledge and practices, are integral to cultural survival. It is vital that their voices are heard in all realms of education, including the academic arena. To have healthy dialogue, we need to hear many voices in the space 'in between'. In this space (between Indigenous, European and multicultural communities), knowledge, culture and respect can merge and understanding can be deepened. For contemporary Indigenous artists, it is crucial to know that there are many artists who see 'through our eyes', who 'experience similar feelings', and who also have an internal spiritual and cultural flame to keep going. Knowing that Indigenous art is strong will sow the seeds of the future and hopefully make it easier for the generations to follow.

Culture lives within us. No matter how much settler society has tried to take away from the Aboriginal community, it continues and survives. Due to the determination and diligence of Elders to learn cultural practices from their parents or grandparents, our culture has continued through all the hardships. The wisdom and strength of Elders deserve respect. Their stories contain important symbolic messages for the continuation of the oldest living and surviving culture in the world. Disconnection has taken place for many Indigenous people in Australia through the Government's assimilation policy. This does not mean, though, that identity or cultural experiences must be lost forever, as many people have reconnected to family and birth right of their cultural heritage.

Symbolism and meaning can be interpreted along with cultural teaching. The river and bush environment is a place of education where stories are told relating to the formation of the landscape. Old traditional stories told by Elders are merged with contemporary experiences which incorporate messages from wildlife. In this context, my interpretation as a conduit between two worlds exists on both physical and spiritual levels. Indigenous people need to be in touch with our communities in order for learning to take place.

SPACES BETWEEN INDIGENOUS AND NON-INDIGENOUS KNOWLEDGE SYSTEMS

Indigenous learning is active. It is lived. Cultural practice cannot be put aside for months and then taken up again. Yet, it survives in people's minds and in their perceptions of the world. In thought, people are culturally connected, and this generates collective strength. I have been guided by my Elders to practice my culture every day, even if it is only one stitch of a basket, or one brushstroke of a painting.

Figure 3. Sites of significance.

Sites of Significance (figure 3) is a work which denotes the traditional creation of possum skin cloak making. Possum skin cloaks were worn by all members of Victorian Aboriginal tribes. The cloaks tell the stories of the land, the family and significant cultural sites pertaining to certain tribal areas. The cloaks were, and still are, a reinforcement of cultural oral history, which relies on intimate knowledge of the land. *Sites of Significance* is a contemporary manifestation of the same and relates to sites along Dhungala (the Murray River), where I have lived for most of my life.

The process of making possum skin cloaks includes a method I learnt from Aunty Beryl Carmichael, the closest family member who has traditional knowledge. The work combines traditional and contemporary practices and incorporates the stories of the waters the two rivers of the Darling and the Murray created with bark ink from trees. The work combines traditional and contemporary practices and incorporates the stories of the waters the two rivers of the Darling and the Murray.

DEEP LISTENING (TREAHNA)

In my research, I have had some profound and affirming experiences, which have led me to trust my intuition and interpretation of cultural signs and spiritual messages. I have learned to listen to internal and external guidance that I receive through my connection with Elders' cultural wisdom, as well as to respect signs and symbols that sometimes go beyond rational understanding. In this respect, understanding and learning can take place at different times, over months or even years. My search for an appropriate methodology, which was sufficiently flexible and culturally congruent, was a long journey.

In the early days of my research, I explored the concept of Heuristic Inquiry (Moustakas 1990). I made a series of artworks in response to the key constructs of the methodology: identifying with the focus of inquiry; self-dialogue; tacit knowing; intuition; focusing; indwelling and the internal frame of reference. This methodology encompassed sensitivity to Indigenous ways of knowing. It also enabled me to develop key markers, which entwined academic research with the vital experience of Indigenous cultural practice.

Later, however, I adopted the Indigenous principle of Deep Listening, *Dadirri*, for my research. *Gulpa Ngawal* is the Yorta Yorta equivalent. It describes a way of learning, working and being together and also works well as a research methodology. *Gulpa Ngawal* is informed by the concepts of community and reciprocity. It means listening with a sense of responsibility to the stories being told. It also means listening and observing the self, and in the context of applying it to research, it means bringing a sense of integrity to our roles as researchers (Ungunmerr, 1999, Atkinson, 2001). Deep Listening stands in a long tradition for thousands of generations of Aboriginal people in Australia. The immersing of all senses to observe, learn, create, share, and grow throughout time is of vital importance to our cultural knowledge. Deep Listening opens up a space to think about experience. It means listening not only with our ears. It involves deep listening with our eyes, deep listening with all the senses. It's connected to a spiritual realm. It can happen in silence. The created space allows individual thoughts and experiences to merge with cultural teachings based on Elders' wisdom.

Weaving the Land (figure 4) portrays the intricate vibrations of the land heard through Deep Listening to land and culture. The weaving texture in this work also refers to the sand hills, where my family's traditional burial sites are. The ground gives life to the trees and, through people, the endless stories of the land are always protected. We are always told that, if we paint our land, our land will remain strong.

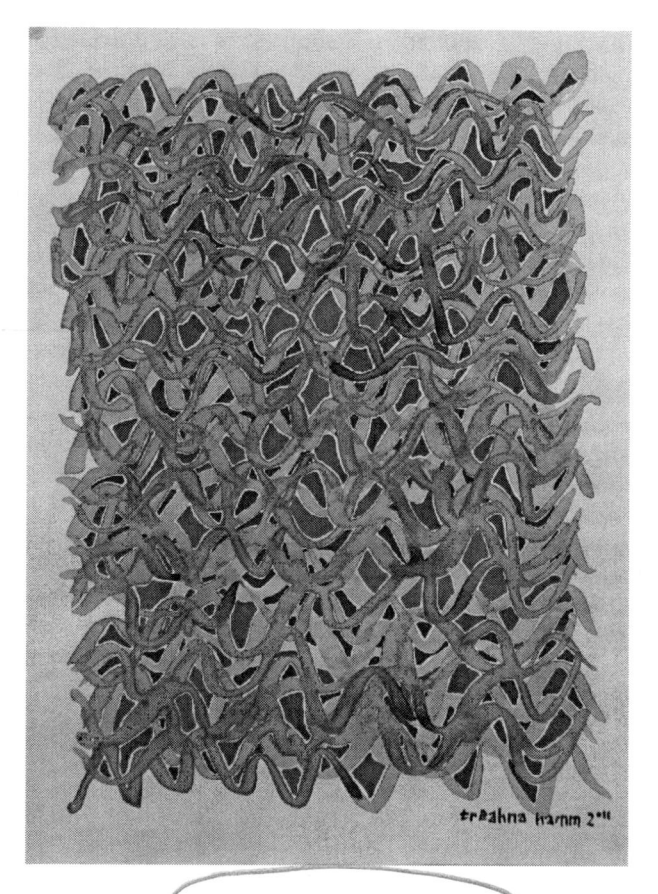

Figure 4. Weaving the land.

CREATIVE REPRESENTATION (TREAHNA)

Creating artwork based on our culture supports the integrity of our culture. The stories may change to adjust to other languages, but, primarily, the artwork itself does the talking. Telling stories, as I normally do, helps me understand my work and other people. We listen to the stories of our families, culture and Elders, which emanate from within us. We live our history. The stories told from past generations of cultural experiences are part of us, and we are part of our Elders and ancestors and the land. Making art allows me to gain insights into a realm of cultural symbols, which surface through my creative practice. This process helps me interpret and make sense of the world.

I find that living my culture through my art affords many special insights of life. I look towards certain Elders to guide me, especially those who live and work within culture. They, too, are guideposts along the journey of life, and they help me to distinguish what I do in relation to my culture and to fulfil the role I have been given in life. I seek support from my Elders' wisdom. I know they have lived through hard times. Our history is something that lives inside all of us.

The courage and love of the Elders give me the determination to help them with the work that they do. Through my artistic pursuits I return respect to them. They need to know that they are respected. To me, creating artwork is the gift I give back to my Elders and the community. As an Indigenous artist, I am connected to all other Indigenous artists throughout the world. It is this brotherhood and sisterhood that we all share. The experience of my research has given me the ability to explore my role in life as an Indigenous woman. Through the artworks I made in my PhD research, I wanted to regenerate culture. I learned from the Elders and from myself. My aim for my PhD was to experience cultural growth and development. This was indeed my experience. The bond that Laura and I shared created connections with community. The Koorie Cohort of Indigenous researchers created something new in the University system, a safe space, in which to learn, create and write. It was not only about an individual narrative, but a community narrative with the Koorie Cohort. Laura and I worked as equals, with no subordination in our roles as candidate and supervisor. Through our conversations, both University requirements and Aboriginal responsibilities could be intertwined. There was a depth of understanding, mutual respect and a support for each other in our roles. It was a successful partnership, which led to the establishment of a strong group able to express themselves at local, national and international events.

Figure 5. Oral Histories.

SPACES BETWEEN INDIGENOUS AND NON-INDIGENOUS KNOWLEDGE SYSTEMS

Oral Histories (figure 5) depicts important cultural sites and knowledge from places along the Dhungala – Murray River. The inspiration for this work encompasses the many experiences of 'being', which denote the totality of community and deep listening to the land, birds, animals and people connected to my tribe. The artwork displays the sensitivity and fragility of this ancient land, and the strength of knowledge, and is surrounded by symbols of personal experience. The use of bark ink within the work also brings into being the experience of gathering cultural knowledge with my Elder, Aunty Beryl Carmichael. Respect for learning surrounds important sites of learning. The river is an important symbol in many of my works. Elders' knowledge, and how I am taught to be patient, surfaces retrospectively and is reinforced through *Oral Histories*. The whole work is like pages of photo albums which have been placed to reflect the importance of observation and Deep Listening to Elders and country.

Dhungala Dilly Bag (figure 6) was created from an idea to weave and sculpt an artwork which highlighted Lake Mulwala, where I was raised, and bring to life the spirituality of the area. Dilly bags were commonly carried by women who collected small amounts of food, such as berries and nuts. The bags were also used to carry other items like reeds for weaving, as well as small stones and shell shards. The basket serves as a metaphor for the 'spirit' and 'spirituality' of the land when walking on tribal homelands. The space between the base of the basket to the top of the woven sky represents 'walking through the land' with spirit.

Figure 6. Dilly Bag.

CONTEXT, PRINCIPLES AND PRACTICE (TREAHNA AND LAURA)

Indigenous participation in academic research programmes in Australia is shamefully low. In his PhD, Indigenous scholar Professor Mark Rose identified the following barriers facing Indigenous candidates in the university system in Australia:

- lack of relevance of content;
- lack of flexibility of structure;
- isolation and alienation;
- demands of community and family;
- inadequate university support mechanisms; and
- institutional racism. (Rose 2003)

Each of these barriers has an alternative, in the form of an enabler, which requires a programme of learning to be relevant, flexible and with a structure that generates a sense of community and mutuality of learning. It requires an infrastructure of support and processes facilitating learning that are cognisant and respectful of Indigenous paradigms of knowing and being.

The Indigenous research participants in Professor Jeannie Herbert's doctoral thesis (2003) also identified several barriers to successful learning in universities. Her research highlights the importance for Indigenous candidates to have 'a sense of their own place' in the university and of the commensurate need for universities to create a place for Indigenous knowledge. This requires universities' values and power structures to transcend those of Western cultural traditions. Herbert acknowledges the importance for Indigenous learners to be able to feel that they are a valued part of a learning community. She also recognises the need for an approach that enables candidates to contextualise learning and to understand relationships between different bodies of knowledge. The successful candidates in her research discovered that they did not have to give up their identity as Indigenous Australians to be recognised as scholars within the academy.

The low participation of Indigenous research students highlights that universities have to demonstrate the will to respond to the expressed desires of the Indigenous community. Indigenous voices in research must grow in volume, in every sense of the word.

Emerging from our own work together, we have identified some *principles and practices* for working effectively as supervisors and candidates in non-traditional doctorates in a cross-cultural context. On that basis, we have developed and applied a framework of practice within a Doctoral Programme that is trans-disciplinary and culturally situated. Its purpose is to:

- incorporate Indigenous ways of knowing into creative research projects;
- provide a developmental infrastructure for staff and candidates, which facilitates ways of working between Indigenous and non-Indigenous knowledge systems in a creative research context;

SPACES BETWEEN INDIGENOUS AND NON-INDIGENOUS KNOWLEDGE SYSTEMS

- create a cross-institutional community of practice of staff, candidates and members of the Indigenous community interested in research; and
- support the development of Indigenous researchers.

The following concepts and implications for practice are introduced in the first semester of the programme and are deepened throughout the candidature.

Theme	*Content*	*Implications for Practice*
Ways of knowing	What is research? What is knowledge? The changing nature of research Identifying beliefs and values Ways of knowing beyond words Knowledge as a social construct Making a difference in research	Documenting the process Situating oneself in the field Discovering research questions in one's practice Responsibilities of candidates and supervisors
Ways of looking and listening	Identifying theoretical foundations to the work Issues of representation Multi-voiced texts (poly-vocality) Multiple perspectives in research Theoretical paradigms and perspectives, e.g., positivism, post-positivism, feminism, critical theory	Deep listening as research practice Undertaking a literature/visual resource review The personal and resource archive Interviewing techniques Research as a relational process Research as conversation
Ways of acting and reflecting	Reflecting on practice, reflection in action, tacit knowing in action Using an art form to explicate meaning and knowledge Linking inquiry to practice Narrative as a political act Relationship of art to research Performative and critical text	Library visit including data bases, copyright issues Locating resources What is the research question? Creating a research design Emerging innovations in methodology Art as a reflective conversation with a situation
Ways of making meaning	Issues of power and politics: who formulates problems? Ethics and politics of research Contestatory values Research as a site for critical conversations The politics of representation Art, practices and politics of interpretation and presentation Reframing constructs of Other	Developing the project proposal Linking theoretical foundations to practice Identification of themes, curation and reflection Developing presentation skills Drawing conclusions and future implications of research

Programme participants collaboratively explore these concepts in ways which embed:

- multiple ways of knowing and modes of creative research practice;
- flexible approaches to learning embedded in practice; and
- pedagogical principles that are holistic, integrated and culturally inclusive.

Throughout the programme, candidates create work which demonstrates their understanding of culturally inclusive, creative research methodology and its connection to the candidates' research topics. The work may be a research proposal document, an artwork, a performance or other media of their choice. Five key aspects of the programme may be helpful to other supervisors and candidates.

1. Facilitate mutual exchange. Frame the supervisor and candidate relationship as a collaboration. Find out what you have to share as the foundational structure of the doctoral work. Candidates and supervisors invite each other into their cultural and creative worlds to share songs, stories, images and poetry related to the conversation.

2. Value whole life experience. Recognise the value of creative and cultural lived experience that Indigenous candidates bring to the academic world. Appreciate the value of the Indigenous candidates' cultural practices, the richness of their knowledge base, and the significance of the research they are undertaking. See beyond student numbers.

3. Create multi-layered systems of support. Foster a community of Indigenous and non-Indigenous students and staff who are interested in exploring innovative approaches to research. Meet regularly in formal and informal settings. Develop systems of collaborative support including advocates within the larger system. Become a strong group with a collective voice that can't be ignored and is deserving of respect and systemic support.

4. Work between knowledge systems. Be open to naming and questioning assumptions about different forms of knowledge. Be willing to explore what we mean by concepts such as scholarship, creativity and research itself. Develop approaches to assessment and research methods which examine underpinning principles, criteria and language.

5. Develop collaborative frameworks of learning. Develop systems of support which encompass collaborative frameworks of learning and partnership models of scholarship. Promote opportunities across disciplines and cultures for on-going dialogue of people who are genuinely excited about each other's work. Be willing to question and expand beyond the systemic power relationships endorsed by the university structure.

All of our work together has been underpinned by the Indigenous concept of Deep Listening, whose core qualities, we believe, have applicability in our lives as community members, within and beyond the university setting:
- Respect underpins our relationship with each other.
- Time is invested in our relationship and the building of trust.
- Our understanding of ways of knowing is broadened and deepened.
- Creativity is embedded into the way we learn.
- A quality of care infuses our relationship and our work with each other.

REFERENCES

Atkinson, J. (2001). Privileging Indigenous research methodologies. Paper presented at the National Indigenous Researchers Forum, September 2001 Melbourne, Australia: University of Melbourne.
Bateson, G. (1972). *Steps to an ecology of mind*. New York, NY: Ballantine Books.
Brew, A. (2001). *The nature of research: Inquiry in academic contexts*. London, UK: Routledge Falmer.
Denzin, N.K. & Lincoln, Y.(2011). Introduction: The discipline and practice of qualitative research. In N. K. Denzin & Y. S. Lincoln (Eds.), *Handbook of qualitative research* (pp. 1–42). Los Angeles, CA: Sage Publications.
Derrida, J. (1981). *Positions* (A. Bass Trans) Chicago, IL: University of Chicago Press.
Dewey, J. (1938). *Experience and education*. London, UK: Collier-MacMillan.
Ellis, C. & Bochner, A. (2002). *Ethnographically speaking: Autoethnography, literature, and aesthetics*. Walnut Creek, CA: AltaMira Press.
Ellis, C. (2004). *The ethnographic I: A methodological novel about autoethnography*. Walnut Creek, CA: AltaMira Press.
Geertz, C. (1988). *Works and lives: The anthropologist as author*. Cambridge, UK: Polity Press.
Gilbert, K. R. (2001). Introduction: Why are we interested in emotions? In K. R. Gilbert (Ed.), *The emotional nature of qualitative research* (pp. 3–16). Boca Raton, FL: CRC Press.
Glesne, C. (1999). *Becoming qualitative researchers: An introduction*. New York, NY: Longman.
Gould, R.L. (1980). *Transformations: Growth and change in adult life*. New York, NY: Simon and Schuster.
Habermas, J. (1987). *The theory of communicative action: A critique of functionalist reason*. Cambridge, UK: Polity Press.
Harris, J. & Huntington, A. (2001). Emotions as analytic tools: Qualitative research, feelings and psychotherapeutic insight. In K. R. Gilbert (Ed.), *The emotional nature of qualitative research* (pp. 129–146). Boca Raton, Florida, USA: CRC Press.
Herbert, J.H. (2003) *Is Success a Matter of Choice? A critique of the commitment of Australian Universities to providing Australian Indigenous students with a range of opportunities relevant to their needs in achieving success* (Doctoral Thesis). RMIT University, Melbourne, Australia.
Houle, C.O. (1961). *The enquiring mind: A study of the adult who continues to learn*. Madison, WI: University of Wisconsin Press.
Jaggar, A.M. (1992). Love and knowledge: Emotion in feminist epistemology. In E.D. Harvey & K. Okruhlik (Eds.), *Women and Reason* (pp. 115–142). Ann Arbor, MI: University of Michigan Press.
Jaggar, A.M. (1994). *Living with contradictions: Controversies in feminist social ethics*. Boulder, CO: Westview Press.
Jarvis, P. (1987). Meaningful and meaningless experience: Toward an analysis of learning from life. *Adult Education Quarterly*, *37*(3), 164–172.
Jipson, J. & Paley, N. (Eds.) (1997). *Daredevil research: Re-creating analytic practice*. New York, NY: Peter Lang Publishing.
Kalantzis, M. & Cope, B. (2000). *Multiliteracies: Literacy learning and the design of social futures*. South Yarra, Australia: Macmillan.

Kincheloe, J. & McLaren, P. (2011). Rethinking critical theory and qualitative research. In N. K. Denzin & Y. S. Lincoln (Eds.), *Handbook of qualitative research* (pp. 303–342). Los Angeles, CA: Sage Publications.

Kolb, D.A. (1984). *Experiential learning: Experience as the source of learning and development.* Upper Saddle River, NJ: Prentice Hall.

Lather, P. (1991). *Getting smart: Feminist research and pedagogy with/in the postmodern.* New York, NY: Routledge.

Lather, P. & Smithies, C. (1997). *Troubling the angels: Women living with HIV/AIDS.* Boulder, CO: Westview Press.

Lee, A. & Green, B. (1999). *Post-graduate studies, post-graduate pedagogy.* Sydney, Australia: Centre for Language and Literacy, University of Technology.

Leonard, D. (2001). *A woman's guide to doctoral studies.* Philadelphia, PA: Open University Press.

Lewins, F. (1993). *Writing a thesis: A guide to its nature and organization.* Canberra, Australia: ANUTECH.

Mauch, J. & Birch, J. (1998). *Guide to the successful thesis and dissertation: A handbook for students and faculty.* New York, NY: M. Dekker.

Maynard, M. & Purvis, J.(1995) *(Hetero)sexual politics.* London, UK: Taylor & Francis.

Merriam, S. & Clark, M.C. (1991). *Lifelines: Patterns of work, love and learning in adulthood.* San Francisco, CA: Jossey-Bass.

Merriam, S. (2001). *The new update on adult learning theory.* San Francisco, CA: Jossey-Bass.

Mezirow, J. (1981). A critical theory of adult learning and education. *Adult Education, 32*(1), 3–24.

Mezirow, J. (1990). *Fostering critical reflection in adulthood: A guide to transformative and emancipatory learning.* San Francisco, CA: Jossey-Bass.

Meloy, J. (2002). *Writing the qualitative dissertation: Understanding by doing.* Mahwah, N.J.: Lawrence Erlbaum Associates Publishers.

Moustakas, C. E. (1990). *Heuristic research: Design, methodology and applications.* Newbury Park, CA: Sage Publications.

Nickerson, E. T. (1993). *The dissertation handbook: A guide to successful dissertations.* Dubuque, IA: Kendall/Hunt Publishing Company.

Rhedding-Jones, D. (1997). Doing a feminist post-structural doctorate. *Gender and Education, 9*(2), 193–206.

Richardson, L. (2001). Poetic representation of interviews. In J.F. Gubrium & J.A. Holstein (Eds.), *Handbook of interview research* (pp. 877–891). Thousand Oaks, CA: Sage Publications.

Richardson, L, (2007). Reading for another: A method for addressing some feminist research dilemmas. In S.N. Hesse-Biber (Ed.), *Handbook of feminist research* (pp. 459–467). Thousand Oaks, CA: Sage Publications.

Richardson, L. (2011). Writing: A method of enquiry. In N. K. Denzin & Y. S. Lincoln (Eds.), *Handbook of qualitative research* (pp. 959–978). Thousand Oaks, CA: Sage Publications.

Rogers, C.R. (1951). *Client-centred therapy: Its current practice, implications and theory.* Boston, MA: Houghton Mifflin.

Rose, M. (2003), *Bridging the gap: The decolonisation of a Master of Business Administration degree by tactical and pedagogical alignment with the capacity building needs of the Aboriginal and Torres Strait Islander Community* (Doctoral Thesis). RMIT University, Melbourne, Australia.

Rosenblatt, P. C. (2001). Qualitative research as a spiritual experience. In K. Gilbert (Ed.), *The emotional nature of qualitative research* (pp. 111–128). London: CRC Press.

Ungunmerr, M.R. In Jennifer Isaacs, (1999), Sprit Country: Contemprary Australian Aboriginal Art. San Francisco: Hardie Grant Books.

Usher, R. (1996). *Adult education and the postmodern challenge: Learning beyond the limits.* London, UK: Routledge.

Van Wagenen, R.K. (1991). *Writing a thesis: Substance and style.* Englewood Cliffs, N.J: Prentice Hall.

West, E. in D. Foley, (2002) 'An indigenous standpoint theory', *Journal of Australian Indigenous Issues,* 5(3),3–14.

BARBARA M. GRANT

16. "NOT ALL ACADEMICS CAN DO IT"

The Haunted Spaces of Post-Colonial Supervision

PROLOGUE: "IT'S NOT LIKE SUPERVISING PĀKEHĀ STUDENTS"

I said [to this colleague], "it's not like supervising Pākehā students. Right from the start, if [this student] gets this doctorate, it will make a difference to not just him, but his whole hapū (local kinship group), his whole iwi hapū (extended kinship group) probably, 'cause they'll be standing up there ... they'll have all these views. The doctorate doesn't just become one person's thing, it becomes something that everybody in that whānau, the hapū, that marae (traditional meeting place), all celebrate and they all own it ... So that's the first thing you've gotta realise. That it's not just a little thing you're doing with [him], it's actually a big thing. And specially because it's on tribal [knowledge], it becomes even more important. Because it may even become part of that tribal story about itself." I mean, this is huge. This is not just petty stuff you're talking about. So there's that aspect.

And I said, "on the other hand, you've got to really hold [the student], you know, you can't just send him off and then expect he'll meet the deadlines and, if he doesn't, then you just forget about him. You gotta stay in touch with him, you've got to look at stuff and give him really good feedback and encourage him ... You gotta go down to [his home town]", I said, "make a trip down there, visit him. Meet his mum. Meet his family, you know, get into his life, become part of it. Because not only will he appreciate it, but you will learn so much about what you're trying to do".

You know, cause otherwise [this colleague will] sit up in Auckland, she wouldn't know what a [tribal concept] was if she fell over it. Let alone a person [of that tribe], you know. But if she goes down there and experiences something of what's happening on the ground, she'll get a little bit more excited about having a relationship with [the student] and holding on to him, you know? ... My colleague was almost appalled by this, that it wasn't just going to be a kind of one meeting every now and then. And it was actually a bit of a life change. Her lifestyle would have to change. Her whole lifestyle. In other words, she would have to drive somewhere, she'd maybe have to stay overnight, she'd have to eat with other people. She might have to actually spend time sitting in their living room, you know, meeting their uncles and aunties and, oh my god, you know other people's lives. I think a lot of academics don't like getting involved with students like that. They think it's inappropriate or something. They kind of just want this academic relationship over this piece of work. They don't

---

A.-Chr. Engels-Schwarzpaul and M. A. Peters (Eds.), *Of other Thoughts: Non-Traditional Ways to the Doctorate: A Guidebook for Candidates and Supervisors*, 279–296.
© 2013 Sense Publishers. All rights reserved.

want the rest of it. But I don't think you can do a really good job with Māori students unless you have got part of the rest of it. (Kate, settler supervisor)

INTRODUCTION

In Aotearoa/New Zealand, settler[1] academics sometimes supervise indigenous (Māori) doctoral students undertaking research that incorporates indigenous knowledge. For many such academics (and I am one), this activity is 'non-traditional': growing up in Aotearoa does not mean that we have entered te ao Māori (the Māori world) nor that we conduct relationships with Māori *as Māori*. Rather, an often-uneasy relationship with our right to be in this land has left many of us uncertain about, even avoidant of, such interactions. More peculiarly, as settler *academics* we are unprepared for this kind of supervision – or even, we might say, actively prepared against it – by the long process of disciplinary training that we undertake to become researchers/scholars. This process has not only shaped our minds to think in certain disciplined ways – for instance, to be sharply aware of the boundaries of 'legitimate' knowledge and suspicious of so-called traditional and/or local knowledges – but also our views about what kinds of relationships are appropriate in academic life. Both forms of training can act as significant obstacles in the supervision of Māori doctoral students. However, a key argument in this chapter is that this need not be the case. Indeed, I want to argue that it *must* not be the case because, as the number of Māori doctoral students increases in our institutions, there is an urgent need for good supervision, not only across the full gamut of disciplines but also in the generative spaces between.

In writing this chapter, I am conscious of my ignorance. For one thing, I have little personal experience with this domain of academic practice: in fact, I have yet to supervise *any* doctoral student from start to finish, let alone a Māori one who is undertaking a project drawing in mātauranga Māori (Māori knowledge and wisdom). But other forms of ignorance are also at play: in my experience, I am more like the reluctant supervisor in the story above than the storyteller. Over the years, I have had opportunities to enter te ao Māori but I have often held back. At the time, I have felt too busy with work, study and family responsibilities to make room for the time and commitment required. No doubt, there are also other more complex reasons, perhaps something to do with a worry about the potential loss of self, of control, that might be entailed. Whatever the reasons, as a consequence, my understanding of te ao Māori is much more limited than it might be.

The expertise that I draw on here, then, is not my own supervision practice but my scholarship and research into the experience of others: I work in the field of doctoral education studies and have engaged deeply with the study of supervision. In what follows, I feature research data from nine settler academics in diverse disciplines (Economics, Education, History, Linguistics, Management, Psychology) and tertiary institutions in Aotearoa. Each was interviewed in 2008 for a project investigating teaching and learning in the supervision of Māori doctoral students (see Acknowledgments, below).

The questions I pursue in this chapter concern matters of settler identity and settler-Māori relationships in a post-colonial society: What insights about this domain of academic practice can we draw that will be useful for other settler supervisors? What does this material have to teach us about the current state of settler-Māori relations in academic settings? These questions are made urgent and interesting by the aspirations that Māori have for higher education, as well as those that higher education has for them (McKinley, Grant, Middleton, Irwin & Williams, 2011). To address the questions, I will now explore some theoretical underpinnings before I engage closely with two published accounts of settler-Māori supervision and compare them with comments by experienced settler supervisors of Māori doctoral students. In closing, I will reflect on the contribution this chapter can make to thinking about pedagogical relations between settler-as-supervisor and Māori-as-student in advanced levels of higher education.

SUPERVISION AS ENTANGLED IN POST-COLONIAL POLITICS: HISTORY, IDENTITY, POWER

My interest here is in matters of knowledge and identity, history and subjectivity, discourse and power, supervision and pedagogy. (Green, 2005, p. 152)

My interest in supervision, like Bill Green's, concerns matters of identity, history and power. Specifically, I want to explore the peculiar condition of being a settler supervisor of Māori doctoral students, particularly where their research has a significant mātauranga Māori dimension. My exploration is framed by a distinctive theoretical stance that has the following elements.

First, supervision is a site of layered and intersecting relationships in which supervisor and student meet, intimately, as embodied subjects in an historical moment and an institutional and disciplinary location (Grant, 2003). While supervision is primarily an institutionally sanctioned, indeed required, pedagogy (through which a student is prepared by supervisor/s for independent research and scholarship, and guided to produce a thesis) other modes of relationship also powerfully constitute the scene. Some are mobilised by students and supervisors' biographical identities, which can only ever partially intersect. Others, even more knottily, are a function of students and supervisors' separate desires for the project of supervision (the working together, the dreams they have for the research itself, for the thesis, the hopes for the life beyond, etc.). In the interactions of supervision, identity, history and power enter at every layer: not only in terms of how student and supervisor subjects understand and enact themselves as 'student' and 'supervisor' *and* as socially positioned individuals (raced, gendered, classed, cultured and so on, for example 'older-Māori-woman-native-speaker-of-te-reo-Māori'), but also in how they understand, what they expect of, and how they conduct themselves towards each other and the research work. The complexity of these intersecting relationships with self and other makes for an unstable pedagogy.

Second, supervision is both insecure as a cultural construct and constitutive of diverse subjectivities. In this sense, supervision is caught up in broader, competing discourses that structure modern life, that make it possible to think in sometimes conflicting ways about ourselves and the other – and our relations – as meaningful and ethical (Grant, 2005). In *Unfinished business: Subjectivity and supervision* (2005), Green argues that the supervision of research higher degrees is as much about the production of academic subjects as of academic knowledge. He goes on to argue that we should conceive of supervision "*ecosocially* as a total environment within which postgraduate research activity ('study') is realised" (p. 153, italics in the original). In this sense, supervision exceeds the boundaries of any particular relationship and even its institutional location as materialised in policies and guidelines. Supervision is shaped by the socio-political boundaries of disciplinary communities that are international and sometimes fractious, competitive and so on. At the same time, supervision is stabilised by a distinctive architecture: the dynamics that occur when an experienced researcher/scholar (in older language, a master) undertakes to initiate a novice (an apprentice) into the norms and modes of producing knowledge within a particular discipline or field of study, as well as by an international, often fractured and fractious, community of scholars. This process is unavoidably confounded with disciplining in two senses: requiring the student to *do* things (be 'obedient' to the exigencies of advanced academic work) and, more, to learn to do those things in ways that are sanctioned by, and recognisable to, that community. Elsewhere, I have argued that these dynamics are suggestive of the mutually constitutive and necessarily agonistic Hegelian master-slave relation (Grant, 2008). They can be uncomfortable for any two adults – and maybe even more so when supervisor-student are also, biographically, coloniser–colonised.

Third, Māori-settler supervision in Aotearoa is inevitably washed with the distinctive post-colonial politics of this place with its particular past. Crucially, there is more than one version of that past.[2] Not all versions are equal and, indeed, some are aggressively contested. When settler and Māori come into close proximity, the difficult and intransigent politics of post-coloniality come to the fore. There is a fundamental asymmetry to the encounter: the historical legacy of the past has worked, in the main, to advantage one group. That legacy and its attendant politics are ever-present in the daily lives of Māori but settlers are often 'oblivious' to them, suppressing or disavowing their effects through a variety of private and public tactics. Local theorists (Bell 2004; Jones 1999; Martin 2000) have explored the nature of the postcolonial conditions in Aotearoa, in particular the responses of settler New Zealanders: they have drawn our attention to complex and contradictory currents of longing, ignorance, grief, hostility, envy, misrecognition, unease, inability to hear, and denial expressed by settlers in relation to Māori desires to be recognised and engaged with *as Māori* within Aotearoa. Nested within this context, the relation between a settler supervisor and a Māori student can be understood as a particular form of post-colonial encounter, an argument I pursue here through views gathered from settler supervisors.

Lastly, following Michael Singh (2009), I want to foreground the generative value of the difficult condition of ignorance I have already mentioned in passing. Ignorance is not easy to accept in an academic culture where authority lies in positive knowledge. It may be particularly difficult in graduate supervision where supervisors likely feel complex responsibilities towards the success of their students' project: ignorance of a student's conceptual work can feel dangerous and frightening. Problematically, it can lead us to see the students as "deficient and lacking" (Singh, 2009, p. 199). Singh draws on Jacques Rancière to argue that ignorance in supervision (for example, the ignorance of an Anglophone Australian supervisor towards Chinese intellectual heritage) can become a resource rather than an obstacle, if self-consciously held as an opportunity to learn from the student.[3]

PUBLISHED ACCOUNTS OF THE SUPERVISION OF INDIGENOUS STUDENTS

In Aotearoa and Australia, an emergent literature gives insights and advice for the supervision of indigenous students. Written from a range of points of view – supervisor, student, indigenous, non-indigenous – this material is typically experience-based rather than researched and almost always implicitly, at least, addresses non-indigenous supervisors.[4] In this section, I explore two published pieces written by settler supervisors in Aotearoa to see what each writer has to teach us about the condition of being such a supervisor.

Settler Writer 1: An Ambivalent Place to be and a Model that Might Help

This chapter is deeply personal. My interest in examining the problematic nature of the construction, production and legitimation of knowledge via the research supervision process is played out against a backdrop of my own ambivalent positioning within a tertiary educational institution. As a Pākehā (white) woman academic, I am invited by Māori students to act as their research supervisor. In these instances, I feel a connectedness with Cathryn McConaghy's argument that "white women are often the 'workhorses' of Indigenous education at all levels" (2000, p. 3). This is not to offer a lament but to signal the inherently political nature of my work as an academic and a research supervisor. Underpinning these broad identities are further complexities and inadequacies. As a researcher my interests lie in two areas: Indigenous women and educational leadership, and the history of Māori education in Aotearoa/ New Zealand. As a postgraduate research supervisor I have responsibility for Māori students and those students are engaged in projects that are for, and about, Māori communities. Yet I question the legitimacy of my role and the institutional authority that permits me to participate in the production of Māori knowledge via the intellectual labour of postgraduate students. Who made these decisions? How were the decisions made that sanctioned my inclusion and participation? (Fitzgerald, 2005, p. 32)

As a Pākehā academic working with Māori research students, I struggle with notions of legitimacy and authenticity. While my academic credentials validate my role as a research supervisor, I am troubled by the fact that I am neither a legitimate nor an authentic guardian of mātauranga Māori [Māori knowledge] and kaupapa Māori [Māori-style] research. (Fitzgerald, 2005, p. 40)

In this "personal" text (a chapter in a book on supervision), we are privy to several ticklish strands that make up the experience of a particular settler[5] supervisor of Māori doctoral students. The dominant tone is ambivalence and uncertainty (noting "complexities and inadequacies", questioning the "legitimacy of my role"), laced with a suppressed sense of complaint: "white women are often the 'workhorses' of Indigenous education". The writer finds herself in a difficult place: instead of feeling the license and authority that should accompany her work as a supervisor, by virtue of her position as an experienced academic/researcher (her "academic credentials"), she is perturbed by a feeling of illegitimacy. She questions not only her own right to be involved in the production of Māori knowledge but also the right of the institution to sanction her work in this domain. Given that most doctoral supervision involves the consent of the supervisor, and that her experience is of being *invited by* Māori students to become their supervisor, she is referring to a more subtle process than one of being forced to supervise Māori research students: she is pointing to wider political issues about institutional care – or carelessness – towards the production of Māori knowledge that would not be the case with regard to other forms of (Western academic) knowledge.

There is an element of contradiction here: the author has chosen to research in the areas of "Indigenous women and educational leadership, and the history of Māori education in Aotearoa/New Zealand", presumably because she desires to contribute to public knowledge of things Māori and/or about the colonial history of Aotearoa. In this situation, presumably she is participating in the production of Māori knowledge – or at least knowledge *about* Māori. This position must be just as problematic as assisting students to produce such knowledge. Moreover, having made such a choice, it becomes easy to understand why the institution accepts her role as a supervisor of Māori research students. In a way, she answers her own question: even though *she* may make a distinction between mātauranga Māori and Western knowledge about Māori, this is a distinction that the academy has yet to fully contemplate.

The focus of the supervision advice expressed in this chapter is a proposal for a research partnership model based on principles of Te Tiriti o Waitangi[6] and designed to avoid "supervision arrangements [that] have the capacity to perpetuate and repeat patterns of dominance and subordination" (p. 40). Developed with the author's Māori postgraduate students, the model is offered as a platform for negotiation between supervisor and student. Under the three principles of Te Tiriti – partnership, protection and participation – the model incorporates a series of questions that incite an active partnership. (Here the author raises important and pertinent criticisms of the work done by me and Adele Graham in the 1990s on written supervision agreements: she points out the limits of the appeal of such a process to Māori – compared with an oral agreement, say – but also the way in which the process inevitably favours the more powerful partner of the 'contracting' pair.) Her model offers non-Māori supervisors a starting point for thinking through their own understandings of what might be involved in supervising Māori research students, as well as a basis for discussion with those students.

Settler writer 2: A Tricky Place to be and a Story that Might Help

This chapter unveils my limited knowledge and growing appreciation for Kaupapa Māori research and places it on "tricky ground" (Smith 2005). I find such an exercise to be both problematic and delicate. I am explaining myself, addressing two worlds hinged by numerous tensions and underpinned by a concern of getting it wrong. This is partly because of who I am, a middle-aged, middle-class Pākehā or non-Māori male. With this status, there are significant ontological and epistemological differences between my Pākehā worldviews, and those of Māori. But, perhaps more importantly, is an acknowledgement that such differences do exist. I can, therefore, provide only a partial and probably cosmetic interpretation of my limited experiences of things Māori. Within Aotearoa New Zealand, one of the biggest challenges we must face is that such differences are not fully understood or even acknowledged by many non-Māori. Throughout our society, there is a "we are one people" position where Pākehā refuse to acknowledge any culture other than the dominant colonial variety. Linda Smith (1999) declares that one of the ways that non-Māori researchers tackle any such investigation is to avoid it. Research related to Māori people and or issues are subsequently filed in the 'too hard' basket. (Pope, 2008, p. 62)

Crossing the cultural fence has, for me, been complicated yet rewarding and erudite, thanks to the many people who have collectively supported what for me, has been a significant challenge. (Pope, 2008, p. 63)

In a chapter for a book on cross-cultural research, another settler author writes here from the standpoint of being a "Pākehā fella", a "white, male, middle-class supervisor" who found himself "in the role of supervisor to several Māori students" (p. 61) working with Kaupapa Māori research methodologies because there are not enough Māori supervisors.[7] He acknowledges that, for him as a settler academic, supervising Māori research students is problematic: "as a Pākehā New Zealander, there are many tensions that I must address and overcome. And perhaps the most difficult concerns the biases I have established while growing and living in a colonial world" (p. 68). The author does not suggest that such biases make us unfit for such a task, but rather notes the importance of settler academics taking an active role in the supervision of Māori research students: "if a research partnership is to firstly be restored and then grow and flourish in my country, it is people like me who must change" (p. 64). A kind of pragmatism – *let's just get down and do it* – infuses his stance, alongside his acknowledgment, even embrace, of uncertainty and his fear of "getting it wrong" (p. 62). In the story that forms the heart of the chapter, there is a sense of excitement, pleasure and satisfaction.

To share his experiences as a supervisor working on "tricky ground", and by way of offering advice to others in a "culturally appropriate way" (p. 61), the author tells a story in which he attends a hui (community meeting) on a graduate student's marae (formal meeting place) where the student seeks community consent for her research. The author recounts the daylong drive with his colleague/co-supervisor, their uncertainty about arriving in the dark, his anxiety about speaking te reo Māori (Māori language) as part of the welcome ceremony. He also describes the opacity the process of the hui has for him: at the end, he doesn't know what the outcome is until his student tells him. It's a story of being willing to commit time and effort and, perhaps even more challenging, to endure uncertainty: to be in a different space/time, and to experience the limits of what a non-Māori can know about the Māori world. The device of the story works compellingly for getting inside the skin of being a supervisor and *feeling* the uncertainty as well as the rewards of stepping into another world. The author talks about the treasures he found in this experience: the reordering of values to prioritise concern for people and the treatment of time such that its passing is secondary to the processes of hospitality, helpfulness and discussion that must take place. His advice, then, comes in the form of a moral tale.

Reading these two accounts, the condition of being a settler supervisor of Māori students seems both difficult and yet exciting. It is traversed by a sense of inadequacy and at the same time, it seems to invite deep (and, for these academics anyway, welcome) personal change. It also opens up satisfying possibilities to participate in political transformation and the redress of colonial harm. Clearly, these possibilities rest on the invitations from and the hospitality of Māori individuals and communities and their willingness to consider mostly mono-cultural (we might say 'ignorant') settlers as allies in their efforts. To me, it seems the first author is more disturbed by the dynamics of the situation and how they position her – we can think about how gender might be implicated here. Certainly her sense of herself as a "workhorse" – a feminine beast of burden – is not echoed in the way the second author represents himself.

BEING IN THE THICK OF SUPERVISION: ISSUES OF IDENTITY AND CONDUCT

In our research into the supervision of Māori doctoral students (undertaken with Liz McKinley, Sue Middleton, Kathie Irwin and Les Williams – see Acknowledgments), we asked supervisors what advice they had to offer others: several 'directions' emerged. Like the prologue, the analysis that follows foregrounds the supervisors' own words: their accounts are thick with nuance that would be unprofitably lost through too much summary and/or generalisation. Indeed, what these colleagues had to say was *always* bracketed by judgment and consideration, by subtlety and shading. For example, there is a world of difference between advising that "you need to be open to becoming part of the student's world" and the delicate process of responding to invitations when they come, more or less directly:

> I wouldn't say to a student, "and now I want to meet your iwi and now I want to meet your whānau". Those invitations come. And I wait for them to come. And they're not necessarily at the beginning of the process, wherever the beginning is. It just happens ... (Rachel, settler supervisor)

Take Your Responsibilities as a Treaty Partner Seriously

> Take every opportunity to affirm the culture and the values because, you know, you're a supervisor who is employed by the university and so on, [but] you're also a Treaty partner. We're still a Treaty partner even to a student and the best thing I think a Treaty partner can do, wherever you're in a position to affirm the culture, then do so in supervision or in talking. Because it's very fragile and it gets knocked all the time in the media and so, if you can take that opportunity, it will bring back hundred-fold. (Arthur, settler supervisor)

> I think one of the things that is really important is that whole notion of guardianship. You know, that's the first thing, that I'm guarding not only this person but the knowledge they have and the knowledge they bring. It's also that kaitiakitanga [guardianship] kinda sense. And the sense of manākitanga, of hospitality. So supervision sessions will start with cups of tea and coffee and sharing some kai. It's not artificial, it's just a very natural thing. And we don't get to the nitty gritty of the meeting for possibly up to half an hour, maybe even longer, when I find out what other things are going on. (Rachel, settler supervisor)

One way to make sense of settler identity that was proposed by some of our interviewees is as 'Treaty partner'. Partnership suggests a network of mutual obligations between settler and Māori; indeed, several supervisors in our study remarked on the notable level of reciprocity they experienced (see Imogen's words in the closing section). In the current context of significant Māori disadvantage, however, we could argue that the onus falls on the settler to take active steps to participate in the redress of such disadvantage. This direction suggests, then, a kind of duty of care towards Māori doctoral students and the wider project of Māori cultural renaissance that many of them are actively seeking to further through their doctoral research: it is a call to go above and beyond what we might normally think of as our duty towards doctoral students in general, for political reasons that are linked to redressing past wrongs and securing a better future for Māori. As Kate argues in the prologue, it is also a call that feels frightening to some settler supervisors as it requires stepping into unfamiliar terrain – with the possibility of obstacles being put in the way of what 'should' be an unimpeded search for truth.

Actively Support the Student's Project and Progress in Ways That Acknowledge the Complexities of Both

Listen carefully to them as students, as people, and try and establish what is it that they're really trying to achieve [through their doctoral work] in its broadest sense. So not just the narrow academic question, but are they trying to facilitate some kind of social change or are they trying to respond to the needs of a given community and so on. If one can hear the contextual issues, it's likely to enrich the supervision consideration of the specific end. (Noel, settler supervisor)

Be generous around timelines and the possibility of other life events being part of the process. [You need] to kind of expand notions of that, I think. (Esther, settler supervisor)

Just try to be sure that, without discouraging them from being inquisitive, you keep their focus on the focus. (Andrew, settler supervisor)

[My advice is] to be patient, to be prepared for delays, to be prepared to fill in a six-monthly progress report and think of words to cover for the fact that there hasn't been quite as much progress as was predicted last time. Because it seems to me that the Māori students I've been involved with have had more complicated lives and, if I had been uptight about it and wanted it all done in three years or five years, it just wouldn't have worked. So take them as they come, enjoy them for what they bring, provide what you can to assist. In the end they are their own person and they have these other lives and there's just absolutely nothing you can do about a daughter with a brain tumour, or a mother with a stroke, or a tribal group that requires your attendance at a meeting. You have to accept this. I would say you have to be prepared to accept that. (Margaret, settler supervisor)

One of the big things is actually not so much the topic but it's the life. It's being sensitive to and aware of all the other pressures that Māori doctoral students are under. That's particularly acute with [one student], but also with this other student too. I know that she was constantly having to make trips [to a remote area] for various marae commitments and it's just actually being flexible and being aware of those pressures and commitments and requests on their time that go above and beyond what Pākehā students have to deal with. (Imogen, settler supervisor)

My understanding is that students feel in a very vulnerable position if the thesis is driving them or coming to drive them to do things or act in ways that're counter-cultural and going to risk upsetting somebody, irritating somebody or finding that there are ten more people they should be consulting. The supervisory role is to support that and to help them to do that, so sometimes it would mean my going with them just to be with them, just tautoko [support], because tautoko without saying anything is very powerful, and I've had to do that, and I've enjoyed playing that role. (Arthur, settler supervisor)

Māori doctoral students are typically older than their non-Māori colleagues and have significant whānau, community and work responsibilities – some are already leaders in their communities.[8] Many of those who come to undertake doctoral-level study have a strong desire to contribute to the betterment of their hapū or iwi, or the Māori people in Aotearoa at large. Their projects are often complexly linked with te ao Māori and engage with tribal knowledges that are more or less public. Moreover, collectively and in common with indigenous peoples elsewhere, Māori have higher rates of health problems and die younger than non-indigenous people – these matters impact heavily on doctoral students and their whānau. In the advice above, we see some potential tensions: between keeping the student on focus and acknowledging the very real demands arising on their time; between the rate of progress the student can make and the institution's norms; between the demands of the supervisor's own life and those of the student's. From the advice given, it seems that sometimes it is important to act as a counterweight to the life demands a student faces while, at other times, it is just as crucial to support the student in taking the time to meet those demands. These are matters of judgment that will be assisted by a more holistic understanding of a given student's situation:

> I often ask a student, "what is your worst nightmare and how can I [make that happen]?" You know, I remember one who happened to be doing a Master's degree at the time. He said to me, "the worst thing you could do is turn up at my house and ask me where my work is". And I did one day. He was horrified. Horrified. ... But the work came in. ... He saw me on his doorstep and knew what I meant by being there. (Rachel, settler supervisor)

Make Space for Māori Ways of Being and Knowing

If the area is in Māori studies itself, we can encourage them really to think about what it is they know by virtue of being participants in Māori culture. (Andrew, settler supervisor)

It's okay to hug and kiss your Māori students in saying hello and good-bye. You feel okay about that, you know, which is a little bit of a difficult situation in some ways, but, if they initiated it .. Make sure it's all very public and safe and just feel fine about that. (Esther, settler supervisor)

[You need] to realise the position that the doctoral student is in sometimes. For example, a kuia (female elder) may have taken up a wrong position from the

> point of view of the student's project, or taken a position that's going to cause some strife to the project or to the person. However, she is the kuia and she is [the student's] kuia, so she's right and she's right in the sense that [whatever it is] is an issue that has to be dealt with. (Arthur, settler supervisor)

> Often at times like that [managing the stress of work, study, home], I'm thinking about one student in particular, I said to her, "well then, maybe you need to go home for a while. Leave the books, leave the writing and go home." Home being the South Island [where her people come from]. So she knew I didn't mean her house here in Auckland, so off she went for a couple of weeks and just did nothing and came back. And was fine, was fine. … And another student had said, "I go home when I need to feel nourished". So she goes home to where she comes from, which is around [the East Coast]. Goes back to the marae, only speaks Māori, does a lot of cooking, goes and visits her father's urupā, her father's grave. And she comes back refreshed. (Rachel, settler supervisor)

The advice here is broad in scope. As we can see from the quotes, making space for Māori ways of being and knowing can range from how you greet a student at the beginning of a supervision meeting, to how you encourage a student to do what is needed in order to stay well and able to work, to how you support a student in dealing with her/his relationships with *whānau* (extended family) and community. Oftentimes a settler supervisor will not understand the situation and the student may not be willing or even able to explain it: Pope says, "many such intangibles will only be partly understood and never completely known by non-Māori" (2008, p. 70). It's a matter of observation, of respect, of trust, a willingness to make mistakes and, if so, to apologise:

> That comes back to my point about asking questions that are respectful, knowing what to ask and how to ask. And sometimes I get it wrong, but realising I've got it wrong and knowing when that moment is. [Then I] apologise. Aroha mai (I'm sorry). (Rachel, settler supervisor)

Remember Your Ignorance and Your Power

> Always take the unknowing position in a [Māori] cultural context, always … Even if you think you know, you don't. And even if you do know, it's not for you to say. … If you take the unknowing position, people will inform you. And don't speak unless asked to, and feel comfortable with going all the way, travelling all the way, sitting silently beside your student and saying nothing, and that's important because you're doing something. Respect elders. I've got a lovely expression that I've picked up along the way: "even if the kuia is wrong, she is right". (Arthur, settler supervisor)

The notion of reciprocity [is central] – the student and the teacher, the learner and the teacher. Because I often see [supervision discussions about mātauranga Māori] as an occasion to learn. Not that I then have the right to repeat. ... It's a distinction, and I've got it in my head: one student talks about Tuhoetanga, that knowledge which is deeply embedded in Tuhoe traditions and Tuhoe tikanga [correct procedure], which is not for me to repeat. And with another student, we were talking about what happens with Nga Puhi, so up North. And I got the sense that this was the stuff not to be repeated, because we were talking about the nature of evidence and how "evidence can say one thing but do you know Nga Puhi see it this way". And her saying that made me think, "this is what I can't repeat, that is how Nga Puhi see this". (Rachel, settler supervisor)

I think it's a hugely important role, the role I play in terms of my contribution to Māori doctoral supervision in the country. It's the key role that I can play that I really love. That sense of being able to hold somebody I guess. I'm seen as a person who has authority and mana (prestige, authority, power) because of my position within the academic Western, the Pākehā academic world. And I think many people feel if they can kind of hold onto my hand, they can do all sorts of things. ... Whereas I think if they let go of my hand and just went off in terms of Māori things, they wouldn't survive. Because *mātauranga* and Māori politics and Māori cultural relationships are such that they don't privilege, or they don't foreground, achievement within an academic context. And so that's what I do. I keep pulling them back into that kind of, inverted commas, 'Western' frame or 'Western' requirement. ... So I am that acceptable face [of the university]. In a sense I am the opposite of the gatekeeper [who keeps people out]; I am the gatekeeper who holds the gate open. I'm very happy to say I'm a gatekeeper, because I think I do a good job on the gate. (Kate, settler supervisor)

One of the other aspects is around the ways of knowing, too, which vary with different Māori students. But, for some, the use of stories and proverbs and more circular forms of getting to knowledge is the way they work: being aware of that and allowing that as a legitimate way of arguing, actually, rather than sort of linear rationality. That's been a major [challenge]. I still feel a bit uncomfortable with that at times as we chatter on with stories for half an hour about this and that and I think, "oh, where is this going?"... But it's about the ways they learn and the ways they express knowledge. Their writing may be like that too and so part of the supervisor role is to manage that a bit, in terms of presenting it in a way that examiners who are another audience can engage with it. (Esther, settler supervisor)

This advice links to the suggestion that we act as a Treaty partner but reminds us of the asymmetry in that partnership: settler supervisors are powerfully situated within the process of doctoral education, yet are often deeply ignorant of te ao Māori. We are cautioned about how we deal with our ignorance, including how we deal with knowledge that is precious to an iwi and shared with us by the students in the course of their research. As Rachel says, we must be careful about what we do with this knowledge – it is not ours to pass on. Yet, we must not let our ignorance paralyse us: being invited to be a supervisor inaugurates a set of responsibilities towards the student, who is dependent on us in this regard, as well as towards the disciplinary community that the student's work seeks to engage with.

You Will Need to Become Part of The Student's World

> I think the supervisor relationship can be a kaupapa Māori context if you want it to be. Try to understand that, if you're in that role, then you are a *whānau* member so to speak and, as a whānau member, you don't have any more power than anyone else. And so, if you're enjoying the privileges that come from that relationship, like being invited places and being entertained and are invited to share in giving specific knowledge, then there are responsibilities that go with it ... you do need to visit people when they're sick, you do need to attend tangi (mourning for the dead) with people. (Arthur, settler supervisor)

> I've been to her father's funeral, I've been to the family home. I mean I do those things because I want to, not because they say I have to. It is [part of the deal] for me. Because, with Māori students, one of the things I've realised over the years, it's not the individual you're supervising, it's the whole. And the whole includes whānau. So I agree to supervise students when I know that I can engage with whānau. (Rachel, settler supervisor)

> In a sense [it's] no different from [any] good supervision. But I think that, especially for a Pākehā supervisor, there is a sense in which in order to supervise – but then again I see it as almost an inevitability – you become part of the student's world. My advice to other supervisors would be to look for that as something important to the process and to use it, not use it, to welcome it as a very significant resource within the supervisory process. (Henry, settler supervisor)

Most of the supervisors talked about the necessity of becoming part of the student's world, of attending key events in the student's life, of meeting their whānau or hapū or tribal board, of being willing to front up and show your face as the supervisor – a direction that lies at the core of Pope's (2005) chapter. That willingness is connected to issues of trust, not only between student and supervisor, but also between a student's community and a supervisor. Where knowledge and individuals are understood to be taonga (treasures) of the community, such trust is essential. Kate said that, in her view, only Pākehā who enjoy the engagement with the student's life and community – "that kind of wholeness of it, that kind of fullness of it and the sort of down and dirty with it" – were able to "supervise Māori students properly".[9]

"NOT ALL ACADEMICS CAN DO IT"

Relax and Enjoy Yourself (But Get Help When You Need It)

Another thing is be relaxed. My view is that anyone who is prepared enough to enrol for a PhD has probably had a diverse set of experiences and is likely to be quite mature, so recognise that maturity and engage in a trusting kind of way. And ask for help where you need it, for example, if you need a complementary supervisor, locate one. (Noel, settler supervisor)

I just say to other supervisors, enjoy it. It's a privilege and it's just such a pleasure and I wish we had more, you know, Māori graduate students, I really do. It's interesting, too, especially as a Pākehā woman, I find. It's interesting that you're constantly reminded of your own limitations in what you know and what your experiences are. And so being tested and challenged on those things is a good thing. It's good to feel like you're on the back foot sometimes. You might know something about the specifics of the topic per se but when it's placed in a Māori context there are other things that, as a Pākehā, you can't access or you just don't have the experience, so there's a lot of learning that has to take place. (Imogen, settler supervisor)

I've been involved with Māori [research in my field] now for 30-odd years, and never once have I regretted getting involved in that because it's been a way into aspects of New Zealand that a lot of Pākehā don't get. I still find it endlessly fascinating. (Andrew, settler supervisor)

Several interviewees advised settler academics just to roll up their sleeves and get involved, that we would find much to enjoy and little to regret. There is a strong sense here of a precious opportunity that should not be missed; at the same time, a likely reluctance or uncertainty on the part of settler supervisors is implicitly acknowledged, reminding us that the wider socio-historical context of our country is not bracketed in academic relationships.

IN CLOSING

In particular, we have in the very presence of international students on such a scale in Australia the possibility of new models of intellectual exchange. We can approach our work not as the simple transmission of Western intellectual culture to a group of people from other backgrounds. We can constitute high-level intellectual work as encounter between intellectual cultures, sharing resources in a much more substantial way than we currently do. (Connell, 2006, p. 32)

I want to rework Raewyn Connell's challenge by replacing "international" with "indigenous" to put indigenous students' contributions at its heart: the growing presence of doctoral students undertaking mātauranga Māori projects in our institutions represents an opportunity for "high-level intellectual" encounter between Western settler and Māori worlds.

Supervising Māori doctoral students opens many generative possibilities for settler academics. Mātauranga Māori research, particularly engaged projects that test the limits of the work on the ground, may present significant challenges to Western intellectual traditions. The confluence of Māori epistemologies with traditional academic knowledges will no doubt be turbulent, and there are likely to be points at which the process stalls. At the same time, a possible outcome is an exciting revival and redirection of disciplinary attention and redrawing of boundaries, as well as the fruitful elaboration of mātauranga Māori. More personally, the supervision process appears to offer remarkable opportunities for identity shift in the settler supervisor – from mono-cultural descendant of greedy forebears to active, increasingly bicultural even, partner in the project of Māori renaissance. Undertaking this role offers some satisfyingly direct connections between academic work and the project of social transformation that many of us recognise as needed for our country's future. It offers opportunities to participate in guardianship of mātauranga Māori and to contribute to the emergence of a generation of highly qualified knowledge workers who are already committed to making a difference to their communities. The experience stirs many feelings in the settler academic breast: from pride and pleasure in our contribution, to ambivalence about our right to do it, to a concern about what we do not understand, and a fear of being misunderstood. The dynamic of enacting our supervisory authority – as we should – while recognising our ignorance and stepping back, to make space for our Māori doctoral students to enact their own authority and knowledge, is a volatile one. We may make mistakes, feel uncertain, hurt or misunderstood: this is also a precarious legacy of our colonial past. What remains, though, is an obligation to get on with the supervision that needs to be done, in a way that does not repeat our colonial history.

ACKNOWLEDGMENTS

This chapter draws upon the *Teaching and Learning in the Supervision of Māori Doctoral Students* research project undertaken by Elizabeth McKinley and Barbara Grant (Principal Investigators, The University of Auckland), Sue Middleton (University of Waikato), Kathie Irwin (Te Whare Wānanga o Awanuiarangi) and Les Williams (Ngā Pae o te Māramatanga). It was funded in 2007-2008 by the Teaching and Learning Research Initiative (project no. 9250, http://www.tlri.org.nz/). Thanks to the nine non-Māori supervisors whose interview data appear in these pages.

NOTES

[1] There are many terms used to describe this group of people – for example, Pākehā (New Zealander of European descent), Kiwi, tauiwi (foreign people or non-Māori), white, or European (as described in *The Politics of naming: Pākehā or what?* seminar, held on 28 March 2012 in the BRCSS Seminar Series, Constructing and Contesting Dominant Identities in Aotearoa). I have chosen to use 'settler' to foreground not only the historical event of colonial settlement and its consequent dispossession of the indigenous people but also the lingering effects of this process. For the record, in the group of non-Māori supervisors whose interviews are drawn upon here, eight out of the nine described themselves as Pākehā.

[2] The work of Alison Jones and Kuni Jenkins (2008) is instructive in this regard: they have sought out archival materials and oral histories to record early Māori engagements with education, showing how it was actively sought and valued.

[3] Singh offers several interesting "working principles" (1999, pp. 195-198) as a starting point for "debate among care-full supervisors conscious of being faced with our own cross-cultural ignorance" (p. 195).

[4] Experience-based accounts by indigenous writers include, from Aotearoa, Joanna Kidman (2007) and Te Kepa Morgan (2008) and, from Australia, Larissa Behrendt (2001), John Budby (2001), John Henry (2007) and Lester-Irabinna Rigney (2002, with Zane Ma Rhea). A team of Australians that includes at least one Indigenous author (Laycock, Walker, Harrison & Brands, 2009) has published a handbook giving advice to supervisors of Indigenous students. Research-based accounts include publications arising from the Aotearoa/NZ project, which had a bicultural research team (Grant, 2010a, 2010b; Grant & McKinley, 2011; McKinley & Grant, 2011; McKinley, Grant, Middleton, Irwin, & Williams, 2011; Middleton & McKinley, 2010), and Michelle Trudgett's work (2011) in Australia (Trudgett is Indigenous Australian).

[5] The author uses the term 'Pākehā' – see Endnote 1 above.

[6] Te Tiriti o Waitangi (the Treaty of Waitangi) was signed between the British Crown and many Māori chiefs in 1840, giving Great Britain formal possession of the islands that became known as New Zealand and subsequently much enlarged settlement of the country. The enactment of the Treaty has been a source of contention for Māori ever since and, in the present, a process of settlement is underway in an effort to redress historical wrongs that contravened the Treaty, especially with respect to land ownership (for information on the Waitangi Tribunal, consult http://www.waitangi-tribunal.govt.nz/).

[7] Kaupapa Māori research methodologies are ways of doing research that are informed by Māori tikanga (correct procedure). Or, as a student in our study said: "Kaupapa Māori theoretically means that, what my tūpuna (ancestors, grandparents) have brought me up with, I will ensure I do with [my research] participants".

[8] The Māori doctoral student profile shows that Māori candidates diverge significantly from average statistics in many ways: women participate in doctoral studies at a significantly higher rate than men; approximately 40% of the total are aged over 40; overall, they have slightly higher first-year attrition rates, similar retention rates, but notably longer completion rates than other ethnic groups, particularly among students over 24 years (Ministry of Education, 2006).

[9] Kate makes an important distinction between students who are ethnically Māori and those who "act themselves Māori". Her interest here is supervising the latter.

REFERENCES

Behrendt, L. (2001). The benefits of a formal mentoring relationship: 'Not my new best friend'. In A. Bartlett & G. Mercer (Eds.), *Postgraduate research supervision: Transforming (r)elations* (pp. 211–213). New York, NY: Peter Lang.

Bell, A. (2004). *Relating Māori and Pākehā: The Politics of Indigenous and Settler Identities* (PhD thesis). Massey University, Palmerston North (Aotearoa/New Zealand).

Budby, J. (2001). The academic quandary: An aboriginal experience. In A. Bartlett & G. Mercer (Eds.), *Postgraduate research supervision: Transforming (r)elations* (pp. 247–253). New York, NY: Peter Lang.

Connell, R. (2006). How to sabotage a PhD. In *Proceedings of the 2005 Quality in Postgraduate Research: Knowledge Creation in Testing Times Conference* (pp. 27–34). Adelaide, Australia.

Day, D.G. (2007). Enhancing success for Indigenous postgraduate students. *Synergy, 26*, 13–18.

Fitzgerald, T. (2005). Partnership, protection and participation: Challenges for research supervision in Aotearoa/New Zealand. In P. Green (Ed.), *Supervising postgraduate research: Context and processes, theories and practices* (pp. 30–47). Melbourne, Australia: RMIT University Press.

Grant, B.M. (2003). Mapping the pleasures and risks of supervision. *Discourse: Studies in the Cultural Politics of Education, 24*(2), 173–188.

Grant, B.M. (2005). Fighting for space in supervision: Fantasies, fairytales, fictions and fallacies. *International Journal of Qualitative Studies in Education, 18*(3), 337–354.

Grant, B.M. (2008). Agonistic struggle: Master-slave dialogues in humanities supervision. *Arts and Humanities in Higher Education, 7*(1), 9–27.

Grant, B.M. (2010a). Challenging Matters: Doctoral supervision in post-colonial sites. *Acta Academica Supplementum (1)*, 103–129.

Grant, B.M. (2010b). The limits of talking about 'teaching and learning': Indigenous students and doctoral supervision. *Teaching in Higher Education, 15*(5), 505–517.

Grant, B.M. & McKinley, E. (2011). Colouring in the pedagogy of doctoral supervision: Considering supervisor, student and knowledge through the lens of indigeneity. *Innovations in Education & Teaching International, 48*(4), 377–386.

Green, B. (2005). Unfinished business: Subjectivity and supervision. *Higher Education Research & Development, 24*(2), 151–163.

Henry, J. (2007). Supervising Aboriginal doctoral candidates. In C. Denholm & T. Evans (Eds.), *Supervising doctorates Downunder* (pp. 155–163). Camberwell, Australia: ACER Press.

Jones, A. (1999). The limits of cross-cultural dialogue: Pedagogy, desire, and absolution in the classroom. *Educational Theory, 49*(3), 299–316.

Jones, A., & Jenkins, K. (2008). Invitation and refusal: A reading of the beginnings of schooling in Aotearoa New Zealand. *History of Education, 37*(2), 187–206.

Kidman, J. (2007). Supervising Māori doctoral candidates. In T. Evans & C. Denholm (Eds.), *Supervising doctorates Downunder* (pp. 164–172). Camberwell, Australia: ACER Press.

Laycock, A., Walker, D., Harrison, N., & Brands, J. (2009). *Supporting Indigenous researchers: A practical guide for supervisors*. Casuarina, Australia: Cooperative Research Centre for Aboriginal Health.

Ma Rhea, Z., & Rigney, L-I. (2002). Researching with respect: Supervising Aboriginal or Torres Strait Islander students. In J. Sillitoe & G. Crosling (Eds.), *Assisting research students from non-traditional backgrounds* (pp. 8–19). Melbourne, Australia: HERDSA.

Martin, B. (2000). Place: An ethics of cultural difference and location. *Educational Philosophy and Theory, 32*(1), 81–91.

McKinley, E., & Grant, B.M. (2011). Expanding pedagogical boundaries: Indigenous students undertaking doctoral education. In A. Lee & S. Danby (Eds.), *Reshaping doctoral education: International approaches and pedagogies*. London: Routledge (204–217).

McKinley, E., Grant, B.M., Middleton, S., Irwin, K., & Williams, L. T. (2011). Working at the interface: Indigenous students' experience of undertaking doctoral studies in Aotearoa New Zealand. *Equity & Excellence in Education, 44*(1), 115–132.

Mead, H.M. (2003). *Tikanga Māori: Living by Māori values*. Wellington: Huia Publishers.

Middleton, S., & McKinley, E. (2010). The gown and the korowai: Māori doctoral students and the spatial organisation of academic knowledge. *Higher Education Research & Development, 29*(3), 229–243.

Ministry of Education. (2006). *Māori in Doctoral Study*. 2 pages. Accessed on 01 Aug 2008 at http://educationcounts.edcentre.govt.nz/

Morgan, T.K. (2008). Reflections on a research baptism by fire. *MAI Review 2008, 1*, 5. Retrieved from http://www.review.mai.ac.nz/index.php/MR/article/view/120/113.

Pope, C. (2008). Kaupapa Māori research, supervision and uncertainty: 'What's a Pākehā fella to do?' In P. Liamputtong (Ed.), *Doing cross-cultural research* (pp. 61–71). Dordrecht, Netherlands: Springer Science+Business Media BV.

Singh, M. (2009). Using Chinese knowledge in internationalising research education: Jacques Rancière, an ignorant supervisor and doctoral students from China. *Globalisation, Societies and Education, 7*(2), 185–201.

Trudgett, M. (2011). Western places, academic spaces and Indigenous faces: Supervising Indigenous Australian postgraduate students. *Teaching in Higher Education, 16*(4), 389–399.

AFFILIATION

Barbara M. Grant
The Faculty of Education,
The University of Auckland

ROBERT JAHNKE & A.-CHR. (TINA) ENGELS-SCHWARZPAUL

17. A CREATIVE JOURNEY: BY MĀORI FOR MĀORI

Interview with Robert Jahnke[1]

TES: *Kia ora Bob, I'm happy that you could make the time to contribute to our book in the end. It matters to me because you were the external advisor to my own PhD, so it is nice to collaborate like this many years later! Now, let me ask what you think about the term "non-traditional" in the title of this book, given that the term "traditional" is so habitually associated with Māori culture?*

RJ: I think of *non-traditional* as something that is not ordinary, something that breaks away from convention – a way of thinking in new and different ways. So, given that a PhD in creative practice is a new phenomenon, I guess *non-traditional* is most appropriate!

In a new and different way of thinking about PhDs – what do you think is the distinctive feature of research at that level? What are the standards and requirements, the principles and their impact? What makes a PhD thesis different from a Master's thesis?

I do not think there is a single formula; there is a different solution to every creative approach. Just one example: over the years of supervising master's degree students, I have come to realise that the approach to creative practice may be kaupapa-driven or process-driven, and in some cases a balance between the two.

Can you explain kaupapa-driven?

Kaupapa-driven work is grounded in issues related to the candidate's socio-economic or cultural reality (kaupapa meaning platform, theme, topic, agenda). Since the majority of students at our School are Māori, they navigate kaupapa in relation to their own being within the context of Aotearoa/New Zealand. For example, a recent student created a body of work about her Tūhoetanga (culture, practices and beliefs of Ngāi Tūhoe of the Urewera region). The project was kaupapa-driven – most important was not the process or technique involved in creating the art, but rather the agenda that informs the work. Therefore, she needed to demonstrate an understanding of her kaupapa. If, on the other hand, the creative project is process-driven, the student must demonstrate an intimate understanding of the process. For example, one of our students experimented with paintings that became three-dimensional reliefs in paint by exploring techniques and materials that would allow

A.-Chr. Engels-Schwarzpaul and M. A. Peters (Eds.), Of other Thoughts: Non-Traditional Ways to the Doctorate: A Guidebook for Candidates and Supervisors, 297–309.
© *2013 Sense Publishers. All rights reserved.*

the paint to set as a solid mass. Or, another example, a student experimented with the potential of fractured light resulting from counter-grinding stainless steel. Sometimes students will just want to use paint as paint, so then they need to be able to control the medium and develop a skill-level that is almost phenomenal. Supervision is in those cases about facilitating their desire and working out suitable standards with them. Sometimes, there will be a coalescence of those approaches: if students have a strong kaupapa *and* a strong medium-based practice, an appropriate consideration of both aspects will be important. And then the question is, should the student explain how one informs the other in the exegesis, or through an oral defence – or is it the examiners' role to work out the overall kaupapa?

That's interesting. You're suggesting a role for the examination that could be quite separate from the exegesis and the work.

With creative research, I think, the written component is an *attempt* – and I use that word deliberately – to create a document that allows examiners to place themselves in a relationship with the practice or outcome. If you bring a person to the product of creative practice, and you remove the exegesis with its access to the kaupapa, all the examiner has to judge is the product, the output of the creative journey. And then all you can do, as an examiner, is to bring to that creative output *your* view of art, *your* aesthetic experience, *your* subjective perspective. So, what becomes immediately apparent when confronted with, say, a painting, is the technical facility, and one can see whether there is a consistency in technical skill or chromatic consideration. I might also gain a sense of the emergence of some figurative theme generated through the arrangement of gestural marks. And I am witnessing a journey towards expressing an idea through the minimal application of paint, through single brush strokes layered over single brush strokes – as ground and gestural marks establish a spatial order. Without the exegesis to lead me, all I can do as an examiner is react to what is in front of me; and for me, the journey is evident in the results of the practice. The question I ask myself is then – has this been a successful journey? I could actually decide that the candidate should pass without even knowing what the kaupapa is.

At that point, can you say that the thesis has contributed to your knowledge, or somebody else's knowledge? To knowledge in a wider sense?

Let's put it this way. If the project is driven by process, the process (or the documentation of experimentation and exploration) can demonstrate, dare I say it, research with paint – this should be totally evident in what the examiner encounters. My question is still: how do we contextualise this process of painting or other creative practice in a written form? How do we achieve a synthesis of content and process? If, on the other hand, the process results from an engagement with a *particular* theme, another layer of complexity is added to the examination process: has the candidate been able to articulate the content and also articulate how the outcomes were achieved? I wonder sometimes, are we examining the product (the creative result) or a candidate's ability to articulate how the result was achieved? There's an interesting dilemma here.

If you had to reduce this to conventional terminology, would you say that one is mastery and the other is contribution to knowledge?

I'll be the devil's advocate here: in many non-traditional PhD theses in fine arts, we are being made to conform to prevailing academic conventions regarding the articulation of the research practice. It has to be done in a form that allows a wider audience to come to terms with the art work. Whereas the counterargument would be that an exceptional piece of work really does not need an explanation (that was the norm in the 1970s, when Elam School of Fine Arts offered a Master's degree that was totally practice-based – I didn't agree with the argument at the time, and I still have problems with it). And there are those rare moments where you can immediately respond to the journey when put in front of a series of paintings – the research in paint. However, given that we *have* to produce a narrative, the question for me is always, how we can assist candidates to articulate their process? One of the things we need to make them aware of is that they can, and must, demonstrate in that document what and how they are adding to new knowledge. That can be difficult because each student has a different approach. I am supervising students who are involved in customary Māori whatu kākahu (woven garments), tāniko (embroidery) and raranga (weaving of mats, baskets, etc.), whakairo rākau (wood carving), tā moko (Māori tattoo), graphic design, ceramics, sculpture, installation, ...you name it.

Māori weaving is an interesting phenomenon today. The practice of weaving generated different forms over time, for example kahu (garments), different styles of cloaks including kahu kuri, kaitaka, and korowai. These became fashionable during a particular period and were subsequently replaced by other fashions. I had a Masters student creating cloaks by innovatively incorporating muka (flax fibre): the whole object was black, and she created fascinating textural changes and contrasts through partial exposure of the muka, or through changes in the directional twist during the whatu (weaving) process. The result was interesting in the way its light and dark textures played with light. Her objective was to create experiments in single colour, and to extend this idea across a range of cloaks. The body of work she created was pretty amazing from a technical point of view. Now, how do you place this work within the context of existing knowledge of kahu? She obviously had to study the evolution of cloaks. Because her practice was weaving, and because the form she was creating was based on a cloak, this was easy: an historical context and a formal language already existed. While black cloaks are not really part of the tradition, the use of black as a colour is significant (and she had to look at that use in its historical context). The body of work she generated was quite exceptional and innovative, I think, in contemporary cloak making. She also provided a written component, which supported that practice really-really well and was articulated well for the examiners to empathise with her journey. However, it's not so easy to deal with historical, customary context when the practice is painting ... So you have these situations where pairing the text with the art work makes absolute sense.

Does it perhaps make even more sense when there are international examiners? Can somebody from outside of Aotearoa make sense of something like kahu without being aware of their local context and tradition?

I guess the written component of the thesis needs to be written in such a way that an examiner can comprehend new work within the context of a tradition. Which brings me to another, related point: the requirement to involve an international examiner in the PhD examination. This condition is problematic for PhDs in te reo Māori (Māori language) because there is a dearth of Māori academics at overseas universities who are both fluent in te reo Māori *and* have the relevant subject knowledge. On the other hand, there is a group of acknowledged tribal experts in te Ao Māori (the Māori world) who not only *have* the requisite knowledge, but are *recognised* as having it – but may not have a PhD (although some have been acknowledged through the award of an honorary doctorate). A PhD in te reo Māori demands a special type of examiner, and that can be in conflict with the requirement to include an international examiner. Soon, Māori PhD theses involving creative practice will require examiners who are fluent in te reo Māori; the candidates may even prefer to defend their thesis in te reo Māori. This is currently happening at Te Pūtahi a Toi at Masters level when the exegesis has been written in te reo Māori.[2] It will be a normal reality in the future for PhDs: if a candidate undertakes research through creative practice in relation to customary kōwhaiwhai (painted patterns used on meeting house rafters), for example, a history, a tradition will have to be considered. Who will be the appropriate examiner in this context? Of course, there is the possibility of apportioning examination tasks.

Does the university pay for translations of the exegesis?

No. If a thesis is written in te reo Māori, it has to be examined in te reo Māori. Principally, we cannot translate it into English because that would be an infringement of the legal status of te reo Māori as an official language.

I was thinking in analogy with a scenario that is quite common, I believe: in many, if not most non-traditional PhD examinations, it is highly unlikely that each of the examiners will be able to cover the entire spectrum of the aspects to be examined. So, practically, one always looks for a combination of expertise in the examiners' team. There will almost always be an implicit allocation of roles.

That's a valid point. We need to ensure that one of the examiners has the subject knowledge, while the other two may have iwi knowledge. For a thesis on tā moko, I recently approached a tā moko expert with a Master of Fine Arts degree who had the prerequisite subject knowledge. But he was unable to examine due to other commitments so that, in the end, we selected a carver with a PhD as the subject knowledge expert. It's not an easy task to find examiners who have both fluency in te reo Māori *and* subject knowledge expertise, you've got to really search around for the knowledge.

For the accredited knowledge.

For the accredited knowledge, that's the critically important point. For some Māori PhDs in fine arts or design, we're going to struggle to find the appropriate examiner. I'm willing to look at other Indigenous examiners, non-Māori that is, because that still supports the kaupapa of the programme, and that's critically important for me.

What is the process and scope of the PhD submissions at your school?

It really depends on the candidate. I was recently involved in the examination of two PhD candidates in fine arts, who had sequential exhibitions over three and four years respectively. I like the model. When I initially floated the idea of sequential exhibitions some years ago, there was a muted response. The majority opted for a single substantive exhibition. But seeing examples of sequential exhibitions recently reinforces my view that this is a good approach. In any event, I encourage my candidates to create work as they go, and to keep a really good record that can be presented as part of the final exhibition. But there will always be different formulae for different candidates to realise both the practice and the written component. Another important point for me is that, because I'm involved in Māori PhDs in fine arts, I'm often going to a Māori perspective. So, all the candidates who come to the Bachelor or Master of Māori Visual Arts (BMVA or MMVA) programmes at Pūtahi a Toi must first and foremost engage with kaupapa Māori, and totally understand it.

This is unusual for an art or design school that is part of a mainstream university structure, isn't it?

It is ... there is certainly a point of difference associated with the PhDs in Fine Arts at Te Pūtahi a Toi. Significantly, the candidates currently enrolled are all Māori, and identify as Māori, and contextualise their practice within a Māori framework.

I find quite often that candidates who have been involved in Māori language acquisition are also well informed about the Treaty of Waitangi and tino rangatiratanga (self-determination). As a consequence, many do not need to use kaupapa Māori methodology because, in a sense, they are drawing on a knowledge base located in Te Ao Māori, anyway. If they're Māori, their navigation of the research is driven by being Māori. Nevertheless, the writings on kaupapa Māori theory are a valuable validation that supports them in their journey.

Is this a good moment to talk about collaboration and communities?

Yes! I have a candidate at the moment who is a jeweller. She has embarked on a very collaborative process. It's probably one of the most collaborative research projects I've witnessed. She's consulting with iwi representatives from Kai Tahu, and because she has connections to a number of hapū (extended kin groups) in Kai Tahu, she has to have an informant in each of those hapū. And, of course, the jewellery she creates is a response to the consultation process – which is about tikanga (correct procedure) and hapū narratives. Her final exhibition will accumulate the knowledge derived from the consultation and connection with hapū. But she also visits galleries and museums all over the country, looking at and responding to taonga (prized possessions) – that's taonga as in adornment – created in Kai Tahu. On this journey, she came across an interesting situation at the Otago Museum. All the other museums allowed her to enter the collections, to photograph them, and to print the photos in her PhD. Only the curator at the Otago museum resists. Ironically, the person who is stopping the process happens to be Pākehā. The old adage, a little knowledge is a dangerous thing … "oh no, you can't do this, it's tapu".[4] But her approach is really about engaging with the taonga physically and emotionally and spiritually, and letting them generate her creative response; engaging with hapū narratives and letting the narratives generate her response. The hardest part of her thesis will be the written component, because she's got so much information …

What makes up a practice-led research thesis? Is it the proportion of creative work and written commentary or context? Or is it about the way questions are raised by the practice? In that case, would the clear articulation of questions arising from practice (and the resulting repercussions in the contextualising material – and vice versa) be one possible 'editing' strategy?

I think it's a good strategy.

Do you have any thoughts about collaboration and how it is incorporated, or not, into the rules of PhD research? Which, after all, is 'traditionally' perceived largely as an individual effort?

Again, I think it depends on the nature of the study undertaken by the candidate, and what they're hoping to achieve. There have been a couple of reasonably successful collaborative projects recently. They weren't conducted as part of a PhD programme, but they could have been. I'm thinking in particular of the collaboration between three Māori artists, Ngatai Taepa, Saffronn Te Ratana and Hemi McGregor. They created a work in response to the Tuhoe raids, called *Ka kata te pō*.[5] At Te Pūtahi a Toi, we haven't had any students collaborating yet, although one current student has collaborated during her PhD tenure and will include the collaborative output as part of her PhD. From a Māori perspective – and here I'm prioritising Māori PhDs – collaboration is fine. It has always been an intrinsic part of Māori practice.

Is occasional collaboration easier to accommodate in a cumulative submission? I'm thinking of Moana Nepia's work, which you examined recently at AUT – if it had been based only on one final piece, would collaboration have made it more difficult to assess?

A cumulative submission makes a lot of sense. There are, of course, different constellations for collaboration. We have to negotiate suitable terms of reference for each single case. If two candidates enrol in a PhD simultaneously and collaborate over the duration of the thesis, there should not be a problem provided the terms of reference are clear. For Māori, it's the way people worked in the past. We were collaborators. I get the sense we've been colonised into creating art that is about the individual – as opposed to working collaboratively on projects.

What is important in selecting, adapting and inventing research methodologies for Māori in creative practice-led research?

I'd take out the word "inventing". I don't think what we do is invent. I'd call it innovation. Moana's exegesis is unique in its structure, its opening by a lyrical narrative introduction. This is like an appetiser, akin to a tauparapara (incantation to begin a speech: when you begin whaikōrero, a speech, you introduce with a tauparapara). It has a nice analogy with oratory, and I like that, it makes it very Māori. The way it is laid out is also innovative: it totally breaks the conventions for the organisation of a thesis ... a brave move to break with tradition. I encouraged one of my candidates recently to be more inventive about his formatting but, understandably, he's a little apprehensive of potential negative repercussions.

I've got another candidate, basically a figurative sculptor, who has an interesting thesis. She works in bronze and creates insects that are native to Aotearoa New Zealand and feature in Māori oral traditions. Part of her research is about their significance within the context of te Ao Māori. It is also about the relationship of Māori and Western science taxonomies. She privileges a Māori view of the world in her juxtaposition of different value systems and curatorial strategies. In creating these insects, she plays on the entomologists' way of presenting insects as species and sub-species. So she presents them in cabinet drawers in distorted perspective: the drawers are presented vertically but look like they're horizontal. The insects are presented according to a Māori rather than a (Western) scientific rationale, emphasising the role of insects as determinants of environmental and seasonal change.

What are distinctive contributions that Māori in creative practiced-led research can make to knowledge production?

Creative ways of generating knowledge – but it depends on the context. I think the thesis based on insects is a good example. One of its contributions to knowledge, I think, is that it will put into a single document, for the first time ever, all historical references associated with Māori insects. While the scientific names are integrally acknowledged, Māori knowledge in relation to those insects is privileged. In other words, it does two things: it addresses the conventions of scientific knowledge – I wish it didn't – *and* it places the insects within cultural narratives. It puts Māori knowledge on a par with scientific knowledge.

Why don't you like the fact that she addresses scientific conventions?

Because I was also forced to comply when I did my PhD.

I'm thinking about this a lot at the moment. The quote from Hannah Arendt that Moana read out during his viva was part of an extended discussion about plurality, and how the creation of a common world requires different perspectives. So, while – for political and historical reasons – the privileging of Māori knowledge makes sense, I think, there is also value in having something sitting next to it that it can have a conversation with, if you like.

That's fine. Let's put it this way: as a protest, I refused to reference the accession numbers associated with taonga whakairo in museums – only to get slapped over the hands. Ultimately, I had to conform. But there is value in having conformed. I have now encouraged one of our students to include accession numbers in his study on Māori pare (door lintels) to assist other Māori in their research. Consistent use of conventions means future Māori candidates involved in similar research will have the cross-referenced information at their fingertips. So, in fact, if one looks beyond being radical or pushing the tino rangatiratanga flag, that knowledge can actually be advantageous for other Māori researchers.

And I would like to think that there is value in understanding the differences between the systems, because each of the names stands for a system.

True, the sculptor's thesis about insects brings together two knowledge systems, two different approaches to knowledge; a kaupapa Māori system and a system that owes a debt to Carl Linnaeus. Ultimately, her creative practice is about inverting a normal curatorial process, which privileges a classificatory system of displaying insects. She tips it on its head to privilege relational Māori systems of recording and naming that are associated with environmental and seasonal changes. The insects are cast in bronze and painted in local colours, while the display cabinets will be painted to simulate timber. The final form of the exhibition becomes in this way also an engagement in trompe l'oeil.

Is there, then, perhaps a synergy between a specific Māori perspective on and appetite for knowledge, on the one hand, and new and emerging fields of research such as creative practice-led research, on the other?

I can't separate the two, because I'm involved in supervising candidates who are Māori *and* are involved in creative research.

We've just talked about the candidate who organises her thesis, at least in part, around finding different ways of classifying insects. I imagine that, whatever comes out of this thesis, there will be an accretion of knowledge that could not have happened had she not taken a radically different view from, I suspect, those common in either knowledge system ... the Western scientific system will have gained, too, won't it?

That part of her thesis is publishable as a book, and it would actually be a very informative one. This candidate is an entomologist by training, an entomologist who is an artist and an illustrator. Not only does she draw all the insects – she also draws on interdisciplinary knowledge and synthesises the fields of knowledge from the perspective of a Māori artist. In the process, she acknowledges artists who also work in bronze, like Elizabeth Thomson and Terry Stringer. This is actually an aspect I encourage all candidates to think about seriously. The acknowledgement of artists who have either used similar processes, or images, or social commentary is a very Māori thing to do. This concerns other Māori artists (kaumātua [elders] and peers) particularly if your kaupapa is Māori, but also non-Māori artists, wherever they might be based – the practice candidates undertake might not necessarily have been undertaken by Māori before. Ultimately, such research is situated and related both to precedents and contemporary practice. So, it is critical that candidates acknowledge those tributaries, that feed their pools of knowledge.

At least designers should know that. Do designers know better than artists?

Not necessarily. My entomologist is keen to leave no stone unturned. She accesses every single publication that features insects native to Aotearoa/New Zealand if she can lay her hands on it. As an avid collector of old books, she has collected every edition of the Williams dictionary (1844),[6] and so is able to track the first appearance of insect names, and all the changes in the information associated with words through time. It is vitally necessary, right at the beginning of a PhD candidature, to research all possible expressions associated with the practice in which the candidate is involved. At the moment, I'm talking to another potential PhD candidate, whose practice is totally unique. To appreciate the uniqueness of his technique, it is necessary to walk past the work because the technique capitalises on light refraction. As part of his research into process, he will look at all artists who engage in using refracted light.

Mark Dorrian from Newcastle University (UK) said in an interview that a PhD supervisor's role is, in the first instance, probably that of a critical respondent who supports questioning and finding direction, as a collaborator. How do you see the role of the supervisor in relation to the candidate and other mentors and collaborators?

I think he's got a very good handle on what a good PhD supervisor should be. In some cases, with candidates who are really in tune with where they are going and what they are doing, we can have – I won't say a heated debate – but we can have a debate that challenges their position in terms of their research approach and direction. One of the things I emphasise with candidates is that they need to be able to justify every position they take, and have the evidence to support it. If that's absent, we enter a process of debating the absence of knowledge about the ideas that inform the practice. Candidates then need to convince me that it's not necessary to have one (at that stage, at least). In a sense, I feel that the supervisor needs to be the devil's advocate sometimes. It's not about being autocratic; it's about building a solid case for the position a candidate adopts as a creative research practitioner.

So, is that about ensuring that the development of the work has a sound base and context?

Definitely, it's about being sound. It is also about trying to think outside the square in terms of 'the position', because you can only rely on kaupapa Māori to a certain extent. I think it's important to realise that kaupapa Māori may not necessarily be the only relevant methodology for Māori creative practice researchers. The entomologist's example is a classic case: because she's an entomologist, a scientist, some parts of her work will be taken care of in that way. But I think the way in which she structures it – prior to turning the whole thing on its head – so that the two knowledge systems are complementary to each other and inform each other, is an appropriate and relevant approach. The mere fact that she has discovered a range of Māori names for insects that are not even in Māori dictionaries is in itself a contribution to new knowledge. But I do think to help her prepare for every possible question in relation to her research undertaking is an important part of supervision.

What are other roles?

I think the best role you can ever have is to be available. Some candidates don't need you as much as others, but I've had candidates texting me or ringing me at home (and sometimes the questions are banal, but it's more about being there and being available). One of the things I find PhD candidates appreciate is that they can send me something and get a response within a week, and often sooner. They need to know what they can expect … particularly when they are nearing completion. It's really about making sure that candidates enrolled in a PhD have the best opportunity, and are given the best chance, to complete what they have set out to do. It is a life's investment that is not only about them, but also about Māori in general.

If we have creative practice-led research, what would be mātauranga Māori-led research ... but I think you've talk about that all the time.

I'm particularly aware of that aspect. When I did my thesis, I wrote a chapter on kaupapa Māori theory and its relevance for Māori visual culture. My supervisor decided that the chapter was irrelevant. He said, "as far as I'm concerned, what you're writing about *is* kaupapa Māori, you do not need this chapter". End of story. This led me to develop my own framework – Te Tātaitanga Ahua Toi (2006) – as a possible model for addressing research in Māori visual culture. Interestingly, if I look at Moana Nepia's approach to creative research in his recent PhD submission, it is about being Māori, it is what Māori do, it is a Māori approach. He began by going home. The narratives he referenced for his methodology were from home. He interacted with the land and the sea at home. His informants were from home. When the work shifted location, it was imbedded in a consideration of the change in iwi context; an acknowledgement of mana whenua (power associated with possession and occupation of tribal land). Another important thing for Māori candidates is to undertake a Māori research methodologies paper. I encourage all postgraduate students considering Māori visual arts study to enrol in one, even though it is optional ... and it has reduced my workload amazingly. It introduces students to the basics of good research practice from a Māori perspective. The Māori research methodologies paper we offer also acknowledges and accommodates students involved in creative practice. It introduces them to library database systems, search techniques, literature reviews, proposal development and ethical considerations associated with research. That means that, by the time they come to me, they've thought about the process and they understand the importance of research conventions. Recently we've had an influx of Pākehā students enrolling in the Māori visual arts paper. What is surprising is that they are prepared to undertake a postgraduate programme that acknowledges an ethnicity not their own, and that they are fully prepared to engage in a Māori environment – even to position their creative practice and research within a bicultural framework.

What do you think about Mark Dorrian's claim that it can be an advantage if a supervisor is not an expert in the candidate's subject matter?

That's an interesting question. I am currently working with several co-supervisors who are not visual artists. I involve them because their area of research expertise will benefit the students. For example, a supervisor with an expertise in the area of ethics and discourse on power will be valuable for students examining power imbalance between Māori and institutions. A Māori language expert's contribution to formulating a visual arts vocabulary is invaluable. Kaupapa Māori experts, and even psychologists, can make important contributions. I find that working with experts outside the visual arts also allows me to maintain focus on the creative component of the research. My co-supervisors include Associate Professor Huia Tomlins-Jahnke (postcolonial discourse), Professor Linda Tuhiwai Smith (kaupapa Māori research), Dr Darryn Joseph (Māori language), and Dr Bronwyn Campbell (psychology and post-structuralism). Using expertise from other disciplines opens candidates' perspectives to matters outside the visual arts, and that is an antidote to my visual arts tunnel vision. I find it is really-really important and helpful to be able to offer students alternative perspectives. A larger team of supervisors is helpful because it allows a broader contribution to a candidate's research project.

Is there anything that I've overlooked in my questions?

The way one supervises will produce particular responses. And I like to think that my approach to supervision is related to being Māori first and foremost. One of the important things for Māori researchers to appreciate is that the knowledge they are researching actually does not belong to them. The new knowledge they might generate comes from engaging with prior knowledge, knowledge that has not only been generated by Māori, but also by other people. And it's always important to remember that, whatever they do, the final exposition they generate is something that they are gifting back to the knowledge community.

Is that part of the difference between 'just practice' and a PhD?

I think it is. I often say to candidates I work with, the reason you are in this situation is because you are privileged. And, in this privileged position as a university student, you have to think about how you got here. It's important that, as part of your journey, you make a contribution back, and to those who are going to follow you. It's like the old Māori adage of "Ehara taku toa i te toa takitahi. Ēngari he toa takitini" (a warrior never stands alone, but stands with many). Basically, my knowledge is not just mine, it is an inheritance from those who have gone before. In traditional Māori society, knowledge was viewed as sacred and as an inheritance from deity. One received the gift of knowledge in a privileged wānanga (school of learning) context. And I think that's important when interacting with Māori PhD candidates: making them aware, not that they have a duty, but that they have put themselves in a particular position – from where they can make a contribution back to their people, their whānau, hāpu and iwi. If possible, I also like them to contextualise their research methodology in relation to significant narratives that are related to their kaupapa. A student I work with will be exploring the creation of movement in a two dimensional plane, and I anticipate that he will engage tribal narratives (either Ngāpuhi or Ngāti Kahungunu ki Mahia) that explore the idea of movement and transition. And there are also narratives about reflection. There are relevant terms, not only in Māori narratives, but also in mōteatea (chants) and in waiata (songs), which relate to movement, particularly with the perception of movement. I say to them, you are Māori and you are engaging in a visual practice, and most of the people who are going to access and read your material in the future will be Māori – and that gives them a sense of connection and belonging to the knowledge that has already been researched and recorded. They are part of this continuity by gifting their work back to Māori – so that the search for knowledge can continue.

NOTES

[1] Professor Robert Hans George Jahnke is Head of Māori Studies at Massey University. The interview took place in Auckland on 1 February 2013.
[2] Te Putāhi a Toi is the School of Māori Studies at Massey University in Palmerston North.
[3] The Bachelor and Master of Māori Visual Arts programmes, which are unique to Massey University, engage contemporary Māori art, Māori language, Māori culture, and tikanga. Students combine theoretical and practical studies to become two- or three-dimensional art practitioners who have a sound cultural foundation for their verbal and visual communication. The course encourages and facilitates interaction with the broader Māori community through exhibitions and community courses. http://www.massey.ac.nz/massey/learning/departments/school-maori-studies/school-of-maori-studies_home.cfm
[4] Quite often, the solution to such a problem is to involve hapū or Māori curators, the Māori staff in these institutions, to act as intermediaries.
[5] The Tūhoe raids refers to a police operation, known as Operation 8, which involved 18 months of surveillance of Māori and peace activist. On October 15th 2007, gun-bearing black-clad police squads woke up residents of Ruatoki in Tuhoe territory, smashing doors and dragging inhabitants out onto the road. Local buses and cars were stopped at road blocks and helicopters hovered over the village.

Presumably, the operation was aimed at persons involved in terrorist military training in the Urewera ranges. See CUTCUTCUT Films (2001). On 22 May 2013, the Independent Police Conduct Authority decided that police acted "unlawfully, unjustifiably and unreasonably" during the raids. See Quilliam (2013).

Ka kata te pō translates as *the night laughs*.

[6] Since its original publication in 1844, this dictionary has been continually updated, increasingly by Māori scholars.

[7] The PhD thesis, *He tātaitanga āhua toi: The house that Riwai built, a continuum of Māori art* discusses the relationships between customary, non-customary and trans-customary Māori art forms.

REFERENCES

CUTCUTCUT Films. (2001). *Operation 8: Deep in the forest*. Retrieved March 5, 2012, from http://www.cutcutcut.com/Operation8.html

Jahnke, R. H. G. (2006). *He tātaitanga āhua toi: the house that Riwai built, a continuum of Māori art* (PhD thesis). Massey University, Palmerston North, New Zealand.

Quilliam, R. (2013, 22 May). Police acted 'unlawfully' during Urewera raids, *The New Zealand Herald*. Retrieved from http://www.nzherald.co.nz/nz/news/article.cfm?c_id=1&objectid=10885376

Williams, H. W. (1844). *A Dictionary of the Māori Language*. Wellington, New Zealand: A. R. Shearer, Government Printer.

AFFILIATIONS

Robert H.G. Jahnke
Te Whānau a Rakairoa, Te Whānau a Iritekura, Ngāi Taharora, Ngāti Porou

Te Putāhi a Toi, School of Māori Studies
Massey University, Palmerston North

A.-CHR. ENGELS-SCHWARZPAUL & MICHAEL A. PETERS

18. EMERGENT KNOWLEDGES AND NON-TRADITIONAL CANDIDATES

Conclusion

Ever since scientific work … has given itself its own proper and appropriable places through rational projects capable of determining their procedures, … ever since it was founded as a plurality of limited and distinct fields, in short ever since it stopped being theological, it has constituted the *whole* as its *remainder;* this remainder has become what we call culture. This cleavage organizes modernity. It cuts it up into scientific and dominant islands set off against the background of practical "resistances" and symbolizations that cannot be reduced to thought. (Certeau, 1984: 6)

The claim of rational certainty advanced in the natural and social sciences has always been questionable, as Paul Feyerabend (1993, originally 1975) and Thomas Kuhn (1970) already argued in the 1970s. Nevertheless, it did contribute to the creation of a vast remainder of thoughts and practices under the general term of culture (social, artistic, ethnic …). At the beginning of the twentieth century, culture – largely perceived as irrational, complex and messy – came to form the background of organised and accredited academic research. Since then, there has been (and sometimes still is) an explicit or implicit expectation of doctoral candidates to settle on one of de Certeau's "scientific and dominant islands". Over the last four decades, though, following Kuhn and Feyerabend's challenges to epistemological, methodological and disciplinary certainties, major changes have taken place. They were reinforced and amplified by the growing importance of the global knowledge and culture economies. The new kinds of knowledge emerging in the wake of these changes are often closely allied with the *remainder*. They openly draw on aspects of irrationality, which had previously been incorporated into the rational system only through the provision of reserves, such as private life, art, and entertainment.

This recent ascent of different kinds of intelligence into the preserves of academic knowledge production presents a chance and a challenge at the same time. On the one hand, these new circumstances provide opportunities for those regarded as Other (as a result of a sustained institutionalised marginalisation of their knowledges) to challenge the mainstream with their renegade knowledges (un-subjugated knowledge, counter-memory, counter-language). Their critical engagement with established bodies of knowledge, literatures and methods, and their introduction

A.-Chr. Engels-Schwarzpaul and M. A. Peters (Eds.), Of other Thoughts: Non-Traditional Ways to the Doctorate: A Guidebook for Candidates and Supervisors, 311–323.
© *2013 Sense Publishers. All rights reserved.*

of different kinds can change the academic landscape. The challenge, on the other hand, is to resist subjugation and co-option; to resist becoming part of what Jacques Rancière calls *the count*, which excludes those *beyond count* who "have no part" (Rancière, 2001: thesis 6/14; 2004: 7); the challenge is to refrain from partaking in exclusive traditions.

One recent tradition (ironically exclusive of *tradition*) was until quite recently largely invisible (tradition "goes without saying because it comes without saying: the tradition is silent, not least about itself as a tradition", Bourdieu, 1977: 167). Its main tenet, that modern societies have freed themselves from the shackles of tradition and, as a consequence, undergo scientific and socio-economic progress at a fast rate, denigrated tradition as an outmoded, backward social phenomenon. Yet, as Timothy Luke argues, tradition was alive everywhere in European societies, as late as 1996, except (in its older forms) in the centre of society and in its institutions (1996: 113). Rather than being without tradition, social institutions had developed their own (modernist) traditions – which meanwhile went without saying. Traditional PhD candidates in Europe, at the time of Feyerabend and Kuhn's challenges, were of Taylor and Beasley's types. In the former colonies, the situation was complicated by the fact that *tradition* as a backward way of living had been assigned to the Indigenous populations (see Edwards p. 56, above).

The term *non-traditional* in this book's title, then, does not refer to a simplistic division of the world into West and non-West, science and non-science. While there are such distinctions, they are criss-crossed by others, in locally specific ways. There are two approximate themes, within the term *non-traditional*, by which we have clustered the contributions in this book. One theme (ironically) concerns members of so-called traditional (ethnic or national) cultures, the other refers to particular research cultures and methods. The first cluster includes researchers from Indigenous, transnational, diasporic, coloured or ethnic minority groups (already, there are overlaps between these categories); the second cluster involves research orientations and methods that arise from, for example, trans-cultural, post-colonial, transdisciplinary and creative practice-led approaches.

Mindful of our own relation to tradition, we encourage in this book an experimental attitude to knowledge sources, processes and creation. There is great value in leaving one's safe and intimately known shores to become estranged from unspoken traditions and to look back from the ocean – another view of the world. A sense of the whole will be different on return.[2] Traditional patterns will shift when they are brought into motion by new researchers and emergent knowledge fields as they raise questions regarding the nature of a literature; the genealogy of a practice; or the status and function of a thesis, exegesis, performance/exhibition, 'the oral' and 'the defence'. This will, in turn, affect the generally held concepts of the scholar and the researcher. An on-going critique of the ideology of the self – as scholar or researcher – helps resist *tying down* knowledge by ever newly invented disciplinary ropes (see Feyerabend, 1993: x).[3]

EMERGENT KNOWLEDGES AND NON-TRADITIONAL CANDIDATES

THE CONCEPTS OF THE SCHOLAR AND THE RESEARCHER

It is remarkable how concepts come into and go out of fashion; indeed, how they are fashioned. The notions of *scholar* and *scholarship* are inseparable from texts. The medieval European university was based on the notion of the text, and faithfulness to the text, which grew out of a long association of commentary and meta-commentary arising from the textual interpretation of the Bible. Today, scholarship implies a relation to textual study based on academic and legal norms. With the establishment of the modern research University (beginning with the University of Berlin in 1811), it could be argued, the notion of *researcher* became more dominant than that of the *scholar* (although the two are often blurred). The term *researcher* takes its cues from notions of research that emphasise method and experiment and the production of new knowledge, rather than from the context of humanistic knowledge based on creative interpretation of texts.[4] The empirical method developed by the early modern research University still had philosophy as its pedagogical paradigm, and its pedagogical forms echoed those of the scholastic University. It appealed to the nature, autonomy and authority of the *scholar*, with its pedagogical forms of examination and genres of academic writing reflecting forms of philosophical reasoning and other practices: the thesis, the dissertation, the lecture, the seminar and so on.

The shift from *scholar* to *researcher* has relevance for understanding larger epistemic shifts from the medieval University (based on textual commentary, oriented and constituted by a literature and canon, and governed by interpretations of a community of scholars) to the modern research University.[5] The latter harnesses the new sciences in the service of the nation and is wedded to scientific method, that is, to hypothesis-testing, the production of new empirical knowledge through experiment and observation, and the further testing and validation of any findings by other researchers.

In Europe, still the silent point of reference for discussions such as this, scholars and scholarship developed alongside new modes of textual production following the invention of the printing press and movable type in the fifteenth century. Soon, academic norms regulating the *literature* were institutionalised in textual layout and commentary, as well as forms of citation (e.g., the convention of acknowledgement, exemplified in the long history of the footnote that began in the Renaissance, or the appeal to past authorities). In a climate where freedom of speech was not customarily observed, or where secret societies existed to protect members from prosecution or criminal action, these norms had important functions. Already in the fourteenth century, academic knowledge in Italy had emerged in learning societies alongside science. Britain, France, Germany and the United States followed suit.

Only in the eighteenth century did one of the basics of modern scholarship, the institution of peer review, come into force at the Royal Society (first at Edinburgh in 1732 and later at London), principally as a means of censorship.[6] The emergence of peer review as the public self-regulation of scholarship by scholars themselves is thus a very recent phenomenon compared with the origin of the University or Learned Society. The historical process, by which a set of standardised expert peer review processes and conventions came to be regularly deployed in the production of journals, is nearly invisible today. These conventions now form a seemingly timeless system, which implicitly asserts a notion of *truth* as the warrant for the validity, authority, textual faithfulness and trustworthiness of claims made by scholars. In part, this system of (often blind double) peer review relies on academic writing conventions that employ standardised forms (e.g., introduction, problem formulation/ question, methods section, literature survey, and analysis of findings). While the standards do vary from discipline to discipline, the world's stock of some eighteen thousand journals (which is growing very rapidly) tends to embody globalised norms of citation, acknowledgement of sources, bibliographical conventions, and section headings. This standardisation not only obscures the gradual, piece-by-piece development of the conventions. Their historical dependency on writing and printing technologies; on the roles of the scribe and scholar; and on the particular forms of reasoning that predated our current forms of academic knowledge production (for which peer review seems so central) is also largely invisible.

Research is partially distinguished from scholarship through an emphasis on methodical experiment and the production of new knowledge (McClintock, 2005). This suggests a greater engagement of researchers in the world. While scholars integrate the findings of a cumulative collection of knowledge, crafting coherent understandings, researchers seeks clear answers and solutions to specific questions and problems, "using peer-sanctioned methods and techniques" (49). Scholars in "the exercise of their craft" must also answer questions, of course, but the relationship of research to its own questions is on the whole of a more instrumental nature – particularly in the research university, whose "faculty members rely on the publication of peer-reviewed research for promotion and tenure" (49). Research "tends to be use-driven, conducive to interested, not disinterested, results, and it accentuates findings with instrumental value directly applicable to a specific form of activity" (49).

Research, thus, is closely related to practice. Meaning a "strict inquiry" in the seventeenth century (and in Old French, a "diligent search", Skeat, 1883: 504), research has an even older reference to Latin *circare*, to circulate and go around (Partridge, 2006: 515). As Jenner suggests (p. 205, above), re-search does not necessarily imply repetition, though it often does: as in a hermeneutic circle, returning to the same position at another level of skill, experience and understanding will, indeed, often amount to intensification. This revisiting of experience is intimately related to the notion of practice Richard Sennett carefully describes in *The Craftsman* (2008). "Going over an action again and again" permits self-criticism, reflection and a modulation of practice from within (37-8).

The development of practice-led research in the last decades, outside of the natural sciences, gives a very contemporary edge to these craft principles. Akin to the conceptual circularity of action-research, creative practice-led research and time-based performance deploy iteration as an increasingly important methodological principle. It seems to reclaim the time, sometimes almost obsessively, that was rationalised out of production. When craftspeople in this historical process turned into designers, the playful element that made their craft an art came under threat (287-8). Prehension became projection, process a project that follows an intention towards a goal. Rules and measurement follow. Sennet makes the case for drawing, against CAD procedures, in architectural design where crystallising and refining architectural sketches by hand as "pictures of possibility" provides the designer with time to get deeply involved, until the object of attention becomes "ingrained in the mind", and, over time, to mature her or his thinking about it (40). "Slow craft time" makes space for reflection and imagination (295). Solutions to a problem (like answers to a question) can uncover new territories through curiosity, an intimate mental bridge between "problem solving and problem finding", which asks both 'Why?' and '"How?' about any project" (11).

While creativity is not the same as research, it shares with research the potential of transformation, of changing the rules of the game. A research thesis (even a traditional one) will exceed already known criteria and rules. It cannot be "wholly described in terms of its audience or context, because this would imply that we knew beforehand what kinds of social relation it would invoke or entail, and to what intellectual purposes it might be put" (Howard, 2007). Non-traditional candidates doing non-traditional research are probably more aware of these conditions. While this may often be a consequence of heightened awareness due to a marginal position in terms of ethnicity, the deployment of the term *non-traditional* certainly does not simply introduce 'culture' as a new power dimension. As the contributors to this book have shown, there are many different margins that can be both productive and disabling. And there are as many ways of dealing with marginality and diversity.

While an *ethical model* of dealing with diversity would proceed with respect and endeavour to change attitudes, it would leave the structures intact. A *radical model* critiques the existing structures and advances claims that there are different ways of knowing (of class, gender, race, etc.) and competing norms regulating the distribution and administration of knowledge (social, cultural, economic, etc.). A *model of openness* recognises that practices are open to change, and can be made to change, by (in this case) precisely the non-traditional candidates that are still on the threshold of the institution. The orientation towards openness aims at the creation of a different scholarly community, while it adheres to, and seeks to protect, some core traditional academic values and practices – all pointing to openness and change – which first allow the endurance of academia through constant modification: criticism, experiment, evidence, justification, dialogue, and a collegiality that highlights the value of a community of peers.

VOICES/TEXTS/OBJECTS/PERFORMANCES

Traditionally, one of the critical notions in relation to doctoral study is that of a *literature*. In the early stages, most doctoral research is defined in relation to a literature – this becomes apparent in the terms *literature survey* or *literature review*. In most disciplines, the *literature* comprises extant written works of superior or lasting merit that helped define the *canon* within a discipline, and the review provides a summary and synopsis of previous research in a particular area. In some areas, the critical review (*review of knowledge*) includes, for example, art works, films, architecture and performances. The review usually also articulates the orientation and shape of the research questions and approaches that inform a particular doctoral research project. These kinds of considerations are addressed in doctoral research manuals. Yet, the notion of a *literature* has far deeper philosophical roots that, properly considered, can partially also help us to understand the origins of the modern research University, as well as the philosophical models and pedagogical practices it has inherited from the past.

Philosophical texts display a variety of literary forms, among them the letter, the treatise, the confession, the meditation, the allegory, the essay, the soliloquy, the symposium, the consolation, the commentary, the disputation, and the dialogue. These forms have conditioned academic writing (and assessment) in the University and their analysis raises questions of philosophical writing and the relation of philosophy to literature and reading (Peters, 2008). Yet what students in the Humanities learn are often standardised formulae for writing. Regarding the essay form, Sean Sturm quotes Pamela Hahn's observation: "tell me what you're going to tell me, tell it, then tell me what you told me" (Hahn in Sturm, 2012). He argues that standardised forms like the *thesis-support form* (Heilker) or the *five-paragraph theme* (Schaffner) derived from such instructions become "so internalized for academic writers as to become, as David Chapman puts it, 'the 'default drive' for expository writing': the form of 'conformity', almost Procrustean in its execution" (Sturm, 2012). There is not much danger for candidates in creative practice areas to be shaped like this, their struggle is often the contrary: to find an order to stabilise (but not to ossify) bubbling ideas.

In one way or another, candidates will learn to negotiate the "forest of signs" (Rancière, 2007) to take up their place amongst their fellow researchers.

> From the ignorant person to the scientist who builds hypotheses, it is always the same intelligence that is at work: an intelligence that makes figures and comparisons to communicate its intellectual adventures and to understand what another intelligence is trying to communicate to it in turn. This poetic work of translation is the first condition of any apprenticeship. Intellectual emancipation, as Jacotot conceived of it, means the awareness and the enactment of that equal power of translation and counter-translation. (275)

However, taking one's place amongst fellow researchers often means in practice adopting a particular theoretical attitude, following a particular writer or artist, or school, or literature, or movement. Departments sometimes have strong affinities (e.g., Continental Theory), and candidates may be expected to align themselves accordingly. It is interesting to note that the contributors to this book refer to a literature in quite different ways: some concentrate strongly on particular theorists or schools of thought – other do so less, possibly because the literature in their field is less solidified and homogenised, or because it is formed by multiple, sometimes even anonymous voices rather than by a few 'great men'.

Traditionally, *the literature* (or *the canon*) has been regarded as the precondition of an academic subject area or discipline. It provided evidence of a specific body of knowledge and served to outline and define the parameters and core concerns of an academic area of study. Non-traditional candidates and non-traditional research areas challenge these notions of *the literature*, and *the canon*, by introducing multiple perspectives and different media through which knowledge may be produced and passed on in a field. An early example of this process is manifest in Ranginui Walker's account (1999) of the development of Māori studies at the University of Auckland. Walker, who had been appointed associate professor of Māori Studies in the Anthropology Department at Auckland University in 1986, relates the story of his and Bruce Biggs' proposal to the Senate to establish a department of Māori Studies.[8] Their proposal was initially thrown out, on the grounds that Māori Studies did not have *a literature*. Walker and Biggs' argument, that Māori knowledge is based on an oral tradition, made little impact. Essentially, Walker and Biggs had to construct a literature, starting from the very first recorded written works, like the Māori Bible and translations by Governor Grey and others in the nineteenth century. Eventually, in 1993, Walker was appointed professor and head of department in Māori Studies.

Similar challenges have been faced by, for example, feminist, queer, post-colonial and creative, professional and practice-led researchers and scholars. In the process, they have re-formed the modes of writing that count as scholarly in the University; proposed forms of knowing and getting-to-know that are image, sound and performance based; formed alliances with knowledge communities outside of the University to conduct participatory and *mode 2* research;[9] and explored the potential of knowing in action, researcher subject positions, distributed knowledge, collaboration, networks and meshworks. On the way, they had to develop their self-understanding as scholars and researchers and their articulation with particular research paradigms, bodies of knowledge and traditions of practice. For creative practice-led research, for example, the nature of the connection between art practice and academic knowledge is still vexing, and some proponents warn that an instrumental relationship would be compromising for both. On the other hand, passing artmaking off as research *per se* would be, as Jan Webb notes, a "category error" that would not serve the creative disciplines (2012: 14). Instead, she suggests that current creative knowledge and methodologies need to be refined better to suit "creative thinking and seeing; reminding the academy more broadly about the extent to which imagination, chance and tacit knowledges actually drive research practice". Making explicit the difference "between professional, aesthetic and research practice", can break down the

> apparent antinomies in which so many find themselves caught. A recrafting of both individual habitus and cultural field has the potential to result in something genuinely new: a new kind of academic who is simultaneously a

new kind of artist, making a new kind of object in a reconceptualised field. (Webb, 2012: 14)

In such reconceptualised fields – how will the examination and distribution of knowledge produced during the PhD research be organised? How will appropriate access be made available and an equivalence achieved between the diverse knowledges produced and submitted (see Brabazon & Dagli, 2010)? In the cultivation of the forest of signs, in which doctoral candidates find and create their paths, there are many questions to be addressed. This calls for "poetic beings who are capable of embracing a distance between words and things, between signs and their referents" (Whittaker, 2011: 92), who can accept the "unreality of representation" and "do not expect words to correspond to the world as it is" – beings who can move between the sea and islands of scientific rationality.

> The ignorant schoolmaster's most scandalous proposition is that this distance between words and things, signs and their referents, makes us all speak as poets – it makes us all try as best we can to tell the story of our mind's adventures and verify that they are understood by other adventurers. (92)

Andrew McNamara calls research that *creates problems* and renders apparent solutions problematic "adventurous research" (2012: 13), which is different from the instrumental knowledge envisaged by university orientations towards "scientism and vocational education" that ties higher education increasingly to industry needs. The homogenisation deriving from the latter eradicates potentially complementary capacities between critical thinking and the quest for new knowledge and excellence (3).

THE UNIVERSITY AND SPACES OF APPEARANCE

Not surprisingly, in the context of the knowledge industries, knowledge production managers deal with principal questions concerning the University (for example, what is the role of doctoral education, what is its relationship with the wider community, and what are the most commensurate contexts, forms and procedures to support it?) with a peculiar mixture of problem awareness and solutioneering: in most countries, only universities can confer the doctoral degree, and they see this as one (if not *the*) activity that defines them as institutions. University staff are also heavily invested in the area, and partially for reasons of personal and institutional status and economic advantage.

Traditionally, the close, master-apprentice relation between supervisor and supervisee is the foundation of the view of the doctorate as a rite of passage, an initiation to the scientific community, the *res publica literaria*. Doctoral education in this view is the ground where scholars can plant their ideas and pass them on to the next generation. (To this day, academics who have long earned their spurs will still, in some countries, be identified by the supervisor of their doctoral thesis; for example "Professor Smith, a pupil of Jones, thinks …", and in German-speaking countries, supervisors would be referred to as the 'doctoral father/mother', *Doktorvater/-mutter*). This rather traditionalist element in doctoral education is, as the language describing it indicates, seen as a private relationship where ideas reign free from interference from institutions. Those faithful to this tradition are very wary of institutions and lawmakers introducing reforms that potentially endanger this tradition. Yet doctoral education is changing fast.

A recent report for the European Universities Association, *Quality Assurance in Doctoral Education* (Byrne, Jørgensen, & Loukkola, 2013), emphasises the core function of doctoral education for the traditional identity of a university. The report goes on to plot relationships between quality assurance and quality culture. It identifies four cultural types that, in one direction, move between professional and management cultures and, in another, depend to a larger or lesser degree on the involvement of staff/faculty and management. The move toward greater management involvement over the past decades is in part a consequence of policy shifts towards the *knowledge economy*, where universities are put in the service of national and regional economic imperatives. In back-grounding these recent changes in doctoral education, the authors refer to recommendations made by the European University Association (EUA)'s 2005 *Bologna seminar on "Doctoral programmes for the European knowledge society"* in Salzburg. The EUA published the Salzburg Principles as a response to the Bergen Communiqué of the Bologna Process, which had called for "basic principles for doctoral programmes". These principles "were instrumental in shaping the reforms of doctoral education" (14). Firstly, they confirm that "the advancement of knowledge through original research" is the "core component of doctoral training" and then, secondly, emphasise the need to embed an expectation in institutional policies and strategies that "doctoral programmes and research training ... are designed to meet new challenges and include appropriate professional career development opportunities". The third principle endorses the

> **importance of diversity**: the rich diversity of doctoral programmes in Europe – including joint doctorates – is a strength which has to be underpinned by quality and sound practice. (European University Association (EUA), 2005)

Principles four and five recognise doctoral candidates as professionals: "early stage researchers", who make a key contribution to the creation of new knowledge, have "commensurate rights". Their supervision ought to be "based on a transparent contractual framework of shared responsibilities between doctoral candidates, supervisors and the institution (and where appropriate including other partners)". Principle six acknowledges that "*different solutions may be appropriate to different contexts*" but advances that "doctoral programmes should seek to achieve critical mass and should draw on different types of innovative practice *being introduced in universities across Europe*" (our emphases). Principles seven to ten address issues of duration, structures, mobility and funding (European University Association (EUA), 2005).

What is interesting about these principles is that, while they recognise the value of 'diversity', they clearly signal a move towards integrated and standardised doctoral principles and practices that unify programmes across Europe and the world – in the name of 'quality'. Perhaps one could argue that there is relative homogeneity within Europe (though that would be contentious), but what happens when such principles are transferred, as they so often have been in the past, to non-European, not-strictly-Western countries? Further, the principles make no mention of the public role of University education. By contrast, the US Council of Graduate Schools pointed out in 2008 that, "fundamentally", "graduate education is about people" and has benefits that "extend beyond the economic realm".

> [It] plays a central role in producing an educated citizenry that can promote and defend our democratic ideals. Scholars educated at the graduate level ... are critically important to our quality of life and the cultural and social fabric of society. (Council of Graduate Schools, 2008)

The role of *the University* as a "critic and conscience of society" (New Zealand Vice-Chancellors' Committee 2012, 2013), called on to give society an awareness of itself (Klaus Heinrich in Narr, 2004), has dropped out of sight in the EUA principles.

How do the conditions of possibility arise that determine whether issues become visible or remain obscure, whether certain orientations and knowledges are in- or excluded? In comparing *spaces of appearance* and *spaces of surveillance*, Xavier Marquez notes that, in spaces of surveillance, norms exist prior to actions. They provide "a standard with which to judge [an] action". By contrast, action in spaces of appearance "is primarily exemplary and either precedes the norm or puts the norm in question" (Marquez, 2011: 23). Spaces of surveillance derive their technologies (e.g., examinations, timetables, and the partition of spaces) partially from religious and military precedents. They constrain freedom and "possibilities for beginning something new" by allocating visibility differentially and disregarding plurality (24).[10] In spaces of appearance, on the other hand, all participants can initiate concerted action, and the power generated amongst them is "produced by people who stand in symmetrical relations of visibility to one another" (13).[11]

New forms of cultural practice are more likely, according to Christine Halse and Peter Bansel, to be based on the networked collaboration of academic communities than on structural rearrangements. Newly created "academic units, research concentrations or centres, departments or faculties" probably end up on the "path of all new disciplines and develop exclusivity, rather than inclusiveness" (2012: 388). Change of the doctoral candidature is better accommodated by growing ethical relationships between "multiple actors and practices that constitute a knowledge community" (388) than by managerial, competitive, and economically driven conceptions. The latter's increasing emphasis on short candidatures and high completion rates triggers attempts to define and implement 'best practice' that might even stultify the doctoral experience.[12] Far more important are contributions that support candidates and their supervisors in understanding their own practices, positions, aspirations, roles and commitments in the context of their institutional conditions, by making practices visible and by bringing them into discussion. This might be best achieved by going beyond the private model of supervision and by formally involving the networks of support many candidates already draw on, as a matter of course.

The pushes and pulls impacting on university environments create tensions and challenging situations for candidates and supervisors. Alison Jones proposes that irresolvable tensions between contradictory positions can produce interesting new knowledge and new ways of thinking.

> All that becomes possible is a tension. Contradictory and irreconcilable realities sit in interminable tension with [each] other. And in the *tension* between contradictory realities is the *ake ake ake*, the endless struggle – to know, to read, to understand, to work with, *to engage with*, others. (Jones, 2007: 10)

NOTES

1. Namely, "disproportionately male, from high-status social-economic backgrounds, members of majority ethnic and/or racial groups, and without disability" (Taylor & Beasley, 2005: 141). See p. 1.
2. This reference throws out a slender bridge to Friedrich Nietzsche's note on estrangement from the present (1996: 195) and Epeli Hau'ofa's reconceptualisation of the Pacific as a *Sea of Islands* (1994).
3. The field of meaning of *guide* includes, via *rope* (Klein, 1966: 686), *showing someone the ropes*.
4. Initially, though, the Royal Society produced new knowledge while the University concerned itself with teaching alone. Only with the emergence of the research University, did the trio of research-teaching-service become normal practice for academic staff. The etymology of *research* in French or Italian reveals its status as a reflective practice. Today, the term fits well with the notion of *search* (and *search engines*) that currently constitutes electronic, online and open research on the Internet.
5. There is no space here to discuss the long interim period of humanist modes of scholarship.
6. Peer review has earlier historical references to Arab medicine where doctors shared notes on patients.
7. Nevertheless, the engagement in creative practice research does require an outward-looking disposition, beyond the experiments of the project itself, to develop an "explicit interpretative-contextual (relational) understanding" (Franz in Durling & Friedman, 2000: 66).
8. Biggs was the first academic appointed to teach Māori language at a New Zealand university in 1951. See Edwards, p. 55, above.
9. See discussion in chapter 10, p. 192.
10. See also Sturm & Turner (2011).
11. Roles and actions are then not predetermined but depend crucially on the structure of the space: "in an egalitarian space of appearance, identity is at its most fluid" (20). Marquez argues that this very fluidity, and the attending lack of control, makes spaces of appearance inadequate for production. However, they lend themselves to "the creation of new roles and rules" (26).
12. Jacques Derrida's account of his own supervision by Jean Hyppolite, in "Punctuations: A time for a thesis" (in Derrida, 2004) is difficult to imagine in today's university contexts.

REFERENCES

Bourdieu, P. (1977). *Outline of a theory of practice* (R. Nice, Trans.). Cambridge, UK: Cambridge University Press.

Brabazon, T., & Dagli, Z. (2010). Putting the doctorate into practice, and the practice into doctorates: Creating a new space for quality scholarship through creativity. *Nebula*, 7(1/2), 23–43.

Byrne, J., Jørgensen, T., & Loukkola, T. (2013). *Quality assurance in doctoral education – results of the ARDE project*

Certeau, M. d. (1984). *The practice of everyday life* (S. Rendall, Trans.). Berkeley: University of California Press.

Council of Graduate Schools. (2008). *Graduate education and the public good*. Washington, DC: Council of Graduate Schools. Retrieved from http://www.cgsnet.org/portals/0/pdf/N_pr_GradEdPublicGood.pdf

Derrida, J. (2004). *Eyes of the university: Right to philosophy (Vol. 2)*. Stanford, CA: Stanford University Press.

European University Association (EUA). (2005). *Bologna seminar on "Doctoral Programmes for the European knowledge society". Conclusions and recommendations.* . Salzburg, Austria: EUA. Retrieved from http://www.eua.be/eua-work-and-policy-area/research-and-innovation/doctoral-education/doctoral-programmes-in-the-bologna-process/salzburg-seminar/

Feyerabend, P. (1993). *Against method: Outline of an anarchistic theory of knowledge*. London, England: Verso.

Halse, C., & Bansel, P. (2012). The learning alliance: ethics in doctoral supervision. *Oxford Review of Education, 38*(4), 377–392.

Hau'ofa, E. (1994). Our Sea of Islands. *Contemporary Pacific, 6*(1), 147.

Jones, A. (2007). *Ka whawhai tonu mātou: The interminable problem of knowing others. Inaugural Professorial Lecture, University of Auckland, 24 October, 2007*. Retrieved from http://www.cs.auckland.ac.nz/webdav/site/education/shared/about/schools/tepuna/docs/Inaugural_Lecture.pdf

Klein, E. (1966). *A comprehensive etymological dictionary of the English language. Dealing with the origin of words and their sense development thus illustrating the history of civilization and culture* (Vol. 1). Amsterdam, Netherlands: Elsevier Publishing Company.

Kuhn, T. S. (1970). *The structure of scientific revolutions*. Chicago, IL: University of Chicago Press.

Luke, T. W. (1996). Identity, Meaning and Globalization: Detraditionalization in Postmodern Space-time Compression. In P. Heelas, S. Lash & P. Morris (Eds.), *Detraditionalization* (pp. 109–133). Cambridge, MA: Blackwell Publishers.

Marquez, X. (2011). Spaces of appearance and spaces of surveillance. *Polity, 44*(1), 6–31.

McClintock, R. (2005). *Homeless in the house of intellect: Formative justice and education as an academic study*. New York, NY: Laboratory for Liberal Learning, Columbia University.

McNamara, A. (2012). Six rules for practice-led research. *TEXT - Special Issue: Beyond practice-led research, 14*(October). Retrieved from http://www.textjournal.com.au/speciss/

Narr, W.-D. (2004, 05.06.2011). *Laudatio für Johanna Kootz zur Verleihung des Margherita-von-Brentano-Preises*. Retrieved 20 March, 2013, from http://www.fu-berlin.de/sites/margherita-von-brentano/preistraegerinnen/kootz_laudatio_narr.html

New Zealand Vice-Chancellors' Committee 2012. (2013, February 14th, 2013). *The NZ university system* Retrieved 18 February, 2012, from http://www.universitiesnz.ac.nz/nz-university-system

Nietzsche, F. (1996). *Human, all too human: A book for free spirits* (R. J. Hollingdale, Trans.). Cambridge, England: Cambridge University Press.

Partridge, E. (2006). *Origins. A short etymological dictionary of modern English*. London, England: Routledge.

Peters, M. A. (2008). Academic writing, genres and philosophy. *Educational Philosophy and Theory, 40*(7), 819–831.

Rancière, J. (2001). Ten theses on politics. *Theory & Event, 5*(3).

Rancière, J. (2004). Introducing disagreement. *Angelaki - Journal of the Theoretical Humanities, 9*(3 December), 3–9.

Rancière, J. (2007). The emancipated spectator. *Artforum International, 45*(7), 271–279.

Sennett, R. (2008). *The craftsman*. New Haven, CT: Yale University Press.

Skeat, W. W. (1883). *An etymological dictionary of the English language*. Oxford, England: Clarendon Press.

Sturm, S. (2012). Terra (in)cognita: Mapping academic writing. *TEXT - Special Issue: Beyond practice-led research, 16* (2 - Special Issue: Beyond practice-led research). Retrieved from http://www.textjournal.com.au/oct12/sturm.htm

Sturm, S., & Turner, S. (2011). 'Built Pedagogy': The University of Auckland Business School as Crystal Palace. *Interstices: Journal of Architecture and Related Arts, 12*, 23–34. Retrieved from http://interstices.ac.nz/published-journals/interstices-12-unsettled-containers-aspects-of-interiority/

Taylor, S., & Beasley, N. (2005). *A handbook for doctoral supervisors*. Milton Park, UK: Routledge.

Walker, R. (1999). The development of Māori studies in tertiary education in Āotearoa/New Zealand (pp. 187–198). In Peters, M. (1999). *After the Disciplines: The Emergence of Cultural Studies*. Westport, CT: Greenwood Publishing Group.

Webb, J. (2012). The logic of practice? Art, the academy, and fish out of water. *TEXT - Special Issue: Beyond practice-led research, 14*(October). Retrieved from http://www.textjournal.com.au/speciss/

Whittaker, M. (2011). *Restaging Rancière: New scenes of equality and democracy in education* (PhD thesis). The Ohio State University, Columbus, OH.

AFFILIATIONS

A.-Chr. Engels-Schwarzpaul
AUT University, Auckland

Michael A. Peters
University of Waikato, Hamilton

INDEX

(Non-English terms in the index are, if not otherwise identified, Māori terms)

academic cultures, 116–117, 123, 183, 187
academic standards, 183
academic writing, 133, 152, 221, 228, 313–314, 316
academy, 54–64, 108–112, 139, 142, 164–165, 172–174, 209–210, 221, 224–225, 241, 252–253, 284, 317
academic, 54–55, 59–64, 69, 94, 101, 103, 117, 133, 136, 139, 174, 248, 279–294
accountability, 58, 172, 218
accreditation, 175, 204
accredited, 301, 311
action, 20, 48, 60, 63–64, 103, 111, 185, 190, 208, 228, 246, 320
acting, 190, 196, 275
adaptation, 58, 84–85
adventurous research, 318
advising, 9, 101–104, 106–109, 111–112, 147–148, 150–152, 154, 156–157, 263, 287
aesthetics, 4, 85–86, 95, 125, 205–206
ako (pedagogy), 76
alienation, 2, 36, 126, 134–135, 138, 164–165
alternative ontologies, 4
ambiguity, 9
analysis, 121, 184, 186, 221, 223
ancestral, 60–62
anxiety, 5, 21, 77, 155, 227, 286
apparatus, 30
approach to knowledge, 148
approval, 119
architecture, 203–206, 209–210, 213–216, 218, 240, 282, 316
Arendt (Hannah), 4–5, 10, 167, 304

argument, 4, 152, 157, 183–184, 187, 190–191, 225, 243–244, 248, 254, 280, 283, 299, 317
art, 239–255
artefact, 172, 197, 206, 210, 225, 243
artist, 20, 85, 93, 170, 208, 234, 246, 250, 260, 265, 268, 272, 302, 305, 307
artist-researcher, 247, 249
artwork, 20, 91, 205, 225, 230, 232, 236, 259–260, 266, 270–273, 276
Asia, 68, 158
assimilation, 70, 78–79, 81, 85, 267, 268
authority, 53, 64, 68, 70, 72, 78, 111, 123, 155, 174, 217, 261, 265, 283–284, 291, 294, 313–314
autonomy, 38, 313
autopoiesis, 186, 197
Baecker (Dirk), 5–6, 167, 171–172, 186–187, 189
Bateson (Gregory), 263
Bhabha (Homi), 9, 71–72
blind spot, 5, 124–127
boundary, 173, 211
Bourdieu (Pierre), 74, 116–127, 312
bricolage, 30, 31, 242
candidacy proposal, 239, 249, 251–252
candidates, 311–321
candidature, 6, 8 19, 46, 69, 103, 109, 163, 222, 251, 275, 305, 320
canon, 185, 313, 316, 317
capitalism, 35
Carter (Paul), 241
ceramics, 299
certainty, 5, 23, 186, 311

INDEX

challenge, 4, 9, 37, 46, 54–59, 62–63, 72–73, 80, 85, 101, 104, 139, 168–179, 183–185, 199, 212, 250, 255, 285, 294, 305, 311, 312, 317, 319
change, 3, 7, 43, 55, 59, 63, 72, 87–88, 93, 116, 119, 123–127, 135, 141, 143, 166, 168, 171–172, 188, 192, 214, 221, 229, 271, 279, 286, 288, 303, 306, 312, 315, 320
China, 67, 73, 77, 87–88, 90, 92–94
choice, 7, 41, 62, 83, 103, 124, 136–137, 193, 226–227, 276, 284
choreography, 5, 19, 21
class, 1, 35, 38, 110, 115–118, 120, 121, 132, 148, 216, 285, 315
co-construction, 152
coherence, 84, 157
collaboration, 85, 103, 147–148, 164, 169, 174, 260, 264, 265, 276, 301–302
collectivity, 53, 71
collegiality, 315
colonialism, 60, 64, 165, 174
colour, 101–112
commentary, 244, 246, 248, 305, 313, 316
commercialisation, 157, 170, 250
community of peers, 315
community, 1–2, 6, 9, 11, 58–61, 64, 72–73, 78, 81, 101–105, 121, 135, 137–138, 141–142, 165–167, 170, 195, 199, 218, 264, 267–268, 282–283, 286, 289, 294, 301, 317, 320
completion, 3, 59, 169, 171, 173, 236, 240, 264–265, 306, 320
concept map, 51
concept, 2, 8, 19, 20, 27–30, 51, 71–72, 74, 76, 80, 87, 91–93, 107, 125, 149, 154–155, 167, 174, 186, 188, 192–194, 196, 204, 210, 213, 229, 233, 259, 266, 270, 277
conditions of possibility, 10, 167, 320

conflict, 83, 125, 204, 245, 300
congruence, 92, 259, 270
connection, 6, 9, 21, 30, 61, 71, 73, 85, 136, 163–165, 169, 208, 213, 227, 231, 236, 246, 248, 255, 266, 270, 272, 294, 302, 308, 317
context, 6, 21, 54, 57, 61, 70–71, 76, 80, 83–86, 89, 95, 103, 108, 109, 115–117, 169, 175, 189, 209, 251, 274, 318
contingency, 112, 119, 172
contribution, 7, 9, 46, 51, 60–62, 138, 168, 196, 206, 248, 293, 303, 307, 312, 320
contribution to knowledge, 71, 92, 205, 243
control, 19, 29, 55, 60, 83, 124, 137, 141, 147, 165, 170, 176, 186, 189, 233–234, 280, 298
convergence (of scientific and designerly approaches, of Science and Design), 187–194
co-operation, 58
co-option, 64, 312
counter-memory, 156, 311
counter-translation, 316
craft, 49, 204, 217, 230, 314–315
creativity, 10, 41, 77, 80, 87, 116, 124–125, 127, 137, 165, 170, 190, 204, 243, 250, 276, 277, 315
creative arts research, 231, 241, 243, 246–248, 252–254
creative practice, 3–4, 7, 8, 20, 80, 83, 89, 94, 126, 169–175, 203, 206, 209, 227, 245–248, 251, 254, 271, 297–298, 300, 303–304, 306–307, 312, 314, 316–317
creative writing, 5, 19, 239–240, 251–252, 255
creative production research, 51, 174, 240–242, 244, 246–247, 249, 251–255
credential, 64, 67, 70, 284

critic and conscience of society, 140, 320
critical framework, 89, 96
Critical Theory, 35–36, 74, 153–154, 221, 263
critique, 35, 89, 206, 315
cross-cultural, 72, 84–85, 93, 95, 103, 215, 260, 263, 274, 285
culture, 266–270
cultural and epistemic traditions, 2, 53–54, 56, 103, 108, 109, 112, 167, 192, 195–196, 212
cultural knowledge, 9, 25, 69–70, 72–73, 76–78, 81, 266, 268, 270, 273
cultural studies, 27, 51, 68, 85, 153, 239
cumulation, 20, 102, 302, 314
Dadirri (Deep Listening), 259, 270
Gulpa Ngawal (Deep Listening), 259, 270
dance, 5, 19, 20, 240, 243
de Certeau (Michel), 311
deconstruction, 30–31, 153–155
defence, 101, 207, 298, 312
deficit model, 2
Deleuze (Gilles), 30–31, 41
Deloria (Vine), 55, 62
Derrida (Jacques), 31, 149, 151, 207, 244–245, 263
design doctorates, 183–199
Design Fiction, 187–192, 194
design research, 43–46
Design-in-Use, 184, 197
desire, 1, 152, 274, 281, 282, 284
Dewey (John), 190, 195, 264
diagram, 91, 97, 207, 214, 224, 226, 245
dialogue, 157–160
diaspora, 27
dichotomy, 204
difference, 2, 6, 20, 48, 63, 67, 76, 85, 88, 103, 133–135, 159, 163–164, 167, 171, 175, 187, 221, 229, 232, 250, 287, 294, 301, 308, 317
digital art, 85

disadvantage, 59, 287
disapproval, 86
disciplinarity. 2, 31, 44, 47, 51, 60, 69–71, 86, 89, 115, 118, 120–124, 133, 153, 158, 163, 170, 176, 183, 185, 192, 204–205, 215, 223–224, 280, 282, 294, 307, 312, 316, 320
discovery, 19, 136, 165, 171, 205, 207–208, 215, 230, 233, 254–255
dissertation, 43–44, 46, 101, 103, 110, 112, 141, 155, 197, 313
distance, 3, 21, 89, 121, 123–124, 150, 164, 166–168, 233, 234, 318
distributed knowledge, 317
diversity, 2, 5, 11, 28, 36, 37, 55, 61, 69, 74, 85, 101, 102, 132, 214, 263, 315, 319
Doctor of Creative Arts, 239
Doctor of Design, 183–199
Doctor of Philosophy (PhD), 115
doctorate, 183–199
documentation, 49, 90, 95–96, 143, 222, 298
Doktorvater/-mutter, 6, 44, 319
domain, 61, 62, 90, 97, 173, 174, 183–184, 187, 189, 193–196, 260, 280, 281
domination, 36, 55, 74, 83
dualism, 38, 187, 199
Durie (Mason), 61
economy, 168–169, 319
eco-socialism, 35
education, 4, 7, 35, 36, 37, 54, 56, 59, 67, 73, 79, 85, 88, 95, 102, 103, 109, 111, 117–118, 132, 143, 148, 151, 170, 187, 195, 283–284,
educational climate, 176
educational institution, 283
elders, 75, 266–273, 290, 305
Elkins (James), 163, 175
embodiment, 209
emerging academic fields, 115–127
emerging discipline, 4

INDEX

emerging knowledge, 163–175
emerging research field, 6, 7, 164, 168
emotion, 21, 37, 41, 152, 155, 240
engagement, 2, 7, 8, 10, 11, 28, 41, 58, 65, 69, 72, 74, 79, 90, 91, 105–108, 110, 112, 117, 132, 148, 153, 164, 165, 167, 169, 171–172, 214, 216, 236, 243, 246, 250, 254, 262, 292, 298, 304, 311, 314
enrolment, 1, 8, 11, 48, 110, 170, 174, 251
ephemerality, 223
episteme, 4, 65, 204, 212
epistemology, epistemological framework, 133–134, 155–158
epistemic heterogeneity, 195
epistemic ignorance, 53, 56
epistemic potentialities, 2, 212
epistemological modesty, 171
epistemological perspectives, 2
English for speakers of other languages (ESOL), 1, 3, 70
ethical consent, 70
ethics, 4, 58, 89, 107, 142, 160, 171, 184, 194–196, 199, 206, 251, 307
ethnicity, 38, 104, 125, 307, 315
ethnography, 90
eurocentrism, 56
evidence, 44, 74, 78, 88, 90, 97, 140, 143, 188, 194, 218, 225, 244, 291, 305, 315, 317
evolution, 185, 189, 299
examination, 3, 19, 48, 55–56, 67, 76–77, 89, 91, 94, 175, 242, 244, 246–8, 291, 298–302, 307, 313, 318, 320
example, 151, 168
exchange, 45, 75, 84–85, 155, 260, 276
exclusion, 126, 135, 173, 265
exegesis, 51, 89, 95–96, 174, 207, 239, 243–248, 250, 252–255, 298, 300, 303, 312
exhibition, 94, 205, 207, 252, 301–302, 304, 312

exoticisation, 136, 139–142
experience, 19, 21, 30, 37–38, 39–40, 49, 53, 61, 68, 71, 80–81, 86, 89, 92, 95, 102, 104, 107, 116, 125, 132, 134–135, 141, 143, 151, 160, 164, 168, 169, 189–190, 199, 193, 206, 208, 213–214, 230, 261, 263–264, 266, 270, 276, 283, 314
experiential (evolutionary) learning, 184, 189–190
experiment, 47, 224, 233, 234, 313–315
expert knowledge, 3
expertise, 84, 86, 88, 147, 186, 199, 215–216, 280, 300–301, 307
exploration, 8, 19, 24, 36, 74, 77, 83, 113, 116, 134, 148, 175–176, 183, 185, 188, 281, 298
exposition, 8, 27–29, 40, 307
facts and values, 183–184, 194–196
Fanon (Frantz), 104
fantasy, 35
feeling, 30–32, 40, 47, 93, 118, 124, 132, 152, 228, 232, 241, 284, 286
feminism, 36–38, 153, 263–4, 275, 317
Feyerabend (Paul), 156–157, 311–312
field, 115–127
field-reflexivity, 116, 124, 127
film, 132, 137, 240, 242, 251, 252, 255
Foucault (Michel), 39–40, 57, 151, 155–157
framework, 2, 9, 19–20, 41, 51, 84, 89, 91, 96, 97, 116, 127, 139, 153, 173, 184, 190–191, 199, 203, 209, 211, 214, 216, 222, 229–230, 235, 241, 246–252, 274, 276, 301, 306–307
Frayling (Christopher), 190
freedom, 47, 55, 57, 63, 83, 138, 227, 243–244, 250, 313, 320
Freire (Paulo), 104–106, 152, 261
friendship, 63, 148
fringe, 7, 10
Gadamer (Hans-Georg), 167, 205, 211, 218

INDEX

gay, 3, 6, 11, 132–134, 138–141, 167
Geertz (Clifford), 89–90, 263
gender, 38, 102, 110, 115–116, 120–121, 125, 134, 148, 286, 315
gendered, 139, 281
genealogy, 28, 157, 312
generative connection, 164
getting-to-know, 2, 167, 317
Giroux (Henry), 35, 36
globalisation, 212–216
glossary, 89
graphic design, 5, 87, 299
Guattari (Felix), 30
guide, 1, 3, 10, 11, 63, 155, 156, 186, 222, 271
guidelines, 151, 183, 204, 212, 227, 249, 282
habitus, 9, 74, 115–119, 124–125, 127, 317
hapū (extended kin groups), 61, 279, 289, 292, 301–302, 308
Haraway (Donna), 36–37
hegemony, 36, 103, 116, 121, 165, 168
Heidegger (Martin), 24, 152, 154–155, 171, 208, 211, 217, 229, 241
heritage, 27, 73, 77, 268, 283
hierarchy, 115, 118, 122–124
historicist, 118, 154
history, 281–283
homogenised difference, 2
humanities, 23, 35, 36, 105, 107, 123, 187, 197, 209, 225, 239, 251, 316
identity, 281–283, 286–293
ideology, 35–36, 56, 157, 312
ignorance, 9, 53, 56, 72–73, 75, 155, 160, 171, 282, 283, 290, 292, 294
image, 221–237
imagination, 10–11, 41, 89, 97, 157, 167, 197, 204, 206, 210, 240–244, 250, 255, 315, 317
improvisation, 172, 185
in-between, 43, 72, 80, 88–93, 193, 216
independence, 37, 134, 164

indigenous, 6, 23–27, 53–65, 74, 83, 165–167, 212, 259–277, 280, 283–284, 293, 301, 312
indigenous doctoral students, 23, 58, 62, 63
indigenous method, 8, 23–26
indigenous thought, 60
industries, 2, 169, 318
inequality, 40, 103, 116–118
infrastructure, 110, 185, 274
Ingold (Tim), 28, 215
Inheritance, 25, 55, 58, 93, 308
initiation, 72, 118, 227, 318
innovation, 74, 76, 126–127, 184, 188, 214, 218, 303
inquiry, 23, 36–37, 55, 71, 76, 101, 103, 126, 132, 137, 165, 170, 174, 183, 187, 195–196, 198–199, 270, 314
installation, 19, 230, 240, 299
institution, institutional, 2, 7, 9–10, 47, 56, 60–64, 83, 101–103, 110, 115–127, 134, 139–141, 143, 151, 156, 159–160, 166, 169–170, 204, 249, 251, 254, 274–275, 281–284, 293, 307, 311–313, 318–319
instrumental/instrumentality, 35–37, 56, 132, 165, 194, 204, 244, 264, 314, 317–319
instrumental rationality, 35
intellectual, 1, 2, 5
interaction, 41–42
intercultural supervision, 67–68, 70, 75, 77–81
interculturalism, 84–88
interdisciplinarity, 44, 51, 69, 169, 192, 305
interior, 86, 90, 92
international students, 3, 96, 148, 170, 212, 293
international, 3, 4, 9, 43–46, 67–70, 74, 115, 123, 137, 139, 148, 272, 282, 293, 300
internationalisation, 1, 11

329

interpretation, 19, 24, 28, 39, 48, 56, 74, 91, 167, 195, 205, 214, 223, 242–244, 265, 268, 270, 285, 313
invention, 36, 170, 204, 206, 313
irrationality, 38, 311
iwi (tribe), 279, 287, 289, 292, 300–301, 306, 308
judgment, 199, 233, 287, 289
justification, 35, 48, 95, 208, 223, 231, 236, 315
kahu (garments), 299–300
Kant (Immanuel), 10, 167
kaumātua (elders), 75, 305
kaupapa (subject, platform, theme, plan or agenda), 19–20, 25, 58, 175, 284–285, 292, 297–298, 301, 304–308
Kaupapa Māori methodology, 301
kaupapa-driven, 175, 297
knowing, knowledge, 102–104
knowledge economy, 169, 319
knowledge gap, 3, 173, 186, 189, 193
knowledge system, 62, 90, 304
Koori (Australian Aboriginal people), 260, 272
kōrero (narrative), 20
kōwhaiwhai (painted patterns used on meeting house rafters), 300
Kuhn (Thomas), 311
Lacan (Jacques), 229, 241, 242, 246
language, 1, 3, 20, 55, 62, 67–68, 70, 74, 76–77, 88–91, 94, 117, 125, 134, 140, 155–156, 166–168, 173, 175, 199, 203, 207, 211–212, 215, 218, 241–242, 246, 259–260, 276, 299–301, 311
Latour (Bruno), 189, 195
learning, 10, 46, 51, 76–77, 79, 84, 91, 94, 104, 109, 116, 126, 133–134, 143, 151–152, 156–157, 164, 169, 171, 184, 189–191, 193, 217, 246, 253, 259, 264, 268–270, 273–276, 293–294

lesbian, 132, 133, 140, 167
Lévi-Strauss (Claude), 30, 90
liberation, 24, 57, 60, 105–106, 154
Lilomaiava-Doktor (Sa'iliemanu), 31
liminality, 72, 170
limits, 3, 24, 29, 31, 39, 49, 54, 61, 80, 102–104, 112, 123, 138, 156, 185, 198, 224, 227, 245, 251, 285, 286, 294
listening, 10, 155, 174, 259, 260, 264–266, 270–273, 275, 277
literature, 2, 7, 23, 38, 44, 49, 77, 104, 132, 133, 141
literature review, 46, 205, 247, 316
Luhmann (Niklas), 186, 196, 197
making, 24, 37, 56, 58, 59, 63, 73, 76, 85, 90, 91
management, 5, 60, 115, 123, 191, 218, 280, 319
managerial, 2, 245, 320
Māori, 5–11, 19–21, 23–26, 40, 53–65, 8, 74–78, 83, 165–166, 170–171, 174–175, 280–294, 297–308, 317
Māori epistemology, 56, 57, 294
Māori ethics, 58
map, 11, 51, 91–92, 96, 97, 168, see also diagram
margin, 120
marginal, marginality, 4, 9, 38, 56, 58, 59, 63, 80, 101, 102, 103, 104, 111, 112, 133, 136, 139–140, 164, 165, 166, 168, 315
market, 115, 122–124, 147, 169, 193, 249
mātauranga Māori, 5, 20, 21, 58, 63, 74–75, 280, 281, 284, 291, 293, 294, 306
material, 10, 19, 20, 28, 49, 103, 122, 133, 137, 139, 141, 142, 154, 164, 199, 209, 215, 217, 241, 243, 281, 283, 308
materiality, 157, 197, 215, 237

meaning, 58, 81, 90, 97, 107, 126, 155, 166, 197, 205, 209, 232, 234, 235, 243, 262, 275
mediation, 11, 63, 121, 134, 173, 189, 206
media, 5, 11–12, 175, 228, 260, 276, 287, 317
medium, 253, 266, 298
mentoring, 141, 148
mentor, 8, 75, 111, 174, 305
metaphysics, 23, 24, 25
methodology, 19, 20, 21, 31, 119–120
methodological, method for thinking, 8, 20, 23–26, 28, 37, 48, 58, 73, 125, 127, 190, 196, 263
mind-map, 91, 92
minority, 3, 4, 9, 67, 83, 85, 93–94, 133–135
mode 2 knowledge production, 187
model, 147, 148, 160, 190, 209, 210
mōteatea (chant), 308
motivation, 39, 44, 46, 59, 60, 151, 217
moving image, 221–237
muka (flax fibre), 299
multicultural, 83, 268
multiplicity, 1, 2, 4, 5, 7, 10, 32, 74, 104, 111, 261, 275
music, 88, 161, 252, 259, 260, 265
narrative, 8, 9, 20, 27, 31, 36, 38, 53, 61, 63, 76, 107, 125, 143, 285–286, 303
negotiation, 78, 79, 83–85, 86, 87, 92, 142, 237, 249, 302, 316
neo-colonial, 11, 61
neo-liberalism, 36, 176
networks, 2, 8, 45, 69, 72, 141, 148, 172, 189, 241, 317, 321
neutrality, 35, 53, 57
Next University, 184–187
Nicolescu (Basarab), 175, 191, 192
Nietzsche (Friedrich), 147, 149, 151, 155, 156, 160
non-traditional, 1–12

non-traditional candidates, 1, 2, 4, 6, 7, 12, 15–179
non-traditional disciplines, 1, 168
not-knowing, 3, 4, 171, 172, 173, 183–184, 186, 187, 189, 199
non-knowledge, 186
Novalis (Friedrich Freiherr von Hardenberg), 8, 23, 24, 25, 26
objectivity, 35, 36, 263
objective, 106, 124, 214, 232, 248, 299
obligation, 31, 71, 174, 226, 294
older student/older students, 8, 39, 40, 41
ontology, 4, 8, 23, 40–41, 48, 101, 229
openness, 6, 9, 10, 11, 21, 28, 54, 81, 87, 96, 164, 211, 227, 228
oppression, 36, 37, 60, 61, 62, 101–102, 105, 106, 126, 133
oral examination, 67
orality, 56
orientation, 2, 4, 8, 25, 40, 60, 83, 125, 126, 133, 137, 140, 147, 152, 263, 315
originality, 28, 37, 81, 89, 105, 118, 122, 172, 199, 205, 244, 249
other thought, 53–65
Pacific, Pasifika, 27, 32, 170, 212, 321
painting, 40, 41, 56, 86, 87, 96, 97, 170, 210, 250, 269, 298, 300
Pākehā, 6, 67, 68, 74, 75, 283, 284, 285, 292
paradigm, 7, 9, 11, 19, 35, 36, 111, 112, 133, 141, 143, 164
pare (door lintel), 304
participation, participatory, 54–55, 71, 79, 117, 124, 164, 169, 176, 197, 317
participatory research, 176, 197, 317
passion, 35–38, 106, 158, 168, 243
pedagogy, 2, 38, 72, 73, 74, 75, 76, 80, 101–102, 105, 106, 107, 109–111
peer review, 125, 157, 218, 225, 313, 314
performance, 221–238

INDEX

performative, 207, 209
perspective, 55–57, 116–119, 263–264
perspectivism, 8, 27–32
philosophy, 5, 8, 10, 96, 115, 150–155
plurality, 206, 304, 311, 320
poetic, 21, 25, 208, 211, 259, 316
poeticisation, 23
poiesis, 204, 208, 210, 212
population, 42, 110, 144, 195, 248
position, 8, 19, 35, 37, 67–70
positivism, 7, 35, 41, 121, 127, 165, 275
possibility, 3, 4, 10, 21, 24, 42, 47, 105, 134, 231, 233, 293
potential, 1, 2, 5, 6, 19, 36, 57, 59, 62, 77, 83, 88, 90, 141
post-colonialism, 4, 11, 67, 69, 70, 81, 83, 165, 174, 282, 312
post-colonial supervision, 279–280
post-colonial theory, 67, 71, 73, 78, 80, 81
postgraduate degrees, 176
poststructuralism, 307
power, 29, 35, 53, 57, 60, 64, 112, 118, 121, 122, 156, 264
power disparity, 36
practice, 2, 7, 9, 20, 30–31, 40, 44, 47, 48–49, 53–56, 60, 63, 70–71, 79, 84–85, 92, 95–96, 105, 108–109, 115, 117–127, 143, 165–166, 169–172, 183, 185, 187, 194, 198–199, 203–217, 222–223, 225–237, 240–255, 259, 268–270, 274–277, 298–308, 311, 313–315, 317, 320
practice as research (PAR), 224, 234, 237, 241, 248
practice-led research, 4, 7, 8, 9, 83, 94, 95, 97, 169, 171, 306, 314
project-led, 48, 203–204, 210
practitioner, 163, 172, 233, 250, 305
privilege, 40, 55, 56, 59, 60, 141, 151, 175, 231, 291, 303, 308

process-driven, 175, 297
professional, 39, 86, 109, 138, 209, 221
progress, 157, 288–289
projection, 191, 192, 194
protocols, 4, 61, 75, 148, 195, 212, 242, 243, 245
public, 4, 7, 28, 39, 97, 136, 152
publication, 12, 44, 89, 111, 141, 174, 305
qualification, 44, 67
Queer, 132
Queer research, 10, 142, 143
Queer theory, 10, 133
questioning, 56, 118, 133, 148, 206, 208, 212, 214, 215, 217, 284
racism, 54, 56, 65, 101, 102, 109, 110, 111, 112, 274
Rancière (Jacques), 10, 171, 176, 283, 312, 316
raranga (weaving of mats, baskets, etc.), 299
rational, 35, 36, 37, 38, 40, 71, 156, 240, 244, 291, 311, 318
reason, 40, 49, 140, 147, 156, 183, 240, 243
reciprocal, reciprocity, 71, 73, 85, 209, 248, 250, 253, 259, 270, 291
reflection, 4, 48, 86, 95, 125, 126, 127, 152, 164, 173, 190, 199, 275
relationality, 86
relationship, 36–37, 275
relevance, 2, 31, 84, 125, 174, 226
relocation, 72, 90, 92, 93, 94, 95, 167
renegade knowledge, 147–149, 156, 158, 311
representation, 271–273
research ethics, 89, 184
research networks, 2, 72, 148
research paradigm, 7, 11, 36, 37, 187, 317
research question, 28, 51, 84, 93, 96, 184, 230

research question model, 174, 225, 245, 247, 248, 249, 253
Research Through Design (RTD), 48, 184, 187, 190, 196
research training, 50, 177, 319
researcher, 313–315
resistance, 35–38
respect, 25, 41, 135, 153, 259, 264, 268
review of knowledge, 21, 176, 316
Ricoeur (Paul), 167
rigour, 54, 59, 63, 101, 142
risk, 3, 9, 63, 76, 78, 94, 135, 186, 218
rite of passage, 318
role model, 8, 44, 45, 47, 48, 50
Romanticism, 241
rules of the game, 119–120
Rykwert (Joseph), 210, 215
sacrifice, 69, 122, 123
safety, 134, 135, 137, 141, 142, 143
Samoa, Samoan, 5, 8, 27, 28, 29, 30, 32, 33, 137, 209, 214, 215
schema, 192, 233
scholar, 24, 35, 37, 65, 68, 91, 92, 101, 102, 110, 148, 152, 282, 313
scholarly inquiry, 71
scholarship, 4, 7, 8, 24, 54, 76, 77, 97, 107, 139, 142, 280, 281, 313, 321
science, 5, 13, 35, 36, 43, 44, 49, 120, 128, 133, 155, 190, 191, 197, 240, 303
sculpture, 125, 210, 240, 241, 299
seeing, 4, 31, 171, 255, 317
self declaration(or Coming Out), 60, 131–132, 136, 137
semiotics, 89, 90, 91, 221
Sennett (Richard), 314, 315
separation, 21, 51, 69, 91, 103, 123, 168, 186, 187, 204, 205, 245, 298
settler society, 165, 175, 268
settler/invader, 68, 71, 72, 78, 79
sexual minority, 1, 132, 133, 134–135, 138, 143, 145

skill, 84, 88, 116, 204, 239, 243, 246, 298, 314
Sloterdijk (Peter), 156
Smith (Linda Tuhiwai), 11, 40, 68, 175, 307
social science, 5, 13, 33, 35, 70, 123, 127, 133, 177, 195, 201
sound, 6, 61, 140, 147, 159, 228, 237, 243, 306
Southern, 9, 67, 68, 69, 71, 72, 81
space, 27, 28, 166, 289–290, 298
spaces of appearance, 320, 321
specialisation, 122
standpoint theory, 264, 278
standard, 2, 4, 7, 43, 48, 56, 59, 70, 79, 148, 172, 184, 298, 314
status, 6, 39, 47, 53, 55, 75, 121, 136, 210, 285, 312
stereotype, 10, 75, 77, 139
stiegler (Bernard), 204
stolen Generation, 264, 267
stoßsätze (sentences that push, German), 8, 23
strangeness, 167
strategy, 9, 30, 55, 79, 86, 87, 95, 124–127, 128, 138, 197, 303
structure, 3, 4, 20, 49, 51, 93, 156, 158, 207, 218, 282, 303
struggle, 19, 35, 90, 105, 232, 245, 252, 254, 263, 301, 316
subjectivity, 41, 42, 71, 76, 150–152, 160, 282, 296
subjugated, 156, 170
superiority, 71, 93, 94, 136, 210, 240, 316
supervision, 157–160
supervision advice, 284
supervision relationships, 7, 38, 59, 119
tā moko (Māori tattoo), 299, 300
tacit knowledge, 71, 94, 209, 241, 317
Tāngata Whenua (people of the land), 53
tāniko (embroidery), 299
taonga (prized possession), 302

INDEX

tauparapara (incantation to begin a speech), 303
te ao Māori (the Māori world), 54, 56, 58, 62, 280, 289, 291, 300–301, 303
te reo Māori (Māori language), 175–176, 179, 281, 286, 300
teaching, 44, 51, 75, 84, 91, 107, 127, 137, 185, 237, 281
techné, 212
technique, 87, 297, 305
technology, 48, 87, 88, 97, 176, 186, 201, 214, 237
tension, 9, 13, 36, 62, 72, 80, 262, 285
testimony, 53
text, 25, 31, 42, 174, 224, 237, 313
theoretical, 7, 19, 23, 41, 48, 74, 153, 170, 243, 251, 308
theory, 2, 35, 40, 41, 44, 70, 71, 105, 148, 204, 214
thesis, 1, 3, 7, 19, 25, 43, 138
thing in common (Rancière), 10
thinking artist, 249, 250, 255
Third Space (Bhabha), 71
thought, 8, 9, 14, 20, 24, 29, 42, 73, 81, 168
threshold, 12, 41, 98, 315
tikanga (correct procedure, custom, practice), 65, 75, 291, 295, 302
tino rangatiratanga (self-determination, absolute sovereignty), 301, 304
tiriti o Waitangi (Treaty of Waitangi), 175, 176, 179, 284, 295
tokenism, 109, 136, 138, 139
tradition, 7, 11, 28, 56, 57, 65, 97, 126, 153, 204, 213, 300
traditional candidates, 1
transcultural, 77, 84–88, 94, 96
transdisciplinarity, 4, 164, 184, 187, 188, 189, 191, 192, 194, 201, 219
trans-domain, 173, 183, 189, 193–196, 200

transfer, 83–98, 185
transformation, 92, 96, 116, 124–127, 264
transition, 12, 88, 94, 193, 210, 221, 308
translation, 12, 83–98, 163–177
trust, 30, 41, 77, 86, 118, 126, 136, 149, 277, 292
truth, 35, 38, 42, 53, 58, 155, 174, 190, 211, 219, 314
truth claim, 35, 36, 121
uncertainty, 3, 6, 9, 46, 47, 48, 80, 88, 171, 172, 177, 201, 286
understanding, 10, 20, 27, 28, 46, 79, 80, 85, 86, 88, 103, 125, 148, 152, 163, 208, 212
unhomeliness, 72, 77, 78, 79, 80, 81
university, 2, 8, 9, 12, 55, 115, 122, 140, 149, 185, 201, 260
usefulness, 70, 168
vā (space, Samoan), 28, 32
validity, 2, 11, 20, 37, 53, 54, 62, 197, 314
value, 7, 27, 40, 53, 62, 96, 103, 116
Varela (Francesco), 1, 4, 13, 186
veracity, 70
video, 19, 21, 230, 235, 236, 238
visibility, 2, 56, 61, 101, 136, 176, 208
visiting imagination (Hannah Arendt), 10
visual arts, 163, 175, 307
voice, 23, 30, 37, 250, 254, 260, 263, 266
waiata (songs), 308
wānanga (knowledge, learning, university), 63, 308
way of knowing, 2, 5, 8, 59, 61, 71, 224, 240, 241, 242, 243, 244, 248
West (Cornel), 154, 161
Western, 2, 5–6, 8–9, 23–25, 54, 56, 59, 63, 65, 67–81, 83–96, 134, 148, 165–166, 199, 203, 211–216, 240, 244, 274, 284, 291, 293–294, 303–304
whakaaro (think, becoming of thought), 24

334

INDEX

whakairo rākau (wood carving), 299
whakapapa (genealogy, genealogical paradigm, inheritance), 19, 20, 25
whānau (extended family), 20, 279, 287, 289–290, 292, 308
whatu (weaving), 299
whatu kākahu (woven garments), 299

Winnicott (Donald), 172
worldview, 23, 54, 56, 58, 63, 83–84, 87, 93, 98, 196, 209, 285
writing, 4, 8, 9, 19, 21, 25, 35–38
YortaYorta (Australian Aboriginal nation), 259, 266, 268, 270